FINDING OTHO

FINDING OTHO

The Search for Our Enslaved Williams Ancestors

Kathy Lynne Marshall

ISBN #: 978-0-9992014-1-1

FIRST EDITION

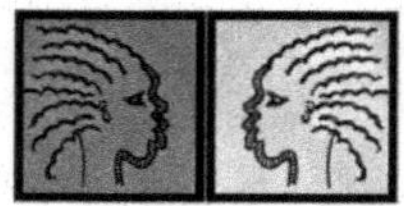

Kanika Marshall Art and Books Publishing

PO Box 1202, Elk Grove, CA 95759-1202

www.KanikaMarshall.com/books.html

Cover design by Kanika Marshall
Artwork by Kanika Marshall and Mary E. Marshall
(owned by Kathy Marshall)

Library of Congress Control Number: 2018913377

Published 2018.

Printed in the United States of America.

Dedicated to the descendants of Otho and Alice Williams.
May this book be a legacy to their tenacity
and encourage the younger generations
to remember our strong roots.

TABLE OF CONTENTS

FOREWORD

Kathy Marshall and I first met via email in 2016, when a librarian in western Maryland, where I live, connected us. As a historian working on slavery in Washington County, I do sometimes get inquiries from people working on their African American family history. However, my correspondence with Kanika—the name by which I know author Kathy—was unique.

Kathy and I began to email back and forth about her ancestor Otho Williams, his possible origins, and family, and some of the myriad questions Kathy was asking, investigating, and hypothesizing about. So many questions! Two things struck me about those questions. One was how few of them I was at all able to help her with. The other was what a fertile investigative brain Kathy has.

She constantly comes up with new approaches to the information, sources, and research problems she has identified. But what impressed me most, as I first got to know Kathy, and still does impress me, was the tremendous range, depth, and dedication of the research she had done. I was somewhat in awe of what she had already accomplished at that point. The story of Kathy's search for her ancestors, which she tells so engagingly and vividly, is one of two stories at the core of this book. The other is the story of those ancestors, most notably Otho Williams.

Of course the Williams family history is part of a much larger story, too: the story of African American individuals and families who were brought to western Maryland in the late eighteenth and early nineteenth centuries; were enslaved in agriculture, domestic service, and—notably in this case—industry; and found various routes to freedom.

As Kathy unrolled her ancestors' story, I kept learning about points at which her family's history touched or intersected with significant aspects of Washington County's African American history. Her great-great-great-grandfather, like so many enslaved persons in western Maryland, had originally come from Maryland's Eastern Shore. He worked in the iron industry that pervaded Washington and Frederick Counties, linking enslaved workers back to African ironworking traditions.

It was Kathy's relative Mary Williams who in the mid-nineteenth century made the intricately stitched white quilt now in the Doleman collection in Hagerstown—one of the oldest items in that important collection. I've seen and photographed that quilt and been moved by its beauty.

Eventually, I had the great pleasure of meeting Kathy in person when she came to Maryland on her 2017 journey of discovery and pilgrimage. That trip, including the delightful day we spent together, is described in this book. But it was only a small part—in a way a culmination—of the years of persistent, patient research that allowed Kathy to tell her family's history. The resulting book, which you hold in your hands, is not only a personal and family chronicle but also a guidebook for others with family histories waiting to be explored. In these pages, Kathy shares many hard-won lessons in genealogy, historical research, and writing.

On the wall above my desk hangs a small gem of an artwork, a metal plaque a little bigger than my palm. On its deep bronze-colored background, branches spring up, bearing round blue fruits. Kanika, the artist who created it and gave it to me on that 2017 visit, told me that it represents the family tree. I keep it where it can inspire my research, writing, and teaching about people who lived and worked in both slavery and freedom. I know that Finding Otho: The Search for Our Enslaved Williams Ancestors will be similarly inspiring to readers, as it takes them along on a quest that is both personal and an important part of our shared American story.

Emilie Amt, D.Phil.
Department of History, Hood College
June 2018

INTRODUCTION

Zebra! Oreo! Uncle Tom! I was called all that in school. For six decades people have been asking me "Are you mixed?"

"No, I'm BLACK!" I responded with a little too much edge in my voice. While perhaps not politically correct to admit, especially in the beginning pages of this book, I still cringe at being asked that question. Why? My barely tanned skin and frizzy hair mark me as being a product of racial mixing, which likely occurred during slavery times in America, sometime between 1619 and 1865. Growing up during the Civil Rights Era of the 1960s and 1970s, "Black is Beautiful" was my credo even though the mirror did not reflect a lush chocolate-brown skin tone.

After so many questions about my ethnic composition, I took a DNA test in May 2012, after retiring from my day job at the California Highway Patrol. "DNA doesn't lie," they say. Those DNA results clearly told the tale of how much cream floats in my African coffee!

Like many African Americans, I have long dreamed of having my Kunta Kinte moment and finding which tribes make up my African DNA and whether we have Blackfoot Indian heritage, as many black people are told. How could I find my enslaved ancestors when I knew nothing about them before the 1870 United States Census?

The fog of historical misinformation has long obscured our path to finding the truth about our African American ancestors, but I was bound and determined to be successful this time. This was the most significant research adventure I had ever undertaken. I wanted to share this exciting experience with you, the reader, hoping you would be inspired to use the hints, tips, and examples in this book to make *your* journey of discovery.

The primary goals of this book were to:

1) Find the parents of my maternal great-great-grandfather (also called "second" great-grandfather), Otho Williams.

2) Determine Otho's slave owner.

3) Write family stories from Otho's descendants' point of view.

4) Determine whether DNA technology—the "in" thing for genetic genealogy these days—gives adequate bang for the buck in proving ancestral connections from Africa and Europe.

5) Validate or disprove our family lore that we get our metalworking and/or mechanical abilities from our enslaved Williams ancestors.

I strove to follow the Genealogical Proof Standard (GPS)[1] for this book, in an effort to establish the reliability ("proof") of my genealogical conclusions, with reasonable certainty. This included conducting an exhaustive research of records, providing complete and accurate source citations, analyzing and correlating the collected information, resolving any conflicting evidence, and ending with a soundly reasoned, coherently written conclusion in the Epilogue.

I planned to travel to Maryland to experience, first-hand, where my Williams family lived in the 1700s and 1800s. The brass ring would be finding their home, smelling the air they breathed, and walking the roads they traveled so long ago. Those rich experiences would enhance the authenticity of this heartfelt book which contains:

- **Part I:** *The Search Begins*: Explores my family-search journey in *Becoming a Genealogist.* The chapter entitled, *Introducing Otho Williams* compares Otho to his 1870 and 1880 neighbors. Chapter 3: *Breaking Down the 1870 Brick Wall* provides useful hints and tips that anyone researching African American ancestry can employ to find slaveowners. Similar techniques may also help immigrants find their ancestors from "the old country."

- **Part II: Bondage 1634-1865:** Chapter 4 examines the environment of *Blacks in North-Western Maryland.* Chapter 5: *The Cream in Our Coffee Wear a Crown?* examines several theories which might lead to uncovering Otho's slave master. Astounding information about Otho's family ties is painstakingly presented in Chapter 6: *1834: The Most Pivotal Year.* Chapter 7: *Does Prince Charming Exist?* and Chapter 8: *Does More Than One Prince Exist?* illustrate the roller coaster ride called African American genealogy, following the clues that lead to unexpected conclusions. We learn more about the two most important women in Otho's life in Chapter 11: *The Mothers' Lineage.*

- **Part III: What Freedom Brings:** Chapter 12 describes how *Emancipation Brings Education.* We explore whether Otho was successful after slavery, who his wife and children were, and how and where they lived in Chapter 13: *The Landowners.* Further, Chapter 14: *Generations of Ironworkers* examines the expertise of African ironworkers and my family's metalworking lineage. Chapter 16: *The Journey Home* chronicles my boots-on-the-ground, research trip to Maryland and Pennsylvania.

- **Part IV: DNA Does Not Lie, Does it?** Encourages the reader to take a short walk on the wild side of DNA research. The tools and techniques presented may be a boon to adoptees, immigrants, and African Americans, especially, but everyone may benefit in using DNA to find their ancestors. Chapter 17: *A Basic DNA Primer* explains the basic concepts of DNA testing. Chapter 18: *Which is the Best DNA Testing Company* contrasts the testing companies used in my research. Chapter 19: *Using DNA to Find Our Europeans* attempts to "find my white people" and Chapter 20: *Who Are Our Africans* to experience my Kunta Kinte moment in finding our African tribal connections.

- **Epilogue:** Contains *It's A Wrap* which recaps this genealogy sleuthing journey, and *Let the Truth Be Told* which collapses the findings of two years of in-depth research and analysis into a cohesive package.

- **Solving Your Ancestral Journey:** Contains brief, one-liner hints and tips to help others embarking on a similar journey of discovery.

When this book was first conceived in 2016, *Part V* would have chronicled the down-home family stories of the descendants of the formerly enslaved Otho and Alice Williams, with separate chapters featuring the lives of:

- My first great-grandfather, Otho Sherman Williams, was the son of Otho and Alice Williams. His Ohio home was a sanctuary for sixteen descendants in the 1930s and 1940s.

- My Great Aunt Reba Williams was the cook for a Pulitzer Prize-winning author, and at the age of 106 was profiled on the Jay Leno TV Show and in Essence Magazine.

- My grandmother, Pearl Williams Carter, was a domestic employee who instilled in her children how to become productive American citizens.

- My Great Uncle, Charles Williams, became a medical pioneer while serving as one of the first black Machinist's Mates in the Navy in 1946.

- My aunt, Lavata Williams, was our illustrious family historian for decades.

- My mother, Mary Ellen Carter Marshall, went from a small-town existence to become a beloved school principal and professional watercolor artist in California.

- My father, Dr. Thomas R. Marshall, brought countless babies into the world while participating in numerous marathons and triathlons around the world. Although not a Williams descendant, he made me possible; thus, he has a place at this table.

- My siblings and I, along with our children are the proud descendants of our ancestors. Never give up.

By the eighth month of non-stop investigation and penning this difficult topic, I had over three hundred double-spaced, printed pages, and was readying the book for self-publication. However, my content editors suggested splitting off the folksy stories about Otho's descendants into a separate book, called *The Ancestors Are Smiling!* That first book was published in July 2017, and was made available on amazon.com and my www.KanikaMarshall.com website.

The Ancestors Are Smiling! contains a collection of uplifting, funny, touching, and sometimes harrowing real-life stories, creatively voiced by the descendants of Otho and Alice Williams. All of the true stories are woven with the African fabric of American historical events. The tenacity of these courageous spirits drove them to ensure that each generation was better than the last.

This book, *Finding Otho: The Search for Our Enslaved Williams Ancestors*, describes the joyous, confounding, exciting, and sometimes painful journey of acceptance of my enslaved Williams ancestral past, using DNA testing to prove family relationships.

I am delighted to have discovered that my ancestors lived near the Potomac River, which was a part of many significant events in American history, including the bloodiest single-day battle of the Civil War at Antietam Hill, only a few miles from where Otho and Alice lived.

Northwestern Maryland was a pass-through on the Underground Railroad for escaping slaves. The Underground Railroad was a secret network organized by people who helped men, women and children escape from slavery into freedom. It provided hiding places, food, and often transportation for hundreds of fugitives who were trying to escape slavery.[2]

Harpers Ferry was at the confluence of the Potomac and Shenandoah Rivers, where John Brown attempted his infamous slave rebellion when twenty-one of his followers attacked and occupied the federal arsenal in Harpers Ferry; their goal was to capture supplies and use them to arm a slave rebellion. Brown was captured during the raid and later hanged, but not before becoming an anti-slavery icon.[3]

By the nineteenth century, slaves and free persons of color could be found in every corner of Maryland, laboring in Washington County's Antietam Iron Works,[4] harvesting tobacco and wheat, caulking ships, and much more. Between all those milestone events and locations, my second great-grandfather, Otho Williams, was born a slave but died a free man who enjoyed some of the benefits to which all Americans are entitled.

Will I ever figure out the entire mystery of my enslaved relatives? Sifting through history books, biographies of runaway slaves, and free persons of color has become a fascinating pastime. Looking through websites that deal with black folk during slavery times wholly absorbs and emotionally drains the brain, as does perusing hundreds of legal and census documents.

Will I ever learn enough about my ancestors to actually see them in my mind's eye and know their personalities?

Truthfully, writing an Introduction early into this ambitious project, I had no idea whether I would be able to connect all the dots to answer my many research questions. However, I strongly believed in the value of presenting my roadblocks and unsuccessful attempts, as well as rejoicing in the many exciting successes.

I wrote this book as though I was sitting in a coffee shop with you, chatting about this research project, and letting you experience the highs and lows of the journey with me. I hope the theories and varied resources utilized in this book will help you research your roots. May this story of discovery and triumph resonate with, and inspire you to search for your family history too.

After all, when the ancestors call, we must listen!

PREFACE

"What are those tiny lights floating in the air?" I asked my cousin Julie, who I'd just met for the first time.

"Haven't you ever seen fireflies before?" she responded, in her charming, mid-western drawl.

When dusk muted the sun's rays on that humid summer night in July 1966, my sister, brother, and I began to see lighted objects flitting about in the air, right in front of our eyes! We tried to catch the gleaming fairies inside our cupped hands. Once successful we carefully opened our hands just a smidgen to peer inside at those miraculous, phosphorescent beings tickling our palms. We lived in California, the Disneyland home of Tinkerbell. However, we didn't imagine that fairies really existed, but here they were in little Mt. Vernon, near the center of Ohio where my mother and her mother were raised.

Three days prior, my mom, sister, brother, and I packed our clothes in brown paper bags for a three-day, cross-country adventure on the sleek, silvery California Zephyr passenger train.

"Tickets please," requested the man in uniform at the doorway of our train car, then he pointed the way to our seats in the back of the train. Our noses wrinkled at the cigarette smoke mixed with sweat and old seat-leather. Lugging our meager bags down what seemed like twenty-five rows, we plopped down in our assigned seats. Mom put as many bags of food and clothes in the overhead compartment as she could, and we shoved the rest of our belongings on the floor under the seat in front of us. Being the oldest, I sat next to the cherished window, sister Carrie in the middle, and three-year-old Greg on mom's lap in the aisle seat.

"All aboard!" shouted someone from outside the train. The doors closed with a *whoosh*, then a chug, chugga-chug chugga-chug sound could be heard as the train pulled out of the station, the metal wheels squealing with the effort of moving the heavy mass from a standing start. We were on our first train ride going cross-country to visit our family. It was the most exciting thing that had ever happened to us, besides the annual visit from Santa Claus, of course.

That first day, the train traveled from Sacramento, south to Los Angeles, then east through the dry, grey-beige, high desert of Nevada. At sunset, the orange-to-red-to-pink-to-shades-of-purple of the sun's dying rays disappeared over the horizon. We marveled at the white expanse of salt flats gleaming in the deep blue hues of the nighttime sky as we passed through the Salt Lake City area in Utah.

"Where's the bed, Mom? I'm getting sleepy!" I whined, at the end of that first day on the train. This was after we had eaten a peanut butter sandwich dinner in our seats, then visited the small bathroom car.

"I thought I told you. This is it. Right here, in our chairs. We can only afford the cheapest seats on this fancy train. That means we have to sleep sitting-up tonight and tomorrow night. We are far from being rich people, you know." Mom spoke quietly so the people sitting in front of us wouldn't know how poor we were.

Mom brought most of our food with us in brown grocery bags. Thankfully, the next morning she let us eat breakfast in the bright and shiny dining car because the milk was cold and fresh there, perfect for our little cardboard boxes of Cheerios and Lucky Charms.

The nearly floorless space between train cars was noisy. It was scary seeing the ground racing underneath between the constantly moving floor plates—that is, if you were brave enough to look down. We kids loved running—technically, it was fast-walking—from one end of the train to the other all day long. We flew from our passenger car, through the bathroom car, the dining car, more passenger cars, a fancy lounge car, the dome car, all the way to the caboose. From the end of the train, we could look back upon the tracks extending way out into the distance. It wasn't until later that I learned my paternal grandfather, Austin Marshall, was a Pullman porter who got to ride trains every day for a living. Boy, was he lucky!

Sitting in the sunny, glass-ceilinged dome car, we had a view like none other. Especially magnificent were the orangey-red, sunset-colored Rocky Mountains as we sped through Colorado. We had to be very quiet and grown up sitting in the popular dome car, or we would be kicked out and be in big trouble from Mom. Nebraska and Iowa whizzed by as we ran from one end of the train to the other, while Mom sat quietly in her seat guarding our rather pitiful worldly possessions passing the time reading, drawing anonymous face portraits, and doing crossword puzzles.

I was the oldest, nine, so it was my responsibility to ensure that my three-year-old brother and seven-year-old sister made it back to Mom safe and sound, and especially without complaints from the other passengers and crew.

We kids were so excited to be visiting our Ohio family for the first time in our lives! It was dusk on our third day as we saw the city lights of Chicago, Illinois. The spicy, smoky odor permeating the massive, high-ceilinged Union Station instantly reminded me of my grandfather Austin's sweet-smelling cigars.

"Here are some Rum Butter Lifesavers and Neccos for this last phase of our trip," Mom said, as she gave each of us some candy to put in our pockets. We clutched our paper bags of clothes as we ascended the four steep steps into the deep green "Philadelphia Flyer." That rickety old train bounced so noisily and forcefully all the way to Marion, Ohio, that we were sure it would break down and toss us out onto the moonlit Ohio cornfields. But we made it in one piece. Thankfully.

Mom's quiet brother, Arthur "Sonny" Carter, picked us up in his 1957 Chevy. We kids shyly told Uncle Sonny hello, and Mom hugged him tight. It only took about thirty minutes to drive to Mom's hometown of Mt. Vernon, Ohio. We primarily stayed with my Grandma Pearl Williams Carter and Sonny in their two-story, deep brown, wood-shingled home on West Walnut Street.

The African Methodist Episcopal church my family attended owned the home and rented it to Grandma for only seven dollars per month. Being a domestic employee all of her life—and the mother of seven children which she generally had to support by herself—she had little money for housing, or anything else.

My mother often told us: "We lived with our grandparents, Otho Sherman—the son of a slave--and Myrtle Williams, in their house for the first fifteen years of my life. Can you imagine? Seven children and my mother living in one bedroom and one small kitchen? We shared one bathroom and a clothes washing area with the eight other people living in the house. This was always a sore spot with me because Grandmother Williams gave us so little space while she had a twenty-foot by fifteen-foot kitchen, a formal dining room, a living room, two small bedrooms off to the side, and three bedrooms upstairs—one for her, one for grandpa, and one for her sons Charles and Robert."

"On the other hand," my mother continued, "going to Grammie Carter's house—my dad's mom—was always so nice, pleasant, warm, and friendly. She treated all seven of us kids so well. We would occasionally spend the night and eat there. She was 90-plus when she died, so she was always 'old' to me. I always said she looked like an aged white-skinned Dutch lady with overlapping braids on the top of her head."

The first full day visiting the Ohio homestead, our first cousins, Jeff, Julie, Everett, and Roy, played with us, and for many days after while our mother relished chatting with her mother, sisters, brothers, and cousins all day and into the wee hours of the night (Figure P.1).

There were so many differences between Mt. Vernon and our west-coast home in Sacramento. A huge coal stove stood in the middle of Grandma's living room. In California, everyone we knew had homes with central heating and air conditioning. We had to walk around grandma's huge, hot stove to reach the kitchen, bathroom, and staircase. We learned not to accidentally touch it as we passed by unless you wanted burned fingers! There was also an old pitted, white, claw-footed tub upstairs, which I feared would walk away with me on its lion feet while I was taking a bath!

Figure P.1. The Marshalls visit their Ohio family. Mt. Vernon, Ohio. 1966. Photograph by Kathy Marshall (not pictured).

We were astonished that there were no fences in the backyards! How do you keep pets and little kids from running away? Everybody in California has a proper fence that clearly delineates your property from your neighbors. Having no fence, though, did open up the space so it looked like everyone had a lovely park in their backyard.

Mom wanted to show off where she grew up, so we walked downtown and bought large jawbreakers and tootsie rolls for a penny at the candy store. At a fragrant bakery, we first tasted the heaven that is fluffy, creamy, chocolate eclairs.

Most of our days were spent in the park down the long street from Grandma Carter's house. This was the same park where our mother and her brothers and sisters spent their childhood, with mom beating other kids at marbles and basketball. They had the tallest swings we had ever seen and believe me we tried hard to swing up and over its metal A-frame foundation!

These were the things I remember most about the small town in the center of Ohio where our mother was born and raised. She lived there until marriage whisked her away to cities along the Pacific Ocean, 2,500 miles away from her loving family.

Even at that young age, I wanted to learn about who Grandma Carter's parents were, and who their parents were. A few years later, in Junior High School, I learned about slavery and began to wonder how many of my family members, besides those of my great-grandfather Otho Williams and great-grandfather Joseph Booker, had ever been slaves.

In high school, there was almost no information about African Americans in so-called "American" history class except two pages about slavery. I began researching black scientists and inventors, and studied civil rights leaders on my own time, then reading those reports out loud in my history classes. I became quite militant, and vowed to one day learn more about my family's history. Now is that time.

Mary Marshall

PART I: TACKLING THE PUZZLE

A genealogist studies an individual's or family's ancestry to trace kinship, lineage, and family history. Genealogists gather their information from such vital statistics as births, deaths and marriages as well as oral family history and genetic (DNA) tests. They must be skilled at multidisciplinary research and often must use computer programs to find the truth. Genealogy is my passion.

Kathy Lynne Marshall, 2018.

Mary Marshall

Chapter 1 - Becoming a Genealogist

* The Early Days *

On July 1976, as fireworks proclaimed our country's two hundredth birthday, I was 19-years-old with my whole life ahead of me. I grew up in the house of an educator, Mary Ellen Carter, and a doctor, Thomas Richard Marshall. There was no way in Sam Hill (as my mother used to say) that my sister Carrie, brother Greg, and I would not attend college.

I had the typical angst of trying to decide which college to attend and which major to pursue, but mom frequently emphasized that we should become well-prepared to take advantage of any opportunity, any door that might open, so we could squeeze in and make our mark on the world. I took general Sociology courses from Sacramento City College to learn a bit of everything from various disciplines.

During the first minute of Psychology 1A class, the college professor—a stern-looking, portly, dark chocolate man asked, "How many of you are shy, and worry that people are always watching you, laughing at what you are wearing, or talking about you behind your back?" Half the class, mostly very young people right out of high school, raised their hand. My hand tentatively went up too. Believe it or not, I used to go a full day at school without speaking to anybody—not one word—I was so petrified of saying or doing the wrong thing.

The professor delighted in chopping our introverted brains up into little bits of gray matter, challenging, "What makes you think everybody is looking at you? It is the height of egoism to think others are constantly thinking about, looking at, or caring about you! People care about their own problems, their own wardrobe, their own self-absorbed thoughts, to be thinking one minute about you." Wow! We of the hands-held-high club were shocked.

That first day of college in January 1975 taught me an important lesson. People really aren't paying attention to me. They are worried about their own lives. There is no reason to continue being shy, now that I am out of high school and an adult going to college. I am no less a person than anybody else. My opinion matters as much as anybody else's. I am just as good as anybody else. That Psych class taught us new adults about ourselves and life more than any other class during my three semesters at Sac City College. I relished every African American History, Women's History, and Anthropology class offered at Sac City, earning my Associate of Arts degree in Sociology in June 1976. "Yes, that was twenty-one units per semester," says this fanatic overachiever!

My mother advised me to pursue a bachelor's degree that would prepare me to get a good job so that I would become a contributing citizen to these United States of America. I promptly enrolled in then-called Sacramento State College for a useful degree in . . . French. Don't ask why (smile). OK, here's the official, honest, and true story. I had enrolled in the International Business Degree program, which required students to become proficient in at least one language other than English and take standard business classes. I had been taking French classes from the seventh through the twelfth grades because I couldn't roll my R's to speak proper Spanish. Admittedly, it would have been much smarter and more useful to learn Spanish here in California, a Mexico border state. *Por supuesto* (Of course!)

My first semester at Sac State was comprised of Accounting 1A (boring columns of numbers), Economics 1A (all about supply and demand), Math 1A (useful review of applied math concepts), French 1A (flamboyant instructors talking about fascinating Paris and French culture), and Computers IA. In 1976, Computer Science consisted of learning about zeros and ones, the basic concepts of computer technology. Back then, there were no personal computers available for the masses, just for the military and some government entities. I struggled to comprehend the complex computer mystique.

After my first year of business and French classes, the college discontinued the International Business degree for some unfathomable reason. I had to choose between those less-than-scintillating business courses and the sparkling language of love. Which would *you* choose?

I was a busy girl. On July 1, 1976, I had also secured a full-time, civil service job with the State of California, working the 3:00 to 11:30 PM swing shift at the California Highway Patrol Headquarters in downtown Sacramento. I made a whopping $525 per month filing accident reports at night, while I went to Sac State full-time during the day. It was the best job to have because once I finished filing each night, I could concentrate on my homework.

On my third night at work, out of the blue, Phyllis, a light-skinned, African American coworker who was probably in her sixties, asked whether I had white blood in my family. Surprised, I respectfully said, "Absolutely not," instead of my usual reply, "No, I'm black!" One glance in the mirror told the tale I was not 100% African, but I actually did not know my family heritage.

* Seeking the Truth *

We lived in Sacramento, 2,500 miles away from Ohio, where the rest of my maternal and paternal families resided. We could not participate in family gatherings, nor hear family stories about those who had gone before us, so I didn't know who my ancestors were. That important question from Phyllis prompted me to write a letter to my Ohio elders asking them about our family lineage. Yes, we wrote letters to family back then because long-distance telephone calls were expensive. My Great Uncle George Booker quickly wrote back that:

> "You have German from my dad 'Booker' and African from his mother, with his father being his owner. Your Grandma Myrtle Williams was African, German, and English. Your Grandpa Otho Sherman Williams was African, Indian, and English."[5]

My paternal grandmother, Daisy Dooley Marshall, living in my birthplace of Cleveland, Ohio, responded with the "we have Indian blood" story that many African Americans who have non-kinky hair hear from their relatives. Believe me, I searched in vain for our (supposed) illusive Blackfoot Native American connection for decades, without finding a smidgen of convincing proof that it was true.

One year after that Bicentennial proclamation of my alleged, diverse ethnic lineage, the TV mini-series *Roots: The Saga of an American Family* aired to grand acclaim worldwide. Based on Alex Haley's book of the same name, it told the story of Kunta Kinte, an eighteenth-century African, captured as an adolescent and sold into slavery in America. Millions of TV watchers raptly tuned in every night to follow his life, and generations of his family, down to his descendant, author Alex Haley.

Wow! Africans actually had traditions, languages, culture, beauty, and an interesting history before being brought to America in chains. Africans in this country weren't always just lowly slaves as usually taught in public schools. Excited, I bought Alex Haley's book and dreamed of finding my tribal affiliations someday. That was the pivotal point when genealogy and family history research became a decades-long adventure for me.

My affectionately called "Aunt" Lavata Williams—actually my first cousin, once-removed—has been our official family historian for decades. One day in June 1982, the elders commanded Lavata to conduct our first-ever family reunion, saying, "Lavata, these children walking around Mt. Vernon, Ohio, don't even know they're related. You know what can come of that. You need to put together a family reunion for the summer of 1983, so everyone can meet."

Back then even adult children were expected to do as they were told, so she did. Aunt Lavata took a genealogy class to learn how to prepare a comprehensive Family History Binder. Because her great-grandfather, Otho Williams, was a slave, it was nearly impossible to find information about him in the era before computers and digital records.

During the summer of 1982, Aunt Lavata interviewed our most-esteemed elders—her mother, Reba Williams, my grandmother, Pearl Williams Carter, my Great Uncle George Booker, and several other family members who were still living in Mt. Vernon, Ohio. "Now Mother, how did you say Margaret Booker brought her family from Virginia to Ohio?" Lavata asked her then seventy-five-year-old mother. Squinting her eyes and bringing her left hand up to massage her temple, my Great Aunt Reba Williams began to speak:

> "Soon after the signing of the Emancipation Proclamation in 1863, Margaret Booker and four of her children climbed onto a buckboard given to them by their former master. Margaret drove by the plantation where her nine-year-old son, Joseph, had been farmed out and quickly picked him up. Our Booker relatives traveled days and slept nights under the buckboard. Crossing into Ohio at Martin's Ferry, they settled in Barnesville, Ohio, about thirty miles from the Virginia border. There, Margaret made a living as a washwoman. In 1881, Joseph and his first wife, Sara Elizabeth Myers Booker (Figure 1.1), moved to Mt. Vernon. Their daughter, Myrtle, who became my mother, was six-months-old."

Figure 1.1. Joseph Booker and Sara Myers Booker, circa 1900. Mt. Vernon, Ohio.

Lavata verified all of their stories with microfilmed census data at the Vital Records Department in Columbus, Ohio. She also traveled to cemeteries in Mt. Vernon and Barnesville, Ohio, to check death records.

She typed up her findings using a manual Underwood typewriter, compiling her efforts into a twenty-two-page booklet of names, dates, and locations containing our Booker, Myers, Jenkins, Walker, and Williams family lines (Figure 1.2).

Sixth Generation

William Booker Scott B: June, 1899, Ill. D: unk
M: unk. C: Barbar Scott, brothers' names unk.

Reba May Williams B: Jan. 23, 1907, Phil. Pa. C: Myrtle L

Pearle Lavata Williams B: Oct. 7, 1908, Phil. Pa.
M: Arthur Taft Carter, Mt. Vernon, Oh.
B: May 2, 1908, Mt. Vernon, Oh. D: unk
C: Norma D., Sara L., Arthur L., Mary E., George W.
Elizabeth A., Dale E.

Jayne E. Williams B: July 23, 1920, Mt. Vernon, Oh.
M: Paul P. Myers, Dec. 1939, Marion, Oh
B: Sept. 1918, Mt. Vernon, Oh. D: 1976, Mt. Vernon, Oh.
C: Saundra L.

Figure 1.2. Excerpt from the Family History Binder prepared by Lavata Williams.

Aunt Lavata printed out copies of her comprehensive binder for each of our families and arranged the entire reunion, held in June 1983 at Mohican State Park, in Lucas, Ohio. About one hundred family members attended, including us, the family who traveled the farthest, from California. Each attendee received a color-coded name tag indicating whether they were from the Booker, Williams, Jenkins, or Thomas family. Each family received a color-coded family history binder with Aunt Lavata's well-researched genealogy information.

"We are a bee-u-tiful people!" (Figure 1.3), proclaimed the son of former slave, Joseph Booker. My Great Uncle George Booker, who was the moderator for this special first family reunion, was a gregarious, well-liked postal carrier in Mt. Vernon, Ohio. "Oh, the stories I shall tell you during this momentous occasion!" Uncle George continued. He certainly made good on his promise. Over the next three hours, he aptly described the Booker family's migration in 1863 from Randolph County,

Virginia, during slavery, and their destination to Belmont County and other counties in Ohio. He concentrated on our family history in Mt. Vernon, Ohio, where most of the family still lived in 1983.

Figure 1.3. 1983 Family reunion at Mohican State Park, Ohio. Photograph by Kathy Marshall (front row, right, in glasses).

We broke bread in the expansive dining room surrounded by large picture windows that looked onto white-bark birch trees that swayed gracefully in the breeze.

Many attendees were meeting family members for the first time. We spent three blissful days in each other's company. The younger kids (meaning twenty-somethings like me) enjoyed going to the rustic rooms of the elders to hear the raucous stories of their youth. Hiking in the lush woods surrounding the Mohican complex, swimming in the clear blue waters of the L-shaped pool, and playing basketball among the forest trees, were among the many outdoor activities that kept attendees of every age constantly busy and happy. The laughter and camaraderie forged new relationships or renewed old relationships in 1983—which we all vowed to continue (and we have over the last thirty-five years).

"It's simple if you are an organized person," Aunt Lavata assured me when I started writing this book in 2016.

Regardless of her glib response, it is still astounding that all of Lavata's research and planning was accomplished in less than one year. It was a phenomenal effort. I constantly marvel at her ability to have pulled it off, mostly by herself before the age of personal computers and cell phones.

Manually searching original, handwritten vital records and census data, along with the inevitable eyestrain from reviewing documents on microfilm, was the bane of genealogists and family historians before computers. Back in the day, genealogists had to travel to the county or state where the records resided. I was fortunate to have access to modern online resources. Computers and traditional genealogical research methods provide our ticket to embark on this journey.

* Baby Steps *

My digital education began in 1979 while working nights at the California Highway Patrol (CHP) as their first Computer Operator. In the basement, down the long dark hall from the dispatch call center, I staffed the first "Help Desk" in our new mainframe computer room. From 3:00 to 11:30 PM I sat in an enclosed room and babysat about a dozen, six-foot tall monolithic computers. They whirred and blinked their Christmas lights as they stored enforcement and personnel data on 10.5-inch magnetic tape reels. I also helped dispatchers around the state keep their brand-new computers and printers up and running. This critical communications link to CHP officers in patrol vehicles ensured they could provide important services to the motoring public in California.

Most of my years with the CHP dealt with computers and data analysis in one way or another. In the Research Unit of the Long Range Planning Section, I gathered and reported various enforcement statistics and evaluated the effectiveness of traffic safety programs. As manager of the Department's Selection Research Program, I provided top management with hiring-related statistical reports.

I spent fifteen years helping create and manage the State Traffic Officer Processing System which managed the progress of cadet applicants who wanted to become Highway Patrol Officers. STOPS tracked the application process, written test results, physical ability test, oral interview, psychological screening, background investigation, medical evaluation, and invitations to the CHP training Academy for one hundred thousand cadet applicants each year.

As part of a Staff Development course, I also created the curriculum for, and taught, basic statistics for ten years to nearly six hundred civilian and sworn employees working in an analytical capacity. The one-day course taught them how to approach and complete written work assignments, which included numbers and statistics. I also created a separate course on how to use the Excel spreadsheet program to better analyze enforcement data and develop charts and graphs.

These experiences prepared me to be comfortable with mainframe and personal computers, in addition to researching, analyzing, evaluating data, and writing technical reports. These skills should have helped me with genealogy research but for some reason this project was not an easy task. In fact, for forty years, I felt like my nose was barely above water in knowing what to do with the volumes of family data I was gathering.

My mother, Mary Ellen Carter Marshall, loved to learn new things. She was the Principal of Camellia Basic Elementary School in a depressed neighborhood in South Sacramento. In 1982, hers was the first elementary school in Sacramento to get Apple computers for a technology lab. She was not one bit afraid of those new devices. She purchased a series of personal computers for her home, loving the technology, especially the digital casino gambling machine programs!

Mom and I were interested in learning more about our family history. She, especially, wanted to track down the father she hadn't seen nor heard from since she was five-years-old in Mt. Vernon, Ohio. What does she remember about her father? He gave her a nickel for her birthday. That's all. What a sad memory.

We began using our personal computers to access the 1880 U.S. Census[6] from the Church of Jesus Christ of Latter-day Saints' brand new "GEDCOM" website.[7] The results back then were difficult to read, but they were certainly better than interpreting handwritten records on rolls of microfilm at the Vital Records office in Ohio. The GEDCOM site was the precursor to the current familysearch.org[8] genealogy website.

It wasn't until 2006, though, when I became an online Ancestry.com[9] member, that I officially started typing our family tree information using the internet (Figure 1.4).

Much of the initial information I key-entered into our online family tree was from Aunt Lavata's comprehensive 1983 Family History Binder she created for our family reunion. I can now easily see all aspects of our family lines in this pedigree view[10] option. This prompted me to find out more about our broader family ties.

In 2009, my youngest son, Matthew, and I flew into Atlanta, Georgia, to visit my first cousin, Julie, and her family. A few days later, we all piled into their blue Caravan for a nine-hour scenic drive from Georgia, through the lush forests and rocky hills of Kentucky and Tennessee, crossing the border with Ohio, then continuing north to Columbus for a family wedding.

Always the multi-tasker, I borrowed my cousin's van the morning of the wedding to attend a "Lett and Myers" family reunion one hour away in Zanesville, Ohio. Incidentally, Zanesville is not only known for its clay potteries (I am a potter) and mixed-race Melungeon[11] population, but it is also where my mother and father met on a blind date in 1952 at the skating rink. If they hadn't met there in little Zanesville, I would never have been born, and this book would never have been published. Surreal!

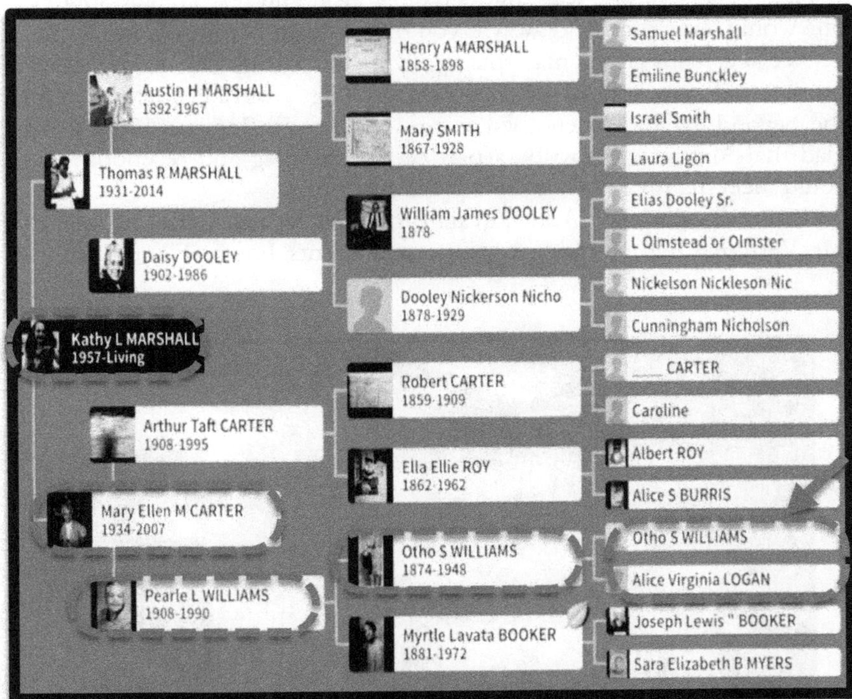

Figure 1.4. Pedigree chart showing Kathy Marshall's relationship to her great-great-grandfather, Otho Williams.

At the Zanesville family reunion, everyone I met was new to me, except for Barbara Nelson, the dedicated family historian for my Myers family line. They had amassed an incredible number of family history binders and quilts. I could only stay a couple of hours, having to drive back to Columbus for my young cousin, Everett's, wedding.

Because my parents, brother, sister, and I lived so far away from the rest of our Ohio family, we missed all the normal family functions like birthday parties, holiday gatherings, helping family when they are sick, summer sleep-overs with our cousins, and even attending funerals to acknowledge our departed loved ones. To be able to participate in the special co-mingling of two young lovers at an outdoor wedding in Columbus, Ohio, was special indeed.

While waiting for the nuptials to begin, we chatted with Aunt Lavata Williams and her mother, the Grand Dame of our family, Great Aunt Reba Williams, who was a mere 102-years-old at the time. Although badly hunched over from severe osteoporosis, Aunt Reba was able to use her walker by herself. She was still incredibly lucid and refreshingly spunky. She would slap your hand away if you tried to help her in any way.

We saw many of my maternal family members that day. I was sad my mother was only able to watch the proceedings from her lofty perch in the beyond, having succumbed to breast cancer in January 2007. I was glad that Matthew got to be a part of the wedding and reception, and could meet many of his cousins for the first time.

The following day, Aunt Lavata drove my cousin, Julie, and me, to Mt. Vernon, Ohio, to visit my great-grandparents' house (Figure 1.5).

Figure 1.5. Otho Sherman and Myrtle Williams housed up to sixteen of their relatives in the 1930s and 1940s in this house in Mt. Vernon, OH, Ohio.

This aging, white clapboard, Cooper-Bessemer Engine Company row structure housed up to sixteen Williams and Carter family members in the 1930s and 1940s. Great-grandad Otho "Sherman" Williams was born in 1874 in Washington County, Maryland. He was the son of former slaves Otho and Alice Williams. Sherman's wife, Myrtle Lavata Booker Williams, was the daughter of Sara Elizabeth Myers and Joseph Booker. Joseph was born a slave in 1854 in West Virginia.

My mother, Mary Ellen Carter Marshall, often told us stories about sleeping in one double bed with three of her siblings at her Granddad Sherman's house. Two other siblings were in a crib, and the seventh slept on a pallet on the floor because she wet the bed. Mom's charming tales and the stories of several other Williams family members and descendants are included in my first book, *The Ancestors Are Smiling!*

During my 2009 visit, Aunt Lavata drove Julie and me to the expansive and restful Mound View cemetery (Figure 1.6) in Mt. Vernon, Ohio, where we left colorful new plastic flowers for our many Williams, Carter, Booker, and Myers relatives buried there.

Figure 1.6. Mound View Cemetery where most Ohio Williams' family are buried. Mt. Vernon, Ohio. Photograph by Kathy Marshall, 2009.

Four years later, in October 2013, I visited my cousin, Julie, to attend the American Association of Retired Persons (AARP) Convention held that year in Atlanta, Georgia. I also rented a car and drove three hours east to Columbus, Georgia, on the Alabama-Georgia border. I spent three days there by myself on a genealogy field trip to research my dad's Marshall family.

With my trusty iPad, I took photos of the Marshall plot in Porterdale's "colored" cemetery, spent one day with the African American History Museum owner, and another at the Georgia State Archives and Library.

Truth be told, I was petrified to be "driving while black"[12] by myself in the deep South. I had read too many historical horror stories about blacks being racially profiled by police, lynched or raped indiscriminately, especially in good ol' Dixie.[13]

I am happy to admit that everyone I encountered in Georgia was as sweet as peach pie. I vowed to go back when it was time to write the Marshall family genealogy book.

* The Journey Begins in Earnest *

I have always been interested in African art and African American history and culture. I established my Kanika African Sculptures art business in 1993 while working full-time, being married to my talented Fire Captain husband, and raising two sons. Creating a gregarious alter-ego for myself—the artist called "Kanika"—allowed me to pop out of my introverted shell.

As Kanika, I use clay, African fabric, glass, stone, and welded recycled metal to create Afrocentric, indoor-outdoor sculptures. Wouldn't it be fabulous to find out through this research that my ancestors were artists, potters, or metal workers like me? But I'm getting ahead of myself.

On May 23, 2012, at 55-years-of-age, it was time to welcome the third stage of my life with open arms and a willing heart: blessed retirement. I was finally living the "American Dream." After so many fulfilling years with the CHP, I was ready to get serious about documenting our family history.

At the top of my list was to give a saliva sample for my first DNA test with the Ancestry DNA company. It took almost eight of the longest weeks of my life waiting for the results—almost as unnerving as waiting for Santa Claus to come down the chimney with my presents. When I opened the email containing my genetic DNA verdict, I gasped. DNA doesn't lie, does it? There was a lot of cream in my African coffee.

It was then that I had to face the fact that maybe I am mixed after all. For the first time in my life, I wanted to find out not only the African component of our ethnic equation but also the white people who gave my family this *cafe-au-lait* skin tone. (Part IV details our DNA results.)

Even though I had stepped up my genealogy activities since retiring in 2012, I had found little more than my Aunt Lavata had discovered decades ago. Do you want to know something terribly embarrassing? Truthfully, I had largely been unsuccessful because of my stubborn resistance to following recommended research protocols. I hope you will learn from my mistakes and avoid these misguided steps.

- All these years I usually did not print out the documents I found because I wanted to save paper. Most of my findings are carefully arranged in folders, by family, inside my laptop computer. The experts stress the importance of printing out documents and organizing them in binders or folders that can be reviewed side by side, to better visualize familial relationships. Plus, if your computer crashes, you won't lose all your research.

- Although many genealogists maintain that familysearch.org contains better sources of data for African American research, I have almost exclusively utilized the user-friendly Ancestry.com since 2006, to access vital records, census documents, my online family tree, and DNA results. After all, I was paying an annual subscription for Ancestry.com—why shouldn't I use it?

- Every genealogy class I attended indicated the importance of reviewing every column in the U.S. Census to obtain valuable contextual information about our relatives' lives and that of their neighbors. We should review at least three pages before and after our relatives' census page, to learn whether other families with the same surname were living nearby. Those could be family members or former slave masters. I did not follow that advice either, instead, mainly only reviewing the gender and ethnicity of people with the same surname.

- Slave research is best accomplished by reviewing the probate, land records, and bills of sale of the slave master. None of my family knew who the slave master was, and I had no idea how to figure out that critical information. So, I never learned how to access those extremely important records until starting this book.

I repeated the same mistakes for years, getting nowhere in the search for my enslaved ancestors. I needed to turn over a new leaf and find other solutions, such as the ones recommended by the experts.

In May 2016, I began living the sixtieth year of my life. A significant feeling of unease crept into my bones and my mind. I realized that if I died tomorrow, all the years of genealogy research would be for naught. My kids wouldn't know what to do with the folders in my computer or with boxes of disorganized records. Forty years of family history would be lost if I didn't do something with it, but what?

In preparation for a June 2016 visit from my Aunt Lavata, our esteemed Family Historian—her first visit since our 1986 family reunion in California thirty years ago—I began madly printing documents from my computer and compiling binders of organized information for five of my family lines. Everyone knows that to be a real genealogist, you must have binders full of printed census records, birth and death certificates, etc., to prove you are using real data and not making up stories about your ancestors' history. I really wanted to look credible in her eyes, so I made the darn genealogy binders and arranged them ever-so-nicely on the bookshelf in my research library (my son's old bedroom) at home.

I soon realized, though, that binders of facts and figures did not present a clear picture of how families are related, even though they are critical to providing proof of our findings. When I leave this earthly plane, I hope my children would not throw those genealogy binders away. Realistically, they don't know what to do with those facts and figures and would likely dispose of my research.

I fervently believed the dry data had to be developed into interesting stories, with photographs and other visuals that anyone can read and understand . . . like in a book. How do I do that?

Why couldn't I figure out how to write a genealogy book about my family? I did that type of research, analysis, and technical writing for decades. I minored in Research Methodology in 1983 for a master's degree in Public Administration. I taught others how to tackle every assignment. Why can't I do it for something so important to me? The ancestors wouldn't let me sleep, whispering "Write our stories, Write Our Stories, WRITE OUR STORIES NOW!" every day since my Aunt Lavata visited me in June 2016. I had to work it out.

Now truth be told, I had already written a dozen hardbound, family history, photo-type books about the lives of my mother (Figure 1.7), father, two sons, and two grandchildren. I had also created several photo-journal books about my travels abroad. Now in my sixtieth year, I want to write a self-published book to be sold on Amazon.com so my family's stories will be out in the world forever.

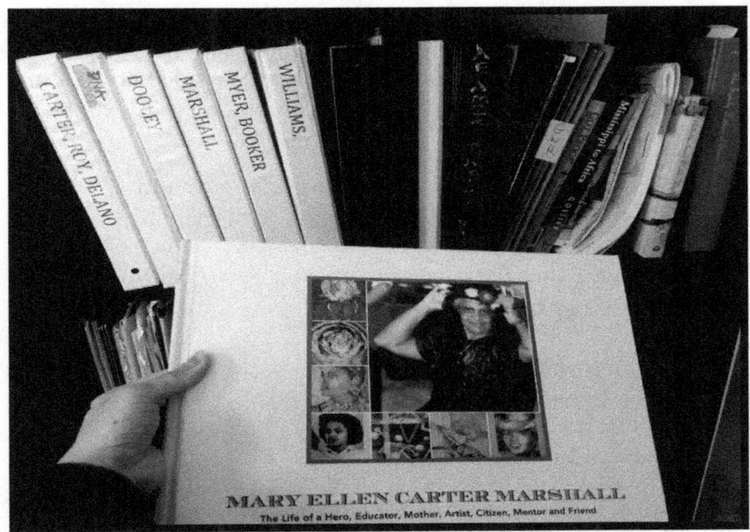

Figure 1.7. Kathy Marshall's genealogy Binders and photo books.

"Sobering" did not describe my discomfort at the outset of this project contemplating that I am the second-oldest left in my father's family and the third-oldest left in my mother's Williams family line since the passing of my 93-year-old Great Uncle Charles Williams in November of 2017. He died knowing his life story was commemorated in *The Ancestors Are Smiling!* That's what it's all about—leaving a legacy.

I have a burning desire to commemorate our living family members in a worldwide forum, as well as those who have passed on. I looked forward to becoming a present-day Hercule Poirot detective, using my little gray cells to uncover the truth of my Williams' family history.

This "*Finding Otho: The Search for Our Enslaved Williams Family*" book will reside in research libraries, be available for purchase on Amazon in hardcover, paperback and eBook (electronic book) format. This book will not only delve into black life in eighteenth and nineteenth century Maryland but could also be used as a guidebook to others on breaking through the "1870 Brick Wall" to shed light on the lives of enslaved ancestors. I also intended to take a dip in the somewhat uncharted sea of DNA analysis for genealogy research.

In my "research library" at home, I had a reasonable collection of black history books from my 1970s college-level African American History and Black Political Thought classes. There were also numerous African art books I have collected over the decades.

To become more familiar with others who have written books similar to what I wanted to write, I began purchasing print and electronic genealogy books from black authors. Their written works served as muses to give me ideas on how to best document my findings. They included:

- *From Mississippi to Africa - A Journey of Discovery* and *150 Years Later: Broken Ties Mended,* by Melvin J. Collier.
- *A Mulatto Slave: The Events in the Life of Peter Hunt 1844-1915,* by Denise Griggs.
- *African American Manumissions in Washington County, Maryland,* by Marsha Lynne Fuller.
- *Cane River,* by Lalita Tadema.
- *Fifty Years in Chains or, the Life of an American Slave,* by Charles Ball.
- *From Slavery to Salvation, The Autobiography of Rev. Thomas W. Henry of the A.M.E. Church,* by Jean Libby.
- *Gleanings of Freedom: Free and Slave Labor Along the Mason-Dixon Line*, 1790-1860 by Max Grivno.
- *Got Proof - My Genealogical Journey Through the Use of Documentation,* by Michael N. Henderson.
- *Incidents in the Life of a Slave Girl,* by Harriet Jacobs.
- *Maryland Women in the Civil War: Unionists, Rebels, Slaves, and Spies,* by Claudia Floyd.
- *Slavery and Freedom on the Middle Ground, Maryland During the 19th Century*, by Barbara J. Fields.
- *The Fugitive Blacksmith,* by James W.C. Pennington.
- *The Life of Olaudah Equiano, or Gustavus Vassa, the African*, by Olaudah Equiano.
- *Their Eyes Were Watching God*, by Zora Neale Hurston.
- *When We Were Colored,* by Eva Rutland.

These riveting and well-documented texts, among many others listed in the Bibliography, became trusted guidebooks for this "*Finding Otho*" research project.

* Starting to Write This Book *

Fast forward to a rainy first day of October 2016. I had seen an advertisement on the "Our Black Ancestry" Facebook page for a webinar that would teach African Americans how to write our family stories. Bingo! That's just what I needed. With much anticipation, I listened to an online presentation from Anita Henderson, creator of the Genealogists' Writing Room[14] organization. She encouraged us to put our family stories into writing NOW, instead of letting others write our history for us.

Anita suggested we start writing what we already knew about ourselves, our immediate family, and other family stories that we already knew well. With her pleasant, upbeat voice, and engaging smile, Anita assured us that not knowing all the answers before starting to write was OK.

Her steadfast recommendation? START WRITING NOW. She said it would be acceptable even if we were never able to connect all the dots to our family beginnings. She indicated that writing about the steps we took to find the truth could be almost as valuable as the actual resolution itself. Dates and places were important, of course, but the *story* is what makes history come alive to the reader.

She affirmed what I believed and feared. When I am dead and gone, my kids and grandkids will not care about the cold facts and figures in my genealogy binders. I am confident they will definitely keep a professionally produced family history book that has pictures and stories of themselves and our ancestors. Being permitted to fail was comforting for a goal-oriented, Type-A person like me.

I realized that Anita uttered the same things I'd read for years in books and heard in genealogy classes. This time, though, I was *ready* to hear it and act on it. This time, the gears turned a notch, and everything finally clicked into place.

Anita's mouth still moved, but I seemed to be having an out-of-body experience. My mind floated just outside my head and my internal artist alter-ego, Kanika, chided me: *Now Kathy, you would never have told your CHP boss, 'Sorry, but I can't finish this assignment because I don't know how to do it.' You have got to pretend the process of writing this book operates like any other assignment.*

I agreed with my impertinent Gemini twin, Kanika: *You are right. I always found a way to finish every work assignment,* and *on time, whether I knew anything about the subject or not.*

The fog in my brain began to clear, and a revelation washed over me. *What if I began to think of my ancestors as my boss? What if I started thinking of writing this book as being no different from completing a CHP assignment? After all, I taught six hundred CHP employees how to research, analyze, and write memos, issue papers, and technical study reports in my quarterly Statistics Class. Writing this book will be simple if I use the same template methodology that I used for every assignment in my work life. And what if I begin to know my ancestors so well that I begin channeling their existence into being, like my author friends say I should be doing? They say the characters in my book should begin talking with me, directing my research, showing me what their lives were like. Yes, I CAN do this!*

By the end of Anita's webinar, I knew exactly what tack to take. A book title hit me right away: "The Cream in My Coffee Wore a Crown." That would be wholly appropriate if my initial theory could be proven that my second great-grandfather, Otho Williams, was fathered by a member of the white Otho Holland Williams family, who had married into English Royalty over five hundred years ago. (More about that revolutionary concept is fully explored in Chapter 5.)

I was ready to write a properly formatted, genealogical research book complete with heartwarming family stories about my enslaved Williams ancestors and their descendants. The book could be used by my family, as well as others who sought ideas on how to break through the 1870 Brick Wall to find their African American ancestors, immigrants who have difficulty finding historical documents, or even adopted people looking for strategies to find their birth parents.

This book would utilize cutting-edge DNA technology to find common African and European ancestors. It would make my family proud. I fully expected the ancestors to perch on my shoulder, helping me all the way to the publishing finish line. "Write our stories, write our stories NOW " they sweetly whispered in my ears.

I transitioned into thinking of the project as being an assignment from the ancestors. They gave me a tight deadline of December 31, 2016, for the first draft and published on amazon.com in early 2017. Understand that I had no idea how to self-publish a book. I was just learning how to write a creative nonfiction memoir storybook! My ancestor bosses had spoken. I could not let them down.

My marching orders were to make the information in the book available to as many people as possible. That meant online, in libraries, in research centers, on my online family tree, as well as a printed book. That approach would accomplish the goal of permanence, allowing our ancestors' stories to live on forever.

At that moment I felt so powerful like I could do anything. Maybe I'd become a missionary for writing family history storybooks! With this book published, I could do speaking engagements at bookstores and genealogy conferences. I could inspire others to do the same thing for their family legacy. Kanika brought me back to earth. *OK now, you haven't even started your first book! No more red Kool-Aid for you!*

The negative self-talk showed up with a vengeance. Why will this effort be any different from your previous failures? Tick-tock, tick-tock. You're not getting any younger. You have to be successful this time. Your ancestor bosses have put their faith in you. They know you are the only one in your generation who cares about this topic enough to dedicate your life to it.

Kanika rose to defend me. "You are more knowledgeable about how to access African American records online now. Plus, you have set aside your thriving art business, to which you have dedicated fifteen to twenty hours per week for the past twenty-three years. You have stopped playing online Scrabble games to wholly dedicate your brain to writing and self-publishing this book. You have vowed to do things correctly this time. I'm confident you can do it."

On that magical first day of October 2016, as if conjured out of thin air, it suddenly became crystal clear how to proceed. The framework for the project, shown in Appendix A, and outline for each chapter appeared in my head as though someone—the ancestors?—were downloading the book directly into my brain.

I created a word processing template, which included the book Title on the first page, followed by a Copyright page, Dedication, Table of Contents, Acknowledgements, Introduction, Timeline, ten Chapter headings for various family members, a DNA chapter, Epilogue, Appendix pages, Bibliography, and End Notes. All I had to do was type my findings and stories into my actual book instead of hand-written notebooks. I initially brainstormed over fifty questions I wanted to investigate (Appendix B).

- How, when, and where did Otho Williams live?
- Who were his parents and where did they come from?
- Who was his owner and how did he treat him?
- Was he freed before the end of slavery?
- Did he fight in the Civil War?
- Did he become a successful person after slavery?
- How did the Williams family end up in Mt. Vernon, Ohio, where my mom was born?

I copied and pasted the questions into the appropriate chapters in the book template. I had begun! It made the most sense to start with the generations closest to me and work backward through the generations, like a pedigree chart, back to my enslaved ancestors. Since we still have three Williams elders alive who remember family life back in the 1930s to the present time, and who can help me get the facts right, that seemed to be the most practical approach.

The memories started to flow. Ah yes. I remembered our three-day, cross-country train trip to Ohio where we met our cousins for the first time in 1966, remembering those phosphorescent fireflies we saw on that first night in Mt. Vernon. I would describe what it was like growing up in a nearly all-white neighborhood in Sacramento, California, during the Civil Rights era, and the excitement of discovering in fifth grade that I was an artist like my mother.

My kids will get a kick out of how I met their dad on a blind date. Looking back, how *did* I ever go to college full-time during the day while working full-time at night? I could write about the tough years of becoming a single mother after my divorce, and then becoming the sole parent when my ex-husband was killed by a drunk driver in 1998.

I must describe the joy when my oldest son joined the Marines in 2003, the pride when my youngest son earned a black belt in taekwondo, and the bliss of becoming a grandmother for the first time in 2008. On fire with enthusiasm, I began typing into the book template the parts of *my* life that the grandkids might enjoy.

I asked my brother and sister to email me their memories, as they might be different from mine. I typed a few of my maternal grandmother's letters in her "Day's Work Raised a Family" chapter in my previous Williams family book, *The Ancestors Are Smiling!* along with notes and transcribed videos about her spunky sister, Aunt Reba Williams, in her "Super Star at 106" chapter in the same book.

I planned to heavily sample my mother's personal journals from her youth and adulthood, as well as excerpts from the photo book biography I created after her death in 2007. Like a mad-woman, I was copying and pasting typed information into the appropriate chapters of my steadily enlarging manuscript.

I even began writing a chapter about my father's life—even though he wasn't a descendant of Otho and Alice Williams. Because both he and my mother made me, he had to have a place in this book. Just like I did with Mom's photo book, I copied and pasted text and images from the oversized photo book I created of dad's memorable life after he died in 2014.

Day after day (and well into the nights), my initial book outline quickly filled out with some measure of detail from the ancestral ether through my fingers into my laptop. I typed the stories I already knew into my book template. That is definitely the best way to start writing a family history book. *Why did I not do this sooner?*

So many exciting, funny, sad, and life-affirming stories kept gushing out of my brain from the elders. Within five weeks, I had written over eighty single-spaced pages, thirty-five thousand words, including photos, charts, and graphs. It was like a manic disco party beating an African rhythm in my brain. Sparkling ideas flew round and round inside my head, landing with a dancer's grace onto the digital pages within my laptop. My body suffered. My gym membership ignored, I got four hours of sleep a night, and existed on chocolate chips and unsweetened yogurt.

In the sixth week of composing, I was printing a copy of my efforts to mail to Aunt Lavata in time for her birthday right after Thanksgiving 2016. I hoped she would correct my mistakes and add more goodies to our family history book.

Surprisingly soon, the stories I already knew were neatly housed in my book. The time had come to tackle the difficult questions for which I had no answers. How does one start writing a research book when you don't know the end of the story? James Ison recommended in his 2016 Roots-Tech[15] keynote presentation that "it's best to actually write as you're doing your research."[16]

That's what I did, writing the book as I found breakthroughs to the many unknowns. It was a veritable roller coaster ride of discoveries and breakthroughs, as well as frustrations with my disappointments when theories did not pan out. But, like the Energizer Bunny, I'd bounce back with new ideas of other approaches to try.

I felt pressured to publish a book about my ancestors knowing this time I must finish or all of the work I'd done, so far, would be for naught. Since it takes six to eight weeks to get the results from DNA testing, I purchased DNA test kits for my three elders—Great Uncle Charles Williams, Aunt Lavata Williams, and Uncle Dale Carter, and several other family members too.

In the past when I tried to find my enslaved ancestors without following the recommended research steps and came up empty-handed, the wise words of Yoda of Star Wars fame chided me: "Do or do not, there is no try."[17]

I adopted a daily mantra: **"I shall diligently follow the advice of genealogy experts and thoroughly search all available resources to write and self-publish a book about my Williams ancestors."**

More than anything I wanted to be like Alex Haley and visit the African tribes, as well as places in Europe where my ancestors lived. I hoped this research would lead me there.

At the outset of this process, all I knew was my current family tree, shown in Figure 1.8. I did not know whether I could answer any of my research questions, but I had to start somewhere. I imagined myself stepping into Mr. Peabody's Way Back Machine[18] and heading to eighteenth and nineteenth-century western Maryland to see what I could discover about what happened to Otho Williams and his family (Figure 1.8), during, and after slavery.

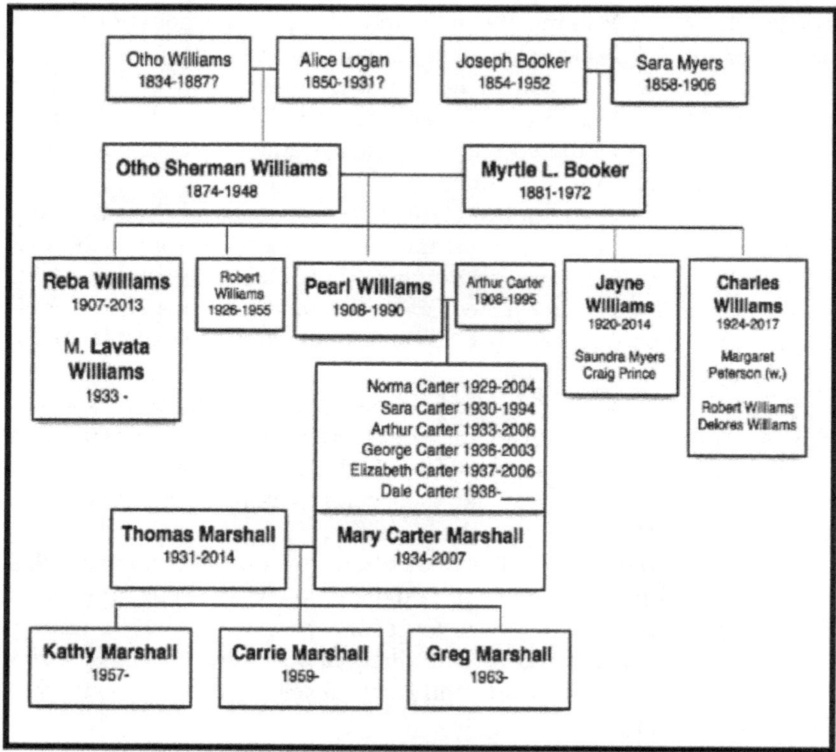

Figure 1-8. Family tree from Otho and Alice Williams' generation down to Kathy Marshall.

Chapter 2 - Introducing Otho Williams

Who was Otho Williams? My elders only knew he was born near Hagerstown, Maryland in about 1834. He had a wife named Alice, and a child named Otho Sherman Williams, who was my first great-grandfather. We also assumed he had been a slave because we could not find him in my records before the 1870 U.S. Census.

I closed my eyes and began to imagine what Otho's life must have been like as a slave. A scene from Roots: The Story of an America Family, began playing in my head.

It was a dusty summer morning. Several bedraggled slaves were in the wheat field below, their overseer cracking the whip to get them to work harder. Was one of those workers my second great-grandfather? I so desperately wanted to find Otho to learn about his life and my Williams ancestors that my eyes and ears began playing tricks on me. As clear as day I heard an indignant voice shout at me from behind my left shoulder.

"What do you mean, 'Finding Otho: The Search for Our Williams Ancestors?' I'm not lost. I'm right here!" I turned around, and materializing out of nowhere, coming slowly into my vision, was an unfamiliar man. He seemed about 5'9" inches tall. He had the trim, muscular physique of many African American men, but with the coloring of a tanned white man. His pate nearly bald, he carried a beige, rumpled hat in his weathered hands. His white shirt with rolled-up sleeves revealed powerful forearms. His pants were made from a coarse khaki-beige fabric, and his sturdy shoes were a dusty-brown. He had a salt-and-pepper mustache that extended just beyond the corners of his thin lips. His dark brown eyes were smiling with upturned creases in the corners.

Was this pleasant-looking, older man my second great-grandfather, Otho Williams, here to visit me and possibly shed some light on his life as a slave? I shivered with pleasure at the possibility.

"I'm so sorry to tell you," I stammered, "but my generation knows almost nothing about you, and neither does my mother's. The four of us elders who are still alive only know that you were a slave born in Washington County, Maryland, in about 1834. We know your wife's name was Alice, and that you had several children, one of whom was my first great-grandfather, Otho Sherman Williams—your namesake.

"Our family historian, Lavata Williams, your great-granddaughter, believes each generation receives mechanical gifts, genetically, from you. *You* are the key. *You* are the star of this book. *You* are the one I want to research and write about, so that my children, and their children's children, will know about your legacy."

"You're pullin' my leg, right?" Otho replied, winking at me. When I slowly shook my head no, the gleam left his mischievous eyes. "You mean my life story did not last after I died? Are you sayin' my children didn't remember me to their children? My life didn't matter at all to my family?" I watched his initial bravado dissolve, leaving his raw emotion bare.

"Now don't say that. I *have* been looking for you for forty years, but I was a child when I started, and you know adults don't pay no mind to children. When I became an adult, I asked Aunt Lavata about you, but she did not know much either."

Trying to comfort the strange hallucination who seemed to be the ancestor I was investigating, I said, "Life happened. I got married and had children. I got divorced when the children were young and had to take on a second job to support all of us. When I could, I did squeeze in genealogy research—that's what we call trying to find out about our ancestors. It wasn't until I retired from my day job that I could start looking for you."

When he remained pensive and silent, I continued. "I plan to begin learning about you by writing down what I *do* know: you and Alice are listed in the 1870 and 1880 U.S. Census. Do you remember someone coming by your house in 1870 asking you all sorts of questions, like where were you born, how old you were, how much your land and personal property was worth, and whether you and your wife could read and write?"

"Nah, I was out workin,' but Alice tol' me a tall white man with a white beard did come by the house one day and asked her a bunch of questions, but she didn't know what they be used for. I never dreamed that talk be used so many years later," Otho trembled while asking. "What year is it now, anyway?"

My answer, "the year 2016" was received with stunned silence as you can imagine when contemplating the 125-year-gap in time. I continued, "The 1870 Census was the first year since slavery that all people were counted by their first and last name, with their sex and an estimate of their age and race, listing everyone living in the same household. I've learned quite a bit about you by reading every category on the census document, keeping in mind that the categories change a bit from each ten-year census to the next."

For years I had been told that one must print out and review several census pages before and after the desired relative's record. That makes it possible to compare the information for the whole neighborhood. If there are other families with the same surname nearby, they could have been the slave master, or relatives. Since Otho has no concept of printers or computers, of course, I left that thought to myself.

"Great-grandpa, people who are experts at finding ancestors told me that some free people might have lived near their former owners to continue working for them as they had when they were slaves. Some of those newly freed men and women might have received land to sharecrop with the former owner, but that kept them tied to the former slave master year after year."

Nodding vigorously in agreement, Otho shouted, "You are right! I know plenty of people that happened to. It's like they get stuck paying their former master but never get ahead." A veil of pain shaded his eyes for a moment, then he quietly added, "That happened to me and Alice with our land."

Trying to pick up his spirits, I told him, "I put together information comparing sixty-seven of your neighbors; about half of them are shown in a chart in Figure 2.1." Otho perked up with his eyes opened wide indicating his interest in what I was about to say, as I pointed to the chart.

"Census data is only as accurate as the person giving the information, whether it was an adult, a child, a family member, or a neighbor. The census taker must accurately record those family details or it's 'garbage in, garbage out.' For example, did they write the correct race and age for each person, and spell the name correctly during a time when most people did not know how to spell their name in the first place?"

With a far-off look in his eye, perhaps remembering something painful in his past, Otho did his best to hide his anger. "That was one of slavery's biggest crimes: not allowing us colored folk to know learnin' and readin' and writin' our name, and understandin' numbers. That's why I made my children walk to that colored school five miles away, so nobody would be able to pull the wool over their eyes when they wanted to buy something at the store, or buy land, or figure out how much seed they'd need to sow on five acres. Me and Alice wanted our children to be smart and do better than us."

I could see and feel the cloud of pain, anger, and embarrassment, hanging around him. A wounded red aura, damaged, and nearly invisible emanated around his backside, leaving him vulnerable to life's hard lessons. He needed a hug, but apparitions have no corporal substance, so instead I changed the subject.

Dwelling #	Head Name	Age	Race of Head	Profession of Head	#People in House	Value of Real Estate $	Value of Personal $	Total Value	Total Value (Average)
273	Keedy, C	42	W	Farmer	7	$15,000	$2,000	$17,000	$17,000
274	Gigous, E	56	W	Keeping house	3			$0	$0
275	Hickman, T	52	W	zCooper	3			$0	$0
276	Thomas, H	58	W	Wagonmaker	5	$200	$100	$300	$300
277	Line, M	50	W	Farmer	10	$24,500	$2,000	$26,500	$26,500
278	Bazzel, M	25	W	Day/farm laborer	4			$0	$0
279	Wigle, J	43	W	Farmer	5	$3,000	$600	$3,600	$3,600
280	Doub, S	64	W	Farmer, Ret.	6	$0	$0	$0	$0
281	Wagner, S	67	W	Farmer	9	$9,000	$1,200	$10,200	$10,200
282	NicodemusJ	48	W	Farmer	9		$1,000	$1,000	$1,000
283	**Douglas,S**	**34**	**Black**	**Day/farm laborer**	**6**			$0	$0
284	Ringer, J	48	W	Farmer	5	$20,000	$15,000	$35,000	$35,000
285	Huffer, A	33	W	Farmer	8	$15,000	$2,000	$17,000	$17,000
286	Huffer, S	35	W	Farmer	4		$1,000	$1,000	$1,000
287	Davis, L	57	W	Keeping house	6		$300	$300	$300
288	Schlosser, E	30	W	Farmer	4		$1,500	$1,500	$1,500
289	Thomas, N	41	W	Farmer	7	$40,000	$14,000	$54,000	$54,000
290	Wastler, J	22	W	Day/farm laborer	3			$0	$0
291	Mumma, N	37	W	Farmer	7	$200	$7,000	$7,200	$7,200
292	Foltz, J	35	W	Farmer	8	$150	$900	$1,050	$1,050
293	Schlosser, J	59	W	Farmer, retired	4	$22,000	$1,000	$23,000	$23,000
294	Finifrock, D.	42	W	Day/farm laborer	7		$100	$100	$100
295	**Cary, M**	**28**	**Black**	**Day/farm laborer**	**3**			$0	$0
296	**Stuart, C**	**26**	**Black**	**Day/farm laborer**	**3**			$0	$0
297	Orrick, G	42	W	Farmer	11		$2,000	$2,000	$2,000
298	Roher, D	24	W	Day/farm laborer	3			$0	$0
299	Baker, L	40	W	Day/farm laborer	9	$200	$100	$300	$300
300	**Williams, O**	**37**	**Mulatto Otho**	**Day/farm laborer**	**3**	**$1,000**	**$100**	$1,100	$1,100
301	KeplingerN	48	W	zBroommaker	3	$500	$100	$600	$600
302	Einberger,H	53	W	Shoemaker	3	$400	$100	$500	$500
303	HammondN	36	W	Farmer	4		$1,200	$1,200	$1,200
304	**Cary, T**	**22**	**Black**	**Day/farm laborer**	**3**			$0	$0
305	Jones, J	62	W	Day/farm laborer	3			$0	$0
306	Groh, J	38	W	School teacher	5		$100	$100	$100
307	**Monroe, P**	**32**	**Black**	**Day/farm laborer**	**5**			$0	$0
308	NewcomerD	56	W	Farmer	7	$34,000	$3,000	$37,000	$37,000

Figure 2.1. Comparison of Otho William's Boonsboro neighborhood wealth in 1870, Part 1, by dwelling number.

"I copied out the page with your family information and about four census pages before and after yours. I typed the last and first names of all the heads-of-household, their ages, gender, race, the number of people in the house, the head-of-household's occupation, as well as the estimated value of their real and personal estate into a spreadsheet," I said as I pointed to each item on the rows and columns, explaining what they said, just as I might to a youngster who hasn't learned to read words and numbers yet. "This chart shows the information by household."

"According to the 1870 Census, you were a 37-year-old mulatto man who lived near the Benevola post office in District 6 of Washington County. That would have included the towns of Boonsboro, Funkstown, Beaver Creek and Antietam. *Antietam?* When I first learned that, it was the first time I realized that my ancestors lived near an important Civil War Battle of Antietam. Before this project, I never thought I would become excited about learning about a war, any war, or whether my ancestors fought in it."

Otho spoke up. "Granddaughter, it was a terrible time. We had thousands of Confed'ret and Union soldiers fighting four big battles in these parts. So many died from guns and more from disease. Soldiers looted our crops and animals. Blood and smells of death were everywhere. Many neighbors wanted the South to win, turning against former friend-neighbors rooting for the Yankees. I'll tell you all about it sometime, but now I want to hear more about your studies and what you found out about me."

"Great-grandpa, I look forward to hearing *anything* you want to tell me about your life!" I said, thrilled to have made the spiritual connection with him. "The 1870 census indicated that Alice was 20- years-old, and you had a one-month-old son named Edgar E. Williams." Otho nodded his head and smiled at the memory of his first-born son. "You were a day laborer working for someone else, right?"

"Mr. David Newcomer," Otho stated with no more description than that.

"When I learned you had real estate valued at $1,000, just a few years after slavery ended, I exclaimed aloud, 'What? My Otho was a landowner?' I was *so* proud of you." Otho beamed at my acknowledgment of his notable accomplishment.

'I learned that your personal estate was worth $100. The census revealed that neither you nor Alice could write, but it said she could read. That's a lot more information than I knew before starting this research journey. I wanted to study whether you were better or worse off than the average person living in your neighborhood. I put all the census information into what we call a spreadsheet." I pointed at my chart in Figure 2.2 and started reading some of the names of his neighbors.

In the next instant, Otho's face brightened, and his eyes twinkled "Ol' Sam Douglas, and Moses and Taylor Cary? Those were some of my best buddies. Them and me and Charlie Stuart and Pete Monroe worked together for the Bakers and the Newcomers, the Souths and the Funks. Yes, there was only a few other colored in the area, so our families stuck together."

"I got lots of useful information from the 1870 and 1880 Censuses. Unfortunately, there was no 1890 Census because most of those records burned. You were not found in the 1900 Census, leaving me to assume you had died sometime in the twenty-year period between 1880 and 1900."

Otho stammered, "I'm sorry granddaughter. I can't help you there. You see, I had a pain in my chest early one morning. It woke me up but there was so much pain, I couldn't speak or move. I can't remember anything else after that, not even exactly when it happened. There was nuthin' for a long while until Alice came along, then my children."

Tears welled in the corner of my eyes knowing the mystery of Otho's death would not be solved that day. "I am so disappointed, great-grandpa that I haven't found out when you died, but let's talk about what I did find, and you correct anything that's wrong, OK?"

"OK."

"To get an idea of how successful you were in comparison to your neighbors, I produced individual and summary statistics by profession, then by the value of their real and personal estate, then by the number of people in each household," showing him Figure 2.2.

Otho's eyes glazed over a bit—like those of the students in my statistics classes at CHP—probably not understanding anything I was saying. I kept talking anyway, hoping it would eventually make sense and get him to talk about his experiences.

"Of the sample of sixty-seven heads-of-household in 1870, almost half were farmers or retired farmers, and one-third were day laborers or farm laborers, including you," I said, pointing my index finger at him. "Three of the remaining neighbors were keeping house, three were wagon makers, two were shoemakers, and there was one from each of the following skilled trades: an auctioneer, blacksmith, broom maker, cooper, miller, retail dry goods person, school teacher, and turnpike gatekeeper. That paints a picture of a neighborhood of active people who provided almost everything a community would need to be self-sufficient." Finished, I smiled and looked directly at him, hoping he would speak.

"That's true," Otho agreed. "We had a lot of people with all sorts of skills in our neighborhood, but everybody was spread out, not like in Hagerstown or Funkstown where peoples' houses was right next to each other. We all had land," he said, standing a bit straighter.

Dwelling #	Head Name	Age	Race of Head	Profession of Head	#People in House	Value of Real Estate $	Value of Personal $	Total Value	Total Value (Average)
314	Hooser, C	62	W	Farmer, retired	4	$6,500	$5,000	$11,500	$11,500
315	Murray, E	62	W	Keeping house	2	$800	$100	$900	$900
316	Kitemiller,D	36	W	Turnpike Gatekeeper	7		$100	$100	$100
317	Stouffer,D	31	W	ZAuctioneer	5		$2,000	$2,000	$2,000
318	NewcomerE	25	W	zDry Goods	6		$100	$100	$100
319	Doub, E	55	W	Farmer	8	$15,000	$5,000	$20,000	$20,000
320	Fasnacht, J	45	W	Day/farm laborer	3	$200	$100	$300	$300
321	Gruber, D	58	W	Farmer	5	$1,200	$200	$1,400	$1,400
322	Maysillas, J	68	W	Wagonmaker	5	$3,000	$400	$3,400	$3,400
323	Maysillas, H	22	W	Day/farm laborer	4		$100	$100	$100
324	Kline, G	54	W	Farmer	5	$9,000	$1,500	$10,500	$10,500
325	Gates, C	43	W	Farmer	2		$80	$80	$80
326	Hammond,J	62	W	Farmer, retired	6	$12,000	$1,500	$13,500	$13,500
327	Hammond,D	28	W	Farmer	7		$200	$200	$200
328	Glose, S	43	W	Farmer	5		$1,200	$1,200	$1,200
329	Eavey, S	50	W	Day/farm laborer	2	$600	$100	$700	$700
330	BomgartnerJ	49	W	Wagonmaker	4	$500	$100	$600	$600
331	Dusang, P	66	W	Day/farm laborer	2			$0	$0
332	Smith, D	43	W	Day/farm laborer	4			$0	$0
333	Summers, I	31	W	Farmer	8		$1,200	$1,200	$1,200
334	Wisonger,S	48	W	Day/farm laborer	8			$0	$0
335	Nikirk, C	22	W	Farmer	4		$700	$700	$700
336	Locke, G	48	W	Farmer	4		$1,000	$1,000	$1,000
337	Gigous, H	33	W	Day/farm laborer	9		$100	$100	$100
338	Stevens, N	45	W	zBlacksmith	9		$100	$100	$100
339	Smith, W	49	W	Shoemaker	8		$200	$200	$200
Average Farming:		**44**			**6**				**$10,888**
Average Tradesman:		**45**			**5**				**$631**
Average Laborer:		**36**			**4**				**$135**
Average Keeping House:		**58**			**4**				**$400**

Total in School	**54**	**15.0%**
Total cannot read	**24**	**6.7%**
Total cannot write	**32**	**8.9%**
Father foreign	**9**	**2.5%**
Mother foreign	**4**	**1.1%**
Total blacks	**21**	**5.8%**
Total mulatto	**4**	**1.1%**
Total households	**67**	**100.0%**
Total neighbors	**360**	**100.0%**
Total males	**195**	**54.2%**
Total females	**165**	**45.8%**

Farmers	31	46.3%
Laborers	20	29.9%
Keeping House	3	4.5%
Wagonmakers	3	4.5%
Shoemakers	2	3.0%
1Teacher, 1Miller, 1Gatekeep	3	4.5%
1Dry goods, 1Auctioneer,	2	3.0%
1Blacksmith, 1Broommaker,	2	3.0%
1Cooper	1	1.5%
TOTAL:	67	100.0%

Figure 2.2. Comparison of Otho Williams' Boonsboro neighborhood wealth in 1870, Part 2, sorted by dwelling number.

I pointed to shaded rows in the chart in Figure 2.2. "Five of the sixty-seven heads-of-household—see these brown lines— were listed as 'black' and only one—you—was listed as 'mulatto.' I never knew whether that description of your skin color was true, or merely the visual estimation of the census taker. Now that I can see you in my mind's eye, you look just like me, tanned from the sun's rays. "I read that a slave's status was determined by the mother. As you know better than I, white women were not slaves, but you had been a slave, so your mother had to be black, right?"

"You know that's right," he agreed. "Those white women were treated like gold inside and outside the house. We colored men could never be caught looking at one of them. We could be whipped, or worse, if we ever dared to speak to a white woman on our own."

I was so excited by now that I delivered a series of rapid-fire questions, not giving Otho time to answer. "Was your father a white man? And who was your slave master? Was he your father?" All my questions about Otho came tumbling out of my mouth like heat-seeking missiles, trying to persuade him to tell me all that I craved to know about him. As you'd expect, there was no answer from the apparition.

Hmmm, Otho seems to be getting comfortable with this story all about him. His previously ruffled feathers seem to be calmed down now. I am starting to get the feeling, though, that he wants to see how my research plays out. I think he won't cut short my efforts and tell me the facts now. No, looking at the smug, bemused look on his face, I bet he plans to simply watch me struggle to find my own answers. Wait! Oh no . . . Slowly fading into the background, he de-materialized completely.

I had no doubt my second great-grandfather would watch and listen to every word during this journey of discovery. I guessed I was on my own now. Sigh . . .

I continued talking aloud, as if to a friend in a coffee shop, further describing my neighborhood analysis, hoping my muse would return to confirm or refute my observations.

Speaking aloud made it easier to hear whether the verb tenses and punctuation were correct, or the sentence needed to be tweaked. Reading my manuscript aloud also helped me synthesize the facts and work out in my brain what Otho's neighborhood was like and how the black and white residents may have interacted with one another.

* A Hard Lesson Learned *

I dissected the 1870 Census in Chapter 2 because it was, with some exceptions, the first time former slaves were counted by name. It was critical to look at EVERY column on the Census.

Genealogists also recommend studying about three pages before and after our relatives' listing in every census to compare and contrast the neighborhood in which our relatives lived. I did not do this important step for forty years, which explains why I got nowhere. I vowed to change my ways this time.

The experts say closely examining the 1870 Census is the most important first step for African American research, if slavery is involved. Looking at the surnames of neighbors could indicate who might have been our ancestors' slave owner. Surnames could also point out other family members. Doing this analysis up front will set the stage for how I should perform future analyses.

Figure 2.1. Comparison of Otho Williams' Boonsboro Neighborhood Wealth in 1870, Part I, by Dwelling Number. This compilation of columns from the 1870 census not only includes information about Otho Williams' family but also forty of his closest neighbors. This visual allows the reader to learn the surnames of those neighbor heads-of-household. This is important to note because some of those people might have been slave owners six years earlier. The chart also reveals the age, race, and profession of the heads-of-household, showing the number of people in their house, the value of their real estate, their personal estate, and their total estate.

The shaded entries in Figure 2.1 specify which neighbors were black or, like Otho, mulatto. This figure is sorted by dwelling number, so one can easily see whether the black neighbors lived in a close cluster, or resided next to the richer neighbors, who could have been their former and/or current employers. For example, black S. Douglass lived next door to farmer J. Ringer, the third wealthiest neighbor in this chart; it is highly possible Douglass worked for Ringer. Otho, was the only non-white who owned real estate and had some personal property. Even though Otho was listed as a day laborer, it is possible he worked his own land too.

Almost three-fourths of the heads-of-household (including Otho) indicated they owned real estate or personal property. The value of Otho's real estate holdings was $1,000; eleven other heads had a lesser land value ($200 to $800), and nineteen others owned more land than Otho ($1,200 to $40,000). Thirty-four people had more personal and eleven reported no personal property.

There was a total of 360 people in the 1870 neighborhood from those sixty-seven households, which means there were five people, on average, in each household. Over half of the people in the neighborhood sample were men. Nine of the 360 neighbors had fathers who came from another country, compared to only four with foreign mothers. Twenty-one of the 360 were listed as black, three were mulatto—all from Otho's family—and the remainder of your neighbors were classified as white.

Fifteen children were in school in 1870, twenty-four neighbors could not read (including Otho), and thirty-two did not know how to write (including Otho, and Alice who could read but not write). Since the neighborhood schoolteacher, Mr. Groh, lived only a few properties away from Otho's family, maybe Alice and their children learned to read from Teacher Groh.

As shown in Figure 2.2, the average household size was largest for farmers with six people living in the house (thus providing a built-in workforce of adults and children?), followed by tradesmen with five people; laborers and those keeping house had four people in the household. As might be assumed, the youngest people, by profession, were laborers, at 36-years-of-age. Farmers were 44-years-old on average, and tradesmen were 45, with those keeping house being the oldest group, at 58-years-of-age.

By 1880, Otho and Alice were still living in District 6, now classified as the Boonsboro area. Otho was a 46-year-old married black farmer working his own land. He still could neither read nor write. His wife, Alice, 29, was keeping house and was the only one who could read. By 1880 she could also write.

Otho and Alice had six sons by then: Edgar E., Samuel M., William F., Otho "Sherman" who was my first great-grandfather, William F.W., and Charles E. Williams. Edgar was a laborer at 10-years-of-age but his younger siblings, who were between one and seven-years-old, remained at home with their mother. Everyone in the household was born in Maryland, as were Otho and Alice's unknown parents.

I did a similar cluster analysis of Otho's 1880 neighbors. As with all censuses, there were mostly the same questions asked of citizens from the previous decade. Unfortunately, the 1880 census did not ask about real or personal property value, but I gathered as much similar data to 1870 as possible, also noting how many of the same people appeared on both of the censuses.

In addition to determining how an ancestor fits in with the community, this type of detailed, household by household comparison also had the advantage of introducing the researcher to the names of neighbors, the types of occupations, the wealth of the community, as well as the ethnic/immigrant diversity of the population of the neighborhood.

This intimate information can become crucial to finding slave owners, family members, and other immediate associates.

Figure 2.2 compares the occupations of Otho's close neighbors in 1870 (and 1880, not pictured). This table gives us an idea of whether the neighborhood was composed of farmers, laborers, skilled persons, or persons keeping house.

There were few new neighbors in 1880 in this small sample of District 6, but three of the six black families from 1870 had moved away for some unknown reason within the following decade. Perhaps due to an aging population, some of the older heads-of-household in 1870 were consolidated into others' homes in 1880, and some of the children from 1870 now had their own households in 1880.

The statistical overview showed a decrease in the percentage of farmers (-8.1%) and laborers (-9.3%) and an increase in the percentage of neighbors with a skilled trade (+2.8) and in those keeping house (+10.2%) between 1870 and 1880.

I had the greatest pleasure in noting that Otho had upgraded his status to farmer in 1880, likely cultivating and harvesting his own land, compared to having been a day laborer for someone else in 1870. On the surface, this is a concrete measure of Otho's success—a promotion, if you will. On the flip side, the notable decreases in agriculture-related occupations may have predicted future trouble for farmers in the District 6 area of Washington County.

After that analysis of Otho's neighborhood and indicators that he had made progress economically after slavery, I felt closer to Otho and Alice and wanted to know more about their earlier lives.

If Otho was a slave, as my family thought, it would not be possible to find him by name in the 1860 census, or any other census before that. Slaves were only regarded as "chattel" property, the same as a cow or furniture, prior to 1865, the official end of slavery nationwide. You would not give a last name to your dresser drawers or your plow in a census report, any more than you would a slave. What did that cruel fact mean? I was at a loss on how to proceed.

Neither my Otho nor Alice are listed by name in the 1850 or 1860 Census indicating that they were, indeed, likely to have been slaves. I was back to the drawing board, where I had been for four decades. You will hear this same "I Got the Genealogy Blues" over and over. How could I get beyond that darn roadblock to find out more about Otho and Alice Williams?

At the time of this writing, we are in the era of Google searches, so I did an internet search for "Otho Williams Washington County Maryland" to see what popped up. I was surprised to see how many men were named Otho Williams in Washington County!

Which, if any of them, was the slave master of my Otho or, dare I presume, the father of my Otho? As with most slave research, I needed to find out who my relatives' slave masters were before more information could be found about my relatives. I MUST get beyond the "1870 Brick Wall" this time!

Mary Marshall

Chapter 3 - Breaking Down the 1870 Brick Wall

A "Brick Wall" is a metaphor used in genealogical and historical research when one reaches a point in their research where he/she is unable to progress further or "dig deeper." All researchers and family historians encounter it. For those tracing African American ancestors, this proverbial brick wall is commonly encountered at the 1870 US Federal Census, a vitally important census particularly for African American research. Since it was recorded just five years after slavery ended, the 1870 census was very often the first official record that recorded formerly enslaved African Americans by their first and last names. The key to African American genealogy research is to trace families from the 1940 census all the way back to the 1870 census. That feat alone is considered a big success.

Source: Melvin J. Collier. March 24, 2012. "Boom! The Brick Wall Came Crumbling Down!" Roots Revealed: Viewing African – American History Through a Genealogical Lens.

Why can't I easily find my formerly enslaved ancestors prior to the 1870 Census? I whined and complained, like a spoiled child, pouting and stamping my feet, wanting what I wanted, when I wanted it. I wanted to find Otho Williams' parents and slave owner. I'd been spinning my wheels on that search for so long. I wanted answers now! My tight shoulders lifted as I took a deep breath, then dropped as a sigh escaped my mouth.

After the 13th Amendment was passed in 1865 to abolish slavery, the 1870 Census was the first to capture information for *all* non-Native Americans. Most genealogists researching African American ancestry hit a "Brick Wall" and had difficulty finding any information about formerly enslaved black ancestors prior to the 1870 Census. Documentation of slave names and family ties was scant during slavery. Slave masters rarely documented their slave or other chattel property descriptively, such as by surname.

Genealogists today are lucky. With the advent of the internet and digitalization of vital records, census, and other genealogy-related documents, African American research becomes more manageable than ever before, but it is still not a straight-forward walk in the park. I'll share the techniques I used to find the parents and slave masters of my Williams ancestors in the hope those steps will help others looking to do the same for their families.

If what you have been doing isn't working well, then try something different. I spent years using the same tool, with few results. I think the for-profit Ancestry.com is a fantastic family history platform because it captures billions of records from every state and many countries. Their web platform can build, manage and share family tree information with other members. Ancestry DNA testing not only provides estimates of ethnicity but can also identify other people who have tested whose DNA matches yours. Their family tree leaf-hints do the work for you in scouring their billions of records to find data matches for you *if* your ancestors are listed in traditional historical documents.

Ancestry offers indispensable how-to videos on youtube.com for every imaginable family history research topic. However, compared to some other sources, prior to 2016 they didn't have many tools available to further African American research.

Part IV, DNA Doesn't Lie, Does it? provides specific examples and much more detail about the offerings of three major DNA companies.

The free familysearch.org website from The Church of Jesus Christ of Latter-day Saints (LDS) was the first public, genealogy-based system at the turn of this millennia. It has a useful "wiki"[19] search tool to find documents about a myriad of topics. Although a free service, you should open an account to view all document contents.

As an example, typing "Kent County" into the "Search by place or topic" of the wiki brings up a "Kent County Genealogy" page which contains: history of the county, specific county locations, cemeteries, church records, court records, family biographies, gazetteers/newspapers, immigration, land records, maps, military information on the major wars affecting county inhabitants, a different set of colonial probate records, tax records, vital records, libraries, free family history centers, helpful genealogy websites, and references. As of 2018, familysearch.org was collaborating with the for-profit Ancestry.com to digitize more records for global use.

The National Archives and Records Administration (NARA) includes another great treasure trove of information. Charged with preserving and documenting government and historical records, NARA increases public access to those resources. Military service and pension application claims are of special interest to African American research for they can contain family, home and occupational information.

Pension application files usually provide genealogy information, often containing supporting documents such as narratives of events during service, marriage certificates, birth records, death certificates, pages from family Bibles, family letters, depositions of witnesses, affidavits, discharge papers, and other supporting papers.

There may be mentions of former slave masters, as well as other enslaved family members, in the case of African Americans who fought in the American Revolution, the War of 1812, the Mexican-American War, or the Civil War.[20]

Many people must rely on paying a researcher to search the original hardcopy pension files because most records are not yet digitally available. However, some are available through the for-fee fold3.com website which makes it a bit easier to find veterans and their application claim forms and records.

Freedmen's Bureau records, more traditionally called U.S. Bureau of Refugees, Freedmen and Abandoned Lands, are becoming more and more beneficial for African American researchers. It was established in 1865 by Congress to help former black slaves and poor whites in the South in the aftermath of the U.S. Civil War (1861-65). Some four million slaves gained their freedom as a result of the Union victory, which left many communities in ruins and destroyed the South's plantation-based economy.

In addition, the Freedmen's Bureau provided food, housing, and medical aid, and offered legal assistance to southerners recovering from the destruction resulting from Civil War battles. The Bureau also attempted to settle former slaves on Confederate lands that were confiscated or abandoned during the war. The bureau was also instrumental in building thousands of schools for blacks who had previously been denied education, and helped to found such colleges as Howard University in Washington, D.C., Fisk University in Nashville, Tennessee, and Hampton University in Virginia.

In the summer of 1872, Congress, responding in part to pressure from white Southerners, dismantled the Freedmen's Bureau.[21] This effectively put the brakes on the forward progress of newly freed African Americans.

The Freedmen's Bureau Digitalization Project was created on "Juneteenth"[22] in 2015 as a set of partnerships between FamilySearch International, NARA, the Smithsonian National Museum of African American History and Culture, the Afro-American Historical and Genealogical Society (AAHGS), and the California African American Museum. With the help of more than 25,000 volunteers, it was completed on June 20, 2016.

Now, the names of nearly 1.8 million men, women and children are searchable online, so millions have access to the names of their ancestors, allowing individuals to build their family trees and connect with their heritage. The http://www.discoverfreedmen.org website is perhaps the easiest way to access these potentially beneficial records. While the Freedmen's Bureau had not yet elicited information pertinent to my family, I referred back to it as more puzzle pieces fell into place.

Genealogy experts encourage finding African American relatives through land deeds, bills of sale, deeds of manumission and other legal transactions. Those original records are generally located at the county or state level, and many are viewable online. Experts proclaim that perusing bills of sale can lead to finding African American ancestors. Great! I would love for someone to tell me the surname of the slave owner so I may access those records. *Do I hear violin music playing a sob song in the background?*

Since October 1, 2016, after viewing Anita Henderson's online writing group "write your stories now" webinar, I forced myself to think and do things in alignment with the genealogical experts' advice.

The official website for Maryland: http://www.maryland.gov produces links to all sorts of information and services, useful maps, links to all county offices, as well as the Maryland State Archives http://msa.maryland.gov, a repository for almost one-half million historical documents that form the constitutional, legal, legislative, judicial, and administrative basis of Maryland's government.

The Maryland Land Records, was perhaps the most oft-used sources for these explorations, through its online www.mdlandrec.net website. It makes available, by county, nearly all original, handwritten land deeds, bills of sale, deeds of manumission, etc. It was not easy to learn how to access these records so I provided step-by-step instructions in Appendix G. This website made all the difference in my success on this project, as fully discussed in future chapters.

Google and other online searches can be *quite* productive. In your computer's browser search box, type "African Americans in county state". For example, searching for "African Americans in Washington County Maryland" brings up a plethora of websites, such as the African American Heritage Guide, Slavery in western Maryland, Doleman Black Heritage Museum, and African American Manumissions of Washington County.

I scrutinized each of those sources for applicability to my project. A collateral benefit to using that approach was finding helpful people in Maryland who went out of their way to aid my search for data about Otho's parentage and slave owner. I truly believed my requests made the local people happy. Perhaps it was an unspoken attempt to right the wrongs of slavery's past or just plain kindness. Be open to letting the locals help you with your family search—everybody wins.

I made several educated guesses about Otho Williams' slave master, then proved or disproved each one based on evidence. My first assumption was that Otho Williams chose to keep the surname of his last slave master when he was freed. That meant I was looking for someone with the last name of Williams because I had no information to the contrary.

It is a common misconception, though, that all emancipated slaves assumed the surname of their last owner. Were that always true, this critical stage of finding slave owners would be far easier than it is in actuality. Ample evidence exists that slaves rarely assumed a surname belonging to their last slave master. Instead, the slave may have used a name which had been in his or her family for several generations. [23] Some runaway slaves changed their names entirely hoping to avoid recapture.

The fact that my Otho named his third son Otho Sherman Williams, further indicated that he may have had some positive interaction with of the white Otho Williams families in Washington County, or someone else with the first name Otho or surname Williams (more on that in Chapter 5).

This inconsistency in how surnames (and some first names) were chosen can make it exceedingly difficult to track enslaved and/or immigrant ancestors. They may have used different names on different documents at different times in their lives. Ancestry.com provides an excellent informational resource on researching African American Ancestry, including identifying the last slave owner.[24] They caution that if a researcher, without good evidence, assumes the owner's name is the same as the former slave, time might be wasted in the pursuit of the wrong family. There are additional naming sources that may be consulted, such as Signature Registers of the Freedman's Savings and Trust Company, ex-slave narratives, and Southern Claims Commission records.

I diligently and doggedly worked through each source mentioned in this chapter determined to find Otho's slave owner and parents.

Meanwhile, I began learning about western Maryland and the life of enslaved and free blacks during the long and inhumane period of bondage.

PART II: PERIOD OF BONDAGE 1664 -1865

1634: 200 settlers found St. Mary's City. Black Mathias De Sousa arrives in Maryland aboard the Ark. As an indentured servant, De Sousa must face seven years of servitude to pay off his debts and earn his freedom.

1663/1664: Maryland legalizes slavery.

1681: Maryland passes a law that children born to free black women and black children of white women would be free.

1776: Continental Congress declares independence from Great Britain. Washington County is created from Frederick County.

1793: Congress passes the first fugitive slave law, which allows for the prosecution of runaways and their return to their masters.

1802: Maryland's General Assembly declares that free blacks cannot vote.

1807-1808: Britain and the United States outlaw the Atlantic slave trade.

1831: Maryland Colonization Society colonizes Maryland blacks in Africa.

1861-1865: As many as 30,000 Marylanders traveled south to fight for the Confederacy, while approximately 65,000 Maryland men, including nearly 9,000 colored troops, served in all branches of the Union military.

1863: The Emancipation Proclamation was signed by President Abraham Lincoln declaring slaves within any State fighting against the Union shall be free. Maryland slaves were not free until 1864.

1865: The 13th Amendment to the United States Constitution was ratified on December 31, 1865, primarily to abolish slavery.

Figure 4.1. Milestone Events For African Americans in Maryland's History.

Mary Marshall

Chapter 4 - History of Blacks in Western Maryland

* New World Arrival *

[Author's note: The following story is basically true, except for the facts about Sally herself. The story is meant to suggest one of the many ways that white women and African men could have commingled to produce children who would become the earliest free blacks in Maryland.]

How did I get into this predicament, you may ask? I am called Sally Smith, an orphan. I turned 16 my last birthday, a couple of months ago. Like many young people, my parents died last year from the pox. My kind neighbors could not take me in, so they encouraged me to indenture myself for the next four years to work for their friend, Thomas Allen. Mr. Allen plans to travel to a place called St. Mary's City in the New World, on the far side of the Atlantic Ocean, wherever that is. He will take me with him.

This 22nd day of November, in 1663, I am standing at the port of Cowes on the Isle of Wight, the coast of Hampshire on the English Channel. Walking up the uneven wooden planks into an uncertain sailing ship, to an uncertain country, and an uncertain new life fills me with dread . . . and, I dare say, a little excitement!

The Ark, our sailing ship (Figure 4.2), does not look big enough to carry all of us to the other side of the world.

On the main deck, there are all sorts of people milling about: English gentlemen with their fine clothing, sturdy Irish lads with dark blue caps, dozens of swarthy bearded sailors, and two other women besides myself.

Figure 4.2. The “Ark” and the "Dove" in a 1934 U.S. commemorative postage stamp.

That elderly man over there told me some travelers are Roman Catholics and Jesuit priests, escaping religious persecution. Others are younger brothers who will not inherit their father’s estate and aim to make their fortunes in the New World.

Only wealthy people can afford the trip, and the supplies needed to cross the ocean and live their first year.[25] It costs about half a year's salary for us workers to get there from England. Those of us without money, like me, are willing to sign contracts to become indentured servants for four or seven years, to pay for our passage.

Two people have darker skin coloring than everybody else. Are they Africans? Look at the golden-brown arms of that fellow over there; his skin glints in the morning sun. The chap next to him has a coppery cast.

The first one has chiseled features, full lips, and a brilliant smile showing gleaming white teeth. If a man could be called beautiful, that's how I would describe him. Oh no! He caught me gazing at him. As I look away, I feel my cheeks getting warmer; I know that means they are flushing redder. What am I going to do? The golden man walks toward me with steady steps, his muscular bare arms swinging powerfully. He has a big grin on his face.

"Excuse me, Miss, may I help you with your bag?" he asked in a lilting form of accented English. "I am called Francisco. I am one of the crewmen and shall be taking this adventure with you. My friend over there called Matthias de Sousa will be an indentured servant of the Jesuit priests on board this ship."[26]

Stuttering, I respond, "Yes, please, uh, and thank you," as I hand him my well-worn satchel containing one dress, undergarments, an old soft-bristle brush, and my mother's silver locket. I follow him downstairs to the 'tween deck of the ship, where most of the crew and poorer travelers are to sleep over the next four months or so on this voyage across the Atlantic Ocean.

We will each have about four feet by six feet of space for our belongings and bed. The richer investors, Jesuits, and Governor Leonard Calvert[27] himself will stay in the larger area under our half-deck. Little did I know at that moment that Francisco and I would occasionally become bedmates, relying on each other for warmth and comfort to weather the stormy winter seas.

Francisco tells me "The Ark—the name of this ship—is about 120 feet long and 30 feet wide, but the Dove over there, pointing to the small ship next to ours, only half this size." He continues, "Both ships will leave England at the same time. Each ship carries food that will keep for long periods without spoiling, such as salted meats, dried grains, peas, and beans. Even water goes bad, so it's only used for soaking dried or pickled meats. We will drink beer and wine, not water, and everyone on board will receive a small daily food ration. The rich passengers are bringing extra food with them, including dried fruits, cheese, breads, spices, wines, ales, sweets, citrus fruits, tea, and a few small animals. Sometimes fresh fish will be caught with hooks or harpoons for all of us to eat."[28]

The ship set sail that afternoon, after the people, animals, suitcases, and crates of provisions were aboard. We waved goodbye to the friends and family members who had come to the dock to wish us safe passage. Knowing we would never see each other again produced tears of regret, but the promise of a new life also produced tears of joy.

Soon after we set sail, the motion of the ocean waves forced non-sailors to the sides of the ship, letting loose their breakfasts into the sea.

Day after day, the normal accepted ways of behaving among rich and poor people were blurred onboard the ship, especially on the 'tween deck. We endured close quarters with about 140 other people.[29] We had minimal food and no fresh water. Many people got sick from the rough seas. There were human smells I never want to experience again! Most of us got along well, although there were occasional scuffles among the men.

The captain decided not to stop at Boavista Island, a Dutch outpost with a lot of salt and goats. Thirty passengers came down with fever after drinking too much wine on Christmas Day; twelve of them died before the new year.

On January 3, 1634, we anchored at the island of Barbados for ten days, where we reunited with the travelers on the Dove and loaded more food and drink. The ship remained at St. Christopher's for ten days in early February, then we arrived at Point Comfort, in Jamestown, Virginia, on February 27th. The Ark and the Dove sailed into the Chesapeake Bay on March 3rd. Father Andrew White celebrated mass on St. Clement's Island on March 25th, marking the end of our long voyage (Figure 4.3).

After a brief three-week stay on the island, we occupied a nearby Piscataway Indian village which had been purchased for us. Where the Potomac River enters the Chesapeake Bay, our new English settlement is called St. Mary's City.

Many of us adventurers became fast friends, now with a common history. A few days after landing, I noticed that my monthly bleeding had stopped and my breasts were achy. I became worried that I would suffer the same horrible death that had beset some of our shipmates before the new year.

I shared my health concerns with Mrs. Anne Cox, describing my symptoms as best I could. Mrs. Cox, a tall, red-haired woman with a rather sallow face, was a few years older than me and had more life experiences than my teenage years. We had become close friends on the long voyage, so I asked what she thought. She pulled me close as if to hug me, then whispered softly in my ear so nobody else could hear, "It probably means you are going to have a baby. I think it would be best not to tell anybody about that right now or you might lose your indenture and be sent back home or be without a job in this new land."

My dry mouth opened with surprise, but no words came to my mind. Nobody back home told me about how babies were made. I had no idea that cuddling with Francisco in that special way on the 'tween deck at night would create a baby.

I wondered how my new employer would feel about this turn of events. I wondered how I felt about it. Should I be sad, or scared, or happy? I worried that I did not know what to expect my body to feel like as time went on. Would I be able to work and support myself with the baby? Would I be forced to give it up? Would Francisco marry me? Would such a marriage be allowed, because he was colored and I white? I wondered what would happen to my baby once it was born; the baby who would be a mixture of Francisco and me . . .

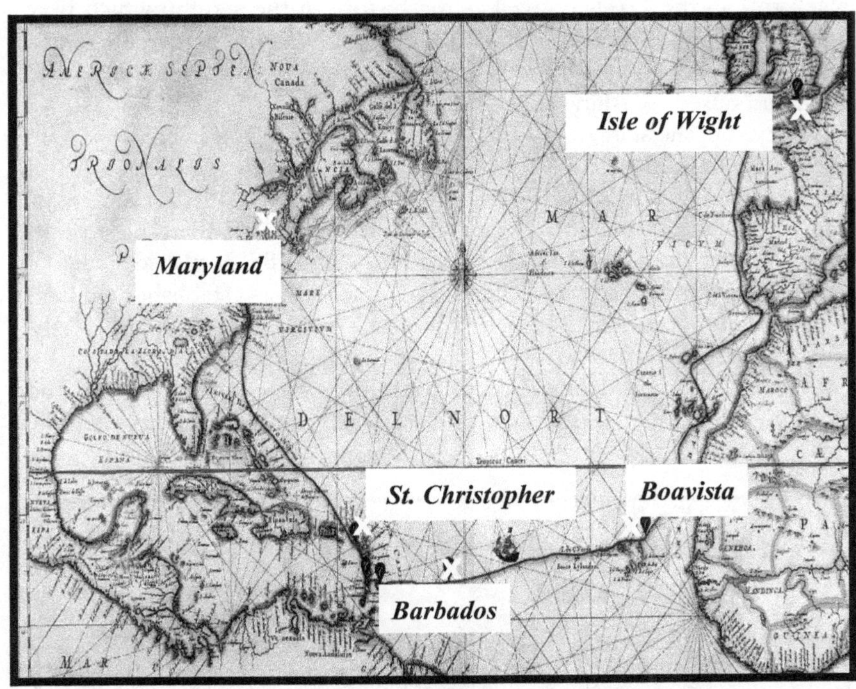

Figure 4.3. Sailing from England to Maryland in 1633/34 took four total months, but only 66 days of actual sailing.

* The New World: Maryland *

How far back in Maryland history does my Williams family go? I believed it possible to get some idea of what their lives might have been like by studying legal documents, personal accounts, autobiographies, newspaper articles, demographic statistics, and other information about black folk in the 1800s, as well as the history of the state in which they lived. During the third month of this book writing adventure, I became immersed in the time and place where my second great-grandparents were born and raised: Washington County, Maryland.

Maryland, the state of my ancestors' birth (Figure 4.4) is a narrow state located in the Mid-Atlantic region of the United States. To the south and west, it borders Washington D.C., Virginia, and West Virginia. Pennsylvania borders it on the north, and Delaware to the east. It was the seventh state to ratify the United States Constitution in 1788. It played a pivotal role in the founding of Washington, D.C., which was established on land donated by Maryland.[30] The state's largest city, Baltimore, is just northwest of Maryland's capital of Annapolis.

Created in 1776 from Frederick County, Hagerstown became the Washington County seat in western Maryland where my Williams family

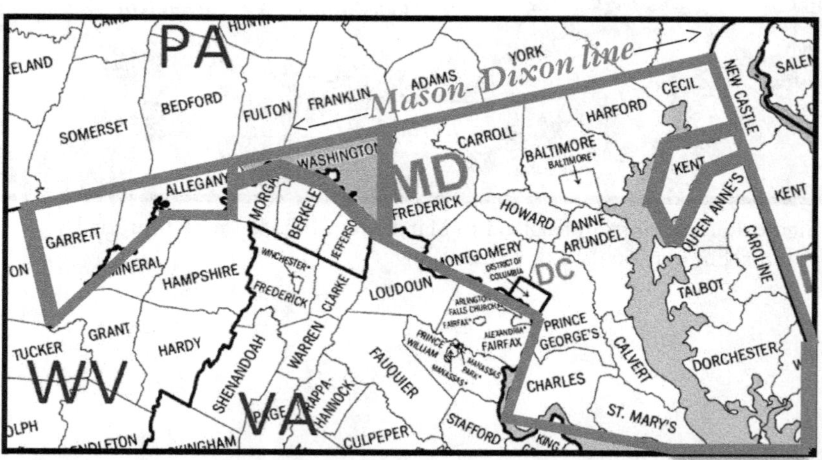

Figure 4.4. Map of Maryland and adjacent States. Source: Marguerite Doleman Museum, Washington County, MD.

lived. One must understand how counties were formed because many documents older than 1776 have names from the former.[31]

I was surprised to find that blacks coming into the state of Maryland were not always enslaved. In 1634, black Matthias de Sousa, who arrived aboard the Ark ship, was an indentured servant who used his wood-working and sailing skills to pay off his debts and earn his freedom during his seven years of servitude with Jesuit priests. In the mid-1700s, most of the English colonists who arrived in Maryland were indentured servants[32] who had served a term of several years as laborers to pay for their passage across the Atlantic.

Back in earliest Maryland times, the line between indentured servants and African laborers, or slaves, was blurry. White and black laborers commonly lived and worked together, and formed relationship unions. During the colonial era, families of free persons of color (FPOC) were formed most often by unions of white women and African men, like the story Sally told in the previous segment. Interestingly, mixed-race children born to white mothers were considered to be free. This helped contribute to the comparatively high proportion of free persons of color in western Maryland.

Prior to this research, I knew nothing about Maryland except that it was a small state, so I had not considered that Washington County's geographical location played such a significant role in the slave trade. The narrow boundaries of northwestern Washington County, at the town of Williamsport, provided a convenient route for runaway slaves from Virginia through Maryland to Pennsylvania.[33] That area had formerly been host to countless American Indian travelers, fur traders, and settlers passing through before it became Williamsport.[34] As a result, there were several slave markets in the county and a considerable presence of slave catchers. These factors forced Washington County residents directly into the slavery-versus-state's-rights debate that was playing out on a national scale.

For more than two hundred years, slavery stood at the core of Maryland's life, as it did with all Southern states in America. Maryland was called the "Upper South," as it was the northernmost state which sanctioned slavery.

Slaves grew the tobacco, harvested the wheat, dug the coal, and smelted the iron upon which Maryland's economy rested. Blacks helped build the Chesapeake and Ohio (C&O) Canal and the Baltimore and Ohio (B&O) Railroad. Blacks cared for the children of their white owners. In their adulthood, many of those children maltreated those slaves who had nursed and nurtured them.

According to "A Guide to the History of Slavery in Maryland," slaves were in the middle of the struggle over freedom that gave the American Revolution, and the Civil War their meaning. As most present-day African

Americans can attest, the struggle for equal rights and opportunity continues long after emancipation.

There was a sickening, never-ending, array of documented efforts at re-enslaving young free persons of color, through the enactment and revival of particularly onerous indentured servitude laws. Sanctioned by the Orphan's Court in 1793 and 1808,[35] those laws allowed the county to remove the children of free persons of color, to work apprenticeships for a specified time-period, without their parents' permission. These heinous, self-serving laws were finally reversed in the federal courts in 1867, but integration and the enforcement of civil rights would not come for another century.[36]

The 1870 U.S. Census in Washington County's District 6 indicated that Otho Williams' family was listed as mulatto,[37] and this started me on a stubborn quest to prove his father was white or Native American. Doesn't being a mulatto mean you are mixed, being part black, part white, or part Native American? Realistically, wasn't it much more likely that a white man had sexual relations with his black or Native American female slave than a white woman commingling with a black or Native American man?

District 6 encompassed the area of Antietam, Boonsboro, Funkstown, and Beaver Creek, to name a few of the small towns south of Hagerstown (Figure 4.5).[38]

My ancestors lived and worked only a few miles away from the bloodiest single-day battle in American history—the Battle of Antietam—sometimes called the Battle to Free the Slaves. This horrific clash between north and south resulted in a combined tally of 22,717 dead, wounded, or missing people.[39]

Truthfully, I had never much cared about the details of the Civil War, just that it resulted in the end of slavery for my people. How exciting it was to ponder the possibility that *my* black relatives may have helped play a part in the destruction of that monstrous form of human bondage. I became *acutely* interested in Civil War history, at least as it may have pertained to my ancestors in Maryland.

No pictures of Otho or Alice had yet been found, nor did I know who his master and parents were at that point. All I could do was continue to investigate what life was like, in general, for African Americans in Washington County, in the early-to-mid-1800s. I hoped to eventually be able to piece together a reasonable picture of the life Otho and Alice led.

Out of a total population of 25,000 in 1830 Washington County, my relatives were among the almost 3,000 slaves, and there were also about 1,100 free persons of color. Irrationally, I found myself naively whining, "Why couldn't my Maryland ancestors have been one of the free blacks?" Heavy sigh.

There were about 103,000 slaves and 53,000 free blacks in the entire state, as shown in Appendix D.[40] Frankly, I was a little surprised to learn there were so many free blacks because Maryland was a slave state even though Maryland technically fought *for* the Union during the Civil War.

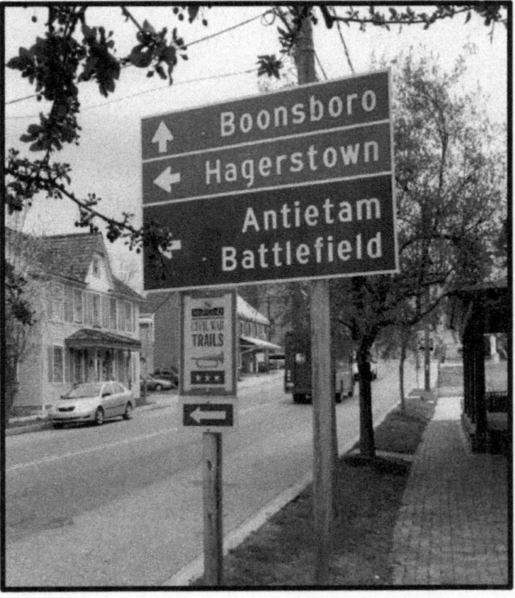

Figure 4.5. Sharpsburg, MD. Photograph by Kathy Marshall.

Many historians believe the proportion of slaves to the total population was lower in the northwestern part of Maryland because there were fewer farmers who grew labor-intensive tobacco which requires more slaves.

Additionally, there were more abolitionists in northern Maryland, being adjacent to the free state of Pennsylvania, thus leading to a lower proportion of whites owning slaves. In 1853, the local *Herald of Freedom and Torch Light* newspaper reported that the number of slaves in Washington County had a total *value* of $317,000.[41] I still cannot stomach the fact that slaves were considered property, just like land, hogs, and farm tools, and therefore had to be *valued* and taxed.

A few slave owners who had to leave the free state of Pennsylvania with their slaves trickled into northern Maryland. Reluctant to surrender their bondsmen and women, some slave masters spirited them to the frightening "Deep South."

For example, in 1791, John McPherson—a future owner of the Antietam Iron Works which became very important to this story—transported his slave, Cyrus, from Pennsylvania to Frederick County, Maryland. Fearful that Pennsylvania's abolition statute would deprive him of the services of a valuable farmhand, McPherson agreed to manumit (free) his 22-year-old slave, provided he "indenture himself to serve the said John McPherson for a term of seventeen years."

Cyrus was not the only bound laborer to cross the Mason-Dixon Line.[42] Pennsylvania had passed personal liberty laws to protect free blacks from being kidnapped into slavery.[43] I thought maybe that's why my ancestor's family moved to Pennsylvania after Otho had died. But I was getting ahead of myself.

Luckily, Washington County has numerous resources for African American genealogy research, and I was skimming through as many as possible. Some of those resources included descriptions of African American records available at the Maryland State Archives. I used The African American Heritage Guide (Appendix C) when I visited Maryland a couple of months later.

Thankfully, the Doleman Black Heritage Museum lists many of their contents online. Reading the Directory of Colored Teachers, I wondered whether Otho's children went to school and whether any of them became teachers in one of those colored schools after slavery.

Julie Saylor, a Library Assistant at the Enoch Pratt Free Library in Baltimore, recommended contacting the Western Maryland Room of the Washington County Free Library in Hagerstown. She suggested checking the Washington County Historical Trust, to locate any properties that my relatives might have purchased. She suggested visiting the Maryland Historical Society to learn about my relative's home and work life.

These were all important founts of knowledge that helped me understand what the locale was like for black people in the 1700s and 1800s, both free and slave. I jotted down notes and typed information into my book template every day to start piecing together a picture of what Otho and Alice's lives were like.

The Allegany County African American History website, created and maintained by Al Feldstein, provides useful information about churches, obituaries, education, and segregation. Even though I was looking for information about Washington County, Mr. Feldstein forwarded my many research questions to Dr. Emilie Amt, Chair of the Department of History at Hood College, in Frederick County.

I am forever indebted to the time Dr. Amt spent in providing me with a litany of additional research sources, actual documents, books to read, and links to other sources. One of her references, a list of 224 slaves who had been manumitted, included their names, ages, and identifying body markings. Dr. Amt helped me decipher a few probate records and land deeds, which were difficult for me to read and understand. She also entertained my many theories about Otho and Alice's parentage and their ownership.

Even though I kept insisting that Otho's father had to be one of the white Otho Williams in the county, Dr. Amt warned me not to get my hopes up too high. Being knee-deep in the same African American history topic herself for a book she was writing, Dr. Amt graciously suggested additional avenues for me to pursue like scrutinizing the 1870 census and contacting expert researchers at the Western Maryland Room Library.

The only thing she could not provide was more time in the day to work on this addictive project.

Back to my history lesson. During the 1800s, Maryland's economy and politics were fractured along regional lines. In the state's northern and western counties, farmers became increasingly dependent upon diversified agriculture, like wheat and corn farming, in which full-time slavery was not required.

On the Eastern Shore, declining tobacco prices and soil exhaustion forced farmers to abandon tobacco, free their slaves, or sell them to the southern states, and begin to cultivate their farms with free black and white farmhands. Even so, in the state's southern counties, tobacco and slavery remained the cornerstones of the agricultural economy.

Slave-owning planters retained their considerable economic and political strength partly through the establishment of the Electoral College, which enlarged their voting power with 3/5 of every slave owned.[44] The Electoral College still plays a formidable role in determining the election of this nation's Presidents.

Slaves became a diminishing portion of northern and western Maryland's workforce as free blacks lived and worked alongside white non-slaveholders. Farmers raising wheat and corn generally hired workers during planting and harvesting seasons, then discharged them after the harvest. Full-time slaves were actually more of a liability to owners who had to feed and clothe them before, during, and after the harvest season.

In Washington County, the slave population peaked at 3,201 in 1820 (13.9% of the population) and had fallen precipitously to 1,435 by 1860 (4.6%). A similar pattern emerged in the adjacent Cecil and Allegany Counties so that one observer wrote, "in the grain and pastoral counties of Cecil and Allegany, slavery appears to be undergoing a gradual extinction."[45] I wasn't sad to read that.

Were Otho and Alice released from bondage before the end of slavery? In my naive mind, being a free person of color could only be a better life than being a slave. I became excited when coming across an 1856 *Herald of Freedom and Torch Light* newspaper advertisement by someone named Otho Williams (Figure 4.6).

For Hire.

A NEGRO BOY, 15 years of age. Enquire of
OTHO WILLIAMS,
Near Williamsport, Md.

April 23, 1856

Figure 4.6. 1856 advertisement in the Herald of Freedom and Torch Light Newspaper.

This advertisement led me to believe my second great-grandfather was manumitted before the end of slavery and had placed the ad himself. Was my Otho in a position to hire other black workers for his farm near Williamsport? Dr. Amt felt obligated to burst what was not be the last bubble of hope on this rocky, unpredictable journey. She told me "no," it was a white slaveholder named Otho Williams (who I am calling FarmerOtho later in this book). She said that particular white Otho Williams often hired out his slaves to work for other farmers. *My hopes were dashed again.*

Slaves with a particular skill—like bricklaying, blacksmithing, welding, or iron smelting—could be hired out by their masters and be allowed to keep a portion of the salary they were paid for their work. With this earned money, a slave could buy clothes, foodstuffs, or eventually purchase his or her freedom, or that of his or her family members. Did my second great-grandfather have a trade where he could make enough money to purchase his and his family's freedom, or were he and his wife manumitted prior to the end of slavery? I had no clue, so the investigation continued into what life was like for blacks in general.

Max Grivno's book, *Gleanings of Freedom,*[46] provides the most descriptive view of the robust agricultural economy of the late eighteenth and early nineteenth centuries in Maryland. He studied the economic status of specific slave owners, like Frisby Tilghman's Rockland plantation in the 1810s and 1820s. Tilghman and his twenty-nine slaves had started a range of agricultural reforms, such as practicing crop rotation, fertilizing the fields with manure and plaster, and experimenting with the latest farm implements.

Tilghman boasted that his estate's 260 acres of improved land yielded 1,100 bushels each of corn and wheat, 400 bushels of oats, and 300 bushels of rye. The plantation's pastures and woodlots were home to extensive livestock herds, including 200 to 300 sheep, 40 to 60 cattle, and 100 hogs. Due to an economic collapse in 1819, caused by domestic and foreign competition, Tilghman's unwieldy workforce became increasingly burdensome. He had made repeated efforts to hire out, or sell, unneeded slaves to "soul drivers"—a person who traffics in the slave trade with ruthless disregard of humane treatment; known for cruelty to prepare the slave for the ill treatment that was the norm in the southern states.

Former bondsman, James W. C. Pennington, whose family belonged to Tilghman, remembered the planter grumbling about owning too many slaves. "I shall have to sell some of you," Tilghman once told Pennington's father, "and then the rest of you will have enough to do; I have not work enough to keep you all tightly employed."

So profound was the terror that gripped slaves at the approach of a soul driver that they sometimes mutilated themselves. When strangers approached a farm in Washington County, a young slave mistook them for slave traders and severed her hand with an axe, thus rendering herself worthless on the market. Fearing sale, a slave confined in the Hagerstown jail took similar action, smashing his hands and head against the prison walls. For most enslaved people, the prospect of being sold "Down South" was unbearable.

The Fugitive Blacksmith,[47] written by James W.C. Pennington, describes his life at the Tilghman plantation, located near where my Otho likely grew up. Pennington wrote that slaves at Rockland were fed salt pork, herring and Indian corn—all part of an allotted 3 1/2 pounds of food provided each week. At times, women slaves used ground corn to make johnnycakes. Slaves were provided with shoes, stockings, pantaloons and a jacket for winter; for summer, they were given coarse linen pants and scratchy shirts.

Slaves were not allowed to attend church on Sundays, although they weren't required to work on that day. Pennington described many incidents of cruelty which compelled him to run away at the age of 21. His adventure from slavery to freedom was absolutely riveting, describing how he evaded capture, making it to New York, taking courses at Yale, becoming a minister, and publishing his autobiography.

Pennington's book, and other written accounts of a similar ilk, helped me understand the uneasy climate of the area in western Maryland where my ancestors lived and worked. Maybe my slave ancestors also lived in a little slave cabin like the one described in Pennington's book, squeezing seven people into a space that would barely fit four. Imagine the insufferable Maryland winters with the snow-chilled wind whistling through the weathered slats of the slave quarters log cabins. And what about flooding in the winter, and caking mud inside cabins that probably had dirt floors?

Reading biographies written by actual runaways, as well as slave narratives, makes their experiences more real, albeit sometimes a little too real. A riveting book, the *Freedom's Gardener: James F. Brown, Horticulture and the Hudson Valley in Antebellum America,* describes James Brown's numerous unsuccessful efforts to purchase his freedom from Susan Williams, the daughter of Otho Holland Williams, one of the several white men who I thought might have fathered my second great-grandfather. Brown kept a diary of his life as a skilled carpenter, as well as his brief adventures on the run from slave catchers, and how he became a rather famous horticulturist.

Through Brown's writings and those of other slaves and free blacks, I was getting an idea of what my relatives' lives might have been like. I was slowly mentally preparing myself for the very real possibility that I would not be able to answer any of my specific questions about Otho. I hadn't found anything substantive in the two months that I'd been writing this book and nothing in the past decade of trying. Living vicariously through the tales of others who lived in the same place, at the same time that my family did, might at least paint a hazy picture of their lives.

I purchased numerous biographies and genealogy books to enhance my understanding of slaves and free persons of color in Maryland. A sampling of my new library books included *The Narrative of Sojourner Truth*, *The History of Western Maryland*, *When I Was a Slave: Memoirs from the Slave Narrative Collection*, *Far More Terrible for Women: Personal Accounts of Women in Slavery*.

I had always assumed it would be better to be free than a slave, after reading about the arch-villain Simon Legree from *Uncle Tom's Cabin,* cruel master Edwin Epps from *Twelve Years a Slave,* and other books that depicted a prototype of an evil, sadistic slave master.

However, it seemed there were plusses and minuses to being a free person of color. According to my readings, because Washington County's slaveholdings were small compared to other parts of the state, and because free blacks were hired out during the intense periods of harvest, they often endured long separations from their friends and families to find work.

The black community was spread extensively over entire neighborhoods and often came together in the region's towns and meeting places where slaves and free blacks could gather to socialize and worship on holidays and weekends. For example, three predominantly "Black blocks" were sandwiched between Summit Avenue and Forest Drive in Hagerstown. This Jonathan Street neighborhood was a settling place for free blacks in the county and was the site of their first churches, businesses and homes.

Despite the challenges of life in a slave society, by 1818, black members of the St. Paul's Methodist Episcopal Church formed their own congregation, called Asbury Methodist Episcopal Church. That building still stands in the Jonathan Street neighborhood. In 1838, some members of Asbury Church seeking more autonomy in their worship, and the right to purchase property, founded Ebenezer African Methodist Episcopal (AME) Church (see Figure 4.7).

The AME Church was a new denomination organized by free African Americans, like Reverend Henry Thomas, who was an ironworker-turned-reverend. Its last historic building was demolished in the 1990s.[48] This sense of community may have been how my second great-grandfather was able to forge social and familial relationships with other black folk, ties that might later result in partnerships after slavery was abolished. I wondered whether any of my family members lived close enough to Hagerstown to have worshipped, married, or been buried at either of these black churches in Hagerstown.

Ebenezer AME Church, torn down in 1910

Figure 4.7. Ebenezer A.M.E. Church, Hagerstown. Source: Western Maryland Regional Library, www.whilbr.org

The Jonathan Street neighborhood also once housed the county jail that held fugitive slaves waiting to be freed, reclaimed or sold on the nearby auction block. I also learned that it was difficult for blacks to live outside this "Black block" so I yearned to find out where, precisely, my family lived in the 1800s.

In 1820, about 74% of free men in Washington County were engaged in agriculture.[49] The county's black population of about 4,130 included more than 1,500 freed men and women by 1840, according to census data. The region's slaves-for-life toiled alongside sharecroppers and tenant farmers, "term slaves," free blacks, itinerant and often impoverished white hirelings, and artisans. Together, they formed a motley crew that one historian likened to a whirling kaleidoscope or "an ever-changing mosaic of unfree and free laborers."[50]

Black and white laborers sometimes forged economic partnerships, friendships, and romances at workplaces and taverns, where they gathered to dance, drink, gamble, and peddle their wares. Those often raucous gatherings brought together people of diverse races and status. The bonds between blacks and whites were not always from necessity. During the early national decades, the workers on the bottom rungs of the economic ladder sometimes formed close, long-standing, friendly, and/or familial relationships."[51]

Max Grivno's "*Gleanings of Freedom: Free and Slave Labor Along the Mason-Dixon Line, 1790-1860*" is set in a narrow swath of territory near the Mason-Dixon Line.[52] More specifically, it focuses on six Maryland counties that abutted the sectional border (Baltimore, Carroll, Cecil, Harford, Frederick, and Washington Counties). Agriculture was the bedrock of the area's economy from the colonial decades through the Civil War. As described by Grivno, in northern and western Maryland, as in other slave-owning places, different forms of labor-control were sometimes locked in competition, but they could also complement one another. For example, the early landowners used indentured servants to augment their slave workforce.[53]

In 1789, Elie Williams (related to several Otho Holland Williams who I believed were involved with my Otho) described how wage labor, slavery, and tenancy worked together on his Washington County plantation. "To enable Dutch John and my Negro men to clean up and sow in good order" and "make other necessary improvements," he needed to bolster his crew with a tenant who would "work the fields, which are not in grain."[54]

Although the composition of the workforce changed over time, employers never stopped splicing together crews from different segments of the labor pool. In 1829, Sharpsburg planter John Blackford harvested his wheat with the assistance of his five enslaved men, four free blacks (including three men and a woman who raked), at least ten white farmhands, and a hired slave woman who cooked.[55] I hoped beyond hope to see my family's names listed in Grivno's examples, but I had to be satisfied with learning about relationships between white laborers, slaves, and free blacks.

Conducting internet searches of farms in western Maryland, I learned that in 1830 it took about 250 to 300 labor-hours to produce one hundred bushels in five acres of wheat, using a walking plow, brush harrow, hand broadcast of seed, sickle, and flail (a threshing tool) (Figure 4.8).

Many farming inventions were being introduced to increase yields so that by 1850 only about 150-180 labor-hours were required to produce twice the amount of corn than with the walking plow, harrow, or with hand planting.[56]

The types of farm equipment used in Washington County could shed light on the type of equipment Otho himself may have used and/or been responsible for repairing. That would go a long way to verifying whether our family story was true that Otho had skills as a machinist or farm equipment repairman.

As Grivno reported, wheat, corn, cattle, and dairy products were the foundation of the region's agricultural economy. Slaves never accounted for more than a quarter of the area's population, and by 1860, their presence had been whittled down to a numerical and statistical nub.

Slaveholders who met the conventional definition of planters (i.e., owning twenty or more slaves) were few and far between. In 1820, 32 of the 1,520 slave owners in adjacent Frederick County were "planters" with 20 or more slaves on a plantation, contrasted to only thirteen of the 732 masters and mistresses in Washington County who owned twenty or more slaves. In 1860, the census recorded only two planters among the 398 slave owners in Washington County.[57] Slavery was inevitably abating.

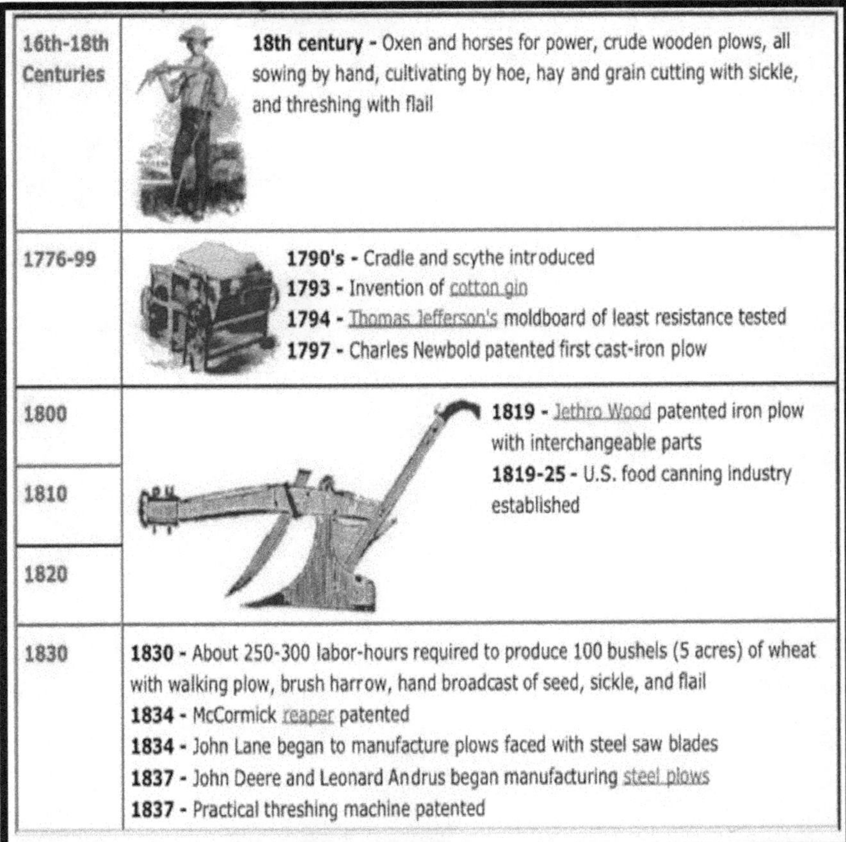

16th-18th Centuries	**18th century** - Oxen and horses for power, crude wooden plows, all sowing by hand, cultivating by hoe, hay and grain cutting with sickle, and threshing with flail
1776-99	**1790's** - Cradle and scythe introduced **1793** - Invention of cotton gin **1794** - Thomas Jefferson's moldboard of least resistance tested **1797** - Charles Newbold patented first cast-iron plow
1800 **1810** **1820**	**1819** - Jethro Wood patented iron plow with interchangeable parts **1819-25** - U.S. food canning industry established
1830	**1830** - About 250-300 labor-hours required to produce 100 bushels (5 acres) of wheat with walking plow, brush harrow, hand broadcast of seed, sickle, and flail **1834** - McCormick reaper patented **1834** - John Lane began to manufacture plows faced with steel saw blades **1837** - John Deere and Leonard Andrus began manufacturing steel plows **1837** - Practical threshing machine patented

Figure 4.8. Farming implements and production in the 1800s. Source: "Growing a Nation: The Story of American Agriculture."

From the time I saw the TV miniseries *Roots* as a teenager and became immersed in Black History classes in college, I had always used the image of one of my pregnant slave foremothers to help me through difficult times. I imagined her being forced to give birth in the planting field, then being expected to start working again after nary a day off for "laying in." [resting after birth]

Whenever I am in pain and want to give up, I think about the strength of my slave ancestors and tell myself to "man up" and try again. Forcing myself to be successful in *"Finding Otho"* displayed that fortitude imparted by my ancestors. I vowed to do everything in my power to finish this legacy book honoring my formidable ancestors!

Chapter 5 - The Cream in Our Coffee Wore a Crown?

Kathy Marshall's "Kanika African Sculptures" created this clay and textile, sculpture of "Queen Charlotte" who was wife of King George III. Charlotte was directly descended from Margarita de Castro y Sousa, thought of as being an African branch of the Portuguese Royal House. Was the Queen of England at the time of the American Revolution really a black woman? Interestingly, writing this book in 2018 saw the Royal Wedding of Prince Henry, third in line to the English throne, to African American Rachel Meghan Markle. Can we prove that the cream in Otho's coffee wore a crown?

The paths I took to find my second great-grandfather's owner and parents have been thoroughly intertwined, convoluted, fraught with difficulty and produced many surprises. Many conducting African American genealogy experience the same results.

Since I knew almost nothing about Otho Williams' parents nor his owner before October 2016, I had to try all sorts of different, creative methods to learn the truth. This chapter explores the avenues I tried. Some were successful, but most turned out to be misguided. This dogged search proved invaluable to finally finding Otho's slave owner. OK folks, take some motion sickness medicine before reading this chapter. It's going to be a bumpy ride.

Serendipity means a fortunate happenstance or a pleasant surprise. Serendipity struck in October 2012 while on a hike at an old silver mine in hilly Nevada City, California. I received an unexpected Ancestry.com message on my smartphone from a cousin-in-law named "Chip" Canty. Chip found one of my Marshall uncles in his extensive and exceptionally well-documented family tree. When he found out I had a then-105-year-old, entirely lucid, Williams relative, he could not believe I wasn't in Ohio interviewing her while she was still alive.

I decided to heed cousin Chip's call to action, and six weeks later, right before Christmas in 2012, I flew into Columbus, Ohio. I planned to interview my indomitable great aunt, Reba May Williams, and her daughter, Lavata Williams, who was our family historian. The day before I was to interview our esteemed elders, my mother's brother and only living sibling, Uncle Dale Carter, drove me to the Ohio History Center in Columbus. We spent the afternoon in the Genealogy Room researching our enslaved Williams family.

The Ohio History Center was beautifully decorated for the holidays. A Polar Express-style model train was chugging around the stately tree, upward along elevated tracks around a snowy small-scale town whose buildings were cleverly made from bark, and surrounded by Douglas fir trees. Jaunty Christmas music filled the entire lobby and wafted into the Library Research Room on the third floor where information about Ohio's history and state government records of enduring historical value are made available. Extensive collections of newspapers, photographs, manuscripts, books, and maps populate the shelves.

Since State Archives and Libraries often have books from other states, I searched for reading material from Washington County and found several interesting tomes. According to the 1880 U.S. Census, I knew that my first great-grandfather, Otho "Sherman" Williams, was born in 1874. All I knew about Sherman's father, Otho, was that he was a mulatto slave believed to have been born near Hagerstown, in about 1834. I was dying to learn if I could find some information about Otho and take that information to my elders the following day. I wanted to discover something new that my Aunt Lavata had not already found about her Williams family.

Unbelievably, in the far corner of that immense Genealogy Room, were several books from Washington County. Oh yes, I received many Christmas presents that day in the Ohio State Archives!

The first book I glimpsed was the *Washington County, Cemetery Records, Volume VI,* which had an index listing for: "WILLIAMS, Gen. Otho Holland, b. 27 Sep 1776, d. 11 Jul 1852." I later learned that he had been the Clerk for the Washington County, Orphan's Court for forty years. That meant he was the highest-level person to sign all Certificates of Freedom and Manumission papers, indenture and apprenticeship papers, etc.

I soon learned the hard way there were lots of white men named Otho Williams in Washington County. I needed to come up with nicknames for each of them to keep them straight in my head. I referred to this Otho Holland Williams as "**ClerkOtho**" throughout this book, because he was the County Clerk.

The second listing I found, also in Volume VI of the same Cemetery Records, had a listing for: *"WILLIAMS, Brigadier General Otho Holland, b. 01 Mar 1749 d. 15 Jul 1794."*[58] (Figure 5.1). Brigadier General Otho Holland Williams was born in Prince George County, Maryland, and was a hero in the Revolutionary War. After the war, he returned to his Springfield farm and bought the surrounding land in 1787 and began laying out the town of Williamsport. He even lobbied his good friend, General George Washington, to make Williamsport, Maryland, the Capitol of our new country.

Figure 5.1. Brigadier General Otho Holland Williams (RevWarOtho), 1749-1794.

I voraciously skimmed several books about this Otho, whom I called "**RevWarOtho**." The most interesting text was a hardbound book produced by Patricia Schooley for the Washington County Historical Trust, entitled *Architectural and Historic Treasures of Washington County.* Thank goodness I brought my Apple iPad tablet to take pictures of the many documents describing RevWarOtho's considerable land holdings, as well as specific narrative passages about him and ClerkOtho that would be useful later.

I also found a third Otho Williams, born in 1785 and who died in 1869. He appeared to have a lot of land near Williamsport, but he did not have the middle name of "Holland." I began calling him "**FarmerOtho**" since I learned he had quite a bit of land which would need many slaves—maybe my relatives—to farm it.

Before visiting the Ohio State Archives Library in 2012, I believed "Otho" was such an unusual name and that Hagerstown had to be a small place because I had never heard of it. Yet, there were three white men called Otho Williams in the same county in Maryland where two of my black Otho Williams ancestors were born and had lived. The search was on to see if there was any connection between them.

I began to loosely form the theory that my mulatto second great-grandfather, Otho Williams, could have been the son of his white slave master, who was also named Otho Williams. Which, if any, of the several white Otho Williams in the county was my relative's father and/or slave master: RevWarOtho, ClerkOtho, or FarmerOtho, or was it an entirely different Otho? Or was it not an Otho at all but a different white man? Gooseflesh on my arms began to tingle at the thought that I might finally find out where some of this light skin color came from.

When I returned to Uncle Dale's house after dinner that eventful day in December 2012, I anxiously began typing "Otho Holland Williams" into my Ancestry.com online family tree, using my trusty iPad. I pretended that RevWarOtho, born in 1749, was my four-times great-grandfather.

Ooh, shaky green-leaf hints[59] upon hints upon hints began to appear on the screen. (a green-leaf hint is an Ancestry.com feature that suggests records that may contain information that is pertinent to your search.) My head was pounding with the flood of mesmerizing ancestral information appearing on my iPad. Generation after generation of white Otho Williams popped up on screen, and I added them to my faux family tree. I could not believe how many generations of "Otho Williams," "Otho Holland" and other "Holland" surnamed family members were found in Colonial America, then from England, dating back to the 1600s, then the 1500s.

Most black people I knew, at least in 2012, usually did not see many of these useful Ancestry.com leaf hints. Why? Because at least 80% of all black people in America were still enslaved by 1860.[60] There was still a lack of digitized slave documentation, even a handful of years ago, which meant there were few, if any, green leaf hints for my family tree before my Ohio trip in December 2012.

The closest approximations of the number of enslaved persons are the 1850 and 1860 Slave Schedules, which contain the gender and age of slaves held by their masters—hardly definitive proof that a particular slave belonged to a particular master. We are totally out of luck if we do not know the slave master's name, which was my case. Other possible data sources included bills of sale or Last Wills and Testaments where enslaved blacks may have been specifically mentioned. But, one must know the slave owner's name to search those documents.

For me to see those brilliant green leaf hints on my iPad next to someone I was researching, was beyond exhilarating! That night, generation after generation of Otho Holland Williams' relatives were filling my online family tree. My tree now had white Williams generations born in the 1700s. Then from Prudence Holland, who married Joseph Williams, the family line went back to their Otho Holland ancestors in England in the 1600s. Hour after hour of ancestral gifts appeared on my iPad screen.

It was soon 3 AM on a snowy morning in Columbus, Ohio. My synapses were firing in my head like high-powered rifles when I learned that Henry Holland, a direct ancestor of RevWarOtho, had married into the English Royal Family when he married Anne Plantagenet in 1447.

What? My black second great-grandfather, Otho Williams, could have been related to English royalty and thus, so could I? Thanks to RevWarOtho, my family could qualify as Sons and Daughters of the American Revolution. If true, I could say, "The Cream in Our Coffee Wore a Crown." I thought that could be a great title for this book! But first I had to prove that the hypothesis was true. And if so, which of the many white Otho Williams living in western Maryland could have fathered my enslaved Otho?

Realistically, since RevWarOtho was already dead by 1794, and my Otho was born in 1834, he was not a candidate to be my third great-grandfather. Perhaps one of RevWarOtho's sons or nephews was part of my family, or was our slave owner. RevWarOtho's son, Otho Holland Williams, was born in 1792, but he died after being thrown from a horse in 1802, therefore, could not have fathered my Otho in 1834.[61]

Another possibility was RevWarOtho's nephew, Otho Holland Williams, born in 1819 or 1820. I nicknamed him **BusinessOtho** because later in life he had amassed a fortune from intelligent business dealings, creating an incredible estate worth almost one million dollars by the time of his death in 1903.

Perhaps three white Otho Williams could have been the father or the owner of my ancestor: ClerkOtho, FarmerOtho, or BusinessOtho. Initially, the theory that made the most sense to me was:

> "In western Maryland around 1834, the 14-year-old son of the slave master spied a slave girl working at his uncle's farm and coaxed (or ordered) her into the barn where he sowed his wild oats. The rape of the slave girl resulted in a mulatto son to whom he bequeathed his proud family name of Otho Williams—my ancestor."

In the chilly wee hours of that morning, covered in a cold, white fluffy quilt, I was punch drunk with dancing green Ancestry.com leaf hints pointing the way to additional research references floating through my dreams. That became my number one theory about Otho's parentage: BusinessOtho was the father! How could that be proven? Upon waking, I found an 1850 Slave Schedule for a "Brig. Gen. O.H. Williams" and, lo and behold, there *was* a male slave aged about 15, which was really close to the age my enslaved Otho would have been in 1850. My theory had the *possibility* of being true.

The next day, I presented my theory of white parentage to my Great Aunt Reba Williams, Aunt Lavata Williams and Uncle Dale Carter. I encouraged my elders to poke holes in the theory and tell me why it was false. They could come up with no specific reasons why it *couldn't* be true. I decided to pursue a course of action to prove or disprove that the 14-year-old whom I call BusinessOtho, son of slave owner Elie Williams, fathered my second great-grandfather Otho Williams. I mulled this hypothesis over for four years, but could not satisfactorily prove or disprove it. I had no other cards up my sleeve and was stuck in limbo at the 1870 Brick Wall for four long, disappointing years.

To my knowledge, there were only three ways to prove beyond a shadow of a doubt that my Otho was fathered by one of the white Otho Williamses who was related to English Royalty, and who was a Son of the American Revolution:

1) Actual documents, such as a Will and Testament, or land records, or a letter specifically indicating my enslaved Otho is the white Otho's son; or,
2) Matching Y-DNA test results for one of the men in my Williams family line compared to those of a direct male descendant of RevWarOtho; or,
3) Finding a living member of the Otho Holland Williams family who will certify that their white relative fathered my Otho.

All three of those methods were the longest of long shots, but they were *possible* until proven otherwise. If I could be sure of who my Otho's slave owner was, I could research probate records, census, and land records, in addition to the 1850 and 1860 Slave Schedules. I could also check and match the information against data from the 1870 and 1880 Census. The most insurmountable problem was not knowing who the slave owner was even after four years of trying to figure it out. More than discouraged, I had to admit I was still at square one.

Even though not positive of my ancestral origins, in 2015 I dared to submit a two-minute video for the "Next Ancestry DNA TV Commercial." With great excitement, I explained my theory of our possible descent from Royalty (Appendix E) and emailed it to Ancestry DNA. I got a call-back and was interviewed in April 2016 via Skype, an internet app that allowed an Ancestry DNA official from San Francisco, California, to interview me. I was disappointed that our video story lost out in the final round of decision-making. Believe it or not, if selected, our commercial would have run on TV stations worldwide during the 2016 Olympics coverage.

After being so happy about my progress during the first and second months of writing this book, a reversal of fortune slapped me hard in the face. During that third month, I encountered several snags while researching the topics for which I did not have answers, namely anything about my enslaved ancestors. It felt like for every step forward I'd take three-fourths of a step backward. That was when the "Never Give Up" motto and images of the "Energizer Bunny" who never stops working, began to stick in my head. I began thinking of the research not just as a book to write, but as a strategy game that I need to WIN!

To revisit the original parentage and ownership theories I had discussed with my elders in Ohio in 2012, I had assumed that Hagerstown was a small town in the early 1830s, so how many "Otho Williams" could be in that small place? Since I believed Otho was such an uncommon name, I also assumed that only a father with that unusual name would name their child Otho too. I was so wrong on both points! Hagerstown is the Washington County seat, so it was an important town of over 25,000 people in 1830.

Dr. Emilie Amt, the expert I consulted with from the Department of History at Hood College kept reminding me that Otho was a popular name in that area.

> "Otho and Williams were both very common names in nineteenth-century Washington County, as you've no doubt discovered. I would not conclude that your Otho Williams was necessarily connected to any particular white Otho Williams unless you have other reason to think so. Black families having the same last name as their enslavers in this County was very rare."

I decided to do further research by analyzing the 1820 U.S. Census. I would never have guessed it, but there were twenty-five people in Washington County named Otho with differing surnames. By 1860, there were at least seventy-three named Otho in the same county. Unfortunately for me, many people—white and black—named their children Otho, probably after the beloved Revolutionary War hero Otho Holland

Williams (RevWarOtho). To this day, there are scads of men named Otho Holland Williams, or Otho something, throughout the United States. Dr. Amt was right.

Certainly, the first name Otho was not as popular as the surname Williams. An internet search indicated that 46% of all Williams in the United States are black (over 716,000).[62]

I persisted in trying to prove my theory, but the abundance of Otho Holland Williamses had made my project incredibly difficult and exceedingly confusing. The esteemed genealogy expert, Tony Burroughs, said that in all the research he has conducted, he has found that only about 15% of former slaves took their former owners' surnames.[63]

Heavy sigh . . . I had no clue how else to proceed, except to continue believing that Otho's father has the Williams surname and, perhaps a first name of Otho. Was I tenacious, exceedingly stubborn, or just plain desperate for information?

Maintaining that course of action was difficult because the census, newspapers, and many legal documents did not differentiate between the white Othos in any special way. I doggedly continued to print census data, death notices, and other records for each of the white Othos, and created a huge binder of papers for each of the white Otho Williams. I was painfully aware as I stubbornly continued the research that *none* of those white Othos was likely either the slave master or the father, but I had to try something.

As already mentioned, the 1850 and 1860 U.S. Censuses had "Slave Schedules" for each slave owner, indicating whether the slave was black, mulatto, male, or female, as well as their age. Unfortunately, none of the slaves' first or last names are included in those Schedules. The Slave Schedules have little actual utility, but they were a resource to explore. I was grasping at straws, so I searched the Slave Schedules more closely.

Because many of us are visual people, I decided to develop a spreadsheet to compare all the white Williams hoping it would help determine the potential slave master (Appendix F). The pendulum swung toward thinking ClerkOtho could be the slave owner, but I wasn't positive.

Dr. Amt again cautioned me to not put much faith in the accuracy of the slaves' ages in the Slave Schedules. Record keeping was generally abysmal, and the slaves' ages were likely incorrect. But I had to try. This trial clearly illustrates what the 1870 Brick Wall is all about. If you don't know the slave owner's name, you cannot access the correct 1850 and 1860 Slave Schedules, or probate, or land records. I felt like a broken record, rehashing the same wrong ideas over and over, going around and around, stuck on one track.

OK. I was ready to try a different course of action, even though it would result in hundreds of extra hours of research which might lead nowhere. I was desperate to find something—anything—this time. I looked at *all* of the Maryland Land Records for Washington County containing the surname Williams, not just those with a given name of Otho or Otho Holland. It took me a while to figure out how to access the land records—an irrational reason as to why I have never reviewed them before this point.

Every state may be different, but for Maryland, land records are digitized in this helpful website: www.MDLandRec.net. Appendix G contains the steps I took to access and print out twenty-five pages of Williams surname land records. At thirty-five records per page, that meant I was prepared to search potentially 735 hand-written land records to try to find *my* Otho Williams mentioned somewhere.

In the seventh column, "Kind of Instrument," I was carefully looking at all the deeds of manumission (D of M) and bills of sale (B of S) first, for they were most likely to involve slave transactions—either the buying, selling or freeing of human "chattel." Be aware that many "Deed" documents also contain slave transactions, so I would likely have to read all of the transactions on many of the pages. Starting with my theory that a white Otho Holland Williams owned my second great-grandfather, I looked at *all* Otho H. Williams' transactions between 1833 and 1865, when my Otho was a slave. There were almost two hundred land records that fit the criteria.

I decided if I didn't find my Otho mentioned in any of those transactions, I would widen the net and examine all other transactions with different first names on those Williams Index pages. I also noticed and paid attention to the surnames of people who had done business with Otho H. Williams, such as Newcomer, White, Van Lear, Funk, Comegys, and Clagett. I soon learned those men were considerable movers and shakers in Washington County.

After printing and carefully reviewing hundreds of legal documents, I had to admit there was no sign of my enslaved second great-grandfather mentioned anywhere in the Otho H. Williams land records. Another heavy sigh.

Not meaning to whine again, but it was extremely difficult to read sometimes light or illegible overly flowery handwriting, not to mention trying to comprehend the legalese contained therein. I kept envisioning clerk Bob Cratchit in the Charles Dickens "A Christmas Carol." We see poor Bob, wearing a thick muffler around his neck, and shabby coat around his shoulders, toiling away in Scrooge's perpetually freezing office . . . forever cold because the obsessively rich Mr. Scrooge is too stingy to buy coal to make a sufficiently warming fire in the office. Poor Bob Cratchit sits on his tall stool at a slightly slanting desk, hunched over a large ledger of oversized papers, his cramped, frozen fingers scribbling legalese with his tattered quill ink pen. That's about how I felt reading those documents—cramped, eyes-strained, cold, and tired.

I soon saw the need to purchase a second computer monitor with a big 29-inch screen to supplement my laptop (Figure 5.2).

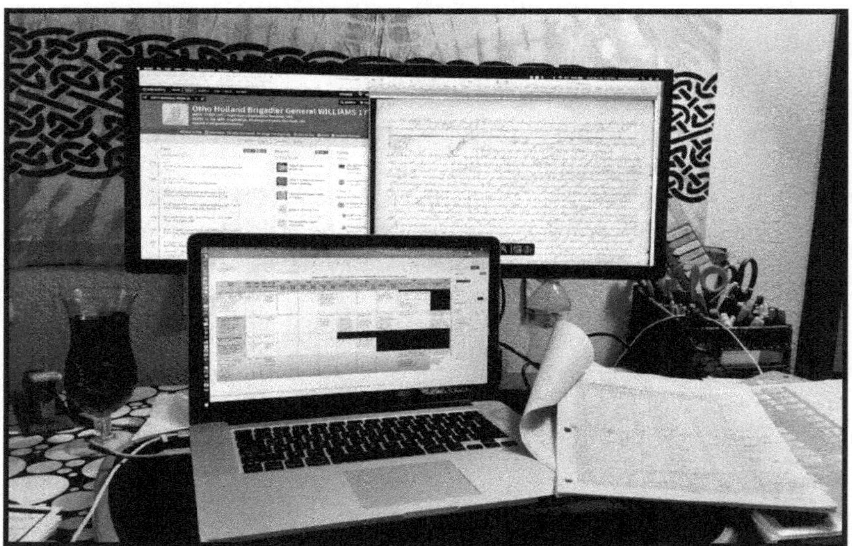

Figure 5.2. View of Kathy Marshall's workstation with 29-inch computer monitor to read land records and other documents side by side.

That helped me view the many computer windows I continually had open: Apple Pages word processing, Apple computer's "Numbers" spreadsheet, Ancestry.com or familysearch.org, Maryland Land Records, and a window for online articles about Maryland. I had to enlarge the land records to see and make sense of what was written.

That land records research and interpretation process was repeated for the *"Wi-Wz, 1776-1932"* Index, in Washington County, containing Williams surnames. Rarely listed was the slave's age, and rarer still, a description of the slave, such as dark mulatto, scar on left arm, etc. I wrote the names and ages of each freed person in the margins of the printed Index pages, (as shown in Figure 5.3) as an homage to their freedom.

General Index to LAND RECORDS—Washington County, Md.—To December 31st, 1911

...cate Family Name by Front Index

NAMES							LAND RECORD		
...mily Names	Given Names ABCDEFGH	Given Names IJKLMNO	Given Names PQRSTUVWXYZ	To or From	NAMES	Kind of Instrument	Book	Page	Year of Record
...ams			Richard	to	Eliza Williams	Deed	I N 3	610	1848
		Llyod		from	John Newcomer	D of M	I N 3	625	1848
	David A			to	John Coss	B of S	I N 3	671	1848
	David			to	David Winters	B of S	I N 3	672	1848
		Mary S		to	Adam Shoop	Deed	I N 3	790	1848
		Otho H		to	William Corby	Deed	I N 3	810	1848
			William S	to	Peter Wolfe	Deed	I N 3	853	1848
		Otho H		from	Zachariah Holland	D of T	I N 3	864	1848
		Otho H		to	Jeremiah Pattison	Deed	I N 3	898	1849
		Otho H		to	George Shafer	Mortg	I N 4	68	1849
			Phinehas	from	Elias Snively	Deed	I N 4	139	1849
			William	to	William H Hager	B of S	I N 4	607	1849
al	David			from	Thomas McCain	B of S	I N 4	681	1850
			William S	from	John C White	Deed	I N 4	790	1850
		Otho		from	Jno Campbell White & wf	Deed	I N 5	211	1850
			William S	to	Henry Brooks	Deed	I N 5	397	1850
		Nathan		from	Benjamin Witmer	Deed	I N 6	152	1851
		Nathan		from	William Faulkwell	B of S	I N 6	259	1851
		Otho & wf		to	John C White	Deed	I N 6	437	1851
		John		to	John W Betts	B of S	I N 6	457	1852
		Owen & wf		to	Zacheus O McComas	Deed	I N 6	498	1851
			Susan F	to	Edward Donelan	Deed	I N 6	557	1852
			Susan F	to	Peter Wolfe	Deed	I N 7	52	1852

Figure 5.3. One of 21 pages of Maryland Land Records for the Williams surname, 1848-1853.

Searching the land records was a laborious process, to be sure, but I was delighted that information was available online instead of having to pay someone to research the information from the county where the records were stored.

To illustrate how challenging, but chock full of information, this exercise can be, I have transcribed one manumission document, issued by ClerkOtho for his slave named Mary in 1817, along with the handwritten deed (Figure 5.4.). *Was ClerkOtho's slave, Mary, my Otho's mother?*

"To all whom it may concern. Be it knowned that I, Otho H. Williams of Washington County in the State of Maryland, for diverse good causes and considerations and at the particular desire of my late wife expressed, previous to her decease as also further consideration of one dollar current money to me in hand paid, have released from slavery, liberated, manumitted, and set free and by these presents do hereby release from slavery, liberate, manumit, and set free my Mulatto girl named Mary being of the age of eighteen years or there about and able to work and gain sufficient livelihood and maintenance by laborer and her the said ..."

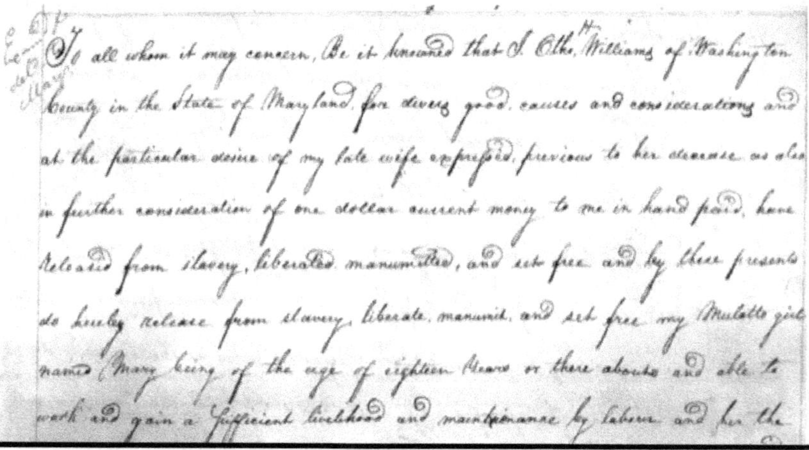

To all whom it may concern, Be it knowned that I Otho H. Williams of Washington County in the State of Maryland for divers good causes and considerations and at the particular desire of my late wife expressed, previous to her decease as also in further consideration of one dollar current money to me in hand paid, have released from slavery, liberated, manumitted, and set free and by these presents do hereby release from slavery, liberate, manumit, and set free my Mulatto girl named Mary being of the age of eighteen years or there about and able to work and gain a sufficient livelihood and maintainance by labour and her the

Figure 5.4. Partial transcription of freedom papers issued by ClerkOtho, Otho Holland Williams, Washington County, book BB, page 995, dated 1817.

Seeing for the first time human beings included in the same sentence as horses, pigs, tables, and knives in a normal bill of sale, made my blood boil and tears well up in my strained eyes. We really were treated like any other property—alive, dead, or inert.

Disappointed that I still hadn't found a record of manumission or bill of sale or land deed of any kind for my Otho, I had to assume he remained a man in bondage until the end of slavery.

So who were those many white Otho Williams in Washington County, Maryland, to *my* Otho?

Was BusinessOtho (1820-1903) my Otho's slave owner or father? My original theory reasoned that my mulatto ancestor was fathered by the teenaged son of slaveholder Elie Williams. He grew to be a powerful shipping merchant and businessman in Baltimore, which is about seventy-five miles away from the Boonsboro area where my Otho may have been born. BusinessOtho did have three black servants working for him in 1850 and only white servants in 1860. It did not appear he ever had any slaves at all. Dejected, I must admit there was no documented proof that BusinessOtho was involved with my Otho in any way. I begrudgingly crossed BusinessOtho off the list as my Otho's slave owner or father.

Was FarmerOtho (1785-1869) the slave owner or father? Looking at the enlarged 1859 Washington County property owner Taggart Map on my wall, it is clear that FarmerOtho was the most likely candidate to own a lot of land and, therefore, the most likely to need slave labor to farm that land. I attributed all Otho Williams census records that had the most slaves to FarmerOtho, but none of his slaves' ages or genders were anywhere close to my Otho. Additionally, none of his land nor probate records contained any information about my Otho, raising serious doubts that FarmerOtho was the slave owner or father I was searching for.

Was ClerkOtho (1776-1852) the slave owner or father? My third theory was that Brigadier General Otho Holland Williams, who was the powerful Washington County Clerk from 1800 to 1845, was the slaveholder and maybe the father. The 1850 Slave Schedule indicated "Gen. O.H. Williams" lived in Hagerstown and had one 15-year-old black male who was close to the age my Otho would have been in 1850. I wondered whether one of his older female slaves—one named Mary—could have been my Otho's mother and/or grandmother. I had great luck obtaining probate information from familysearch.org for almost every other white Otho I was following, but not for ClerkOtho.

I finally threw in the towel and paid the Maryland State Archives $35 to hand-search their records to obtain ClerkOtho's Will. At the beginning of the fourth month, I received a big manila envelope from Maryland . . . but there were only two pieces of paper inside: my original information request form and the letter stating they could not find any evidence of a Will for ClerkOtho. How is it possible that an important lawyer like him, the Clerk of the Orphan's Court who signed thousands of legal documents during forty-five years of service, did not have a legal Will or Testament? ARRGGGHHHH. I cannot describe the depths of my abject disappointment and anger. I could not believe that I was no closer to finding out anything new about Otho and Alice Williams than when I started the book-writing process.

Dr. Amt kept reminding me to consider that the white Otho Williams families might have had nothing to do with my black family.

This and the following items are all about the white Otho Williams families. One can speculate endlessly about their slaves, but what is the evidence that links your second great-grandfather to a white Otho Williams at all? The similarity of name is not that evidence . . . You may have that evidence and not have shared it yet . . . Your research is very complex, but I think the weak link is the connection between the white Otho W's and your ancestors. I'm just not seeing that you've found that connection yet. (By connection I mean parentage or ownership--or both.)

After spending prodigious amounts of time and effort and tears and sleepless nights, I was getting nowhere with those white Otho Williams families. I had been beating a dead horse. That meant the cream in my coffee did not likely wear a crown, nor was there any connection to royalty, nor membership in the Daughters or Sons of the American Revolution after all. Another audible exhale. I needed to regroup and turn my energies and speculation to another theory.

Chapter 6 - 1834: The Most Pivotal Year

- Andrew Jackson was the President, Martin Van Buren the Vice-President, John Marshall was the Chief Justice, and the Whig Party was officially named.
- A land record dated 1834 detailed the purchase of several household items and a cradle.
- The author's second great-grandfather, Otho Williams, was born in 1834. Nearly one hundred years later, Otho's great granddaughter, Mary Carter Marshall (the author's mother), was born in Mt. Vernon, Ohio.
- A Will dated 1834 named ten slaves, seven of whom became the pivotal focus of this research.
- Margaret Booker, Kathy Marshall's other maternal third great-grandmother, was born a slave in 1834 in Virginia. In 1863, her heroic migration with her newly-freed children, from the plantation in Virginia to Barnesville, Ohio, started a new era for our family.

Figure 6.1. Milestone events in 1834.

Why was I persisting in trying to find a blood ancestor from Europe, especially after denying any such relationship existed for most of my life? One look in the mirror confirms I am not 100% African, no matter how much I celebrate my natural curly frizzy hair, wear African garb and create African-inspired art sculptures in my Kanika African Sculptures business. Am I "mixed" after all?

My Uncle George Booker had revealed in a 1977 letter that my second great-grandfather, Otho Williams, had African, English and Native American blood. The 1870 Census indicates that Otho was a mulatto. Therefore, I assume Otho looked like he had a parent who was African, but who was mixed with white or Native American blood.

Early on in this research, I learned the designation of "mulatto" was based solely on the visual estimation of the census taker at the time. There was no formal investigation which proved a light-skinned person had a non-black parent. My exhaustive search has found NO evidence that any of the white Otho Williams in Washington County had fathered or owned my second great-grandfather. I had to consider other possibilities for his parentage and ownership. A slave could not own another slave, according to Maryland law,[64] but a free black person could. Time for a new theory: Could a free black person be Otho's owner or parent?

During the antebellum period between the War of 1812 and the Civil War starting in 1861, Maryland had the largest free black population in the United States.[65] As detailed in Maryland Population Statistics (Appendix D) there were 83,942 free blacks in Maryland prior to the Civil War, compared to 87,189 enslaved—nearly half free and half slave.

According to African American historian, Marguerite Doleman, almost ten percent of blacks in Washington County bought and/or sold land and some owned slaves, perhaps buying their family members out of bondage. As shown in Figure 6.2, most Washington County blacks in 1870 were born in Maryland, and 132 owned property. I hoped beyond hope to find that my relatives were among those landowners.

Being a free person of color was not a bed of roses, as I soon learned. Many slave owners feared that free blacks would persuade their enslaved brethren to run away from their masters. Many whites believed free blacks had to be totally excised from the state of Maryland in a "send them back to Africa" movement. To that end, the Maryland General Assembly authorized an 1831 census to aid in the effort to resettle recently freed slaves and other free African Americans to Liberia, Africa.[66] Marylanders saw colonization in Africa as a means of curtailing the growing free black population.

Enough Maryland blacks sailed to Africa that a "Maryland District" was created in Liberia, West Africa, and a special "1832 Census of Negroes" was generated for Harford, Talbot, and Somerset counties.[67]

Who were these free blacks and did any of them have anything to do with my Williams family?

In the third month on this project, I ordered the book of "African American Manumissions of Washington County," compiled and written by Marsha Lynne Fuller, CCGS.

African American Manumissions

1870 Town	People	Born in MD	Own Property
Sharpsburg	178	164	6
Williamsport	373	267	10
Hagerstown	878	785	66
Clear Spring	338	269	17
Hancock	252	189	6
Boonsboro	114	111	5
Cavetown	22	22	1
Rohrersville	43	42	2
Leitersburg	14	11	0
Funkstown	102	87	5
Sandy Hook	146	89	2
Tilghmanton	90	84	2
Wilsons	79	77	5
Ringgold	0	0	0
Indian Springs	61	34	3
Beaver Creek	133	132	2
Antietam	3	3	0
TOTAL	2826		132

- Data compiled by Marguerite Doleman, Hagerstown, Maryland

Figure 6.2. African American property owners in Washington County, MD. Data compiled by Marguerite Doleman, Hagerstown, MD. Source: "African American Census of Washington County for 1860 and 1870."

It arrived like a beacon of light in the middle of my fourth frenetic month on this project. Frankly, I was at an extremely low point emotionally, having made less headway than desired in finding useful qualitative information about my Otho's day-to-day life.

As I flipped languidly through the pages of that shiny, red, wonder-book, it was apparent that anyone doing serious research on African Americans in Washington County *must* obtain this goldmine of a publication. It contains a Guide to Manumission Laws, African American population statistics, original slave documents, newspaper articles, and some photos of enslaved and free African Americans. I felt the most important aspect of the book was the transcriptions of actual manumissions of formerly enslaved people dating from 1806 to 1862. The Otho Holland Williams, whom I called ClerkOtho in Chapter 5, testified to hundreds of these Slave Manumissions between 1806 and 1845 until he retired as County Clerk.

Fortunately, there were several people with a Williams surname listed in the red African Manumissions book Index (Figure 6.3), but no Otho Williams was found in the Index, or anywhere else in the book. Drat! It wouldn't be as easy as I had hoped.

Williams, Aaron B53b
Williams, Amanda, B116c
Williams, Edward E., A28b
Williams, Edward G., A28a
Williams, Elia, B1b
Williams, Elizabeth, B116c
Williams, Harriett, B15a
Williams, Henry, B55b, B81c
Williams, Jane, B116c
Williams, John, B116c, B144b
Williams, Margaret E., B173b
Williams, Mary F., B84c
Williams, Mayberry, B116c
Williams, Nathan, B58c
Williams, Samuel, B121b, B129b

Figure 6.3. Williams surnamed African American Manumissions, Washington County, MD.

Upon receiving the Manumissions book and reading the Williams-surnamed people, I soon discovered most of them didn't mean anything to me because I had so little information about my enslaved family. I only knew a few tidbits from the 1870 and 1880 Census.

As my research progressed and questions were answered, I found myself rereading the Manumissions book over and over leading me to uncover more names of potential family members each time the book came under scrutiny.

I wondered whether my Otho at one point had a different last name other than Williams like some other researchers had experienced. There were a few black Othos in the book, but with different surnames (e.g., Otho Snyder, Otho Sewall, Otho Strite). I made a note to research those other Othos in the future if I didn't find more information about my Otho soon. One thing was clear. To be successful in finding my Otho, I must search additional resources.

Looking at the Maryland Land Records again, I found a "Certificate of Slaves" from 1825 which listed sixteen slaves who were brought from Virginia into Maryland by Catherine Shearer. She freed many of those slaves within two years of being in Maryland (Appendix H). Of course, I wondered if any of those people were my family members. Once again, like a broken record, no Otho Williams found anywhere.

One of Catherine Shearer's freed persons was a fellow named Nathan Williams who was eleven-years-old in 1825 when he was brought into Maryland. Nathan certainly did not squander his chance to become part of landowning America. While I didn't know the source of his wealth, starting in 1847, Nathan began buying the freedom of other slaves, as well as buying land tracts and selling parcels of land to other freed people. Nathan Williams purchased one of the most long-lasting historical landmarks in the county: Fort Frederick State Park.

According to the Washington County African American Heritage Guide:

"The land that is now Fort Frederick State Park was once owned by a free African American named Nathan Williams. Fort Frederick was built in 1756 during the French and Indian War. The fort was also used during the Revolutionary War and the Civil War. Williams was considered the second wealthiest African American in Washington County. He bought the property and used it as farmland. During the Civil War, Williams produced food which he supplied to both the Union and the Confederate Armies. He helped escaping slaves get through Maryland. Fort Frederick State Park was owned by Nathan Williams' family of free blacks and mulattos from 1860 to 1911."

Nathan is the dignified, white-haired man in Figure 6.4. His wife Ammy, seated in the center, was a slave who Nathan bought from a neighbor in 1847 for $60; he bought other slaves too. The family continued farming there until 1911. Nathan Williams' cabin was located where the parking lot now sits in the center of Figure 6.4.

I expressed my disappointment and anger to one of the docents-dressed-as-a-soldier working at the fort. "I cannot understand why they didn't renovate Nathan's cabin like they did the rest of the buildings instead of tearing it down for a parking lot. After all, Nathan Williams' family were the capable stewards of that property for over fifty years. The National Park Service missed an incredible opportunity to study the lives of an important African American family."

Searching the Maryland Land Records with a finer-toothed comb, I noticed several recurring people with the Williams surname, but with a first name other than Otho H, including Elie, Susan, Richard, William, Eliza, Ann, Hillary, John, Henry, Edward, Hannah, and James Williams. Scrutinizing their land transactions, it seemed those individuals were Caucasian, and most were directly related to one of the white Otho Williams or Otho Holland Williams men.

There were three persons of interest with a Williams surname, some of which are shown in Figure 6.3. They were buying and selling land and/or purchasing the freedom of other blacks from 1834 to 1865: Nathan, Prince, and Samuel Williams.

The first name, Nathan Williams, was the ex-slave who purchased Fort Frederick and other properties, and the freedom of other slaves (who may have been his family members). The other two names—Prince and Samuel Williams—must be white, or free blacks because slaves could not own property.

Figure 6.4. Photographs by Kathy Marshall from Fort Frederick Visitor Center, Williamsport, MD. 2017.

The second fellow, named Prince Williams, purchased household goods, furniture, and a cradle for $30 from John Cox in 1834. That was the same year my Otho was likely born. Prince also purchased property in Funkstown in 1842. Was Prince Williams setting up a family household for a newly born child named Otho, as well as for Otho's mother? I kept that exciting possibility in the back of my mind as I continued to research more Williams land records.

The third person that came into my radar beam was Samuel Williams. I already knew from the 1880 Census that my Otho's second oldest son was named Samuel Williams. Since it was common for blacks and whites to name their children after relatives, I began looking for all land transactions by Samuel Williams, thinking he might be a relative.

The first land transaction with the name Samuel Williams was a Deed of Manumission in 1853 for Catherine Campbell. However, it seemed that particular Samuel was a white man, after reading the particulars of the transaction.

I previously noticed an entry involving "Samuel from John Ingram" in the Washington County Book of Manumissions, dated 1854, but it didn't seem to be pertinent to my research at that time. But now I perceived that the verbiage in the land deed was the same as the language in the Book of Manumissions:

> "A Negro man, named Samuel Williams, was manumitted and set free by John Ingram by Deed dated the sixth day of April 1854, and recorded in Liber I.N. No. 8, one of the Land Records of said County, reference thereto being and will more fully appear. The said Samuel is now 35 years of age, 5 feet 5 inches high, has scars under [?] each [?] jaw and dark complexion."

Could Samuel Williams be related to my family? I had been having more downs than ups with many of my theories bottoming out leaving me craving answers I could not produce despite my diligent efforts. The potential new avenue of Samuel Williams as a possible connection jump-started my excitement hoping it might shed some light on my Otho's slave owner.

I was on fire again, this time to begin a search for a white Ingram family with someone named John Ingram. I printed the Maryland Land Records Index for the Ingram surname, listing all of their land deals from 1787 through 1882. *Hmmm.* They only had three Deeds of Manumission: one in 1848 for Mary Williams, one in 1854 for the above-mentioned Samuel Williams, and one in 1860 for Margaret E. Williams. Words cannot describe how disappointed I was not to see a Deed of Manumission for my long-sought Otho Williams, but I thought I was on to something big which spurred me to begin an Ingram search anyway.

Searching census records for the Ingram family in Washington County resulted in an 1860 U.S. Census listing a Rachel, John, Benjamin, and a 21-year-old black "servant"—no longer a slave—named Margaret Williams. There was no mention of an Otho Williams in the Ingram's 1860 Census record (Figure 6.5). Another heavy sigh escaped my mouth. Maybe the Ingrams were not Otho's owners after all.

Wait just a minute, let me recheck the Book of Manumissions. There was a Margaret Elizabeth Williams in the Index. Her manumission revealed:

> "Margaret Elizabeth Williams was duly manumitted by John and Benjamin **Ingram** of said County by Deed bearing the date the 29th of May 1860 . . . The said Margaret Williams will be 21 years of age on the 30th day of September next, she is 4 feet 10 inches high, has a mole on the chin and two moles on the left cheek, and one on the right hand, near the thumb, of a light copper color."

Was Margaret Elizabeth Williams somehow related to my Otho, like maybe a sister who was born around 1840? I began examining the Ingram Land Records Index more scrupulously. There was an "Agrmt" in 1834 between Joseph Ingram and someone named Jacob Jeffries that suggested the Agreement was part of **Joseph Ingram's Will** which was setting Jacob Jeffries free in 1834.

Do you see why it is necessary to read almost every land transaction for the Williams and Ingrams families? Slave-related information can be stuck inside the most unusual places.

Who was Joseph Ingram, born in 1762 and died in 1834? Did he have any relationship to my Otho, either as his owner and/or his father? After constructing a faux family tree for the Washington County, Ingram family, I understood that Joseph Ingram was married to Rachel Perrin (1774-1830) and was the father of ten children, including:

> William (1790-1863), Elizabeth (1795-1878),
> John (1796-1862), Sarah Ellen (1799-1847),
> Cynthia Ann (1800-?), Rachel (1803-1843),
> Benjamin (1809-1861), Edward (1812-1883),
> Joseph Ingram (1813-1890), Elizabeth (1825-?), and
> Catherine Ingram (1827-?).

How interesting: Joseph died in 1834, the same year my Otho was likely born, according to the 1870 Census. Is there anything in Joseph's Will that mentions my Otho?

Using the familysearch.org website, my fingers couldn't type fast enough trying to find Joseph Ingram's 1834 Will and other probate records. If his Will mentioned one slave being granted freedom in an "Agreement" instead of a "Deed of Manumission" could it also mention additional slaves?

The following partial transcription of Joseph Ingram's April 15, 1834, Will (Figure 6.6) describes how he disbursed seven of his slaves to seven of his ten children who were still living with him at his 246-acre Meadows Green property near the Beaver Creek. That property was initially surveyed for Joseph's grandfather, John Ingram, in 1785.[68]

That revealing Will document included what Joseph Ingram labeled as "my young family of Negroes."

At the beginning of that new year, in January 2017, I wondered, *Could this finally be the "Smoking Gun" I had been seeking for so long?*

JOSEPH INGRAM'S WILL:
Dated: Apr 15, 1834, Book D Page 101 (D-101, img 78)

- William gets $2,952 and land in Ohio
- Give John, Benjamin and Edward 246 acres, Meadow Greens Plantation,
- Elizabeth Huyett gets $500 and a horse
- Susanna Swope gets $1,000
- Sarah, Ellen, Rachel, Cynthia Ann and Catherine each $500 stock
- Sell rest of property in 3 months, except for Negroes
- Negro **Charles** shall act for himself and work where he pleases
- **Pegg** shall remain a slave and pay Executors $1 per week for support. Her children shall be given to Joseph's children if they want them.
- My young family of Negroes (none of these blacks should be sold out of state):
  - John to take S
  - Benjamin to take **Henry** (Harry?)
  - Edward to take **Hez** (Hezekiah?)
  - Sarah Ellen to take **Mary**
  - Rachel to take **Patcey**
  - Cynthia to take **Matilda**
  - Catherine to take **Margaret** (Prince's wife or daughter?)
- **Jacob Jeffrey** to be freed
- Ready money in the house should pay for the above (slave?) legacies

Figure 6.6. Joseph Ingram's "Young family of Negroes" in his 1834 Washington County, MD, Will.

There are several names listed in Joseph Ingram's Will. The names in bold typeface appear to be slaves: Charles, Pegg, Sam, Henry, Hez, Mary, Patsy, Matilda, Margaret, and Jacob Jeffrey. Same ol' same ol' as my Great Aunt Reba Williams would always say: I did not see my Otho listed there. Perhaps he was born just after the Will was issued (hope springs eternal).

Hmm, this is interesting. I did see a slave named "Hez" listed ("Edward to take Hez").

It is important to remember genealogy discoveries do not always occur in a cut-and-dried, straight-forward manner. In this case, a few weeks previous I had discovered that my Otho Williams was involved in a land purchase with someone named Hezekiah Williams. They had purchased 1.5 lots of land in Funkstown, in 1868.

The 1870 Census indicated that Hezekiah Williams could have been born in 1831, during the time Joseph Ingram was still alive. Hence, the "Hez" listed in Joseph Ingram's Will may be the same Hezekiah I had hoped was Otho's brother. Or, was the Hez in the Will a different relative, like an uncle of my Otho Williams? I did not know, but I continued searching the Ingram probate papers with relish.

I had already stated that a Margaret Elizabeth was living as a servant in the Ingram household in the 1860 Census, and I had guessed she might be my Otho's sister. But wait a minute, according to her manumission document, Margaret Elizabeth was stated to be 21 in 1860. That meant she was born around 1839, which was five years *after* Joseph's Will. The dates do not add up.

Could the Margaret who was given to Joseph's daughter Catherine actually be the *mother* of the 1860 servant named Margaret Elizabeth? Could she also be the mother of Hezekiah and, dare I say it, the mother of my heretofore unfound Otho? That was obviously an unproven, elastic stretch in logic, but possible.

Or could the slave named Pegg in Joseph's Will—Pegg being a nickname for Margaret—actually be the mother of all of Joseph's "young family of Negroes" and possibly my still-unfound Otho?

Was I grasping at straws (which can sometimes lead to a breakthrough) or could the "young family of Negroes" be *my* family members, as shown in Figure 6.7? That theory had real possibility of being true, not wannabe true, but truly true. I exploded into the Happy Dance! 1834 offered an invitation to be my favorite year ever.

I basked in the glow of the *potential* find for just about sixty seconds. No, I couldn't relax. Nothing was proven yet! There was a lot of conflicting information there. Was Margaret Elizabeth born prior to April 15, 1834, while Joseph Ingram was still alive, or was she born in 1839 as some documents suggested? Was Joseph's Will modified after his death? Who is the Margaret E. mentioned in Joseph's Will? And why is there no mention of my Otho? Are these not his family members after all?

What about all the other people listed in Joseph's Will: Charles, Jacob Jeffrey, Matilda, Mary, Henry/Harry, Hez, and Patsy? Were they Margaret's siblings, her children, her parents, or a combination of them all? Was Joseph Ingram merely the owner of these slaves or was he someone much more *personally* involved when he says "my" young family of Negroes?

Some colleagues with whom I discussed this case felt Joseph's terminology could indicate he was their biological father. Was Otho's father one of the white Ingrams, or someone else entirely? No more questions!

I took a break to relax for the rest of that blessed day in the energy center of my home, surrounded by my African artwork, the sun streaming through the blinds as I savored two squares of Trader Joe's dark chocolate and a petite glass of sweet ruby port wine on my shockingly red couch.

I basked in the exciting new possible discovery that Pegg and Margaret, slaves of the Ingram family, "might" be my third great-grandmother and my second Great Aunt, respectively, or some other relatives that I had only to precisely identify.

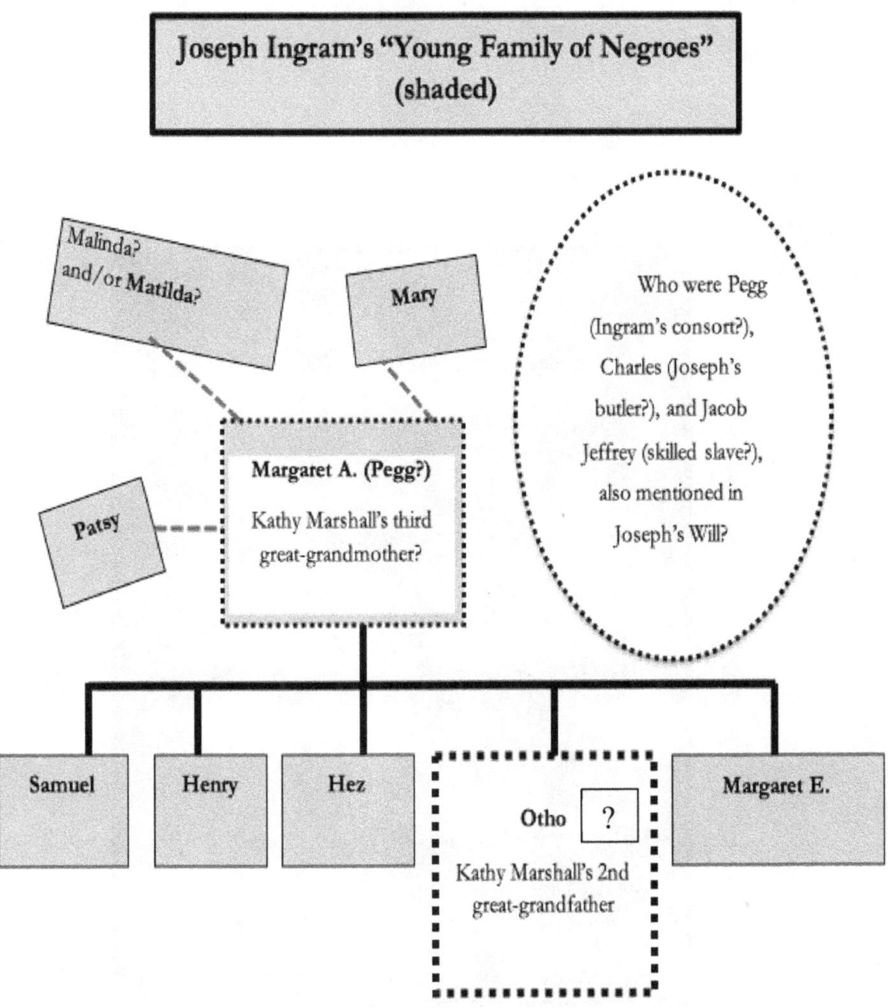

Figure 6.7. Joseph Ingrams' "Young family of Negroes" & their relationship to Kathy Marshall.

Mary Marshall

Chapter 7 - Does Prince Charming Exist?

"So, you finally found out about the Ingrams, did you? It's about time, little girl," rumbled a voice as deep as velvet, out of my line of sight.

I jumped out of my seat from the dining-room table strewn with research materials, ink pens, yellow highlighter, my printed draft manuscript, genealogy books from other authors, the dictionary, my lap-top computer, and a glass of water. "Who's there? Is it my Great-great-grandpa Otho again?"

"Guess again. Let's just say I'm gonna' hep ya figure out this mystery ya got here tired gal," intoned the disembodied voice.

How did he know I had been losing sleep these past several months, diligently searching land and probate records, leading me to new key players in our heritage story? After discounting ties with any of the white Otho Williams in the last chapter, learning about real estate mogul, Nathan Williams, and former Ingram-slave, Samuel Williams, I had just decided to zero in on a free black man named Prince Williams.

"Now ya talkin'!" came the melodious voice again, interrupting my thoughts.

I turned around, coming face-to-face with the apparition of an attractive ebony man nearly my height, about 5'6", standing in front of my refrigerator, to the right of the table which had become my preferred book-writing space. The man had close-cropped, wooly grey hair, receding a bit from his hairline. His smiling full lips surrounded sturdy white teeth that had a slight gap between the two front teeth, just like my sister's smile before she had braces which obliterated her African dental origins.

His almond-shaped brown eyes were clear and intelligent, as he seemed to take in the technological advances of my kitchen gadgets and television in the living room without a qualm. He had a chiseled "GQ Magazine" face with angular cheekbones and a prominent forehead. He had broad shoulders and muscular arms that extended from his short-sleeved white cotton shirt that was tucked into the narrow waistband of his coarse pants.

When he turned around to look at my house, I could see he had the trademark, rounded, "bubble butt" common (and desired) among many African Americans. His long fingers could easily reach an octave plus three keys on my piano. I restrained myself from asking him to prove my guesstimating at the piano in the next room.

Bringing me out of my observational reverie, he said, "I want to be here for this part of your search."

Am I asleep or merely having a nervous breakdown? Am I seeing and hearing this apparition—someone different than Otho? I have only been getting five hours of sleep each night, juggling my many genealogy, art, family, and boyfriend responsibilities. Wait? Am I finally becoming a real writer who sees her characters as clearly as if they were alive?

"That last idea sounds good. Let's go with that one, little girl," evidently listening to my thoughts; he added, "Tell me what you were about to do before you saw me."

As if it wasn't the craziest thing to do, I responded, "Well, I was going to write in my book that a man named Prince Williams bought $30 worth of household goods from John Cox in 1834.[69] That included: three beds, three hives of bees, two hogs . . ."

"And one cradle, right?" interrupted the hallucination.

"Uh, yes, how did you know a cradle was described in my transcription of the sale," I said pointing to the text in Figure 7.1 "Can you read it?"

"Gal, you know I can't read!" he said, a bit irritated. "It was against the law to teach slaves to read and write, and even though I am not a slave now, I never had the time to go to school. I had a family to support. Anyway, I guess they thought we'd take over the world or something if we had as much learning as they did," he said, still irritated with me and the fact that black people were intentionally kept illiterate.

I chuckled and said, "Some still feel that way today---that black folks should just be quiet and keep on working." That brought a knowing smirk from him. All of a sudden, I felt a little tingle in the back of my brain. My synapses began firing like a shotgun, hoping to hit the target and connect the dots. *Could Ebony actually be my great-great-great-grandfather, Prince Williams, finally making an appearance in my psyche? I can see him in my mind's eye now, and hear him too. Maybe I can get some answers to my burning questions from him. Yes!*

"So, what all does this here paper say? It's been many years since it was written, you know," he asked, becoming a little less gruff with me, waiting for me to reply.

I couldn't stop smiling, being in the presence of my Triple G grandfather at last.

Believe it or not, my present-day fiction author friends were aghast when they learned I hadn't already drawn a detailed picture of each of my ancestors, and carefully described their personalities and characteristics. They said a *real* writer must "know" their protagonist and *plot* the story arc before starting to write. They must use the character's *voice* and mannerisms to tell their story. Well, that was my problem. I knew nothing about my ancestors aside from the scant information that the 1870 and 1880 Censuses provided, and I didn't want to make anything up. It had taken quite a bit of time to learn enough from various sources to begin channeling my ancestors' existence into being.

Transcription of Prince's Household Goods Bill of Sale, Maryland Land Records, Book PP, Page 118, 1834

The request of Prince Williams, the following bill of sale was recorded May 12, 1834. Know all men by these presents that I, John Cox, for and in consideration of the sum of $30 current money in hand paid by Prince Williams, both of Washington County, in the state of Maryland . . . I, the said John Cox do hereby acknowledge, have granted, bargain, and sold, and by these presents, do grant bargain and sell unto the said Prince Williams, his executors and administrators and assigns, all the goods and chattels hereinafter mentioned and set forth, that is to say three beds, bedsteads and bedding, three hives of bees, two hogs, one cradle, and scythe, two touring scythes, one corner cupboard, one stove, one bureau, six chairs, one chest, one large iron kettle, three iron pots, one grindstone, one meat tub, and all my household and kitchen furniture not above stated, that is to say cups and saucers and plates and dishes of every description, all of which property is now in my possession, to have and to hold all and singular above mentioned property, to the said Prince Williams his executors and administrators and assigns forever ...

Figure 7.1. Prince Williams' 1834 bill of sale for household goods.

What helped me envision the spirit of my ancestors was a 2018 movie about Charles Dickens, entitled "The Man Who Invented Christmas." In it, the main characters, Scrooge and Marley, and poor clerk Bob Cratchit and his family, began appearing to Dickens as semi-transparent people who told Dickens how the story "A Christmas Carol" should be written.

Visualizing how characters could be imagined as real people helped me conjure up my ancestors too, allowing me to let them tell their tales.

I read aloud the partial transcription of my third great-grandfather's 1834 land deed, as he requested (Figure 7.1). "Triple G, may I call you that instead of great-great-great-grandfather? Were these items purchased to provide a home for an infant born in 1834, named Otho Williams, your son, who would become my second great-grandfather?"

Prince did not respond right away—whether from not understanding what I meant by Triple G, or some other reason, I did not know, so I continued speaking. "There's another recorded land deed involving you, dated eight years after that. On March 11, 1842, you recorded the purchase of lot 143, and half-lot 144, in Jerusalem (now known as Funkstown). Let's see, your property was located between Green Street and, uh . . ."

"East Cemetery Street," offered Triple G. "In Funkstown, all full lots are 82 feet and 6 inches wide by 231 feet in length, slightly less than half an acre. The entire one and one-half lot purchase was about two-thirds of an acre if I remember right." [70]

"Excuse me, sir, may I continue?" I answered, enjoying this game of verbal tennis.

"Certainly Miss," he deferred and winked at me.

"The land record says you purchased this property from John Sharrer and his wife Anna for '___ [blank] dollars.' Triple G, there is no indication that you were charged anything for this property. Is that true? Was the land given to you for free, or was that 'blank' just a mistake? What type of relationship did you have with the Sharrers? Were they connected to Catherine Shearer who brought sixteen slaves surnamed Williams from Virginia in 1825 and freed most of them within two years?" I rattled off question after question, as they came up in my mind, not allowing him to answer.

He piped in on cue, "One of Catherine's slaves from Virginia was Nathan Williams,[71] but I did not know him or the others that well. I adopted the last name Williams a few years after I was freed in 1812 at Antietam Iron Works, after working there for several years. Can you guess why I chose the last name Williams?"

I volleyed, "I have no idea, but I am dying to find out. Did it have anything to do with Otho Holland Williams, the County Clerk who signed your Freedom Paper in 1812? Or was it for Brigadier General Otho Holland Williams who fought in the Revolutionary War? Why did Negro Prince choose the surname Williams and when did you adopt it? Won't you just tell me?"

As he shrugged his broad shoulders and scrunched up the right side of his face in a smirk, he shook his head no. Darn!

So I went back to my previous question. "If I may (Prince smiles at my gumption), did the Sharrers sell you their property because you were related to those Virginia slaves in some way?"[72] No response. "Were you working for the Sharrer's on that Funkstown property before they sold it to you?"

Prince studied me from head to toe but still didn't answer. I felt that he was psychically *willing* me to understand, to find the truth on my own, for he knew it would be a sweeter victory that way. I wanted the answers *now*, forget the sweet victory.

There was electricity in the air, sparking the tungsten inside my head. The Tetris[73] video game pieces were dropping into place, one by one. Like his apparition son, Otho, I had a sinking feeling that Prince wanted me to puzzle out his story by myself. I changed the subject, hoping to trap him later. "Triple G, this type of family history research does not always progress cleanly from Point A to Point B," gesturing with one hand that Point A is close to my body, then moving my arm away to represent Point B, which is the faraway goal I am trying to attain. "Breakthroughs often happen out of sequence, sometimes after seeing the same information several times before the light bulb clicks on, offering brilliant clarity to the truth." *Oops! He has no idea what a light bulb is, but since he's not questioning me, I am going to continue trying to pry as much useful personal information out of him as I can.*

"A little while ago, I found an 1868 land deed involving an Otho Williams and someone named Hezekiah Williams. They purchased your same lot 143 and half-lot 144, but I could not determine what the handwritten deed meant. I never have a problem asking people more expert than me for guidance, so I asked online kindred spirits on the 'Our Black Ancestry' Facebook[74] page to interpret what the land deed said. I know you don't understand what Facebook is, but just know that several knowledgeable people explained to me that Otho and Hezekiah were somehow tied to *your* estate. I just knew there had to be a really strong connection between you, Otho, and Hezekiah Williams, but what was it?" I asked, looking straight into his sparkling eyes.

Prince flexed his cheek muscles just a tad, as though he was trying hard not to smile an acknowledgment that I was getting close to the truth, but he kept his ample lips tightly closed.

"It seems more and more likely that the 1834 purchase of household goods was *definitely* connected to the birth of my Otho that year, but how can I prove it?" I mused out loud.

"Why don't you look at those Wills Records again," Triple G innocently suggested.

"Oh, good idea." I retrieved my printed copy of the Maryland Register of Wills Records Index for people whose surname began with a "W", lived in Washington County, and had a probate record[75] between 1777 and 1850. "I saw there were two entries for Prince Williams, as shown here," I said pointing to Figure 7.2.

DECEDENT.	DATE OF DEATH	WILLS. Date of Probate.	WILLS. Liber	Folio	EXECUTORS AND ADMINISTRATORS.	DATE of ADMINISTRATION
White Peter		Feby 11. 1785	A	108	Margaret & Peter White	Feby 12. 1785
Wagner Philip		Aug 10. 1787	A	147	Rebecca Wagner	Aug 10. 1787
Watkins Peter					John Protzman	June 25. 1792
Waltz Peter		March 17. 1808	B	154	Mary Waltz	Mar. 17. 1808

1. Williams, Prince May 22, 1843 D 494 John Ingram May 23, 1843

DECEDENT.	DATE OF DEATH	WILLS. Date of Probate.	WILLS. Liber	Folio	EXECUTORS AND ADMINISTRATORS.	DATE of ADMINISTRATION
Winebrenner Philip					James K. Mood	Dec 23. 1851
Wineoff Philip		Sept 17 1861	E	565	Philip H. Wineoff	Sept 23. 1861
Wright Peter		May 12. 1868	F	201	William T. Hamilton	May 18. 1868
Williams Prince					Edward Ingram & Benj. J. Huyett d.b.n.c.t.a.	Aug 11. 1868

2. Williams, Prince Edward Ingram + Benj. Huyett Aug 11, 1868

Figure 7.2. Maryland Register of Wills Records, 1629-1999, Washington County, MD, Will Index 1777-1850, p. 204.

My finger moved along the entry labeled **1. Williams, Prince.** "One Will indicates the date of death was May 22, 1843, with John Ingram designated as the Administrator, and the Will was dated May 23, 1843." [76]

"The second Prince Williams entry did not have a dated Will but listed Edward Ingram and Benj. [Benjamin] Huyett as the Executors on August 11, 1868. I had wondered whether there two Prince Williams—maybe a father and a son—or only one Prince Williams who had initially written a Will in 1843, but modified it for some reason in 1868?"

As usual, Triple G was silent, his eyes boring through me, egging me on, with the corners of his mouth ever-so-slightly stretched upward.

The thought that something momentous was about to happen had my heart palpitating from excitement. "I searched online and found Prince Williams' Will and transcribed it in Figure 7.3."

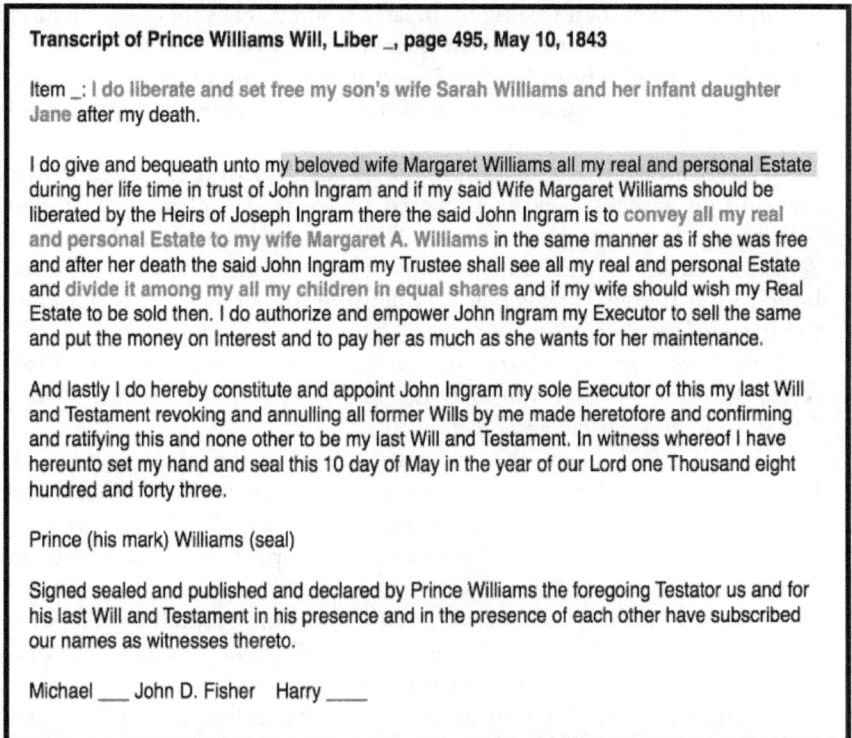

Transcript of Prince Williams Will, Liber _, page 495, May 10, 1843

Item _: **I do liberate and set free my son's wife Sarah Williams and her infant daughter Jane** after my death.

I do give and bequeath unto my beloved wife Margaret Williams all my real and personal Estate during her life time in trust of John Ingram and if my said Wife Margaret Williams should be liberated by the Heirs of Joseph Ingram there the said John Ingram is to **convey all my real and personal Estate to my wife Margaret A. Williams** in the same manner as if she was free and after her death the said John Ingram my Trustee shall see all my real and personal Estate and **divide it among my all my children in equal shares** and if my wife should wish my Real Estate to be sold then. I do authorize and empower John Ingram my Executor to sell the same and put the money on Interest and to pay her as much as she wants for her maintenance.

And lastly I do hereby constitute and appoint John Ingram my sole Executor of this my last Will and Testament revoking and annulling all former Wills by me made heretofore and confirming and ratifying this and none other to be my last Will and Testament. In witness whereof I have hereunto set my hand and seal this 10 day of May in the year of our Lord one Thousand eight hundred and forty three.

Prince (his mark) Williams (seal)

Signed sealed and published and declared by Prince Williams the foregoing Testator us and for his last Will and Testament in his presence and in the presence of each other have subscribed our names as witnesses thereto.

Michael ___ John D. Fisher Harry ___

Figure 7.3. Transcription of Prince Williams' 1843 Will.

Is he listening to me at all? I'll wager he does not know what "online" means, but he didn't ask, so I will continue my assessment.

"Let me take over now," the ebony apparition said, no doubt tired of my endless guessing about the past.

"But you can't read," I countered.

"I don't need to read. I know exactly what happened in 1843. It is *my* Will, remember? First of all, I freed my son's wife, Sarah Williams, and her infant daughter, Jane."

"What?" it was my turn to interrupt him. I couldn't ask the questions fast enough. "You mean you were a slave owner? That's incredible! Who was Sarah? When did you buy her . . . and from whom? How did you earn the money to buy her in the first place? And who was your son?" I was aghast!

Many present-day African Americans cringe at the thought that their black ancestors could have been slave owners. However, in many cases, free blacks bought their enslaved relatives to protect and keep them safe within the family, then freeing them later when it was safe to do so. Since Prince wouldn't answer any of my questions, I chose to assume Sarah was a family member whom he freed, and that was the extent of his slave ownership. *Hmm, I wonder why you didn't buy the freedom of your wife or your other children?*

"Listen, little girl, it's my turn to tell *my* tale," he scolded affectionately, cracking his knuckles, as he prepared to speak. He cleared his throat, "Uh-hem, the second part of my Will left my beloved wife, Margaret A. Williams, all of my real and personal estate during her lifetime. I had hoped John Ingram, or his heirs, would free her, or at least let her enjoy the fruits of my estate."

*I noted something very important in what he just said. Prince specified his wife was named Margaret "**A.**" not Margaret "**E.**" as appears in Joseph Ingram's "Young Family of Negroes." What might that mean?*

"Say," I asked, "does this mean the 'Pegg' in Joseph Ingram's 1834 Will is your wife, Margaret A. Williams? Was Margaret E. your daughter, and *possibly* the sister of my Otho Williams?" Prince's head starts to move around, like one of those bobble head dolls people put on the dashboard of their car.

"Are you shaking your head yes or no, or just getting a kink out of your neck? This is all too confusing, Triple G!" He kept rotating his head yes, then no, so I didn't know what to think.

I continued, "OK, for now in this book I shall call your wife 'Margaret' and your daughter will be 'Margaret E.' Williams unless I can prove differently. How does that sound to you?" I extended my hand, palm up to Prince indicating it was his turn. Would he say something helpful to enliven my search?

Prince took the bait. "The third part of my Will tells you I had more than one child. I told John Ingram to sell all my real and personal estate and divide it among *all* my children in equal shares. So, the big question that you must have by now, my darling girl, is . . . who were 'all' of my children?" He sat down in the dining room chair across the table from me.

"You are right, Triple G," I eagerly responded, "There is nothing in the 1843 probate record that answers that question. So, who were *all* of your children?" Like an obstinate little boy, he refused to open his mouth, shaking his head no, no, no. I continued speaking about a different topic, thinking I'd be able to trap him later into revealing some really good information.

"There were two pages of Inventory describing your personal holdings at the time of your death on April 4, 1843." I transcribed many of those items in Figure 7.4.

Inventory of all and singular goods and chattels of Prince Williams deceased is appraised by David Funk and Joseph Wheeler this 15th day of June 1843. Total value $56.13.

7 common chairs	2 sickle	1 lot bottles
1 chest	1 lot store boxes	1 rolling pin
1 tunnel Bell	1 lot milk crocks	1 lot tubs & bucket
1 Looking Glass	1 walnut table $13	1 do milk crocks
5 Window Blinds	1 lot buckets 3 1/3	1 meat tub 50
1 plate stone, dishes	2 skillets, pots, pans	1 spade & shovel
1 wash stand	1 ham 25	1 maul & wedges
1 bedsheet and bedding	1 broom & basket	1 wheel barrow
1 lot soup 40, 4 barrels 25	1 pail & rake	1 large iron kettle
1 cradle 12 1/2	1 lot blacking Brushes 6 1/4	1 lot corn in the ground
1 coffee mill	1 lot knives, forks, spoons	1 Hog
1 bread basket & bucket 25	1 lot carpeting 12 1/2	1 Tinplate Stove

Figure 7.4. Partial transcription of Prince Williams' estate inventory, 1843, by Jacob Shoop.

Prince affirmed, "Yes, I had chairs, beds, cooking stuff, a coffee mill, carpeting, window blinds, farming tools, and a hog.[77] You can get a pretty good picture of my life by looking at the things I owned, can't you?"

"Triple G, I am embarrassed to admit that I had ignorantly assumed you would not have had the niceties of carpeting or blinds at the windows. In reality, you had many of the same household items and yard tools that I have today, although, most of us nowadays do not have a live hog or a meat tub in which to butcher it.

The fact that you had milk crocks (plural) makes me wonder if you stored milk from a neighbor's cow, maybe for your growing children?" My voice elevated the last word in a question, "children?" Of course, Prince would not give me a confirmation or denial of whether any of his children lived with him at the Funkstown property, or whose cow was milked for what purpose. One step forward, three-fourths of a step back. That had become the story of this devilishly interesting but difficult writing project.

I asked, "You had one lot of corn in the ground. That made you a corn farmer, right? Were you also skilled in other areas, like bricklaying or blacksmithing?"

When I looked up from my notes, he was nowhere to be seen. He'd done a disappearing act just like his son, Otho, had done in Chapter 2. He didn't even say goodbye. Disappointed, but what a rush to finally experience Prince as a live character. It made it easier to imagine the type of person he might have been.

Since Prince was not listed in any U.S. Census for Washington County that I could find, I also did some research on Funkstown to get an idea of the possible employment opportunities he may have had as a free black man, besides being a corn farmer.

The village of Funkstown was bounded on three sides by Antietam Creek. Since its very beginning, Funkstown was known for its mills. Their first mill was built in 1762. It was a flourmill operated by Henry Funk. By 1785, then-called "Jerusalem" the village was home for an iron furnace, brickyard, powder factory, grist and woolen mills and a host of inns and shops. The last mill built in 1859 was a flourmill which burned in September of 1929 (Figure 7.5).[78]

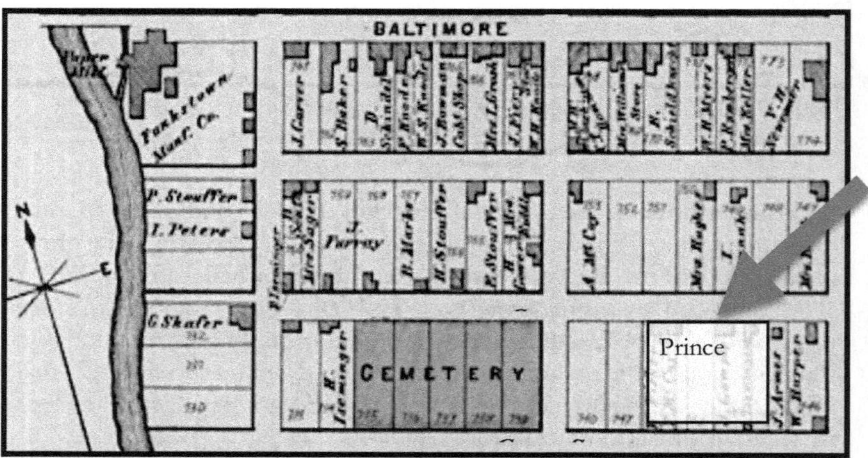

Figure 7.5. Partial map of Funkstown, 1859. The Williams lived between Cemetery and Green Streets.

By the neighborhood analysis performed in Chapter 2, thirty years after Prince bought his property, it was clear that half of the area's sixty-seven neighbor heads-of-household were comprised of persons skilled in many occupations besides farming, e.g., wagonmakers, shoemakers, one auctioneer, a blacksmith, broom maker, cooper, miller, dry goods person, schoolteacher, and a turnpike gatekeeper.

Among Prince's probate records was a bond[79] to pay the taxes and unspecified claims against Prince from a dozen local men such as Henry

Funk, John Newcomer, and Dan Schnebley; all debts totaled $151.87. That left a paltry $50.33 to be passed on to Prince's widow, Margaret Williams, in 1843.

In 1868, Prince's Bequeath to Heirs (Figure 7.6) indicates how much money his *five* living children would get after all his debts were settled. Therefore, I now knew who Prince's estate was claiming as his natural children (at least those who were still alive in 1868 when his estate was settled). They were Samuel, Henry, Hezekiah, *my* Otho, and Margaret Elizabeth Briscoe.

Transcription of Prince Williams Bequeath to Heirs

Source: Maryland Register of Wills, August 11, 1868.
Bond: Vol. G Folio 550, Inventory: W-19, Sales: Y-658-664, 1st Account: 24-308

[Editor Note: When Prince's wife, Margaret A., died in 1868, the remainder of Prince's estate was sold and distributed to his heirs, as he directed in his 1843 Will. The August 11, 1868, Attorney Bond for this transaction cost an astonishing $1,200 to handle the probate/sale/distribution.

Amount brought forward $726.90 and distributed aggreeably to the Last Will and Testament of Testator as follows viz:

Samuel Williams:	$145.38 [Ed: wife Sarah freed by Prince in 1843?]
Henry Williams:	$145.38
Hezekiah Williams:	$145.38 [Ed: wife Minta Galloway]
Otho Williams:	$145.38 [Ed: wife Alice Logan]
Margaret Williams Briscoe	$145.38 [Ed: husband Abraham Briscoe]
Total disbursed:	726.90

State tax on C _?_ 1/10 of $86.06 = $8.61

Figure 7.6. Prince Williams bequeathed an equal share of his estate to his five living children, distributed in 1868.

At that point, I concluded there was only one Prince Williams who died in 1843. There was no new Will in 1868, but there were five pages of personal inventory items, compared to only two pages from 1843. Someone had been quite busy buying goods in the twenty-five years since Prince had died.

According to custom, when a person died, their estate would be sold publicly, and the proceeds of the sale used to pay off any outstanding debts, taxes, and legal fees. The remainder of the estate would be distributed as stated in their Will.

Hallelujah! I finally had proof that Prince and Margaret were legally *considered* to be Otho's parents. In his Will, Prince Williams indicated he had more than one child ("children") that would benefit from his estate when his wife, Margaret died. Prince's estate was disbursed in 1868 to five children whom the executor, Edward Ingram, regarded as Prince's children, but was his assessment correct?

My second great-grandfather, Otho Williams, was listed as a child of Prince and Margaret Williams in the disbursement. However, whether Prince was the blood father of all those children is debatable. Still, it was time to celebrate a hard-won victory!

I was shocked at how much of Prince's estate the Ingram lawyers claimed—a $1,200 bond— thus leaving his five living children a paltry $145.38 each. It seems Prince's actual estate was valued at about $2,000 upon his death, (about $31,000 in 2017 dollars). That was a decent sum of money in 1843 for a black man.

On a hot and sticky summer morning on September 12, 1868, a crowd lined up at 9:00 AM to participate in a public sale of Prince Williams' real and personal estate (Figure 7.7). An advertisement in the *Herald and Torch Light Newspaper* regaled the public with the "comfortable one and one-half story log dwelling house, and lot and half lot of ground" for sale, as well as various household goods such as beds, chairs, carpet, bureau, safe and wardrobe. The description indicates there was a small back building with a good garden and excellent well water near the door. There was also corn in the ground for sale.

"Who will bid $2 on the interest in a lot of corn in the ground?" the auctioneer called out in a loud, sing-song voice. It was the first item on the 180-item inventory list. Several interested persons raised a numbered stick to bid on the item. Then the auctioneer increased the bid higher and higher, with Noah Jackson being the highest bidder for the corn interest for $6. An assistant recorded the name of the winning bidder and bid on the Sales Inventory list, continuing until all items were sold.

Many of the goods sold for less than a dollar, with a total of $102.89 garnered from the sale of Margaret's personal property. Her daughter-in-law, Sarah Williams (the one who had been freed by Prince), bought the safe for $2.25 and a large quilt for $4.00. Margaret's son, Henry Williams, bought a tub for $1.70. Daughter Margaret Elizabeth Williams Briscoe bought the bureau for $4.75 and her mother-in-law, Mrs. Briscoe, made the costliest investment of the day spending $17.00 for 34 pounds of feathers. Son Otho Williams bought the wardrobe for $1.80 and 20 yards of carpet for $7.40. The advertised ten-plate stove went for $10.25 to Margaret's son Samuel Williams. [80]

ADMINISTRATORS' SALE
OF
REAL AND PERSONAL PROPERTY!

By virtue of an order of the Orphans' Court of Washington County, the undersigned as Administrators, *de bonis non*, of John Ingram, late of Washington County, deceased, will sell at Public Sale, on

SATURDAY, SEPTEMBER 12TH, 1868,

all the Real Estate of Prince Williams, late of said county, deceased, consisting of a

HOUSE AND LOT,
AND
HALF LOT OF GROUND,

situated in Funkstown, Washington county, and recently occupied by Margaret Henson, deceased, and adjoining the properties of Abram White and Mrs. Fisher. The improvements consist of a comfortable one-and a half story

LOG DWELLING HOUSE

with small BACK BUILDING, with a good Garden and excellent Well of Water near the door. This property is very pleasantly situated on one of the back streets, and can be made a very desirable home.

The above property will be sold subject to an annual ground rent of one dollar per lot.

THE TERMS of the Real Estate, as prescribed by the Court are: One half of the purchase money to be paid on the day of sale, or on the ratification thereof and the balance in one year with interest from the day of sale, the purchaser or purchasers to give note with approved security for the deferred payment, and on the payment of the whole purchase money a good and sufficient deed will be executed.

Possession will be given upon receipt of first payment.

Also, at the same time and place will be sold the Personal Property of said deceased, consisting in part as follows;

1 BUREAU, 1 SAFE, 1 WARDROBE,

3 Bedsteads and lot of Bedding, such as 1 Feather Bed and Pillows, Bed Ticks, Sheets, Quilts Comforts, &c 1 Stand, 1 Dining and 1 Kitchen Table, Queensware ½ dozen Chairs, 1 Rocking do., lot of Carpet,

1 TEN-PLATE STOVE AND PIPE,

1 IRON KETTLE,

CORN IN THE GROUND,

and many other articles not necessary to mention

TERMS—Cash for the Personal Property, and no goods to be removed until settled for. Sale to commence at 9 o clock on said day.

EDWARD INGRAM,
BENJ I. HUYETT,
Administrators *De Bonis Non* with the Will annexed
August 19, 1868

Figure 7.7. Herald of Freedom and Torch Light Newspaper, 1868 Sale of Prince Williams' Estate.

I noticed that many of the purchases were made by people with a Williams surname: Henry, Hez, Minta, Otho, Sarah, and Margaret [Elizabeth] Williams Briscoe. However, there were many others who purchased Margaret's worldly goods: Mrs. Briscoe, Tobe Briscoe, next door neighbor Mrs. White, etc. While I do not recognize some of the buyers' names at this point in my research, I realize they may become important in the study of my family's ties and close friendships.

Sons Otho and Hezekiah purchased their parents' Funkstown property for $690 in 1868.[81] According to the terms for real estate in the newspaper advertisement, the winning bidder "had to pay one half of the purchase money to be paid on the day of sale, or on the ratifications there of and the balance in one year with interest from the day of sale the purchaser(s) to give a note with approved security for the deferred payment, and on the payment of the whole purchase money a good and sufficient deed will be executed. Possession would be given upon receipt of the first payment."

The land purchase transaction that I had seen a month before, between Otho and Hezekiah Williams, now makes perfect sense: Prince's sons wanted to keep his property in family hands.

Prince trusted John Ingram to handle his affairs and to free his wife, Margaret, sooner rather than later. A manumission document was never found proving the Ingrams freed his widow. However, the 1850 Census indicates she was a free woman living in the Funkstown property that her first husband had provided for her.

Having a publicly viewable family tree online resulted in a serendipitous event that certainly furthered my progress. In the fifth month on the project, I received an unsolicited, but welcomed, email from genealogist, Carol Wait. She was investigating the Ingram family when she found my public family tree on Ancestry.com, which contained information about the Joseph Ingram's family. I had been contemplating whether one of the Ingram men was the father of my Otho and some of his siblings, so I have tentatively listed Joseph Ingram as Margaret's father and slave master on my working family tree.

Carol gave me a huge present. She revealed that the burial record for Prince Williams had been incorrectly transcribed from the church document. "Prince" was erroneously listed as "Bruce" Williams in the Ebenezer A.M.E. Cemetery records; the error had also been incorrectly typed into findagrave.com, an excellent online source for cemetery records. Someone at the Washington County Historical Society had noticed the mistake, corrected the typed transcribed record with updated death information in pencil, and updated the online findagrave.com record (Figure 7.8). What incredible luck!

Carol also told me that Margaret Williams had married William Hanson (sometimes spelled Henson) and that she was also buried in the Ebenezer AME Church Cemetery, located in the Jonathan Street colored neighborhood of Hagerstown. That welcomed correspondence introduced invaluable information that Margaret had remarried after Prince died.

Prince
Bruce Williams, age ca. 60yr, - D. Apr. 4, 1843.

Mary E. Barnum, age 85yr, 7mo, 16da, - D. Dec. 20, 1855.

Malinda Williams, dau. of Prince and Margaret Williams,
age 21yr, 11mo, 24da, - D. May 11, 1859.

Mary Luisa Thomas, age 16yr, - D. Feb. 13, 1861.

Margaret Henson, wife ofWilliam Henson, age 72yr, - D.
Aug. 5, 1868.

Eliza Lucy Robeson, age 23yr, 9mo, 28da, - D. Aug. 10, 1864.

Widow of Prince Williams, m. Wm. Henson after Prince's death

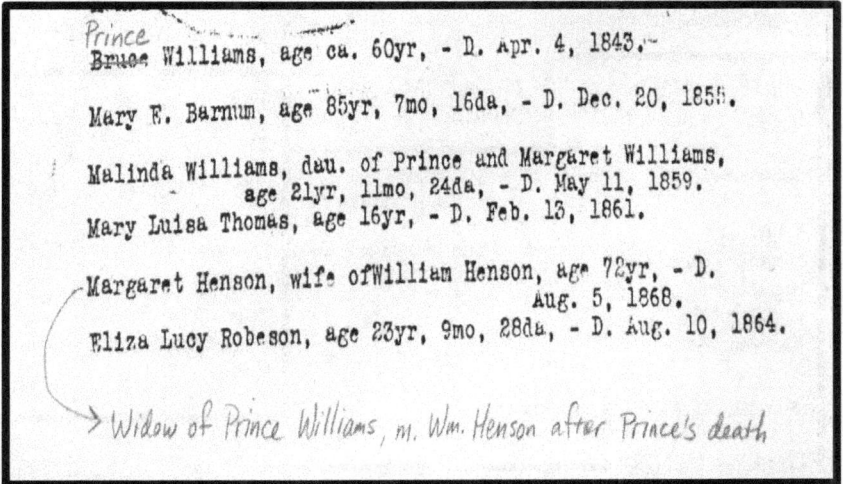

Figure 7.8. Cemetery records, Hagerstown, MD, district 21, p. 60.

Additionally, the cemetery record indicated that Margaret Williams Hanson was born in 1796, the same year John Ingram, executor of Prince's estate, was born. So many connections! I had estimated that Margaret was born in about 1800 since her child, Samuel, was born in about 1818. The cemetery record confirmed she was born before 1800. The Ebenezer AME Cemetery record indicated Prince was born in 1783. Having confirmation of both of my third great-grandparents' birthdates was rewarding. I am indebted to Carol for this remarkable happenstance.

I recognized that this chance meeting was likely engineered by the ancestors anyway (smile).

As mentioned earlier, Margaret Williams was listed in the 1850 census. She was living with William Hanson and her and Prince's daughter, Margaret Elizabeth Hanson, in the Funkstown property. Therefore, Margaret had to have been freed at some point before 1850, as only free people may be listed in the U.S. Census.

In the seventh month, I searched church records while at the Historical Society and Western Maryland Room in Hagerstown, as part of a genealogy adventure.

As shown in Figure 7.9, I learned that a woman named Malinda Williams (1837-1859) was also buried in the Ebenezer Cemetery, and was reported to have been the daughter of Prince and Margaret.

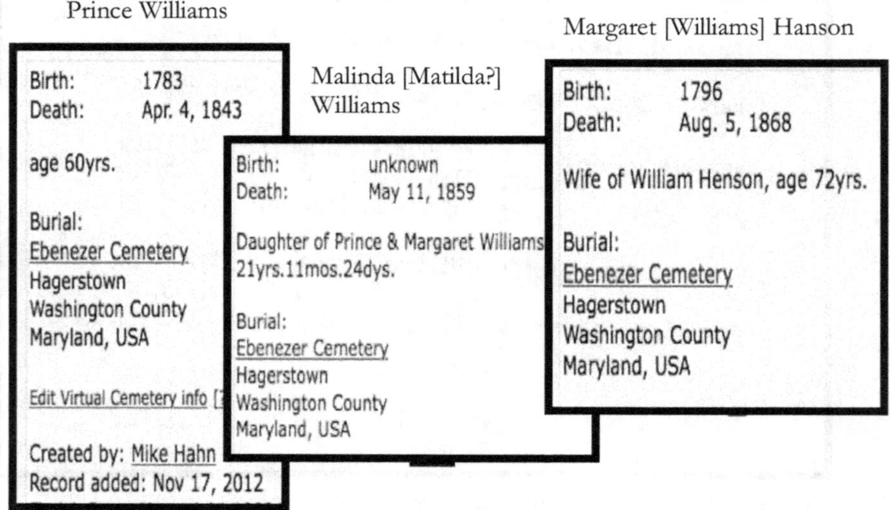

Prince Williams
Birth: 1783
Death: Apr. 4, 1843
age 60yrs.
Burial:
Ebenezer Cemetery
Hagerstown
Washington County
Maryland, USA
Edit Virtual Cemetery info
Created by: Mike Hahn
Record added: Nov 17, 2012
Malinda [Matilda?] Williams
Birth: unknown
Death: May 11, 1859
Daughter of Prince & Margaret Williams
21yrs.11mos.24dys.
Burial:
Ebenezer Cemetery
Hagerstown
Washington County
Maryland, USA
Margaret [Williams] Hanson
Birth: 1796
Death: Aug. 5, 1868
Wife of William Henson, age 72yrs.
Burial:
Ebenezer Cemetery
Hagerstown
Washington County
Maryland, USA

Figure 7.9. Prince, Malinda, and Margaret Williams buried in Ebenezer Cemetery, Hagerstown, MD. Source: findagrave.com

However, there was no slave Malinda listed in Joseph Ingram's Will, nor in Prince Williams' Will. Malinda was born in 1837, which was after Joseph Ingram had died. She passed away in 1859. Maybe that was why Malinda is not listed with Sam, Henry, Hez, Otho, a Margaret Elizabeth when Prince's estate was distributed in 1868. Or, perhaps Malinda was incorrectly listed in Joseph's Will as "Matilda." An official printed cemetery record found at the Washington County Historical Society clearly indicated Malinda was Prince and Margaret's daughter.

The Ebenezer Cemetery first began interring people in about 1840. Therefore, Prince Williams was among the first to be buried there in 1843. In fact, of the sixty-five memorials found online for that cemetery, Prince holds the record as the oldest burial date, aside from a woman named Ruth Cook.

I theorized that if Prince and Margaret were buried at Ebenezer, it was likely they were parishioners there and knew the other Ebenezer members well, including the ex-runaway, ex-ironworker, and esteemed founder of Ebenezer AME Church, none other than the Reverend Thomas Henry who wrote *From Slavery to Salvation, The Autobiography of Rev. Thomas W. Henry of the AME Church.* An edited copy of his book, with an historical essay by Jean Libby, was gifted to me by the public historian and activist Jean Libby herself after I spent an engaging afternoon with her at her Northern California home in 2017.

The relationship between Reverend Henry and my family is further explored in Chapter 14: *Generations of Ironworkers.*

* Unmasking the Prince *

Who exactly was Prince Williams who first appeared to me in the 1834 Maryland Land Records? Where did he come from and was he born a free man or manumitted? Looking for "Prince Williams" in the *African American Manumissions of Washington County* book, I did not immediately see his name in the index. I cannot adequately convey my disappointment.

I decided to read the *Manumissions* book anyway from cover to cover to learn about each of the many hundreds of slaves who were freed between 1806 and 1860. By devouring every descriptive manumission statement, I found several names that would have otherwise gone unnoticed from just looking in the Index. This exercise also served to help me become knowledgeable about the people living in the county.

Lo and behold, on the third page of Book A, for the manumission entitled A9a, there was a description of a "Negro Prince," as shown in Figure 7.10.

Was that text describing my third great-grandfather? The Certificate of Freedom was given to free Negro Prince in 1812, testified by County Clerk Otho Holland Williams (yes, this is the same "ClerkOtho" mentioned in Chapter 5).

That critically important Freedom Certification was legally required to be presented to any white person who requested proof the free black person was not a runaway slave. That identification document indicated that Prince was 28-years-old in 1812, thus making his birthdate sometime around 1784 (his Ebenezer Cemetery record indicated he was born in 1783, so the dates are very close). Further, that said Prince was born in Kent County and was sold by his former [unnamed] master, for an [unnamed] term of years to McPherson and Brien at the Antietam Iron Works (located in Washington County, Maryland).

Described as being "of a Black complexion"—what I interpreted as ebony—would lead one to believe that Prince's parents were probably both darker-skinned blacks, not mulattos, and not whites. While Prince's physical description may have thoroughly discredited my theory that a white man fathered my Otho, who was described as a mulatto in the 1870 Census, I was more than thrilled to learn that one of my Williams relatives was actually a free black man!

A9a State of Maryland, Washington County, Towit:
I hereby certify that negro Prince the bearer hereof, is a free Man, that he has satisfied me by sufficient evidence , he was born in Kent County State of Maryland, that he was sold by his former Master for a term of years to McPherson and Brien at Antietam Works in Washington County and State of Maryland, with whom he finished his servitude.

The said Negro Prince is about twenty eight years of age, of a Black complexion, about five feet six Inches high, has the first joint of his left thumb off; no other notable mark perceivable. Test O.H. Williams Clk
certificate given 8' Jany. 1812

Figure 7.10. Negro Prince's Certificate of Freedom issued by Otho Holland Williams, 1812.

Perhaps even more unbelievable was the realization that my third great-grandfather was an ironworker, just like me. You see, I use a welder with recycled steel in many of my mixed-media outdoor art sculptures. Was Prince sold to the Antietam Iron Works by his former owner to learn a useful trade, or for some other reason? What tasks did he perform at the Iron Works?

Maybe Prince was apprenticed, and not actually sold on an auction block, sometime before he began working at the Antietam Iron Works. The Law of 1793 allowed the Orphan's Court, or a Justice of the Peace, to order involuntary indentures of children falling within the following categories: orphans whose inheritance was insufficient to maintain them, illegitimate children, and children whose parents were too poor to support them.

An 1808 supplement to the law of 1793 singled out free African American children and provided for the indenturing of "the child or children of lazy, indolent, and worthless free Negroes," who could not financially support their children. Since most free blacks were denied the economic opportunities available to white Marylanders, they were constantly at risk of having their children taken and indentured without their approval.[82]

An indenture could be seven years for whites, or for many blacks until they were 28 or 31 years of age.[83] Was Prince a slave born in Kent County whose unnamed owner sold him to the Iron Works? Or was Prince merely a child of free blacks who was deemed by the Orphan Court to be inadequately caring for him? Is that why he was freed at the age of 28 in 1812? I need more information to definitively determine who Prince's former master was, how Prince came to be at the Antietam Iron Works, and what he learned there.

Until more pearls of wisdom could be found, I decided to settle down with a See's Candies chocolate peanut crunch bar and a small glass of sake on the comfortable, bright-red couch in the energy center of my house and reflect on all I had learned.

I now knew Prince Williams was born in 1783 in Kent County, died in 1843 in Washington County, and was buried in the Ebenezer AME Church Cemetery in Hagerstown. Prince was working at the Antietam Iron Works for a period of time, and was freed when he was 28-years-of-age in 1812. He was described as being 5' 5" tall, of a black complexion, with part of his thumb cut off. I felt like I was getting to know him.

Prince Williams was associated with the white Ingram family who may have let him cohabit as man and wife with their slave Margaret. They may have lived in a slave cabin on the Ingram's Meadows Green property, in the rural outskirts of the town of Boonsboro, close to Beaver Creek.

Prince and Margaret had five still-living children together: Samuel, Henry, Hezekiah, Otho (my second great-grandfather), and Margaret Elizabeth Williams, as specified in the 1868 distribution of Prince's Will. However, they may also have been the parents of Mary F., Patsy, Malinda/Matilda Williams. I was more than gratified to finally, at last, be able to plug in a third generation onto our family tree (Figure 7.11).

After five months of exhausting research, the most important initial two goals for this book had been achieved. I found Otho's parents and his slave owner. My family could reasonably infer that my fifth goal of having a metalworking ancestor, like many of his Williams descendants, was true.

I guess we do have royalty of a sort in our family after all: my third great-grandfather, "Prince" Williams.

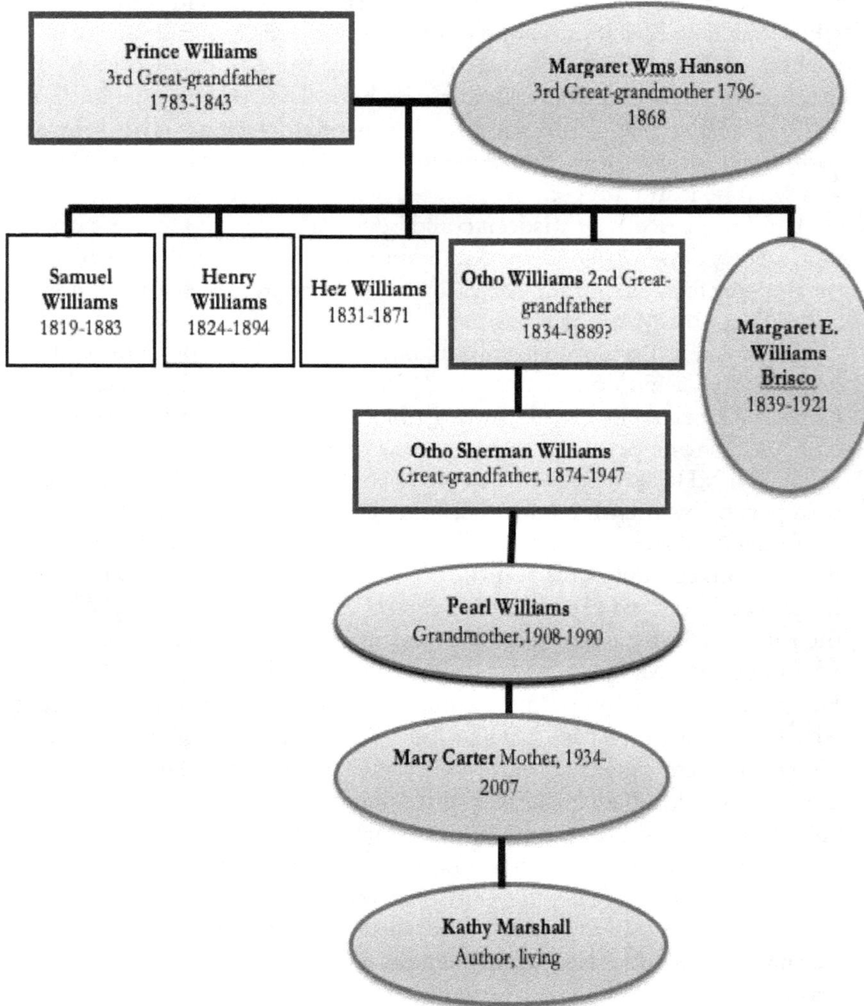

Figure 7.11. Six generations of Kathy Marshall's family.

Chapter 8 - Does More Than One Prince Exist?

Kanika African Sculptures, "The Griot" welded steel, Ceramic Tile, Glass, Synthetic Hair. 60"x20"

* Who's Your Daddy? *

My batteries were fully charged again knowing that my third great-grandfather was a free black man named Prince Williams. My third great-grandmother was Margaret Williams, an enslaved woman in the Ingram household, who married William Hanson after Prince died in 1843. She lived for about twenty-five years on the Funkstown property that Prince had purchased for their family in 1842.

Should I be greedy and attempt to go back even further in the Williams ancestral line? Let me tell you this genealogy work is addicting. There are always more clues to follow and puzzles to solve.

Many convoluted paths were traveled in an attempt to find Prince's parents and his slave owner. This chapter chronicles my attempts to find more about Prince Williams: why did Prince choose the surname "Williams"? Who were his parents and his slave owner? Why and how did he get from Kent County to Washington County? I developed many theories for each of those questions.

I will briefly discuss the positive or negative outcome of each question, in hopes that you, the reader, may incorporate these possible avenues into your family research.

In 1805, the Maryland General Assembly passed a law that would identify free African Americans via a Certificate of Freedom. It would also control the availability of these freedom papers because, as the law-makers explained: "great mischiefs have arisen from slaves coming into possession of certificates of free Negroes, by running away and passing as free under the faith of such certificates."[84]

The law required African Americans who were born free to record proof of their liberty in the county court. The court would then issue them a Certificate of Freedom.

If the black person had already been manumitted, the court clerk or register of Wills would look up the manumitting document before issuing the Certificate of Freedom.

A typical certificate not only indicated how the individual became free but also listed physical characteristics that could be used to establish his or her identity. These attributes included age, height, complexion, hair color and texture, as well as any distinguishing scars and/or marks.

Prince's Certificate of Freedom (Figure 7.10) certainly did shed a light on what he looked like (e.g., 5'6" tall, of a Black color, and with part of his thumb cut off) and what he may have done for a living (e.g., sold to the Antietam Iron Works for a period of years).

* What's in a Name? *

A vexing question from the beginning of this project had been the derivation of the Williams surname. My ancestor was called "Negro Prince" on his 1812 Freedom Paper, but he was going by the name Prince Williams on an 1834 land record. He gave the surname Williams to his children with his wife Margaret (and his Williams name was passed down through generations of my maternal family). When did Prince adopt the Williams surname and why?

As briefly mentioned in Chapter 3, only a tiny percentage of freed slaves in western Maryland took the surname of their slave owner. Knowing where the last name "Williams" came from could help determine Prince's parents, to uncover another generation of ancestors.

Was Prince's choice of surname derived from the white Otho Holland Williams family about whom I had incessantly theorized had been his owner in Chapter 5? Perhaps Prince was paying homage to the Washington County Clerk Otho Holland Williams (ClerkOtho in Chapter 5), who signed his, and nearly every other manumission document from 1800 to 1845.[85] Or maybe the surname came from Joseph Williams who signed many of the probate records in Kent County, where Prince was born, in the earliest years of the nineteenth century.

Jean Libby, Public Historian and expert on African ironmaking in Maryland, brilliantly hypothesized that "The possible reason the Williams surname was selected is, I believe, because that is the name that appears on everyone's freedom papers that they are required to carry and submit to any white person who demands them. I believe he [Prince] adopted it as a symbol of the establishment so that he can be inconspicuous as he goes about the business of free life—buying property, getting married, etc."

I chose to adopt Jean Libby's erudite theoretical assessment. It could also explain why Prince named one of his children "Otho Williams" which carried the mystique of white power and American heroism attributed to the Revolutionary War Brigadier General Otho Holland Williams (RevWarOtho in Chapter 5).

It is important to remember that Prince was not born a Williams, but adopted that surname sometime between 1812 and 1834. We may never know the true reason why "Williams" was chosen to represent Prince's familial legacy, but the difficult impact of his choice of surname on Y-DNA testing is thoroughly discussed in **Part IV: DNA Doesn't Lie, Does It?**

* Theories: Can a Prince Be Owned? *

To find anything about Prince's parents and potential siblings, I needed to know precisely where he lived as a child and who his owner was. His Certificate of Freedom merely stated that "he was born in Kent County, State of Maryland, that he was sold by his former master for a term of years to McPherson and Brien at Antietam Works." It gave no clue as to who the former master was or how old Prince was when he was sold to the Antietam Iron Works. We only knew he was 28-years-old in 1812. We had no idea whether Prince was sold at the age of 10 or 20 before he began working at the Antietam Iron Works. We also have no idea who sold him or why.

With Sherlock Holmes' signature deerstalker hat firmly on my head, several possible hypotheses about finding Prince's parents and slave owner materialized. A myriad of ideas is provided in this chapter to share how various possibilities can be proven or discredited. Please do not become too attached to the details of the earliest theories. The truth is summarized at this chapter's end.

Theory #1: Slave Owner with the Surname Williams or Ingram in Kent County

Since Prince and his previous owner lived in Kent County, my initial theory was that the owner's surname was either Williams or Ingram. Searching all land records in Kent County with the surname Williams and Ingram prior to 1812 (Figure 8.1), did not produce any bills of sale or manumission records involving a slave named Prince. There was a probate record for Edward Ingram of Kent County, dated December 1, 1806, in which three slaves were included in his estate inventory: a 24-year-old slave woman named Margaret (possibly born in 1782), a 4-year-old slave girl named Hannah, and an 18-month old girl named Ann.

Liber J.F.B. No. 1, Folio 35, Ingram, Margaret A.
Liber J.F.B. No. 142, Folio 35, Ingram, Sarah
Liber _, No. 1, Folio 70, Ingram, Robert
Liber _, No. 6, Folio 13, Ingram, Elisabeth
Liber _, No. 8, Folio 315, Ingram, Edward
Liber B.C., No. 6, Folio 266, Ingram, James

Figure 8.1. Kent County, Ingrams Will Index.

Was Edward's slave, Margaret, the mother of my third great-grandmother, also named Margaret who was born in 1796? That theory yielded few evidentiary results that Prince's owner from Kent County was surnamed Williams or Ingram. However, I kept the slave, Margaret in my mind's eye.

Theory #2: Look for a Prince Williams Born in 1763 or Earlier

Since my Prince was born in 1783, I am looking for his father, possibly with the unusual first name of Prince, and surname Williams, who might have been born in the previous twenty-year generation, i.e., earlier than 1763.

Lo and behold, typing "Prince Williams" born in about 1763 into an Ancestry.com search resulted in several different men with that name. See Figure 8.2 for how I illustrated my conjecture each of them might be my third great-grandfather.

While I could find no other census, marriage or death records for Prince, I did find a present-day Prince Williams living in Baltimore. I contacted him through his LinkedIn social media account. He was originally from Fort Worth, Texas, and most of his Williams family live in Illinois, therefore, he was not a contender for my Maryland Williams family tree.

The second candidate was a Prince Williams born in 1764 in Cecil County, listed in the 1830 through the 1850 Census, indicating he was a free man. Is it likely the free 19-year-old Cecil County candidate could have impregnated a black female slave? Could a child of a free father and slave mother have been sold to an indenture at McPherson and Brien's Antietam Iron Works sometime before 1812 when my Prince was freed?

Additional circumstantial evidence for this theory asserted that Cecil County is located just north of Kent County where my Prince Williams was born, and just south of the Pennsylvania border. Was it possible this Cecil County Prince could have lived in, or visited, Kent County in 1783 and fathered a child with a slave there?

An extensive descendancy analysis for the Cecil County Prince was attempted, with the goal of finding family members who might be alive today, with whom I might be able to compare DNA results. To my delight, I was able to contact one descendant for the Cecil County Prince Williams. Alas, his DNA did not match mine, nor any of our ten other DNA-tested Williams family members.

Another Prince Williams was living in New York by 1850, but he was deemed not pertinent to this Maryland research.

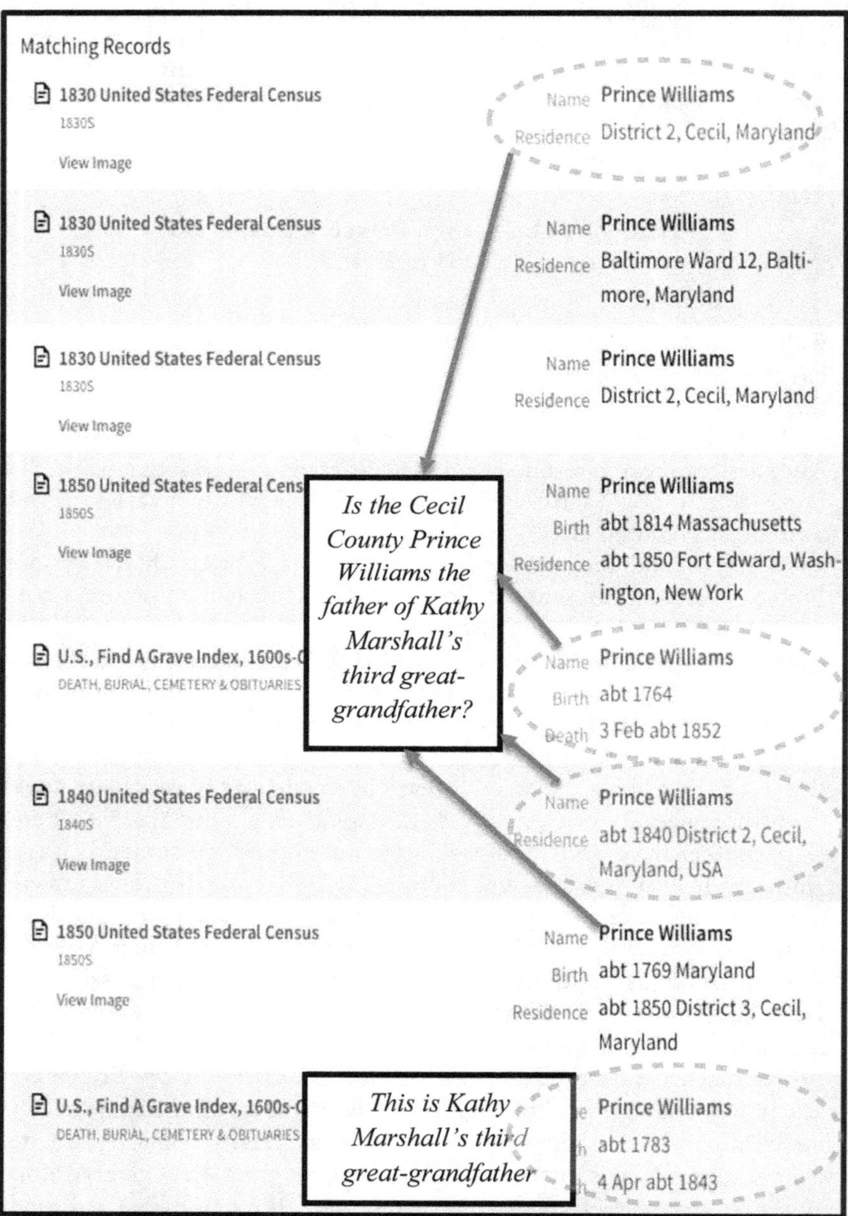

Figure 8.2. Maryland search results for Prince Williams. Source: Ancestry.com.

Theory #3: Look for Prince in Tax Records.

Many genealogists recommend looking at tax records since slaves were considered a commodity to be taxed. Tax records might tell how many slaves were owned and might contain the names of the slaves.

I looked at 1783 through the 1830 tax records for the various owners of the Antietam Iron Works to get a better idea of the slave workforce of former owners Joseph Chapline, Samuel Beall, Jr., David Ross, Richard Henderson, John Brien, John McPherson, and John Brien McPherson.[86] None of those records clearly indicated that Prince was one of their slaves/employees (but it is possible that he was).

Only five Maryland counties recorded their slave assessments separately in a series called "Assessment Record, Slaves": Frederick, Kent, Montgomery, Talbot, and St. Mary's.[87] A typical record lists the election district, the year the assessment was taken, the slave owner's name, the first name of the slave, and the slave's age, sex, and value. The assessments were arranged by election district and then by the name of the slave owner. Unfortunately, those records were only for 1860 or later; Prince Williams died seventeen years before the 1860 slave assessment, so this information was not pertinent to this project.

Theory #4: Look for Negro Prince in the Probate Records of White Owners

"Prince" was an unusual first name for slaves in Maryland. Therefore, I theorized the name Prince could have been passed down from generation to generation I my family. Perhaps the original slave brought from Africa (or the Caribbean) to North America was an African Prince or was renamed Prince by his new slave master. It is, admittedly, a huge stretch in logic that will be difficult to prove, but I want to search the internet to determine how many slaves were named Prince in various Maryland counties.

Permutations of "Negro Prince" and "Kent County" along with other combinations of keywords invariably returned search results containing annoying listings which included "Prince George's County" or "Prince William County." Plenty of horses named Prince popped up, but rarely a Negro named Prince. However, when a positive "hit" occurred from the Google search, I felt it was more likely to be worthy of further consideration. I was overjoyed to receive interesting results; results which might support this theory.

Since there was a dearth of documentation for most of our black ancestors, we must allocate a good portion of our research to investigating their white captors and their close white associates and friends. I did find a few potentially useful results from slave owner probate records from the mid-1700s in various counties. The following chronological results of slaves named Prince in Maryland probate records "could" be my Prince's father or grandfather.

A. In 1735, Kent County, William Comegys bequeathed a slave named Prince to his son William Comegys.[88] This struck me as being possibly pertinent for three reasons:
1) It was issued in Kent County where Prince was born;
2) Perhaps Prince's surname comes from his master's first name "William";
3) William Comegys' son, William II, had a son-in-law named George Briscoe. My Prince's son-in-law was a black man named Abraham Briscoe. So, were the white Comegys and Briscoes friends who had slaves, and who moved from Kent to Washington County, in the latter decade of the 1700s? Was the Prince mentioned in the 1735 Comegys' Will an adult male who was born before 1715? If so, could he have been the father or grandfather of my third Prince who was born around 1783?

B. In 1737, Kent County, Frederick Hanson left a slave named Prince to his wife, Mary.[89]

C. In 1741, St. Mary's County, Richard Hopewell bequeathed to son Joseph two Negro men, named Prince and Caesar.[90] The term "men" would indicate they were likely older than 20-years-of-age and, therefore, born prior to 1720. As discussed in Chapter 10, there is an interesting nexus between the Hopewell's slave, Letty Ann, who married Isaac Warfield in 1854. Letty Ann and her daughter, Letitia Warfield Barnum Diggs, were well-acquainted with my Otho's sister, Mary F. Williams. Did this suggest the Hopewell slaves migrated from St. Mary's to Washington County?

D. In 1745, Cecil County, John Pennington left Negro Prince to his son Benjamin for life. To his wife he left two Negroes, Cesar & Diner.[91] Was this the same "Caesar" from the 1741 Hopewell Will?

E. In 1746, Kent County, Jacob Glen, left Negro boys Joe, Hark, and Prince to his sons Samuel, Johannes, and Nathaniel.[92] Could Glen's Prince be my Prince's father or grandfather? Is that why my Prince named his oldest son Samuel?

F. There was also a 1747 Will from Mary Hanson leaving slave Prince to her daughter Ann.[93] Is this the same Prince that her father, Frederick, left her in 1737? This is interesting because "Hanson" is the same surname of William Hanson who married my Prince's widow, Margaret Williams.

Were the black and white Hansons, Comegys, and Briscoes all friends in Kent County who moved westward to Washington County, in the late 1700s? Could the Prince mentioned in the 1747 Will of Mary Hanson actually be the father or grandfather of my Prince who was born in 1783? Could the Comegys and/or Hanson Prince be the same one mentioned in several references about Africans and slaves working at the Principio and Valley Forge Iron Works in the 1730s through the Revolutionary War? (More information in Chapter 14.)

G. In 1755, Kent County, Vincent Hatcheson[94] bequeathed to wife, Rachel, a Negro "man" Caesar and Negro "woman" Pina (Diner?). Vincent also willed to daughter Rachell a gold ring with a stone, a cow and calf, six sheep, and Negro "boy" Prince [perhaps born between 1735 and 1750]. Did Vincent Hatcheson purchase, or somehow inherit slaves from John Pennington's estate (Theory D)? Could the "boy" Prince in Vincent's 1755 Will be the son of the "man" Prince from Hopewell's 1741 Will (Theory C)?

H. The 1801, Kent County, probate inventory of Elizabeth Hanson described a seven-year-old slave named Prince in her estate.[95] Could this boy have been the eldest [heretofore unknown] son of my Prince? Could he have come from a long line of Hanson human property, dating back to Frederick Hanson's Will in 1735?

I always wondered why my Prince had not named his eldest son Prince instead of Samuel. Could my Prince, born in 1783, have fathered a child in 1794 when he was 11-years-old when Elizabeth Hanson's young boy-slave Prince might have been born? It is unlikely, but entirely possible that an 11-year-old could father a child.

Two other interesting coincidences are that: 1) John Page was the executor of Frederick's estate and was a witness to Mary Hanson's Will signing, and 2) payment was made to John Carvill from William Hanson's 1709 estate. The Page and Carvill names became pertinent to this research in Theory #5.

I. In 1803, Kent County, John Frisby had forty-three slaves in his estate inventory, including a 38-year-old slave named Prince.[96] Could this 38-year-old have been the father of my Prince? Frisby's holdings also included a 34-year-old slave named Sam, a 35-year-old slave named Zeke (could that be short for Hezekiah?), and a newborn named Henry, which were the names of three of my Prince's sons.

Frisby also had a 50-year-old slave named Peg. Could she have been the mother of my third great-grandmother Margaret (also known as Pegg)? I know this may sound far-fetched, but until absolute proof can be found, every possibility must be considered.

Then I found an 1803 deed from Vincent Hatcheson, delivering land to William Briscoe, from the deceased William Hanson.[97] Dr. Henry Briscoe was on The Ark sailing from England to the first Maryland settlement in 1634. The essence of this thought is there were long-lasting relationships between black and white Briscoes, Hansons, Hatchesons, Ingrams, Hopewells, Pages, and Williams. They all had a slave named Prince.

Why were people with the surname Briscoe dancing all around the above-named Comegys, Frisbys, Glens, Hansons, Hatchesons, Hopewells, Ingrams, and Penningtons? A free black man named William Hanson married Prince's widow, Margaret Williams. Prince's daughter, Margaret Elizabeth, married Abraham Briscoe after the Ingrams freed her in 1860. Briscoes purchased some of Margaret Williams' property after she died in 1868.

What were the connections between these white men who owned slaves named Prince? Did the families lend, trade, or give their slaves to each other, without officially selling them? Were there four generations of slaves named Prince between 1715 and 1803? Every answer created more questions. It was time to explore a new theory while keeping these scintillating questions in the back of my mind.

Theory #5: Was There A Son Named Prince Williams

It was my unproven theory that the first name "Prince" was passed down from generation to generation in my mother's Williams family. So why does it seem Prince and Margaret did not name one of their sons Prince? Maybe they did, as shown in the very interesting document in Figure 8.3. It indicates that a father named Prince Williams, and his wife Margaret A. Williams, had a son named Prince Williams who was born in 1825 who married Sarah Williams and had a child named Jane. Prince, Sarah, and Jane were living in Cecil County in 1863.

We knew that my Prince Williams' 1843 Will clearly stated he purchased the freedom of Sarah and her daughter Jane and that she was the wife of Prince's [unnamed] son. Was that unnamed son actually named Prince Williams who was born in 1825, lived in Cecil County in 1863, but died in 1868? If so, that would explain why that son Prince was not listed in the 1868 disbursement of father Prince's estate along with Samuel, Henry, Hezekiah, Otho, and Margaret Elizabeth Williams.

So maybe the Cecil County Prince Williams family *is* somehow related to my Williams after all. I needed to closely examine the other records attributed to this one (for example, the 1840 Census), and other sources in Washington D.C. through 1891.

Name	Prince Williams
Spouse	Sarah Williams
Father	Prince William
Mother	Margaret A. Williams
Children	Jane
Birth	1825 - USA
Death	1868 - Maryland, USA
Residence	1 July 1863 - Cecil, United States [1830 - Cecil, USA] [1840 - District of Columbia, USA] [1857 - United States] [1866 - USA] [1870 - USA] [1877 - USA] [1878 - USA] [1880 - USA] [1886 - USA] [1891 - USA]

Figure 8.3. Prince and Margaret's son, Prince Williams? Source: Ancestry.com

Theory #6: Review Kent County Negroes, Slave/Free Files

In addition to the normal probate records like wills, inventories, sales, and debts, Kent County also has separate chattel record files for "Negroes, slave and free" for 1775, and also for 1790 through 1898. I used familysearch.org to find these useful records (Figure 8.4). [98]

A typical chattel record lists the names of the buyer and seller, their places of residence, the items sold, the amount sold for, and the date of the sale. When a slave was sold, the record usually gave the first and last name of the slave. That resource theoretically included all transactions concerning black people, such as bills of sale, manumissions, and distributions of probate records. Unfortunately, the records were indexed by the names of the buyer and seller, not by the name of the slave sold. That meant every single record must be reviewed to potentially find the desired slave name.

I attacked that "Negroes, slaves and free" index several times in the fifth and sixth months of work on this project, but it was so labor-intensive that I rarely got far before my mind strayed onto different topics. Determined, I vowed to look at every record, no matter how long it took.

There appeared to be no specific format for writing inventory records in Washington and Kent Counties. Slaves were more often listed near cattle, as opposed to tools, forks or bed pillows; however, that was not always the case. The latter-day researcher must potentially read through every single handwritten line in probate records and bills of sale to find the desired slave names.

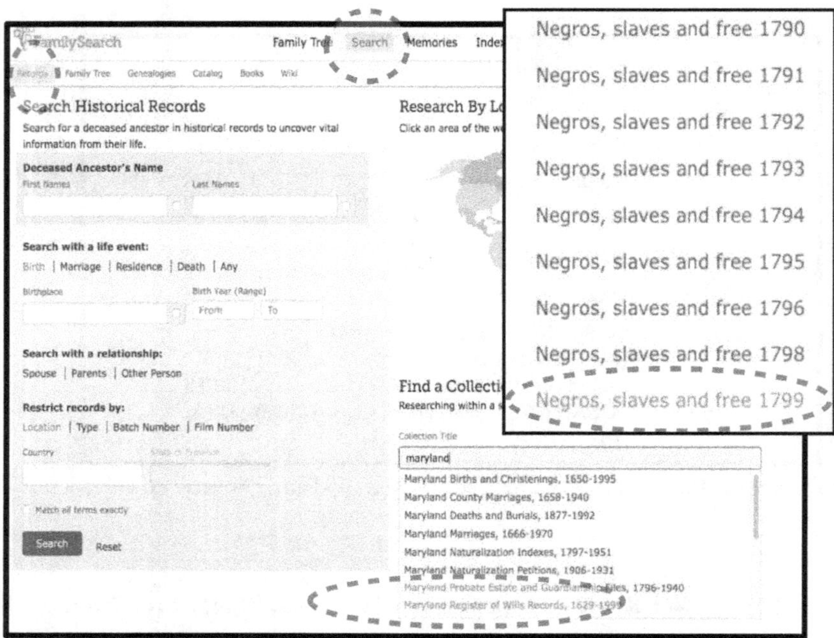

Figure 8.4. Kent County "Negroes, Slaves and Free" index. Source: www.familysearch.org.

I forced myself to tackle each of those files until I had read every line in every "Negroes, slaves and free" document to find my Prince. After many weeks, I saw a shocking entry in image 27 in the 1799 folder (Figure 8.5).

> Kent County to wit:
> John Carvill Bound in #10 to the State of Maryland to be levied of your body goods and chattels lands and tenements for the use of the said State on condition that your Negro Isaac will personally appear at the next County Court to be holds on in and for the said County then and there to testify in behalf of the said State against **Negro Prince the slave of Benjamin Hatcheson** of this County and not to depart these without leave of the court taken and acknowledged this 9th Day of August 1799. Before Joseph Williams.

Figure 8.5. Maryland Register of Wills Records, 1629-1999 Kent "Negroes, Slaves and Free," 1799, Image 27.

There was another disturbing entry in image 30 (Figure 8.6).

> Kent County to wit:
> **Benjamin Hatcheson** bound in #10 to the State of Maryland to be levied of your body goods and chattels lands and tenements for the use of the said State on condition that his Negro **man** named **Prince** shall appear at the next county court to be hold on in and for said county to answer for an assault and battery made on Negro Isaac the slave of John Carvill of Chestertown (?) County of and in the meantime to keep the peace and be of good behavior, but more especially toward Negro Isaac. Taken and acknowledged this 21st Day of July 1799. [Heard] Before Joseph Williams.

Figure 8.6. Maryland Register of Wills Records, 1629-1999 Kent "Negroes, Slaves and Free." 1799, image 30.

It seemed that when my third great-grandfather, then-called Negro Prince, was a rambunctious youth, he assaulted another slave named Isaac. That was not an auspicious revelation to cheer, but it explained so much. You see, John Carvill, mentioned a few pages ago in Theory 4.H., was Slave Isaac's owner; he was mandated to let Slave Isaac testify against Prince **in a court other than Kent County**. The pieces of the puzzle were beginning to fit as to why my Prince, born in Kent County, ended up in Washington County. With a sick feeling, I continued to look through the documents in the 1799 file to see if there was more damaging evidence that my then 16-year-old ancestor was not always the upstanding individual I had imagined him to be. But then again, we do not know the circumstances of the assault.

After reading Max Grivno's stellar *Gleanings of Freedom* book, I could fathom how such an altercation might have occurred. Grivno offered that "during the turn of the 19th century, a growing chorus of agricultural reformers, evangelicals, and industrialists argued that all workers—black and white, free and enslaved—must be broken of their intemperate habits."

The linkages among drinking, gambling, petty theft, and a poor work ethic were apparent to both employers and slaveholders. They were convinced those habits led to rebelliousness and fighting amongst their workers. Throngs of African Americans flocked to towns on holidays and weekends to escape the isolation of rural life. In 1798, the grand jury commissioned several constables to disperse the "disorderly meetings of Negroes and other ill-disposed persons, who frequently collected in numbers on Sundays and Holy Days in Frederick and other towns."

I suspected that black folk—who had been offered by their masters a severely skewed strain of the Christian religion (i.e., if you don't run away from your masters, you might get into Heaven) to mollify their subjugated slave state--regarded joyously celebrating their Lord in song and merriment on Sundays as a release from the difficulties of their unequal station in life. I bet blacks would not have considered their adulation to be "noise" as some white onlookers maintained.

But with the addition of alcohol, perhaps after the worship, one could understand that altercations such as that between Negro Prince and Negro Isaac could have easily occurred. There were many other possible reasons for their violent disagreement, of course, including fighting over a woman, lack of payment for a gambling debt, or normal man-boy play fighting that escalated into an actual brawl, but no further specific information was found about this particular assault.

* Solved! *

While I was dismayed about the stain on my ancestor's character, I was overjoyed to have finally solved the question of Prince's slave owner. As of 1799, Benjamin Hatcheson from Kent County was my Prince's slave owner! That hard-won revelation opened up a whole slew of additional questions.

Did Benjamin Hatcheson have other slaves who could be related to Prince? Did Prince grow up in the Hatcheson household or was he originally owned by any of the slave owners described in Theory 4, e.g., Hansons, Pages, Comegys, Hopewells, or Penningtons, or Frisbys? Was Prince *genetically* tied to the Hatchesons who originally came from Ireland? Is that why I have some DNA from Ireland?

Who were the Hatchesons? To learn whether their other slaves might be related to my Prince, I did a quick Google search. I found that Benjamin Hatcheson was born in 1759 in Saint Paul's Parish, Kent, Maryland The 1800 Census, the only one found for Benjamin Hatcheson, indicated he had ten slaves and thirteen other free white persons living in his household in Kent, Maryland.

There was another astonishing Google result: "Kent County—Sheriffs—Maryland State Archives." Yes, voters appointed Benjamin Hatcheson to two multi-year terms to serve as the Kent County Sheriff, between 1794-95 and 1797-1800.[99] The role of the county sheriff in the early 1800s was significant: "an office of great dignity which included that of tax collector and financial agent of the county" (Williams, 1906).[100]

Imagine how embarrassing it would be for the Sheriff of Kent County to have his slave (Prince) beating up the slave (Isaac) of another member of the community? Because he was the Sheriff, I imagined Benjamin Hatcheson could not adjudicate an allegation of assault that involved his own slave. Mr. Carvill, the owner of the assaulted slave, was directed to allow Isaac to testify against Prince in another county, presumably for a hearing of the facts and the administration of punishment. I was never able to find out any more about the testimony, or where or when the hearing was held.

Thankfully, there were several Kent County land records which included Benjamin Hatcheson but generally in his Sheriff capacity. Many of the transactions suggested that the Sheriff was confiscating real and personal property from debtors to pay off their debts. Interestingly, if I read the texts correctly, some of those absconded properties seemed to end up in the family coffers of various Hatchesons.

Benjamin Hatcheson himself was often testifying in court defending his own indebtedness, as shown in the partial 1796 resolution from the Maryland General Assembly in Figure 8.7.[101]

RESOLVED, That if Benjamin Hatcheson, of Kent county, shall enter into bond, with two or more sufficient securities, to be approved of by the treasurer of the eastern shore, for the sum of five hundred and twenty-eight pounds two shillings and eight-pence current money, with interest from the first day of September, seventeen hundred and ninety-two, it being the balance due from him to the state of Maryland for arrearages of taxes for Kent county, on or before the first day of March next, that the treasurer of the eastern shore, or the agent for the time being, be authorised to take the said bond, payable to the state of Maryland, giving three years for the payment of the said balan

Figure 8.7. Sheriff Benjamin Hatcheson defends his own indebtedness to Maryland General Assembly.

Did Sheriff Hatcheson find it expedient to sell the troublemaker Prince to the highest bidder, and was that bidder McPherson and Brien, co-owners of the Antietam Iron Works? Unfortunately, I could find no specific bill of sale or legal proceeding which documented the sale or transfer of Negro Prince.

A reference in an 1806 Kent County land record alluded to the "late" Sheriff Hatcheson,[102] which explained why there was no 1810 census record for him. I didn't know exactly when, where, or how he died. I could find no death certificate or probate records for Benjamin Hatcheson, nor how or when my Prince happened to become property of the Antietam Iron Works owners.

There were some non-cited, Ancestry Family Trees that listed Benjamin and his wife, Martha, and their four Hatcheson children: John Richard (b. 1786), Martha Ricaud (b. 1798), Avrilla Osborn (b. 1799), and Benjamin Osborn (b. 1801). Benjamin's parents were Martha Ricaud and John Hatcheson, both born in 1735 in Kent and married there in 1758. I needed more information than that to learn whether any of the Hatchesons had slaves who might have been related to my Prince.

Benjamin's brother was Richard Hatcheson. Richard had twenty slaves and seven free white persons in his household, according to the 1800 Census. In addition to being a farmer, Richard was also a member of the House of Delegates in 1802, 1803, and 1804.

Appendix H, Kent County, House of Representatives Delegates, clearly indicated that the Hansons, Comegys, Briscoes, Hatchesons, and Frisbys all had close ties with one another as delegates for the state of Maryland. It was debatable whether sufficient evidence proved those friendships led to the buying, selling, trading, or loaning my enslaved ancestors.

While at the 2018 RootsTech Genealogy Convention in Salt Lake City, I made a couple of trips to the most well-known genealogy library in the country: The Salt Lake Family History Library. While trying to find information about Otho Williams' wife Alice Logan Williams, I found an unexpected "Maryland Probate and Estate Guardianship Files, 1796 to 1940, Kent County" document dated 1795. Benjamin sold forty-one slaves to brother Richard Hatcheson, as shown in Figure 8.8. Were any of those slaves related to my Prince Williams or were they slaves confiscated from various debtors by Sheriff Hatcheson, then sold to his brother Richard to gain money to pay off his own debts?

I needed to find out more about the Hatcheson family. Always in the back of my mind was the question "Who are my white people?" If the Hatchesons were genetically tied to my family, I wanted to learn as much as possible about their migration patterns. I wanted to conduct descendancy research to find present-day Hatchesons whose DNA might be compared with my family's DNA.

Maybe Richard and Benjamin's father, Vincent Hatcheson's Will would lead me to more answers. Vincent was not only mentioned in Section G of Theory #4, but he was also chronicled in the *Early Colonial Settlers of Southern Maryland and Virginia's Northern Neck Counties.*[103] Variously spelled Hatcheson, Hutcheson, Hutchinson, Atchinson or Acheson, Vincent Hatcheson was born before 1701 and died in 1756. His estate left adult slaves **Cesar** and **Pina** to his wife Rachael, and a boy slave named **Prince** to his daughter Rachael.[104] I did a few handsprings, feeling like the bouncy Tigger, Winnie The Pooh's excitable buddy. Do you understand what this might mean?

Name	Age	Value	Name	Age	Value	Name	Age	Value	Name	Age	Value
Charles	43	$140	Ebenezer	5	$50	Tom	17	$250	Mint	26	$100
Chester	40	$150	Jerry	3	$20	James Cutter	65	$0	Juliana	15	$130
David	36	$200	Richardo	9	$80	Joe	36	$120	Rachel	14	$130
Isaac	25	$250	Jonas	2	$10	Jacob	22	$250	Peggy	15	$130
Michael	32	$220	Clinton	0.8	$1	David	22	$250	Hoefs (?)	11	$80
Stephen	22	$250	Phillis	70	$0	Stephen	20	$250	Maria	9	$60
Harry	20	$250	Beck	45	$60	Bill	8	$80	Caroline	6	$40
James	25	$250	Phillis	45	$30	Gustaves	7	$70	Beck	6	$40
Abe	18	$250	Phillis	32	$80	Owen	4	$30	Louise	3	$15
David	18	$250	Doll	28	$120	Perry	7	$70	Harriott	6	$40
Maria	4	$20								TOTAL:	$4,816

Figure 8.8. Benjamin Hatcheson sells 41 slaves to his brother, Richard Hatcheson, in 1795.

One could muse endlessly that Vincent Hatcheson's 1755 Will did or did not provide enough proof that his adult slaves, Caesar and Pina (probably born before 1730), were the grandparents of my Prince Williams (1783-1843), and that Vincent's boy slave named Prince (born before Vincent's death in 1755), could have been the father of my Prince Williams.

I had documentation that my third great-grandfather, Prince, was owned by Benjamin Hatcheson, as of 1799. A 1755 probate record indicates that Benjamin Hatcheson's father, Vincent, willed a boy slave named Prince to his daughter. It was not much of a stretch to imagine those two males named Prince in the Hatcheson household could have been father and son, one born before 1755 and my Prince in 1783.

Therefore, I planned to plug another generation into my family tree, with a fourth great-grandfather named Negro Prince, born sometime before 1755!

"Hey, batter, batter swing!" I was feeling lucky, or drunk from my possible fourth great-grandfather find. I was going to swing the bat, hoping I hit a home run, but realizing the odds were that I'd miss the pitch, or strike out entirely. Here comes the wind-up . . . and another hypothesis.

For this book edition, I assumed my Prince's mother was a slave of Benjamin or Richard Hatcheson, perhaps the 45-year-old Phillis, or 45-year-old Beck, listed previously in Figure 8.8. They were two of the forty-one slaves that Benjamin sold to his brother Richard in 1795. Those two women would have been 33-years-old in 1783 when my third great-grandfather, Prince, was born.

There was also a 32-year-old named Phillis who would have been 20-years-old in 1783. She, too, could have been my fourth great-grandmother. I swung the bat again. There were three women named Phillis in that 1795 transaction. It was possible they were the great-grandmother, grandmother, and mother of my Prince.

While I was unable to find more than probate records or other documentation to fully validate those estimates of parentage, for the moment I chose to hypothesize that Caesar and Pina, or one of the women named Phillis, were my paternal 5th great-grandparents. That theorized family tree is presented for scrutiny in Figure 8.11. What would you conclude, given the same data?

I intend to prove or refute the assertions on this page in a future Second Edition of this book. You know the drill by now: red couch, scrumptious dark chocolate, and red wine, rejoicing another possible breakthrough for this, the biggest genealogy adventure of my life.

Why can I never seem to just sit back and enjoy a genealogical breakthrough for more than a few minutes?

I pondered the question that most African American genealogists want to know: where in Africa did my ancestors come from? Presuming my theory that Caesar and Pina or one of the Phillises were my fifth great-grandparents was true, and knowing that Prince Williams was described as "of a black color," was it possible that Caesar and Pina, or their parents, were brought to Maryland in the early 1700s directly from Africa, or via the "Middle Passage"[105] of the Caribbean or South America? After all, Kent County is at the mouth of the Chesapeake Bay, the entry point to the port of Baltimore.

Were Caesar and Pina, Vincent Hatcheson's slaves, among the unfortunate enslaved Africans stolen away to America? Did they and their son bring ironmaking knowledge to Maryland, as Jean Libby and others purported that skilled African ironworkers were specifically brought to America? That thrilling possibility is broached in Chapter 14 *Generations of Ironworkers*, as well as in **Part IV: DNA Doesn't Lie, Does It?**

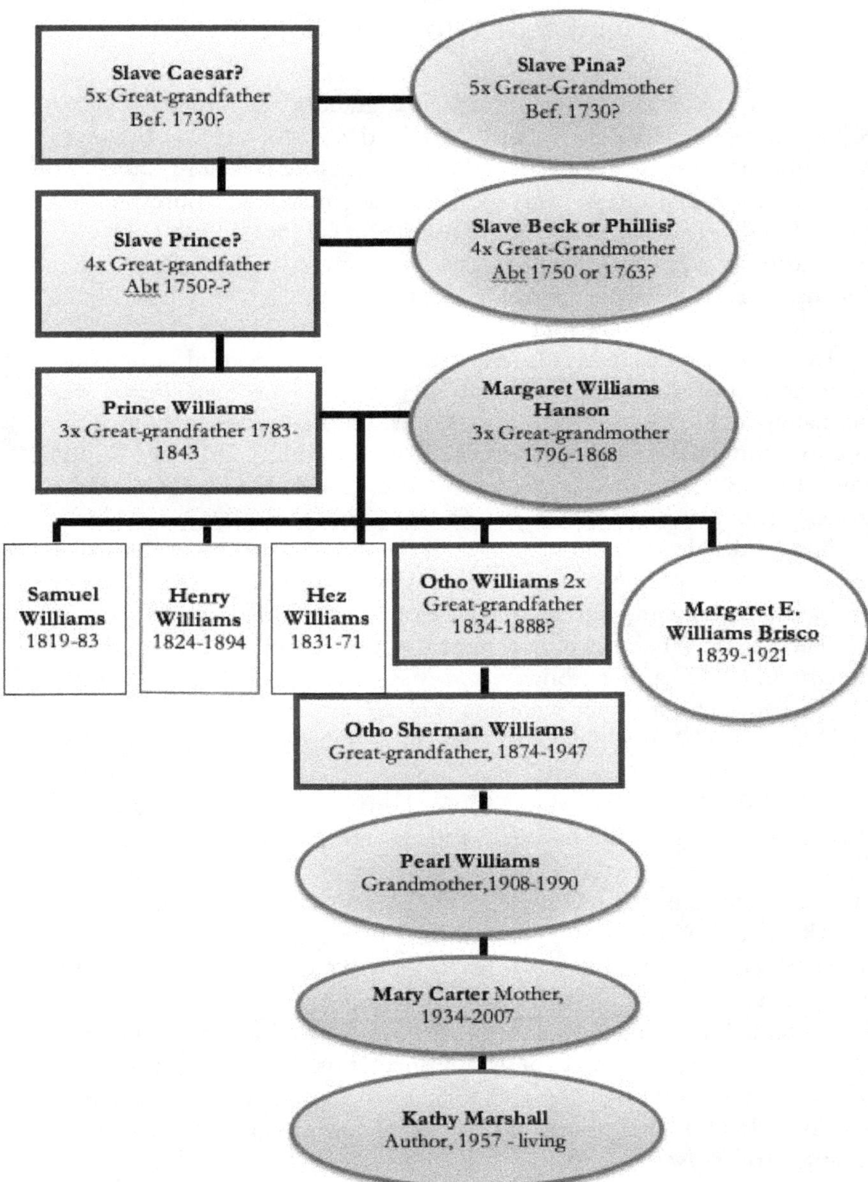

Figure 8.9. Eight generations of Kathy Marshall's ancestors [Note: the 4th and 5th generations are still somewhat theoretical].

* A New Palace for the Prince *

So how and when was my third great-grandfather, originally called Slave Prince, born in Kent County, Maryland, sold for a term of years to the Antietam Iron Works after his scuffle with Slave Isaac in 1799?

I had looked through every possible Judgment and court file that I could find online from Kent and Washington Counties. I had contacted historical staff from both counties, as well as some of my genealogy expert friends, to learn of other possible sources which might clarify how Prince came to be a free man. Nix, nada.

I was pretty discouraged and frustrated not to find any court references or other records that explained how or when Slave Prince was ultimately sold to the Antietam Iron Works. The earliest transcripts of the county court and estate cases appealed from the county Orphan's Courts started in 1806, which was likely long after my Prince was sold to the ironworks.[106]

Next, I decided to examine the land, census records, and probate files for each owner of the Antietam Iron Works to see if a bill of sale or probate record mentioned the purchase of a slave named Prince between 1799 and 1812. What a web of intrigue that turned out to be. High rollers bought and sold various ironworks in Maryland in the 1700s and 1800s. My questions about Prince were unanswered.

Prince's 1812 Certificate of Freedom indicated he was sold to McPherson and Brien at Antietam Iron Works, but those men did not own the Iron Works until about 1806. Sheriff Benjamin Hatcheson was dead by 1806, but I could find neither death nor probate records for him.

Were Sheriff Hatcheson and McPherson and Brien acquaintances, business associates, or relatives? Kent County was on the east side of Maryland and Washington County on the west, but the geographic distance was only 150 miles, so they could have come into contact with each other.

It seemed the *how* and exactly *when* Prince got to Washington County, might have to stay a mystery for now. Prince's possible experiences as one of sixty black workers living and toiling at the massive Antietam Iron Works and village is explored in Chapter 14 *Generations of Ironworkers* and Chapter 16 *The Journey Home.*

Chapter 9 - A Day in the Life

For all the accounts of slave life I had read, what follows is my take on what daily life may have been for my enslaved ancestors in the Ingram household. The cast of characters in the following creative non-fiction story is: Prince and Margaret Williams' children, in order by age: Samuel, Matilda, Patsy, Mary, Henry, Hezekiah, Otho, Malinda, and Margaret Elizabeth.

Ingram children are in order by age: John, Sarah Ellen, Rachel, Benjamin, Edward, Joseph, and Catherine Ann.

Charles Solomon was a free man living in the Ingram household.

"Mary!" yelled an agitated female voice from somewhere upstairs.

"Yes, Miz Sarah, I comin' up." Her blue and white gingham apron flapped against the baluster as she rushed up the polished wooden stairs, holding a tall glass of freshly made apple juice. She hurried to deliver the beverage to her mistress who was waiting in her bedroom at the end of the second-floor hallway, in the sprawling, brown-shingled, Ingram farmhouse.

"Now Mary, how many times do I have to tell you to have my juice on the bed stand before I wake up?" Sarah Ellen Ingram affectionately chided her 20-year-old slave girl on that chilly March morning in 1840.

"I sorry, Miz Sarah. Rooster din't crow this mornin', so I woke up a might late. I dressed as quick as lightnin' and ran to the big house fast as I can. The alley be mighty muddy, so it took a while to wipe ma' shoes clean before comin' in. Mama 'ready got the fire goin' and started cookin' the bacon for breakfast." The unmistakably addictive smell of sizzling meaty pork clung to the folds of Mary's checkered dress and wafted up the stairs.

"I help Mama lift that heavy skillit for the eggs before I started on your juice," Mary explained to her spinster owner. "I boiled some sweet yeller apples and a little bit of the tart green ones last night, then mashed them good this morning. I hope you like the juice, ma'am."

"Well, at least you took care to remove the seeds this time," Sarah Ellen said, gulping the last of the pulpy liquid and wiping her chin with the towelette Mary handed her. "After I eat, I want you to show me again how you did that scallop stitch on the pretty quilt you made for your bed last year. I want to try it myself."

"Yes, ma'am. I be glad to," Mary said, happy to receive a compliment. "Mama say vittles be ready in 'bout ha'f a hour. You want me to help ya git dressed now?"

"Help me up out of this bed, and get me that pink dress with the white flower bodice.

"Yes, ma'am." Mary rifled through the closet looking for the right dress. She helped Sarah Ellen out of the big poster bed, turning back the covers and offering her hand to steady her. Mary gave Sarah the white ceramic chamber pot to use, then helped her take off her sleeping gown and wash up. She handed her mistress clean white undergarments, and helped Sarah Ellen into the dress, fumbling a bit with the ten small white buttons at the back. She tied a pink sash around the bodice and a big bow in front.

As Sarah Ellen sat impatiently on the low stool in front of her mirror, Mary combed her owner's thin, sandy-colored hair, then wrapped it into a tight bun at the nape of her neck, holding it in place with hairpins.

Downstairs, the enslaved matron of the house, 44-year-old Margaret, and her 11-year-old daughter, Margaret Elizabeth, were busy preparing a hearty breakfast for the entire Ingram household and its slaves—seventeen people every day. This included their unmarried 44-year-old master, John Ingram, his brothers Benjamin, 31; Edward, 28; and Joseph, 27; and John's three unmarried sisters, Sarah Ellen, 41; Rachael, 37; and Catherine Ann, the youngest at 13-years-of-age, lived in the house too.

There were also nine enslaved Williams family members and a 60-year-old former slave named Charles Solomon, who looked forward to eating the meal which produced enticing aromas throughout the house.

Margaret called to her eight-year-old son, who was playing outside, neglecting his daily chores. "Hezekiah, where's that milk? Margaret Elizabeth might need to churn more butter before breakfast."

"OK, I goin' git some right now, Mama," he said over his shoulder and skipped toward the twenty foot wide by thirty foot long cow barn which stood at the far end of the gravel path, about 200 yards from the big house. The pig pen, chicken coop, and barn were built as far away as possible from the main living quarters so putrid manure smells would not offend the sensibilities of the Ingram ladies, or other visitors.

Otho's brother, Hezekiah, was usually responsible for milking the cows in the early morning and late afternoon. He only had time to milk one right now. He would do the rest after breakfast. Grabbing a warm teat with each hand, he squirted the milk into a large metal jug. The milking complete, he called to his brother, Henry to help him load the heavy jug into a small red wagon and pull it along the pathway to the kitchen door.

It had rained hard the previous night, turning the thinly graveled path into a muddy, rutted mess. It took the two of them to haul the wagon over the ruts.

Five-year-old Otho, the subject of this book, was playing with sticks in the mud instead of doing his chores. Exasperated, Margaret yelled, "Otho, fill this basket with eggs right now, and be careful not to break 'em this time." Taking the straw basket that could hold about twenty-four large, speckled-brown eggs, Otho headed to the chicken coop. He enjoyed reaching under the warm brown feathers to find the oval treasures. They would become sunny-side-up eggs for the Ingrams, and scrambled eggs for the Williamses. He scattered chicken scratch for the hens adding water to some of the cracked corn and other grains mixture to make their favorite mash. Otho did not look forward to cleaning the nesting area later that day, but it was important to keep their coop clean.

"Malinda, go to the cellar and get two jars of jam," Margaret directed.

"Yes, ma'am. Do you want the blackberry and peach?"

"No, plum and peach."

Every morning, 20-year-old Matilda made sure the mouth-watering smell of freshly baked biscuits pleased Ingram's noses as they made their way down from their bedrooms.

Full-figured Patsy, 21, set the breakfast table just so, and lit the dining room fireplace for the comfort of the Ingrams. She would serve the family and take care of all their food and beverage needs. Her younger siblings would clear, wash, and dry the Ingrams' dishes. Any uneaten food, along with scrambled eggs, oat porridge and fatback, would be eaten by the Williamses for breakfast.

Early the previous winter, squeals had pierced the crisp air as the Williams men, and Margaret had slaughtered, cleaned, skinned, eviscerated, and butchered[107] about two dozen, 250-pound, splotchy, white hogs.

Margaret and two of her adolescent daughters rubbed bay salt and salt-petre into the hog parts as a preservative, then they pushed pieces of the pork fat and muscle through a meat grinder. Using well-cleaned hog intestines as casings, they hand-mixed fennel seed, parsley, sage, pepper, and salt into the ground hog-meat. The meat-filled casings were twisted twice every four inches to form long sausage links. Margaret hung the aromatic ropes in the six-foot square smokehouse, which was located next to the outdoor summer kitchen. The sausages would cure for several months in the colder weather. Everybody knows the sweltering Maryland summer heat makes it impossible to keep foodstuffs from spoiling, so meats eaten during the spring and summer months were often preserved the prior winter.

When the leaves turned yellow and orange last fall, the Williams women "put up"[108] luscious sweet blackberries, tart red cherries, juicy dark-blue plums, and Garnet Beauty fuzz-less peaches, for jams and jellies. They pickled cucumbers and canned dill and sweet pickles. Root vegetables like carrots, potatoes, parsnips, and beets were stored in the cold cellar for eating throughout the winter and spring. Cabbages were eaten fresh, usually in coleslaw, from June through September, and sauerkraut was canned for winter and spring meals. Beans and peas were generally harvested and canned before mid-September every year. Squash and pumpkins were harvested through October and November and stored with sweet yellow and tart red apples in the cellar for eating during the winter and spring seasons.[109]

That meant in March 1840 there were apples for Sarah Ellen's juice, seasoned link sausages, sunny-side-up eggs, warm, buttered biscuits with plum and peach jam, and oatmeal porridge Margaret made for the day's morning breakfast.

John, Benjamin, and Edward occasionally supervised the farm, but because they were lawyers, they were more often managing their J&B law firm in Boonsboro. They executed wills and all manner of probate records for the citizens of Washington County. Benjamin was also a convention delegate for the Whig Party. The brothers regularly worked with the County Register, William Logan and the Sheriff's Office to sell the properties of debtors.

Except for former slave Charles Solomon, who was allowed to do as he pleased after breakfast, the Williams men, and Joseph Ingram prepared for a freezing day in the fields.

Prince Williams, 57, and his eldest sons, Samuel, 22, and Henry, 16, did most of the heavy labor around the farm. "OK boys, it's time. The winter hay crop has to be cut and baled. Eighteen acres need to be cleared for planting corn, forty-three for wheat, and three acres cleared for rye." Joseph said.

In western Maryland, corn, wheat, and rye were huge agricultural staples used for cereal, flour for bread and cakes and, of course, for whiskey. Grain crops required large gangs of workers to harvest the fields in August through September, and sometimes into October.

Max Grivno wrote in great detail about the difficulties of securing and keeping gangs of black and white, free and slave, farmworkers. The Ingrams likely had some of those same problems on their 246-acre farm.

A menagerie of tools of all shapes, sizes, and purposes were found on the Ingram Farm, including a digging iron, crowbar, sledges, mauls and wedges, axes, a grindstone, a cross-cut saw, grain cradles, mowing scythes, forks, rakes, shovels, hoes, and wooden planks. They had a two-horse sleigh, one buggy and harness, two farm wagons, three grain ladders, one windmill, five plows, two harrows and four spreaders. For the six head of horses, there were bridles, halters, collars, harnesses, and riding saddles ready for use.

Therefore, the Williams and other slaves must have been well-versed in caring for horses and cattle, farming grain crops, fixing metal equipment, and managing the farm, skills that would help them successfully act on their behalf after slavery ended.

"Henry, later today, you need to re-shoe Betsy's left hoof. And while you're at it, forge some more horseshoes in case we need extra when we start the plowing next week," said Prince, picking a bit of morning fatback from his teeth with a piece of straw.

There was an outbuilding behind the slave quarters which was used as a smithy for ironworking. Sometimes acrid smoke could be seen and smelled as the pig iron was heated and pounded into horseshoes, tools, or other shapes needed on the farm. Prince most assuredly taught his sons to use the wrought iron blacksmith's tools, small forge, and simple bellows to aerate the fire. They learned how to shoe horses, repair broken farming implements, make nails, and fabricate new metal parts. They, in turn, passed on that knowledge to their sons, who would do the same for their descendants until the present day.

After the breakfast dishes were cleared, Margaret interrupted young Otho and Hezekiah, who were playing tag outside, to ask "Have you boys fed the animals yet?" The young men were expected to feed and care for the thirty-nine head of hogs, and workhorses, in addition to the seven milk cows, four steers, one bull, and the chickens. That task would keep them busy for a couple of hours, in between playing tag. "We gonna do it now Mama," they chimed in unison chasing each other to the barn.

The female Ingrams stayed in the house reading or writing notes, or sometimes they asked Charles to drive them in the carriage to visit their society friends. The Ingram women occasionally used the spinning wheel to make special threads for their embroidery work. Generally, their life was quiet and uneventful. Rachel and Sarah Ellen never married.

In contrast, the female Williams slaves were constantly busy behind the scenes doing all the work of the household—hand-washing the clothes and sheets and hanging them to dry in the cold March wind. They heated irons in the fireplace and ensured the clothes were ironed, folded, and put away. They cleaned boots and shoes, which were always caked with mud from the graveled pathway outside the main house.

The Williams sisters made all the beds and cleaned all the rooms in the house. They kept the furniture dusted and polished and beat the dust from the rugs. They, or the youngest sons, brought wood in from the wood bin next to the outdoor cooking kitchen and kept the fireplaces lit and cleaned out.

The Williams women took care that the cow's milk was stored properly and made into butter and cheese.

They ensured the food in the cellar storage was inventoried and safely maintained, so the family had enough until the next harvest. They sewed, mended clothes, and darned socks. Traveling with and without the white Ingrams, they drove the horse and buggy into Hagerstown or Boonsboro to shop for various and sundry groceries, like sugar. Of course, they were responsible for dressing, tressing, and bathing the female Ingrams.

And last, but certainly not least, all of the enslaved Williams had to immediately respond to every request, order, or admonition from their white masters.

My family members had not a moment to themselves, except on Sundays when they were generally free to do as they pleased after the Ingrams were served breakfast. On the day of rest, they were allowed to use the horse and buggy to enjoy services at the Ebenezer A.M.E Church in Hagerstown.

They could make crafts, like quilts, baby clothes, and baskets, to be sold in the local marketplace. Or they could sell foodstuffs grown in their little gardens. Monies they received from selling their goods would be theirs to keep.

Since it seems the Ingrams may have been more lenient than most slave masters in the area, my family could choose to spend Sundays visiting their friends. Of course, the Ingrams expected dinner to be prepared, but it could be lighter fare than normal.

When Sarah Ellen died in 1847, her slave, Mary F. Williams, valued at $300, was freed by John Ingram in 1848. Mary continued living and working at the Ingram Farm. I cannot prove whether Mary had a *personal* relationship with either of the Ingram bachelors, John or Benjamin, in that house. I shall continue to research whether the descendants of the Ingrams match my family's DNA.

It is known that Mary was an accomplished quilter (Figure 9.1).

Mary maintained friendships with the black Warfield and Letitia Diggs family who were profiled by Dr. Emilie Amt as parishioners of St. Mark's Episcopal Church.[110]

Letitia's mother was Letty Ann Hopewell, who may have been owned by the same Hopewell's discussed in Theory 4.C of Chapter 8. Did the Warfield, Hopewell, and Williams women become friends at the Ebenezer A.M.E. Church in Hagerstown? Was Mary related in some way to Hopewell-surnamed slaves, perhaps as Letitia's aunt or her godmother?

Samuel was freed by John Ingram in 1854 and moved his wife Sarah and daughter, Jane, to his property in Funkstown, as explored in Chapter 13 *The Landowners*.

Margaret Elizabeth was freed in 1860 and was a servant in the Ingram household in 1860. She married Abraham Briscoe and moved to Funkstown. It is unclear whether she was born in 1839, as stated on her manumission document, or earlier, because she was mentioned in Joseph Ingram's 1834 Will.

The fine stitching, including Mary F. William's own signature and the date of the quilt, authenticated this quilt as a piece made before the Civil War. The timing of its construction as well as the gifting of this quilt imbue it with a deeper significance than most quilts. It is not just an example of women's folk art. It is a piece of antebellum history held by an African American family. Mary Williams, sister of Otho Williams, made this "Freedom Quilt" in 1848, the year she received her freedom. She later gave the quilt to Letitia Diggs (pictured) as a wedding gift, who in turn gave the gift to Letitia Comer. Mrs. Comer gifted it to the Doleman Museum.

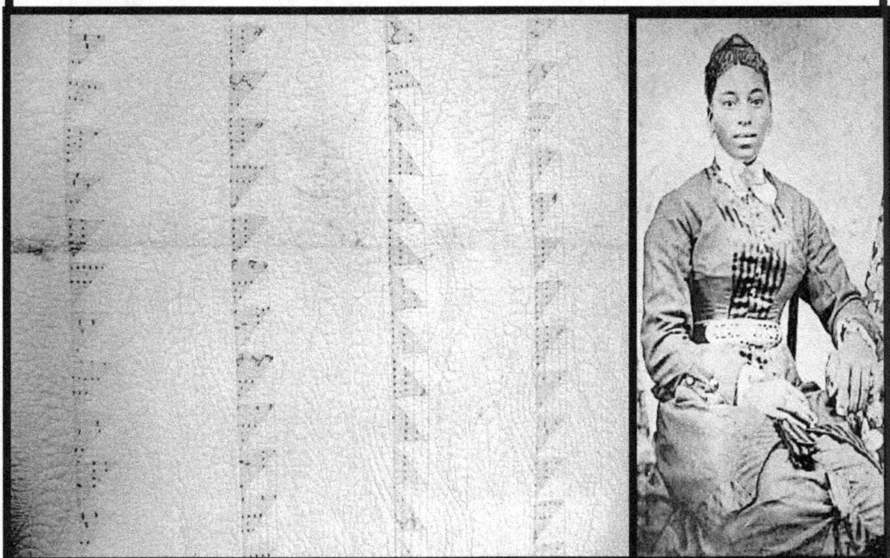

Figure 9.1. "Freedom Quilt" created by Mary F. Williams in 1848. stored at the Doleman Museum, Hagerstown, MD. Photograph courtesy of Dr. Emilie Amt.

* The Ingram Farm *

I had to determine where, exactly, Otho worked and lived as a slave to help determine what his daily life was likely to be. That simple question was more complicated than I ever dreamed it would be. Information about the personal property of the Ingrams (Appendix I) helped to paint a reasonable picture of what the daily lives were like for my family.

We are fortunate that the National Register of Historic Places inventoried the Ingram-Schipper Farm (Figure 9.2), where my family was enslaved. It was designated an historical landmark in 1979. There are ample architectural descriptions of the buildings, fairly clear photographs, and maps of the property layout. The house is located about 1/2 mile west of Maryland Route 66, about 1/2 mile south of its intersection with US 40, situated on the eastern bank of the Beaver Creek.

Figure 9.2. Ingram-Schipper Farm, Boonsboro, MD, 1979, where the Williams Family was enslaved. Courtesy of the National Register of Properties in Maryland.

The main "mansion" structure supports a two-story, four-bay brick dwelling with white trim. A two-bay frame edition at the west end of the house links it with a brick summer kitchen. The house features a Victorian-period, flat-roofed, one-story porch and a slate roof. Near the house are a number of early outbuildings, including a brick kitchen and wash house, three log buildings, one of which has a fireplace and appears to have been a dwelling (Figure 9.3), and a large stone barn.

Figure 9.3. (Upper) Ingram Farm, near the Beaver Creek, Boonsboro, MD. Photograph by Kathy Marshall, 2017. (Lower) Courtesy of the National Register of Properties in Maryland.

The outbuildings were regarded as outstanding examples of early log construction still in existence in 1979.

As shown in Figure 9.3, from the upscale Meadows Green housing development overlooking the Ingrams red brick home (upper photo, left) and outbuildings where Otho Williams' enslaved family lived and toiled in the mid-1800s. Imagine that those meadows (upper photo, right) were covered in hay, wheat and corn fields, toiled by the slaves. In the bottom image, imagine 36 pigs, 6 steers, 7 milk cows, and horses in these pens bordering the dirt roadway from the "Big House" going alongside a storage building, toward the barn. It is likely the chicken coop and pig-pen were at the far end of this gravel path. Yes, my enslaved family toiled along that graveled pathway.

On the largest plantations, housing for slaves was often a large barracks-like structure fitted with bunks and occupied solely by men. Women, children, and the elderly lived some little distance away in small wood cabins barely a step above the barn that housed the horses.

In the smaller "farms," there were often single log cabins for the one to five slaves that the average person owned in Washington County, Maryland. Figure 9.4 is a photograph of one of three slave structures on the Ingram Farm in Boonsboro, Maryland.

Figure 9.4. Slave cabin on the Ingram Farm, Boonsboro, MD. Courtesy of the National Register of Properties in Maryland.

While Joseph Ingram left the 246-acre Meadow Green property to his three sons, he allowed his unmarried daughters to reside in half of the "mansion house" structure until their marriage.[111] It was to his seven children still living at home that Joseph bequeathed Margaret and Prince's seven children. Much of the Ingram's former acreage was sold by Edward Ingram to their next-door neighbor, David Fahrney by 1867 after Benjamin and John Ingram died in 1861 and 1862. The Fahrneys sold parcels of the property to others. Many years later, a land developer built numerous, spacious 5,000 square-foot, $500,000+, mini-mansions on one-acre lots, in an upscale development keeping the "Meadows Green" name.

It seems that Henry was still a slave of the Ingram family until emancipation, but because he was never mentioned in other Wills, I mused that he was serving as an apprentice for a cobbler/boot maker. I also wondered if Henry was disabled in some way. While Otho, 28 and Hezekiah, 31 were each appraised at $275, Henry, 18 was appraised at just $50. An 1862 Maryland Land Record[112] entry indicated 38-year-old Henry Williams was sold by John Ingram to their next-door neighbor, Clarence Fahrney on whose former property still sits a six foot tall, six-foot wide and deep crypt containing the remains of eight members of the Ingram family.

An interesting "Order of Publication" issued in 1894 provided a lot of detail about Henry's life, including his wives and many children, and several land transactions he made. It indicated Henry still owned the property granted him by Daniel Fahrney, his last slave master.

Prior to reading this interesting piece of information, I incorrectly thought my Otho's brother could have been the black Captain Henry Williams who drove a riverboat up and down the C&O Canal.[113]

While all the puzzle pieces were not exactly in place, we had a clearer picture of the daily lives of my enslaved family members on the Ingram Farm in the 1830s through the end of slavery.

Compared to other families who were split up and sold away to parts unknown, it appears that my family was kept together, generally working for the Ingram family or their acquaintances.

In my mind's eye, while visiting their compound during a genealogy tour to Maryland in April 2017, I envisioned my family members walking along the 100-foot alley from the slave quarters to the big house, sometimes carrying loads of wood or pails of milk from the barn where the cows were milked and the hogs fed. I saw my third great-grandmother, Margaret, as she cooked the summer meal in the outdoor kitchen. I imagined seeing my great-great-grandfather, Otho, walking the horses back to their stall after plowing the meadows, readying the fields for planting corn or wheat. This was a visceral experience which I would not have missed for the world.

Figure 10.1. Unidentified African American soldier in Union uniform with wife and two daughters, circa 1863-1865. Courtesy of Library of Congress. This image was found in Cecil County, Maryland, making it likely that this soldier belonged to one of the seven U.S.C.T. regiments raised in Maryland. Source: Matthew R. Gross and Elizabeth T. Lewin, 2010.

Chapter 10 - The Civil War: Who is the Hero Now?

* Civil War Battles Too Close To Home *

What? My enslaved family lived near the Civil War Battle of Antietam? In early April 2017, I visited the site where my family had been enslaved in the early-to-mid-1800s. Standing on a hill overlooking the Ingram Farm I wondered what it must have been like then, for slave and free, white and black, Union and Confederate, to live through that grueling period in American history. I tried to imagine hundreds of soldiers on the grassy meadow below with my family among them.

"Yes, it was only a few years ago, but I remember it so well," mused my second great-grandfather, Otho Williams, as he suddenly popped back into my consciousness. "The lives of all people were terribly affected by Civil War fightin' that happened all around Washington County, between 1861 and 1863, but especially in Sharpsburg, Hagerstown, and Funkstown, where my family lived and worked.

"The Battle of Antietam Hill, where I heard almost 23,000 people were killed, wounded, or missing on September 17, 1862, was only a few miles from this spot right here." Turning around with his arms spread wide, taking in the meadow and buildings on the Ingram's "Meadows Green" property, he said, "Folks sometimes called it the Battle of Sharpsburg, or the Battle to Free the Slaves.[114]

"I can tell you it was a horrible time," Otho said as he removed his crumpled hat and rubbed his tanned, nearly bald head. The sound of Great Crested Flycatchers and Wood-Pewee songbirds caught Otho's attention as they flew overhead toward the nearby C&O Canal. (That important man-made waterway extended from northern Washington County, twelve miles away to its southeastern border into the Potomac River, almost to Washington D.C.)

Otho's sable brown eyes followed the birds' flight into the cloudless sky, as he composed his thoughts about the Civil War.[115]

I wanted to make this important chapter about the Civil War more interesting and personal, so I was more than happy that Otho decided to drop by, if only in spirit, to paint a picture about what the war was like, too close to his home.

We were standing in the broad, flat meadow at the Ingram's Farm (Figure 9.3). Otho was taking a break from checking the corn crop. There was no breeze and the flies buzz-buzzed and landed artfully on his sweaty arms, tasting his salty goodness.

"Ya' have to understand," he started, "that Hagerstown's location at the border between the anti-slavery north, and pro-slavery south, made the city a primary staging area and supply center for four major battles during the Civil War."

After gulping water from his flask, seeking to hydrate his parched 5'9" slender frame, he resumed speaking, "Ya must remember that almost half of Maryland citizens were Pro-Confed'ret and the other half were Pro-Union. Neighbors who'd been friends up to that point suddenly looked at each other with suspicion. Us slaves was in the middle of it all. People who were already free also had a tough time with those white folks fighting about whether we should be free or not. I was still a slave, always been a slave, always wanted to be free, but I din't dare run away for fear of what might happen to my sisters and brothers still living here. The Ingrams were pretty nice to us, compared to most white folks, so we all stayed put.

"Throughout the Civil War, private doctors and other citizens helped men from both the north and south, in a number of places. The Bethel African Methodist Episcopal Church volunteered to use their building as a smallpox hospital when the deadly pox spread throughout the town. Ebenezer A.M.E. Church, where my family worshipped, did the same. Did you know that slaves were not allowed to learn to read or write?"

I nodded my head, yes.

He continued, "Cuz I couldn't read at that time, I had to depend on others to tell me what was in the newspaper. I heard the *Herald of Freedom and Torch Light Newspaper* wrote several articles in September 1862 that described the Battle of Antietam.[116] Near as I can recall what people told me, and what I remember when it happened, our men of the Army of the Potomac got to the fields of Antietam well-fed and well- equipped."

"What do you mean by 'well-equipped?'" I asked.

"Soldiers received about three pounds of food and water each day. The army brought along more than three thousand wagons and maybe thirty thousand horses and mules . . . 'least that's what local people said. Yes, Lawd, some food was, what's the word, 'requisitioned' from the local farmers, whether we wanted to give it to them or not. The amount of personal property, like horses, cattle, hogs, sheep, corn, and hay, taken from our farmers, was enormous. The whole lower portion of Washington County was stripped of nearly everything. What our local people would do for food during the approaching winter in 1862, Gawd alone knew," Otho said with a far-off look in his eyes, obviously remembering the hunger and privations he had experienced during wartime in his once-beautiful homeland.

"What did people do with all the soldiers who were hurt?" I wanted to know.

"Hospitals were in nearly every farmhouse to the north and east of the battlefield. The wounded was also taken to Sharpsburg, Williamsport, Hagerstown, Boonsboro, Keedysville, and Middletown. Many hospitals were set up in barns or houses, and the wounded could also be found in churches, stores, sheds, carriage houses, corncribs, stables, and mangers, in the open air, under tents, or simply laid out on haystacks in fields and orchards. The conditions at those field hospitals, well let's just say, a lot of wounded din't survive, let me tell you. Ohh, the never-ending groaning and screams of the wounded would ring in our ears all night and all day."

"I can't imagine seeing all those sights, sounds, and smells from the fighting," I admitted.

"Aarrgghh," Otho exhorted, screwing up his face into a mask of disgust. "Animal crap, and the swarming flies and other insects that loved it, were everywhere. And the smell, oh the horrible smell of it all . . . death, dying, crap, soldiers throwing up, rotted animals, every smell for miles around was just awful!

"The lack of air movement and enough light, and the fact that many men lay almost on top of each other in filthy, blood-caked uniforms did not help. Many eventually died from typhoid fever and di–ree–a, not from their actual wounds. Sadder still, those diseases and conditions spread and killed many local citizens. I think that's what happened to Massa Benjamin and his brother Massa John Ingram who died in 1861 and 1862. They was both buried in the cement family crypt on the hill over yonder, overlooking the meadow where we are standing right now."

"Yes, I was standing next to the crypt a few minutes before you appeared, reading the names of the Ingrams who were interred in that huge rock-like coffin. It was extraordinary for me to be so close to them after having done so much research to learn about who they were so I could learn about who *you* were, great-great-grandfather," I said with a smile. Otho was still thinking about death and dying, so he did not pick up on my sentimentality.

"Let's see if I can remember this right," Otho said, with a look of concentration furrowing his brow. His index finger was casually perched vertically between his nose and chin, as he struggled to put his thoughts into words.

"Only a few blocks away from Daddy's property, the Battle of Funkstown took place on July 10, 1863, I think it was. It started as General Robert E. Lee's Army retreated toward Virginia in the week following the Battle of Gettysburg. Our Army of the Potomac—the Union forces—attacked the rear guard of the Confed'ret Army, but there were a lot of Confed'rets in Funkstown then. They threatened any Union advance against General Robert E. Lee's important position near Williamsport and the Potomac River. I don't remember the names of all the leaders, and what all that they did, but by early evening, the Union Army began withdrawing south towards Beaver Creek coming closer to us."

"What did the troops do for food?" I asked, having a hard time imagining how the basics of food, water, and elimination (latrines/pits dug into the earth), were dealt with.

"Hundreds, maybe thousands, of tired, hungry troops, and their horses needed water and food every day. They tore through *these* fields here, right next to Beaver Creek, between Funkstown and Boonsboro. They took nearly everything that was ready to harvest, including our prized peaches that I carefully pruned the winter before to get a really good crop. No, there was none of Mama's peach pie or preserves in 1863," Otho said, shaking his head.

"The soldiers killed some of our hogs and demanded they be butchered and immediately cooked for the starving troops. All of us Williams had to pitch in and help get the soldiers whatever they asked for. We didn't mind at all, though, because the Union Army was fighting to free us slaves . . . or so we thought."

"How did you feel when you learned the Emancipation Proclamation did *not* apply to you here in Maryland?" I hesitated to ask.

"I cannot describe how disappointed and ANGRY we Maryland slaves were when we found out President Lincoln's Proclamation didn't count for us. It only freed the slaves from those blasted Confed'ret States! Even though Maryland had slaves, and half of the residents were Pro-Confed'ret, the State of Maryland was fighting on the Union side, and so us slaves was not freed."

A heavy sigh escaped through his dry lips. He had to take a moment to calm himself down. Reliving the intense emotions of that time was obviously difficult for him.

"Anyway," he continued, "in 1864, Hagerstown was invaded again by the Confed'ret army. They levied a ransom of $20,000 and a large amount of clothing, in what they called 'retribution' for the destruction of farms, feed, and cattle in their home areas further south. I didn't care what happened to their homes, just what they was doing to us here in these parts." Otho finished his story and took another swig of water. He placed his hat back on his head, satisfied he had told the tale of war as best he could.

* The Black Presence in Western Maryland Civil War Battles *

During the first years of the Civil War, Maryland slaves who escaped from their owners to join the federal army were usually returned or incarcerated as runaways. By July 1863, despite the protests of Maryland's governor and slave-owning Unionists, the federal government began actively recruiting slaves as well as freemen soldiers to fight on the Union side (Figure 10.2).

Figure 10.2. US Colored Troops Recruitment Poster. Source: Supervising Committee for Recruiting Colored Regiments, Philadelphia, PA, circa 1865.

Believed to be physically and spiritually unfit as fighting men, they were initially confined to non-combat jobs. However, African American soldiers were eventually given a few opportunities to prove their mettle on the battlefield. They distinguished themselves in May 1863 when they bravely attacked, across open ground against Port Hudson on the Mississippi River in Louisiana.

A month later, black troops made another valiant charge when they stormed Fort Wagner near Charleston, South Carolina. This famous attack was depicted in the 1998 movie "Glory," about one of the first military units of the Union Army, during the American Civil War, to consist entirely of African American men (except for its officers), as told from the point of view of Colonel Shaw, its white commanding officer.[117]

The United States recruited six regiments of African Americans from Maryland as part of the newly established U.S. Colored Troops (USCT). Maryland blacks joined the U.S. Marine Corps and the U.S. Navy.[118] Approximately 186,000 African Americans served in the USCT volunteer cavalry, artillery, and infantry units. The enlistment of free blacks and slaves was considered to be a key to winning the war. By the end of the Civil War, roughly 179,000 black men (10% of the Union Army) served as soldiers in the Army, and another 19,000 served in the Navy. Nearly 40,000 black soldiers died—30,000 from infection or disease.[119]

One of my questions at the beginning of this research was whether my Otho, or any of my Williams family members, had fought in the Civil War. Once I found that brothers Henry, Otho, and Hezekiah were still slaves in 1863, according to the probate records of his owners Benjamin and John Ingram—and no military records were found for them—I had to conclude the three had not served directly in the military. However, as described earlier in this chapter, they were certainly impacted by Civil War battles in their homeland.

I searched long and hard to find out whether Otho's older brother, Samuel, had served in the Civil War. Samuel would have been about 44 in 1863. There were conflicting military records regarding several, colored, "Private Samuel Williams" who served.[120] One Samuel Williams mustered into the 2nd USCT in Arlington, VA, another into the 6th from Frederick, Maryland. There was also a Private Samuel Williams, born in the correct year, 1818, but in Salisbury, Maryland, which was far from Washington County, therefore, unlikely my Samuel ancestor.

There was no military record for Otho's possible brother named Prince who was born in 1825 (Figure 8.3). However, there was a fellow named Prince Williams, born in 1843, who was in the U.S. Colored Troops and did fight in the Civil War. I was unable to prove whether he was related to my family or not.

Finally, there was an interesting story regarding Henry Williams. One Thursday night during my fifth month on this project, I found a forty-two-page pension file for Easter Briscoe Williams, the wife of someone named Henry Williams. Was that my Otho's brother?

Upon further scrutiny, I noticed the pension file was actually for the Revolutionary War. Yes, a "colored" man named Henry Williams fought for this country in 1777. What? A relative of mine fought in the Revolutionary War? That meant our family could qualify to be Daughters and

Sons of the American Revolution. I was overjoyed! But no, I had incorrectly calculated Henry William's relationship to my family. That Henry was actually related to the family of Otho's brother-in-law, Abraham Briscoe, who had married Margaret Elizabeth Williams. I was crushed. This journey had more ups and downs than a painted horse on a Merry-Go-Round.

After many thrilling "almost was" moments, it did not appear that any of my William's ancestors registered for, or served in, the Civil War.

M. MARSHALL

Chapter 11 - The Mothers' Lineage

* The Search For Alice's Beginnings *

Really now, why is it so difficult to find historical information about women? Women bear children and, in most societies, generally raise them too; this includes caring for babies and toddlers, getting them to and from school, helping them with homework, etc.

In most societies, women are to this day still responsible for taking care of the household, including cleaning the house, washing and ironing and putting away the family's clothes. Many women are still tasked with feeding their families, including growing vegetables, cooking meals, and cleaning up afterward. In many places, women must work outside the home to earn money for their family, in addition to those many other varied tasks.

It is undeniable that women are the backbone of humanity. Yet the critical contributions they make are considered to be "women's work" and therefore usually undervalued and unappreciated.

Like children, women are to be seen and not heard in many places in the world.

There is unequal pay for comparable work, where women in the U.S. who work full time year-round are only paid eighty cents for every dollar paid to men[121]—and for women of color, the wage gap is even larger. Among women who hold full-time, year-round jobs in the United States, Black women are typically paid 61 cents, Native American women 58 cents and Latinas just 53 cents for every dollar paid to white, non-Hispanic men.[122]

There are laws in some countries that prohibit women from voting, testifying in courts, buying property, or having a voice in daily decisions that concern the family they serve so diligently.

When most women marry, they take on the husband's last name. Therefore, it is difficult to find historical documents with their maiden names. These are some of the reasons that it is difficult to find genealogical records about women. For African American women there is the additional hurdle that slavery imposes on genealogists searching for historical information about their enslaved female ancestors.

I met my two most important goals in the fourth month of starting this book project—fleshing out a credible story about Otho Williams' parents and his slave owner. But because the subtitle of this book is *The Search For Our Williams Ancestors*, I also wanted to find juicy tidbits about the two main women in Otho's life, namely: wife Alice Virginia Logan Williams, and his mother Margaret A. "Peggy" Williams Hanson.

Surely, that would be the chocolate buttercream icing on this marbled cake. It was disappointing to be these many months into this adventure and still know almost nothing about the parents, siblings, or childhood of either woman. I felt as if I was waiting for Godot,[123] waiting endlessly for an unchanging situation to change when it was clear the answers to my search might never come!

Who were Alice Virginia Logan's parents? If she was a slave, who was her slave master? Where was she born and raised? Did she live with any brothers and sisters? How did she meet Otho? I still hadn't been able to definitively answer any of those questions, despite overturning every stone and following every breadcrumb in my research.

Time to go back to the basics. I'd learned I often found overlooked clues when I reviewed previous research material. What *did* I know about Alice's early life? My second great-grandmother was only 17 when she married 33-year-old Otho Williams on November 2, 1867, in Washington County, Maryland.[124] The original marriage documents were destroyed in a fire, so I didn't know any more facts about their marriage than the date and the county.

I closed my eyes and breathed a few deep breaths to shake off the distress. I sank into a sleepy reverie when I heard a disembodied female voice getting louder and louder with every word as she glided towards me through a drizzly curtain of lavender fog.

"Well, I can tell you all about that blessed day, for it was the day me and my Otho got married."

I presumed that it had to be Alice Virginia Logan, herself! A gossamer wedding dress hugged her petite waist and ballooned out around her hips, cascading daintily towards the ground which, in my imagination, was strewn with rubies under her feet. Feathered wings at her shoulders resembled those of an opalescent butterfly. She was definitely a stunning vision to behold.

In a high thin voice, the fairy Alice asked, "Did you know that both of Otho's parents were members of Ebenezer A.M.E. Church—the one on Bethel Street in Hagerstown?"

While some might jump, shriek in horror, or rub their eyes in disbelief, I was not surprised to meet my second great-grandmother that way. After having channeled Otho and Prince, I didn't want to get too excited because she might abandon me like they did before I got answers to my many questions.

"Yes, I know about their close connection with that church. I am delighted to meet you and would love to learn more about your and Otho's wedding day."

Alice continued as though I had not spoken, "Mama Margaret—that's what I called Otho's mother because she cared for me as tenderly as my mother did when she was alive—wanted us to wed at Ebenezer Church.

As you probably know, the Williams family had been among the first parishioners there when it opened in 1839. Prince and the Reverend Thomas Henry were not only friends but both had been ironworkers, so they shared that skill and love of metalworking. Prince was one of the first to be buried in that cemetery, four or five years after it opened. Otho's sister, Malinda, had her final rest there too in 1859, and my champion, Mama Margaret, was buried in a plot next to Prince and Malinda Ebenezer in 1868, the year after we married.

"Speaking of marriage, November 2nd was a typical, chilly, fall day in 1867. It was so beautiful outside. The orange and red foliage from the maple trees, mingled with the spotted lime-yellow oak leaves, gracefully drifting on the light breeze, eventually floating to the ground. It was like someone had tossed colorful petals at our feet as we walked from the buggy to the church. A dove cooed as we passed by as if to remind me these were my last moments as a single girl. When I made the return trip to the buggy, it would be as a married woman with my new husband on my arm.

"Mama Margaret and her second husband, William Hanson, brought me to the church in their well-worn buggy at 11:00 AM, from their Funkstown home, three and a half miles away. William helped me down from the chariot onto the drier cobblestones in the street, so my dress would not get dirty."

"Great-great-grandmother," I asked, "who gave you away that day?"

"I walked arm-in-arm with the charming William Hanson who had agreed to stand in for my father. Three years after the end of slavery, Otho and me could finally legally become man and wife, at last.

"I wore a flowing white dress like this one." She pointed to the dress in the picture in Figure 11.1, open on my research table.

Figure 11.1. Wedding couple that could have been Otho and Alice Williams. Courtesy of the Archives at the Library of Virginia.

"Don't you love how the bodice is cinched just above the waist, with that sweet little bow in the front? Even though my shoulders were bare, it was still a modest gown that Mama Margaret helped me make. There was a bit of blue tulle netting at the sides of the bodice that flowed down the front of my dress. And of course, white gloves covered my fingers and wrists. My mother-in-law pomaded my hair and styled it in perfect black ringlets that peeked out from under the headpiece. The veil trailed down my back. I felt like a queen for the day. Don't you love it?" she asked, smiling coquettishly.

"Indeed, you would have been lovely in that dress, I responded. I had a hard time finding pictures of weddings of black people—you called yourselves colored back then—after slavery ended when many slaves 'jumped the broom'[125] to signify they were married. I'm glad this picture looks about right."

Alice resumed, "Yes, it is very close to my actual dress. My husband-to-be wore his black Sunday-go-to-meeting clothes that Mama Margaret had pressed just so, and he bought a black top-hat for the occasion. Otho was so handsome, so confident, so happy, so ready to be married to me. He held my trembling right hand in his. I smiled at him under my lacy veil during the entire ceremony, waiting nervously for the part when we would both say, 'I do.' What if he backed out? What if this was just a dream? What if the reverend wouldn't marry us for some reason? What if

I can't be a good wife? What if . . . I needn't have worried. My sure and steady Otho came through and proclaimed loudly 'I surely do!' to the judge, me, and all of our friends and family in the church, and all my worries were replaced with a wide smile.

"After we made our pledges brother Hezekiah, the best man, gave Otho a silver wedding ring to place on the fourth finger of my left hand. When the Reverend pronounced us man and wife, Otho carefully lifted my veil and quickly kissed me in front of our friends and family who clapped and chided, 'It's about time, old man!' for Otho was about twice my age. That was the moment I went from being the 17-year-old Miss Alice Virginia Logan to being Mrs. Otho Williams. Our many friends and family hugged us, and everybody was all smiles."

I asked, "Did you have the ceremony of throwing your bouquet, or jumping the broom as in slavery days?"

"Yes and no," Alice responded. "My single female friends jumped all over each other in an un-ladylike fashion, I must say, to catch my small bouquet. My best friend, Frannie, won out and would be the next to marry, according to the catch-the-bouquet tradition. We did not jump the broom like people did during slavery times because now we could be married like regular white folks. They would never do such a thing. We wanted our simple wedding to be dignified. I cannot describe how happy we were that day. We had the rest of our lives in front of us, with all the possibilities in the world," Alice finished her description of the wedding, tears welling in her translucent eyes, as she turned and glided away.

"Wait!" I cried. Just as I was about to ask Alice who her parents and slave owner were, she vanished in a poof of mist. Just as I predicted, I was on my own in unraveling Alice's family lineage.

According to the 1870 U.S. Census, analyzed in Chapter 2, Alice was born in 1850 (that census did not capture birth location). Alice was keeping house while taking care of a newborn son they named Edgar E. Williams. She could read but not write and was described as being a mulatto, which made me assume she had a light skin color.

The 1880 census indicated Alice and her parents were born in Maryland. Alice could read *and* write, was listed as being black, and had five sons by then: Edgar E., Samuel M., Otho Sherman (my first great-grandfather), William F.W., and Charles E. Williams. Mary Irene was born in 1880 after the census taker's visit, and in 1883, a daughter named Alice Virginia Williams joined the family. My Uncle Dale Carter said they usually called the latter daughter "Virgie." I kept that "Virgie" nickname in the back of my mind when searching for records regarding Alice Virginia Logan.

Alice and some of her family were found in the 1900 census, and a revealing document from 1908 answered many of my questions about her, but I will talk about those important items in Chapter 15, *The Great Migration*.

I found plenty of interesting things about Alice's adult life, but what about her childhood, her parents and siblings? How and where did she and Otho meet? Our ancestors left breadcrumb trails of documents in various places. A consultant at the Sutro Library in San Francisco recommended I search for Alice Virginia Logan in all Maryland counties and the bordering formerly free states of Pennsylvania, West Virginia, Virginia, and Ohio.

Google search and numerous genealogy websites gave no information about my Alice, even trying permutations of "Alice Virginia Logan," and "Virgie Logan" born between 1845 and 1855 in Maryland, West Virginia, Ohio, and Pennsylvania. I had not found any direct hits that met the desired criteria, not in any county, or in any state.

Even though this was not my primary directive for this book, I felt driven to find *something* about Alice's early past. Here are four theories I explored to see if we could find Alice's parents and siblings, her slave owner (if she had been a slave), or anything substantive about her early years before marrying Otho in 1867.

Theory #1: Alice Was a Free Woman Prior to 1865

This first theory assumed Alice was born free, or manumitted at some point, before the end of slavery. The comprehensive *African American Manumissions of Washington County* book listed only two "Alice" entries: Ardenia Alice and Alice Jane Miles. This suggested to me that neither Alice nor Virginia seemed to be common names for black women in Washington County, at least not among free black women. There were no people surnamed "Logan" anywhere in the book, but I could not yet conclude Alice was a free woman.

I checked the 1850 and 1860 Censuses for Alice, Virginia, or Virgie Logan, who lived in Maryland or the adjacent states of West Virginia, Virginia, Pennsylvania, and Ohio between her 1850 birth year and 1864 end of slavery. There was an Alice Logan in Cecil County in 1850 but she was 35 then, and my Alice was newly born in 1850. It *is* certainly possible that this Cecil County Alice Logan adult was the mother of my Alice, but I could not confirm that in time for this book.

There was an Alice Logan in Baltimore in the 1870 Census, but she was 16 and white. By 1870, my Alice was living with Otho, so the Baltimore Alice could not be my family member.

There was a mother and daughter named Alice in the Peter Logan family in 1880, but my Alice was living with Otho in 1880, not with the Logan household.

I also checked the Freedmen's Bureau in vain for "colored" people surnamed Logan in Maryland.

Further, looking at military records for Logans in Maryland and adjacent states in the hope of identifying Alice's father, resulted in no Logans in the military who were black, colored, mulatto, or Negro. It is possible that a white Logan in the military was Alice's father, but I could not prove it yet.

Alice may have been a free 10-year-old girl in the 1860 census, but may not have been enumerated, like Prince Williams, and many other free black people were not counted in the census for some unknown reason.

Finally, in 1850, an adult woman named Rachael Logan lived in Hagerstown with William, Sallie, and Robert Logan, a woman named Mary J. Grey, and an 11-year-old named **Alice L.** Grey who was born in Maryland and attended school in 1860. There was no indication of Mary or Alice's race, so I presumed they were all white.

Was my Alice Virginia Logan the daughter of Mary Grey (whose maiden name was Logan and who later married someone surnamed Grey?) If true, then my second great-grandmother may have been white, or so white-looking that the census taker assumed she was white. I could not prove or disprove that interesting supposition that Alice was a free woman, so I shall presume she had been a slave.

Theory #2: Alice Was the Slave or Daughter of a Logan in Washington County

Next, I considered the possibility that Alice was born in Washington County in about 1850, and was the slave of someone surnamed Logan. The most obvious and likely solution was that Alice was the slave of the County Register William Logan. That powerful man signed nearly every probate record in Washington County, including Joseph Ingram's 1834 estate and Prince Williams' 1843 Probate records.

In fact, William Logan signed many other probate records that lawyer/sons John and Benjamin Ingram facilitated. Did the Ingrams and Logans have more than just a professional relationship with William, bringing their slave-servants with them to social gatherings where they could have interacted? Conversely, did their slave-servants meet at the Ebenezer Church or other social functions in Hagerstown and Sharpsburg? Or had Otho been hired out to work for William Logan, as he had been to Benjamin South? Is that how Otho and Alice met? Being nearly twice Alice's age, was this Otho's first marriage, or did he have another wife that I didn't know about? I would have loved another transcendental visit from Otho or Alice.

Barring a spiritual mind meld,[126] I attempted to perform a descendancy analysis, exploring the Logan and Williams family trees in a top-down method, from Alice, down to her children, then her children's children, etc., with the hope of finding present-day Logan scions who matched my DNA. There were so many black Williams in Maryland that I had difficulty ensuring I was finding the correct ones. At that time, I was unable to prove or disprove the theory, but it seemed most likely that Alice's slave master was associated with William Logan, for the reasons mentioned above.

I printed an index of all Washington County land records from 1787 through 1865 involving all persons surnamed Logan to find a bill of sale involving someone named Alice, Virginia, or Virgie. There were about a hundred Logan land deeds during that period, but only a handful of records involved slaves in some way, and none involved a slave named Alice, Virgie, or Virginia Logan in Washington County, Maryland.

Theory #3: Alice Was the Slave of a Logan in Another State

The 1870, 1880, and 1900 U.S. Censuses all agreed that Alice was born in Maryland. Nevertheless, it was possible Alice was owned by Logans who lived just over the border into Virginia (other adjacent states to Maryland were non-slave states), but I could not prove or disprove this possible theory.

Theory #4: Alice Was the Slave of Someone With a Non-Logan Surname

Many people had regular contact with the Ingram family—like the Funks, Keedys, Souths, Newcomers and Bakers. Did any of them have a slave named Alice Virginia Logan? Would other white movers and shakers in the county trade or lend their slaves to or from the Ingrams for short or long periods of time?

Since Otho Williams was often hired out to various families, perhaps one of them had a slave girl named Alice who turned Otho's eye when he was hired out to work for her master. Since the Bakers and Newcomers were Mennonites, whose religion generally did not support slavery or discrimination,[127] it is unlikely they would have been Alice's owner.

There were 113 mulatto females in Washington County, Maryland, according to the 1860 Slave Schedule. I studied the slave owners of sixteen mulatto females between the ages of 8 and 12, which would have approximated Alice's age in 1860. Three of the sixteen were crossed off the list because I noted they were living next to their former master in 1870, during the same time when Alice would have been living with Otho

Williams. Could one of the remaining 13 mulatto females from 1860, aged 8 to 12, have been my Alice Williams? It was possible, but more information was needed to prove it.

The elephant in the room is that I have no idea whether Alice began using the surname Logan after emancipation for any particular reason. She literally could have chosen that name on a whim. It did not need to have been associated with a slave owner or parent surnamed Logan.

* Who Was Margaret A. "Peggy" Williams Hanson? *

While we do not know much about my third great-grandmother's childhood or parents, there are several interesting documents which do paint a picture of her being an industrious woman who made the most of her circumstances during the period of slavery and afterward.

An Ebenezer Church Cemetery record indicated that Margaret was born in 1796, died in Funkstown in 1868, and was buried in the church cemetery in Hagerstown, Washington County.

Margaret may have "married" Prince Williams sometime before their first child, Samuel, was born in 1818.

Records suggest she may have born ten or more children, including Samuel, Patsy, Matilda, Malinda, Mary, Henry, Prince, Hezekiah, Otho, and Margaret Elizabeth. Some, or all, of those children *may* have been fathered by Prince Williams.

Joseph Ingram's 1834 Will inferred that "Pegg" (a nickname for Margaret) was an older domestic house slave. He specified that "My black woman Peggy shall remain with my exec (the executor was John Ingram) as a slave and work for anyone of the family that she sees proper, or any other person who the family approve of, and she is to be rewarded for her services by those persons she labors for, and the said Peggy to pay to my exec one dollar per month to be a support for her in case she becomes unable to labor."

That statement leads one to believe that Peggy had been part of the Ingram family for quite some time and that she had some measure of power, or standing, within that family. However, it was possible that Joseph's "young family of Negroes" could have been *acquired* [purchased, traded, bequeathed by someone else] before his death in 1834.

Since the Will says Peggy "should be rewarded," it implies she was paid for her services, which is unusual for a slave. A slave might be allowed to make extra money on the side by selling handmade crafts or food, but to be paid for their normally expected work in the slave master's house was unusual. For example, daughter Mary created intricate quilts that she may have sold for extra money. If Margaret was paid for her work in the Ingram home, she could have amassed some measure of personal savings of her own, with which she could purchase clothes or other items she might desire.

If Margaret wasn't freed upon Joseph's death, it could simply be a result of an 1826 law which forbade owners from selling slaves who were over 45; she was 47 when Joseph Ingram died in 1834.[128]

Margaret was a slave of the Ingram family until Prince died in 1843 when he requested the Ingrams free her or let her live as though she were free (Figure 11.2). She married William Hanson before 1850 and lived for twenty-five years in the Funkstown home Prince had purchased for her.

Figure 11.2. Inspired by "Free women of color with their children and servants." by Agostino Brunias.

* What May We Surmise About Margaret's Parents and Childhood? *

I could not prove, but surmised, that Margaret could have been born in the Ingram household in 1796, and her unknown mother and father could have been slaves of Joseph's father, John Ingram, who died in 1809 in Washington County. John's parents were Peasly Ingram and Ruth Hammond, and their parents were born in England.

There was an older slave in the Ingram household, Charles Solomon, who was born in 1780 and freed in 1834 upon Joseph's death, whose Will stated: "Charles shall act for himself and work as he pleases."

Another slave, Jacob Jeffries, was also freed upon Joseph's death. Since the Ingrams had a track record of keeping their slaves for a long period, could Jacob have been Margaret's brother? Was Charles Margaret's father who had served the Ingram family for many decades? Charles Solomon and Otho's sister, Mary, were free blacks listed in John Ingram's home in 1850.

Searching the 1850 Census, I noted with interest that there were 1,828 free black people in Washington County, Maryland. The vicinity of Boonsboro, near the Ingram home, included the mulatto family of Lavinia, Mary A., Mary C., and Samuel L. Solomon, who were assumed to be the children of Ingram's former slave, Charles Solomon (were they related to Margaret?).

Living close by them was Sarah Williams, 38, who was freed by her father-in-law, Prince Williams, in 1843. Sarah's husband, Samuel Williams, was freed by the Ingrams in 1854. Next door to Sarah was a white man named Jacob Bear who was living with a mulatto woman called Lydia Haden.

Several black and mulatto family surnames were likely acquaintances, or perhaps close friends, of my Williams family, including: Bell, Briscoe, Brooks, Brown, Coffees, Dorseys, Douglass, Gates, Gross, Gwinn, Helms, Keys, Keyser, Matthews, Phoenix, Ringgold, Shorter, Thomson, Washington, and Wolfe families. Otho's youngest sister, Margaret Elizabeth Williams, freed in 1860, would marry Abraham Briscoe that same year. It seemed that Boonsboro might have been a safe haven for free blacks and perhaps more humane towards slaves.

A free person of color like Prince married to a slave like Margaret could have been fraught with insecurity that endangered a family life constantly threatened with possible upheaval.[129] In cahoots with the 1831 send-free-blacks-back-to-Africa movement, free blacks were invited to renounce their freedom, in a ploy to keep them from being separated from their spouse/family.[130] In some cases, when an enslaved spouse was threatened to be "sold South," the free spouse attempted to purchase their freedom—an attempt that was often denied by the slave owner. Did Prince attempt to buy his wife's freedom like he did his son Samuel's wife, Sarah? Did Margaret live in constant fear of losing her kids, or were the Ingrams "kind masters" who wanted to keep their family together?

It seems Prince and Margaret were luckier than most free/slave married couples. Except for periodic hiring out of sons Samuel, Otho, and

Henry to work for other whites, the Ingrams seemed to allow the Williams family to live together at the Ingram Farm. That means Margaret could have had the pleasure of mothering her own children. That is not a flippant statement. Many slave women had their children torn from their breasts on the auction block, but Margaret was able to hold her children close. She may have had to care for, or wet-nurse, the white Ingram babies, as well as her own.

* The Race Card *

A critical question that fueled my initial research still loomed large in my head: "who are my white people?" Eleven of my present-day Williams family members have inordinately high percentages of European DNA. Did Prince or Margaret, and/or their children, have an equal mix of African and European blood?

Otho and his brother Henry were listed as mulattos in the 1870 Census, and Samuel was described as a mulatto in the 1860 census. Margaret Elizabeth was reported "of a yellow or light copper color" according to her 1860 Manumission document. Was the father of Otho, Hezekiah, and Margaret Elizabeth a white man, or a mulatto, who created mixed-race babies with Margaret?

The 1868 distribution of Prince's Will by Edward Ingram indicated that Samuel, Henry, Hezekiah, Otho, and Margaret Elizabeth, were Prince's children. However, Prince was described as being "of a black color" on his 1812 Freedom Certificate, so was he the blood father of all of Margaret's children, even the ones described as mulatto? The other five children who weren't mentioned in Prince's Will are presumed to have died before 1868 when the estate was distributed. Was Prince the father of all ten of Margaret's children? Does that infer that Prince's wife Margaret was light-skinned, possibly half-white? Is that the only way that so many of their children could be regarded as mulatto?

No, Margaret was described as "black" in the 1850 and 1860 Slave Censuses, as well as in Joseph Ingram's Will where he says, "My *black* woman Peggy." That indicated to me that Margaret was of a darker hue, just like her husband Prince. How, then, was it possible that nearly half of their children—Otho, Henry, Hezekiah, and Margaret E.—were described as having a lighter skin tone? Were some of them fathered by one of the Ingram sons still living in the household—John, Benjamin, Joseph, or Edward—or some other white man? Figure 11.3 illustrates this niggling question.

The elephant in the room was certainly one of my most coveted unanswered questions about Margaret. Were either of her parents white?

Did Joseph Ingram (1762-1834) share his essence with Margaret's mother? Were John Ingram and Margaret brother and sister, born in the same year of 1796? DNA testing might be able to confirm that assertion if I can find a DNA match from present-day Ingrams to my family.

Nicka Sewell-Smith, an expert on African American genealogy and DNA analysis, advocates examining the married surnames of female family members to attempt to find common ancestors that may be validated by DNA research. Therefore, I chose to employ a descendancy analysis for Joseph Ingram and his wife, Rachel Perrin (1774-1830). I studied their children and all of their male and female descendants, keeping in mind the married surnames of Joseph Ingram's daughters, including Huyett, Ingram, Oswald, Price, Swope, and Ward. Could I find a DNA match to me from their current-day family?

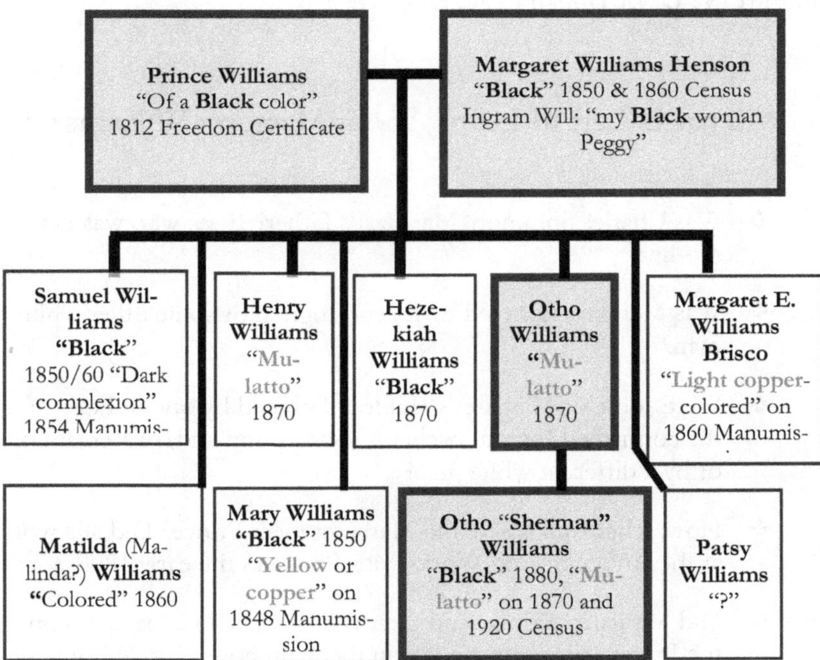

Figure 11.3. Documented skin pigmentation of Kathy Marshall's ancestors.

Could Margaret have been a forced, or consenting concubine of Joseph Ingram, or his sons John or Benjamin Ingram? Some experts in Maryland and at the Oakland, California, Family Life Center suggested to me that by Joseph specifying "my young family of Negroes" in his 1834

Will that perhaps the slaves Margaret Elizabeth, Patsy, Matilda/Malinda, Hezekiah Harry/Henry, Samuel, and Mary may have been Joseph's *children*, as well as his property.

One of my contacts in Maryland indicated it was common for a master to refuse to sell his "favorite" (i.e., concubine/consort) slave. Was Joseph the actual father of many, or all, of Margaret's children prior to his death in 1834, even though Prince's 1868 estate claimed five of them as his own? Maybe that's why Prince bought the freedom of daughter-in-law Sarah, instead of his wife's. Perhaps owner John Ingram refused to sell Margaret.

I have not yet found probate, or other documentary evidence to confirm that Margaret, or her four mulatto/copper-colored children, were related to the Ingrams by blood.

I was hoping DNA testing would confirm whether or not we were genetically related to some other person of European descent on my Williams family line. I planned to explore that concept later in the book in **Part IV: DNA Doesn't Lie, Does It?**

* What Is Left to Learn About Margaret Williams? *

- Was Charles Solomon, Margaret's father? If so, who was her mother?
- Was Margaret fathered by Joseph Ingram or some other white man?
- Were some of Margaret's children fathered by one or both of the confirmed Ingram bachelor sons—John and/or Benjamin, or by a different white man?
- How, when and where did Margaret meet Prince? Did she work at the Antietam Iron Works with Prince in the early 1800s?
- Did Margaret, Prince, and their children live in a log cabin on the Ingram property, or, live in the main house for 24 hours per day service to the Ingram family?
- Can DNA analysis find answers about Margaret's parents?

PART III: WHAT FREEDOM BRINGS

Imagine a life in which you cannot read or write, where you sign your name with an X to vote, exchange money, or buy land. This was the reality for many African Americans in Maryland before and during Reconstruction, the period of readjustment from 1856 to 1877 following the Civil War. While Maryland established a public-school system in 1864, education remained segregated and unequal. African American schools were besieged by discrimination, from arson of schoolhouses to landowners' refusals to sell plots of land for the construction of the schools. The African American communities banded together, providing housing for teachers or school supplies. Despite these struggles, the 1870s and 1880s were described as "great periods of hope for African Americans."

Source: Historical Society offers glimpse of African Americans during Reconstruction, by Clara Vaughn.

Mary Marshall

Chapter 12 - Education and Equal Rights

* Educating the Newly Freed Citizens *

I can imagine how my ancestors would have received the news of their emancipation. "Glory be and hallelujah! We is free! We is free!"

Freedom came to Maryland's slaves in 1864, one year after President Lincoln signed the Emancipation Proclamation. That decree only applied to states fighting *against* the Union. Maryland, which fought *with* the Union, saw their slaves remain in bondage until the Maryland Constitution was changed to free them.

The newly-freed joined those who had already savored freedom and who had established communities in rural areas or towns. In many cases, there was a core of black families, free before the Civil War, in possession of land or other resources on which to build. These examples included Samuel Williams, Nathan Williams, and my third great-grandfather, Prince Williams, mentioned earlier in this book.

There was little civil recourse for the ill-treatment many blacks received at the hands of white employers, neighbors, and even county governments. For more than two hundred years, slavery stood at the core of Maryland life. Slaves grew the tobacco, harvested the wheat, dug the coal, and, like Prince Williams, smelted the iron upon which the economy rested. Slaves helped build the C&O Canal and the B&O Railroad, and they cared for their white owners' kids. It would not be easy for the whites in power to welcome newly freed blacks into an equal American life. Most ex-slaves did not know how to read or write because it was illegal to teach them when they were bondsmen and women.

To help prepare these new citizens to participate in American life fully, the Bureau of Refugees, Freedmen, and Abandoned Lands—more commonly known as the Freedmen's Bureau—was created by Congress in 1865 to address issues of "Reconstruction"[131] in the South. The Freedmen's Bureau's greatest impact was perhaps the establishment of freedmen's schools.

An 1865 Maryland law required that school taxes collected from black landowners "shall be set aside for the purpose of founding schools for colored children." Given the small number of black landowners in Washington County, only about 132 in 1870,[132] the school taxes collected for colored schools were minuscule.

In February 1867, the Washington County School Board minutes recorded: ". . . the appropriation made in November to Colored Schools shall be equally divided between Williamsport and Hagerstown." A year later they paid to the county colored schools the laughable sum of $25 apiece. Based on this, as woefully inadequate as it was, the Board reported to the Freedmen's Bureau that it had "paid what the law allows for these schools." According to the Freedmen Bureau's local agent in Harpers Ferry, this was the only county in Maryland to have allocated *any* money at all to the establishment of colored schools. Tolson Chapel, in Sharpsburg, was one of the first A.M.E. churches to be used as a "colored school." It still exists today as a historical site open to the public (see Figure 12.1).

The Tolson's Chapel trustees and congregation knew that education, so long denied to African Americans, both slave and free, was key to economic growth. Ignored by the county school board, they offered their Tolson's Church building to house a Freedmen's Bureau school. On an April morning in 1868, eighteen young African American students began their lessons in this new school, with their much-ostracized-by-whites teacher, Ezra Johnson. Twelve of the new students had been enslaved only four years earlier.[133]

The 1900 Census indicated that Otho's children all knew how to read and write. Did they start learning those skills in the mid-1880s at the Tolson school, or another colored school closer to their home? Tolson's, at 111 High Street in Sharpsburg, was about nine miles away from Otho's property near Benevola-Newcomer Road, so it was likely his children could not attend there regularly unless they could travel by horse.

Efforts at re-enslaving young black men and women through a revival of the 1793 and 1808 indentured servitude laws were reversed through the use of a *writ of habeas corpus* in the federal courts. Interestingly, the white Otho Holland Williams that I called ClerkOtho presided over the Orphan's Court from 1800 to 1845. It was ClerkOtho who testified on Prince's 1812 Freedom Certificate that he was a free man.

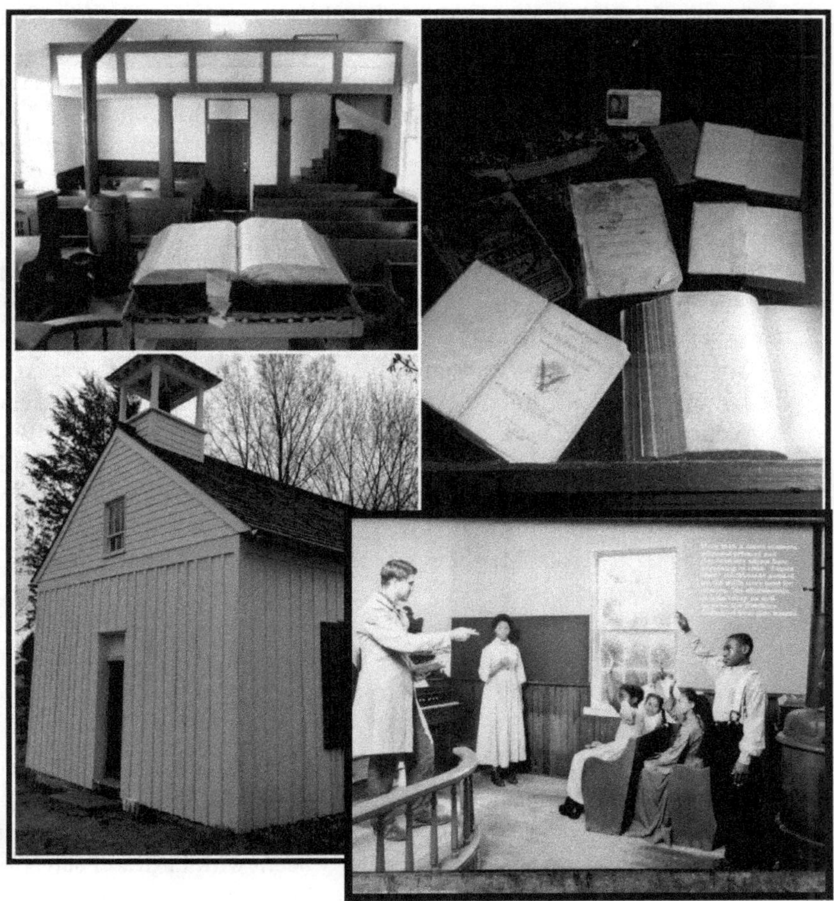

Figure 12.1. Tolson's Colored Church reenacted, Sharpsburg, MD. Photographs by Kathy Marshall, 2017.

The struggle for equal rights and opportunity would continue long after emancipation. I did learn that Otho's brother, Henry Williams, had a daughter named Katie Williams, who became a teacher at the colored school in Beaver Creek during the 1907/1908 school years.[134] My mother, Mary Ellen Carter Marshall, would have been gratified to know that her first cousin twice removed, Katie Williams, was an early educator for formerly enslaved people. My mother was a highly regarded Principal of a 90%-minority elementary school in the Sacramento Unified School District in California.

I can only think my formerly enslaved ancestors would be gratified to learn that several of their progeny became educators. My Great Uncle Charles Williams was a Metal Shop teacher in New York. My "Aunt" Lavata Williams was an elementary school teacher in Columbus, Ohio. My mother, Mary Ellen Carter Marshall, became a principal, and my sister, Carrie L. Marshall Malenab, became a vice-principal in the Elk Grove School District near Sacramento, California.

The subject of education was always the primary topic of conversation in my mother's house when all of us kids met there almost every Saturday. She taught us early on that getting a college education was our key to being successful in America.

My mom earned an Associate of Arts (AA) degree in Liberal Arts, a Bachelor of Arts (BA) in Early Childhood Education and a Master of Arts degree in Administration. I earned an AA degree in Sociology, a BA in French, and a Masters in Public Administration. Sister Carrie earned a BA degree in International Relations, a Teaching Credential, and an Administrative Credential. Brother Greg earned an AA degree in Fire Technology. My son Matthew earned an AA, BA, and Masters in Computer Science.

* New Black Voters *

During the Civil War, Maryland had seriously considered secession. There was a large population of black slaves in Maryland's southern and eastern counties, while its northern and western counties were populated largely by immigrant farmers of German descent with far fewer slaveholdings. As a result, the state was divided on the issue.

Tobacco farmers in southern Maryland felt more kinship with the Confederacy, while those in the northern and western counties were more aligned with the Union. Ultimately, Maryland decided against secession, but never fully supported Lincoln and the Republican party. Because Maryland had never seceded from the Union, it was not subject to the reconstruction policies passed in Congress, and ultimately it had no will to adopt a policy of universal manhood suffrage, which would have allowed *all* men to vote. The issue would have to be forced.

However successful the Republicans may have been nationally, the state of Maryland was experiencing a resurgence of the Pro-South Democratic party with their Governor Thomas Swann and control of the state legislature.

The Republicans, sensing the dismal political future they faced, resolved to seek suffrage for the 39,120 black males in the state, figuring this could help tip the scales in their favor and regain control at the state level. They knew they would have to seek black suffrage at the national level by promoting the recently proposed 15th Amendment which would force Maryland into Negro suffrage, despite the wishes of the Democratic political bosses that would control the state with an iron fist for the next thirty years.

Three-quarters of the states had ratified the 15th Amendment, and it became law on March 30, 1870. As we can see in the art and newspaper articles, it was celebrated with a great deal of hope and good feeling towards the newly enfranchised black race. For Maryland blacks, the atmosphere was one of a new beginning. While the 13th Amendment (which ended slavery) was important, the rhetoric which surrounded the 15th Amendment sparkled with idealism and hope.

Frederick Douglass demanded that Negroes seek "education for their children and money in their pockets" or they would not become independent voters. All the speakers that day agreed that this promise must, and would be, carried out. The celebration of the 15th Amendment was full of hope. Some African Americans were voted in as Senators and Representatives as a result of Reconstruction—a bright period after the Civil War in which the states formerly part of the Confederacy were brought back into the United States.

But as with any wish for perfection, reality always falls a little short. While voter turnout among blacks was very high in the 1870 congressional election (and elected at least one Republican Congressman), by the 1890s there was much talk of disenfranchisement for blacks.[135]

I found an interesting document regarding this topic. The 1877 Jury List for Washington County, Maryland, compiled by the Clerk to the Office of the County Commissioners, was made up of the "male taxable or residents" of the county "not over the age of sixty-five years, nor under the age of twenty-five years." From this list, the Circuit Court judges selected those of "intelligence, sobriety and integrity" to serve on juries. The list, therefore, is a useful genealogical tool, adding to the information about the inhabitants of Washington County.

The 1870 Census records a county population of 34,712. The Jury List includes 4,826 persons 25 to 65-years-old, who were taxable, i.e., they owned property. Unless Washington County broke from Maryland State Law, all of the members of the Jury List should have been white.

Amazing! There was an "Otho Williams" on the Washington County Jury List for the Boonsboro District in 1877. My second great-grandfather was the only Otho Williams living in the Boonsboro area, making it likely that my formerly enslaved relative was on that Jury List ten years prior to the "whites only" statute being removed from the law!

My mother served on the Grand Jury for one year in Sacramento, California, and would have been proud to know her great-grandfather could not only vote, but also did his civic duty and served on a jury if called.

* New Opportunities: Marriage, Work, and Land Ownership *

At the end of the Civil War, all black people were finally legally allowed to be married. As slaves, with the permission of their owners, they could "jump the broom" in a ceremony which represented the wife's commitment or willingness to clean the courtyard of the new home she had joined. Many legal marriage ceremonies after slavery were performed by the Freedmen's Bureau. It is entirely possible that Otho and Alice Williams were married in 1867 by the Freedman's Bureau, or at Tolson Chapel, but most likely they were married at the Ebenezer A.M.E. Church since Otho's father was among the first to be buried in their cemetery.

Once freed, four million enslaved people suddenly faced stark decisions. Many wondered where they would go, what they would eat, and how they would survive. Some stayed on plantations working as sharecroppers. Others fled for a "promised land," hoping to find jobs in cities. Some freedmen tried to scrape together nickels and dimes to buy land, creating all-black communities and towns across the country, where black people, sheltered from a white world, would run stores, banks, post offices, and schools.

I tried to find out what Otho did for a living immediately after emancipation. Was he a laborer for someone else, or a farmer on his own land? Or was he perhaps skilled in a trade like blacksmithing, bricklaying, or equipment repair? Did Otho continue to hire himself out to Mr. Benjamin South, who owned a farm near Funkstown and had paid the Ingrams $10 per month for Otho's services during slavery? I found no proof that Otho was given a portion of the wages he earned working for other masters. However, it was common practice for hired-out slaves to be paid a percentage of their earnings, and to continue working for their former masters or employers after slavery was abolished. The 1870 Census listed Otho as a day laborer, but he had promoted himself to farmer on his own land by the 1880 Census.

Deborah A. Lee, a historian in Virginia who worked with the *Journey Through Hallowed Ground* project, said. "They (blacks) would build buildings, whether it was a home or a fellowship hall. Because some of them were working to earn a living during the day, they would raise community buildings at night. There is a story of one church where the women would hold lanterns, so the men could work in the dark."

"Often," Lee said, "freedmen paid a premium for land—even from those sympathetic to them. Blacks often paid more for land than white people would, but owning land was very important to them. They wanted to develop their autonomy and independence as much as possible."[136]

By 1888, at least two hundred black towns and communities had been established nationwide. Some were modeled on black towns that had been formed after the American Revolution and during the antebellum era—from the late 1700s to 1860. In "*The Black Towns*," Norman L. Crockett wrote that not much was documented about daily lives, aspirations, and fears of the people living in such towns as Blackdom, New Mexico; Hobson City, Alabama; Allensworth, California; and Rentiesville, Oklahoma. Residents failed to record their experiences, and whites were not interested in preserving and collecting material on the black towns."

"Many of the black communities were tight-knit, rural, and centered around school and church," said Susan Pearl, a historian at the Prince George's County Historical Society in Maryland. "The first thing they would build was a church or a Freedman's Bureau school. That happened in Chapel Hill," a Prince George's community that freed blacks founded in 1868.

As described in the next chapter, *The Landowners*, my ancestors may have experienced similar unfair land transactions. But when you want to play with the big boys, sometimes you choose to make sacrifices to stay in the game.

Figure 13.1. Kathy Marshall at Otho and Alice Williams' five-acre property, Barnes Road, from the Old Roxbury Mill to Boonsboro, MD.

Chapter 13 - The Landowners

On a crisp, gray day in early April 2017, my guide/friend, Jane, drove me past Baker Hill—as the locals call this area, because many who live there descend from the Edward Baker family.

We rode down the gently winding two-lane Barnes Road, which used to be called "the public road on the way to Roxbury Mill" in the 1800s. It was bordered by pines and a forest of still-denuded deciduous trees. Jane and I seriously considered that my family traveled that same route nearly 150 years ago, perhaps in a horse-drawn wagon or buckboard, or by foot.

The meadows and leafless bramble bushes still thrived at the edge of the roadside, but now there were power and telephone wires overhead, buzzing with current technology.

Originally owned by the powerful Funk family, we passed several charming brick and stone homes dotting the luscious green meadows located near the Beaver Creek. Their property was later sold to the Keedy family. I wondered whether Otho and his sons worked for the Funks or Keedys during or after slavery. There were probate and land records involving their and my family names, so I imagined they did.

The sweet chirping of unseen birds was heard through the open truck window as we drove through that bucolic setting. We parked near the five-foot tall, black rock that officially describes the beginning of Otho's property (Figure 13.1). We passed a modest, two-story, white vinyl-siding house that sat next to a cream-colored house. Both structures were likely log cabin homes under the modern vinyl siding.

Rumors persisted that there was once a hand-dug well and an old house on the original property inhabited by Otho and his family until 1889 or so. It had been torn down long ago. We spoke in a reserved tone, as you would in a church, as we walked on the mowed portion of unimproved land which had been part of the five acres purchased by Otho and Alice Williams in 1869. I sank to my knees and kissed the ground upon which my formerly enslaved ancestors walked, toiled, and triumphed, for many years in the nineteenth century.

* Memories of Daddy's House *

The feeling was unmistakable. It was the presence of an ancestor. I sat on the grass, closed my eyes, and allowed a vision of what it might be that he wanted me to see.

Otho and Hezekiah stood outside the open front door of the small, whitewashed log cabin home. They hugged each other for a long time, tears welling up in their now-mature eyes.

"I still can't believe Mama is gone," said Otho, wiping his eyes. "Lord knows she was the glue that held our family together through thirty years of slavery, the Civil War coming to our doorstep, floods, as well as being a witness to our blissful marriages."

"I know what you mean, brotha," Hezekiah sat down on the front steps, his long legs splayed out in front of him, baking in his dark blue pants. His lanky torso leaned back against the door jamb, outstretched arms jutting from his sweat-stained, short-sleeved cotton shirt. He wanted to hide in the shade of the prickly pyracantha bushes bordering the front door landing. The first week of August was especially hot and humid. Rivers of perspiration beaded on his forehead, and upper lip. He moved to the porch swing where the temperature felt like it was a few degrees cooler.

Otho spoke up, "When Daddy was gone to the Antietam Iron Works and his other jobs for so many months at a time, Mama was always at the farm, directing us, keeping us together, and keeping us safe. Yes, she had to yell at us knuckleheads sometimes to make sure we was doing our chores. But she never let our spirits get low while we worked from sun-up to sun-down. Do ya remember when Mama would sometimes bring out a cool glass of fruit juice while we was plowing the fields, or she'd have a wet cloth waiting to wipe our faces when we came in at night?"

Hez nodded his head. "Yeah, she'd sing a pretty song in the morning to get us out of bed, or tell us stories about the old days when she was a little girl playing with her mama's hair after dinner. Even after Daddy died and Mama moved away to this house in Funkstown, she left sister Mary in charge of us kids who were left at the Ingram farm. She still made sure we was all doin' good."

"Yes, our beautiful mama always stayed strong," Otho said, the corners of his mouth turning upwards in the hint of a smile. How did she fix her hair in braids 'round her head, dress herself, light the kitchen stove, and brew the coffee before anyone else got up? She found a way to praise those Ingram girls when they got on her last nerve with their constant requests and orders. Her faith in the Lord that something better would come along paid off. She was so happy when she moved in here after Daddy's deathbed wish made her a free woman."

"Yeah, Hez. Remember when all those men started coming 'round the house, bringin' her flowers and gifts? They was sweet-talking real hard once it was known Mama was a widow with this nice piece of land! Big William Hanson, with those size thirteen feet and ham-sized arms, won out, even though he was six years younger than Mama. I am glad he made her happy for---what was it---something like twenty some odd years before he died?"

Hezekiah nodded his head. "Mama was more than ready to become a real wife who could live with her husband every day, not just stealing a few hours here and there, while living on someone else's farm, and taking orders from other people.

You could tell she was happy the last twenty-five years of her life, living every blessed day exactly as she wished, thanks to the money and property Daddy left her. When she wanted to paint the outside of the house white, she hired someone to paint it. When she wanted to stay in bed on a rainy winter day, she snuggled up an extra hour. When she didn't feel like cooking breakfast, she put the coffee pot on the stove and drank the bitter brew. If she wanted a new dress, she could buy whatever she wanted from the dress shop in town."

"Mama and William both kept this place up. I am thrilled we could buy these lots and keep them in the family, brotha." Otho hugged his brother again, smiles overtaking his tear-stained tanned face.

The siblings walked through the open door into the now-silent house sitting on half-lot 144. They had just purchased it, along with adjoining lot 143,[137] after their 72-year-old mother, Margaret, died on August 5, 1868. Otho, now 34, and Hezekiah, 37, were landowners! They owned the property at 25 East Cemetery Street, between South Antietam and South High Streets (Figure 13.2). They would live in this house with their respective wives, Alice Virginia and Minta, and Minta's elderly father, James Galloway.

The new property owners proceeded through each room, remembering how their mother would cut freshly baked bread on the wooden counter in the bright yellow kitchen. She set the dining table with her canned peach preserves, freshly churned butter, and small white ceramic plates with cobalt blue flowers.

They passed into the living room, imagining their mother sitting in the overstuffed rocking chair, her current knitting project waiting on the seat.

Each of the two bedrooms had a double bed covered with the light summer quilts created by their talented sister, Mary. Each sparse room contained a three-drawer walnut chest hand-made by William. An oil candle rested on the top. That their mother loved red and yellow flowers was evident in her choice of window curtains, as well as the cloth curtains that hung in front of the three-foot-wide closets.

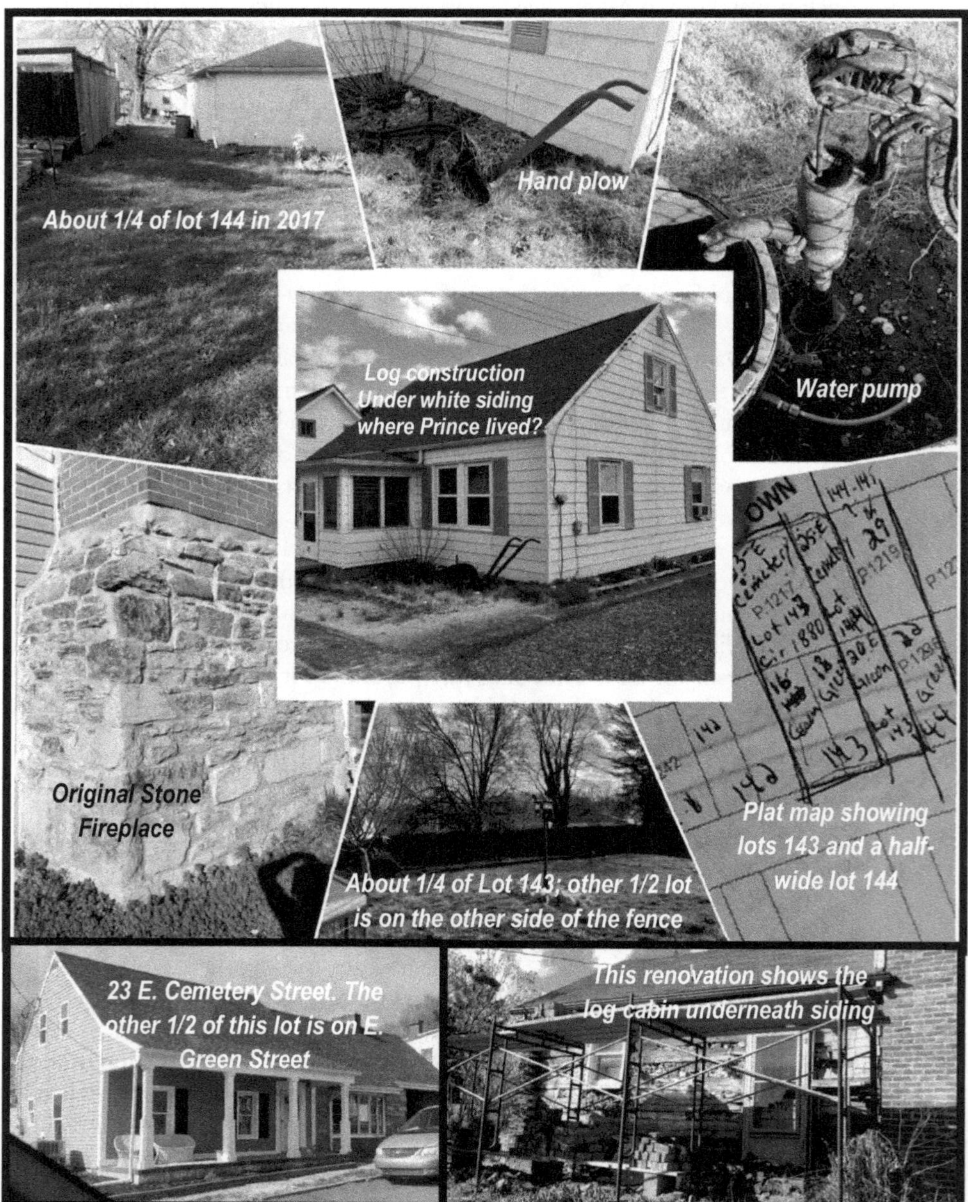

Figure 13.2. Funkstown lots 143 & half lot 144 purchased by Prince Williams in 1842, re-purchased in 1868 by Otho and Hezekiah Williams. Photograph by Kathy Marshall. 2017.

Stepping outside the empty house, fragrant smells from their mother's rose garden masked the odors of the water-closet located on the other side of the massive rock chimney. The brothers surveyed the five-foot corn stalks, which created a nearly impenetrable field of yellow-green colors almost ready for harvest.

Otho spoke to his mother's spirit. "I always dreamed, but never actually believed, Mama, that I would own land and property one day, but I did not think it would be at your expense. The Ingrams sometimes sent me and Hez to work for other white folks. I did some farming for them and used my skills as a blacksmith to fix their tools and shoe their horses, and the like. We grew up with those people coming around to the Ingram farm, doing business with Massa John and Massa Benjamin. They liked me, and I liked them well enough.

"When we was free after slavery, Massa John gave Hez and me some of the money we earned over the years, so we could buy this property for $690. You know, Mama, I been a hard worker after I growed out of my wild youth, and I always wanted my own farm. I try to be the man that you and Daddy raised, providing for my wife and, I hope, children in the future. Now, I want to buy more property and be a successful man." Otho finished his heartfelt soliloquy, happy with himself and the promise of a bright future.

The next morning, Alice and Minta cooked a breakfast of buckwheat pancakes, smoked bacon from last winter's curing, freshly laid eggs from the hen house out back, black coffee, and fresh peaches. They ate in virtual silence, each of them contemplating the altered trajectory of their lives. After the dishes were cleared by the women, Otho leisurely strolled out of *his* house, surveyed *his* land, and went next door to speak with Mrs. White. He had known her for years, as she was the same age as his mother, but this time he was the man of *his* own house. After acknowledging Mrs. White's condolences about Margaret's death, Otho began speaking to her about his dreams for the future.

"You know, Mrs. White," he started in an unusually low officious voice, "when Daddy bought this property in '42, there was only one structure here, this small log cabin house. Daddy tried growing wheat and rye that first year, sure, but I think corn grows best. Hez and I plan to build some more small homes on this land, split the lots so they can be sold separately, then buy some more land somewhere close by so we can do some real farming."

Mrs. White nodded her head as he spoke, listening to the grand plans of this man she had known since he was a rambunctious boy. *Margaret and Prince would be proud of Otho's gumption, but I hope he doesn't take on too much too quickly.*

After wishing Mrs. White a good day, Otho strode over to *his* dirty hand plow sitting in the front yard. He ran out of time to clean it the last time he had used it. Now that it was *his* plow for *his* land, he took it to the hand pump to be washed. Clasping the curved, slender iron handle attached to the pump, he raised it up, then down, up and down, until the water gurgled from the deep well that his father, Prince Williams, had dug in 1842.

Water splashed from the spigot into a waiting wooden bucket in which he had placed the muddied end of the plow. Otho used a chisel to scrape off hardened dirt from the plow blade and handles, then dampened a rough cloth to remove the last of the dirt clods and other debris. Once the plow was clean, he smeared a layer of oil over the entire tool to prevent rusting, then stored it in the front yard, satisfied that his plow was ready for its next use. [See the center photograph in Figure 13.2]

Otho and Alice enjoyed living in Funkstown with neighbors who would become close friends. Alice had moved in with Margaret, Otho, Hezekiah, and Minta when they married in November 1867, but now it was *their* home.

The four of them sat in the backyard reminiscing that first day as landowners. Otho began, "Remember when mama would pack a picnic lunch of roasted chicken, fresh peaches and cherries, and her light and flaky buckwheat biscuits after the church service on Sundays? We would walk the few miles to Beaver Creek with a blanket and fishing poles and come back home with two fish for each of us. Wading in the creek bordered with cool, leafy green shading us from the hot sun, was my favorite place to be on muggy summer days."

Hezekiah said, "I enjoyed sitting on the edge of the bank with a fishing pole, staring into the slowly moving greenish-blue water. It was so peaceful. I did not worry about anything but putting a red worm on the end of my hook and casting the pole into the smooth water."

"Ha! Remember that time you wasn't paying attention and fell in the river and was yelling like a baby because you didn't know how to swim?" Otho chided his older brother whose blushing fair complexion betrayed his embarrassment.

Hez responded, "I never been so scared in my life! I thought my heart would burst out of my chest. After that, I had that Newcomer kid to teach me how to float in the water in case that ever happened again. If we have kids, I'll teach them too."

"Daddy was smart to buy the property here. Living in Funkstown has real benefits. Because the town is bordered on three sides by Antietam Creek, and the creek meets up with the Potomac River twelve miles away, there was plenty of water for farming, and boats to move all sort of items—wood, grain, metal—up and down the state." The Antietam Creek was as a water source for grist mills.[138]

* A Place of My Own *

Months after his mother died, Otho met up with an old acquaintance, Nathan Williams, at the Ebenezer Church in Hagerstown. The usual small talk about the cold weather in early 1869 brought Otho to say, "I've been working at the iron furnace and the powder factory in Funkstown, as well as my small lot of corn at home. My dream is to buy another piece of property and become a farmer on my own land."

Nathan was the richest black man in Washington County, Maryland. In 1860, he had purchased the deteriorating 585-acre Fort Frederick, near Williamsport, for $7,000. During slavery, he had enough money to purchase the freedom of his family members, just as Prince had bought and freed his son Samuel's wife, Sarah.

"I had to laugh," Otho chuckled to Nathan, "when Jerry Thomas asked if I was the Otho Williams who owned the tract of land called the 'Garden of Eden'—you know, that large fruit orchard in Williamsport. Jerry read in the *Freedom and Torch Light Newspaper* that the land was deeded from John C. White & wife to Otho Williams in 1865. Well, it is true that I do live next door to Mrs. White, but no, I cannot even *think* about affording that huge property! It must have been one of the several rich white Otho Williams who lives here in Washington County."

Nathan was highly regarded in the eyes of colored and white citizens alike as a professional land mogul, and Otho felt safe in asking for Nathan's advice.

"Nathan, I must admit, now that I have tasted what it feels like to be a respectable landowner, I want more. Just like my brothers, Samuel and Henry, who are buying and selling small tracts of land left and right. I want to feel like I am as good as, and crave to be treated with respect, like any white man. I *have* to purchase another property, but which one? What would you recommend, Nathan?"

"Hmm . . . I recall hearing Ann Catharine Beeler is looking for someone to buy five acres of land for $1,100 near the Beaver Creek. It's on the public road leading from Roxbury Mills to Boonsboro. Do you know the area I'm talking about?"

Otho shook his head no, but exclaimed, "Five acres of land? Now that *is* a decent-sized piece of property, compared to my little part of an acre in Funkstown. You say she wants eleven hundred dollars? Too bad. We spent all our savings to buy mama's place," said Otho with a loud sigh.

Nathan moved a little closer and lowered his voice. "Let me tell you a little secret, my friend. Get you some white folks who like you and have them go with you to the bank. Ask them to tell the bank manager what a hard worker you are and how you will certainly be able to pay back a mortgage loan. Buy one piece of property and work it. Work it hard. Then a couple of years later, sell it for a higher price, pay back the bank, then do it again with a larger piece of property."

The mogul continued, "That's how I built my estate after Catherine Shearer brought me and my brothers and sisters from Virginia to Maryland in 1825. She helped me get my first piece of land and look at me now." Nathan turned around in a circle with his arms outstretched so Otho could admire his fine suit and polished shoes.

"Hmm, maybe me and Alice best look at the land first to see if we like it."

"Sounds like a smart idea, but don't wait too long," Nathan warned. "I've seen the land myself. There is a small house and a well on one side of it. There's a big—maybe eight-foot tall and round, craggy, black rock at the edge of the road. You can't miss it. Trust me, my friend, this property will be snapped up being so close to the mill and Beaver Creek. Well, good luck to you Otho," were Nathan's parting words, as he sashayed away to speak with some other friends leaving the church.

After this fortuitous meeting, Otho went home straight away to get Alice. He would take her to see the black rock property that very day.

Three weeks later there was pandemonium in the Williams' Funkstown house. "Oh, Otho, is this dress dignified enough? Do I look all right? Is, uh, this hat OK?" stammered Alice, getting herself more and more nervous as she finished pressing Otho's black suit, that was normally only worn to church and funerals. Alice was afraid her youth and inexperience would somehow jeopardize their ability to get a bank loan for the five-acre property they wished to buy that day.

"You look fine, Alice. Don't worry," Otho tried to calm his wife, who at 19-years-of-age had never been involved in a loan, or deed, or any bank transaction. She could read but not write her name; Otho could do neither. Both of them spent time combing their hair and making sure their fingernails were trimmed and clean, and their ashy skin was well-oiled. They wanted to be sure they looked the part of landowners as if the decision to loan them money hinged on their appearance alone.

When their neighbor and advocate, Mr. David Newcomer,[139] came in his buggy to pick them up at 10 AM, he carefully explained the deed reading and signing procedure to Alice. Twenty minutes later, the three of them were sitting in the bank office, listening to John H. Lakin, J.P. read the surprisingly short deed verbiage, transferring the five-acre property from Ann Catherine Beeler to Otho and Alice Williams.[140] Pointing to the place on the deed papers that had to be signed, Judge Lakin said, "And so, Mr. and Mrs. Williams, it is time to sign or make your mark on this line right here." Otho and Alice each made their mark on the appointed space. "The deed will be recorded nine days from now, on April 13, 1869," continued Judge Lakin.

The deal was done, just like that. Simple. Now Otho would learn whether he and Alice would sink or swim as multiple property owners.

* How Does Our Garden Grow? *

One year later, on April 23, 1870, screams pierced the quiet of the early spring morning.

"Look into my eyes, honey chil', and breathe, breathe," the neighborhood midwife told Alice. Sweating, writhing, panting, moaning, gasping at yet another sharp pain rippling through her belly, Alice didn't think she could survive another minute of labor.

Milder contractions had started during the middle of the night, but now the squeezing, gripping pains in her stomach came every seven minutes or so. Brother-in-law Hezekiah went to get the midwife when the sun's rays stretched their warm, yellow arms out from their nighttime blanket.

Fluffy feather pillows propped behind Alice's back helped her sit upright in the marriage bed, letting gravity help the straining baby inch downward, little by little, as the hours passed, oh so slowly. Like the old African way of squatting on one's haunches to let gravity encourage the birth canal to open, sitting upright in bed could help speed up delivery. That's what the midwife had told Alice's sister-in-law, Minta, who was helping during the long labor process.

Alice's stalwart supporters tied damp washcloths around her forehead and replaced them often to cool her heated efforts. The ladies kept up a steady stream of conversation to help keep the mother-to-be's mind off the incessant, rhythmic tightening inside her belly, as the baby's head began to wedge lower into the birth canal.

This was Alice and Otho's first baby. Alice was not quite 20-years-old and had no idea whatsoever what the birthing process would be like. Two hours of agony stretched into four, the contractions getting stronger and stronger every few minutes. The midwife told Minta to boil water and have clean cloths ready, as she inserted a finger in the canal to get a better idea of how things were progressing.

Otho, the nervous father-to-be, found refuge outside the hustle and bustle of the house, astounded that his otherwise quiet wife could yell like a banshee.

To get his mind off the ordeal, he decided to fire up his small smithy and make some horseshoes for his neighbor, hoping the hammering would drown out his wife's alarming cries. He wanted his brothers, or friends, or even their neighbor, Mrs. White—anyone—to join him outside. He wanted someone to make some noise, tell him some jokes, *anything* to cover up the frightening sounds coming from his house. Alas, nothing seemed to overshadow his wife's keening.

Otho didn't know what was happening inside his house. Was his wife alright? Was the baby alright? He knew many women had died in child-birth. Was Alice dying? Helpless to reduce her pain or hurry the birthing process along, or save her, not knowing was worse than knowing.

Towards noon, the screams stopped. It was rather surreal not to hear them anymore. Now it was too quiet. Otho hoped everything was all right, but he didn't dare go inside to check. What if the baby had died? What if his beloved Alice had---no, he could not imagine it.

Just then, a high, piercing sound, like a bird strangled in the talons of an eagle, or a sickly tomcat, came from inside his house, then everything was quiet again, followed by another wailing sound and another.

A few moments later, Minta rushed outside to where Otho was standing, her face wan from fatigue, but with a broad smile on her face. "You have a strong son, brother-in-law. Alice will be fine, with rest. We are cleaning up the baby and Alice right now. I'll let you know when you can come in to see your boy." With that heartening news, Minta turned on her heels and jogged back to the delivery room. Otho had a son. A new generation had begun.

Edgar E. Williams was a strapping boy who latched onto his mother's breast soon after birth. The midwife taught Alice how to nurse her child, how to fold a cloth diaper into thirds, how to place the baby's buttocks in the center of the folded cloth, then tie the ends around his waist to keep the cloth on. Alice learned how to clean Edgar after he had soiled his diaper, how to bathe and clothe him. The oval wooden cradle purchased by Otho's daddy, Prince, in 1834, would be used to rock baby Edgar.

Alice and Otho were very happy about their new addition, but oh how wonderful it would be if their parents could be alive to witness this miracle of life, their descendant. They hoped Hez and Minta would have babies soon, so Edgar would have playmates. Little did they know they would have many babies in their lifetime: nine Williams children born between 1870 and 1883.

Otho did his best to make enough money by working different farming and blacksmithing jobs. As a day laborer in the early 1870s, he worked to feed his wife and the babies who joined their family every couple of years.

Samuel M. was born in 1872, then Otho Sherman Williams—who became my first great-grandfather—came into the world in 1874.

William Franklin Wheeler Williams arrived in 1877, but died in 1882 "near Benevola, August 4th, five years, eleven months, and four days," according to his obituary in the local *Herald and Freedom Light* newspaper.

Charles E. Williams, born in 1879 had passed away sometime before his 21st birthday. My Great Uncle, Charles Elmer Williams, who was 92-years-old when told his life's story was commemorated in my first book, *The Ancestors Are Smiling!* was named after his young uncle.

Finally, Mary Irene, their first baby girl, was born in 1880, followed by Alice Virginia Williams in 1883. Two other babies were stillborn.

It was clear. Otho needed to make more money to pay the taxes each year on his property and feed and clothe his family. It was an emotional decision, but Otho and Alice, and brother Hezekiah and Minta, decided to sell the family's Funkstown home that their daddy had originally purchased in 1842. They received $475 from their old friend, Jeremiah Balls. The money from the sale was split between the brothers and helped Otho's family exist for a few more years.[141]

"Winter is coming" whispered the trees as their leaves turned their reddened faces toward the waning autumn sun. The crisp, cold nights in the fall combined with bright, sunny days to spur the production of red leaves in the sugar maple trees lining many roads in western Maryland. As much food as possible was stored in the cellar, for the old folks knew in their bones this weather was worse than usual.

Hushed voices became more insistent as the mercury dropped night after night and fluffy white snowdrifts covered the meadows like dry confectioner's sugar floating from a sifting sky. Bitter cold set in—15 degrees below zero. Two feet of snow forced the cancellation of New Year's celebrations in 1880.[142] These ominous conditions were a precursor to difficulties about to beset my ancestors and many of their neighbors.

* The Tide Turns *

As many a planter knows, farming revenues are often related to weather and national economic conditions. At the end of the 1870s, it seemed the Williams' fortunes were starting to grow. In 1879, a $600 mortgage was made by Otho and Alice unto Joseph Eavey who bought out Catherine Beeler who sold them the original $1,100 five-acre property. If the Williams defaulted on the promissory note to pay the remaining $600 back, they would forfeit their five acres of land adjoining the lands of David Newcomer, Samuel and Andrew Funk, and others owning property on the public road leading from the Roxbury Mill [present day Barnes Road].[143]

Soon after that, they received an offer too good to be true. Samuel and Mary Funk, and Andrew and Catherine Funk—neighbors who were movers and shakers in Washington County—offered Otho and Alice nineteen acres of land situated on Beaver Creek adjacent to his existing five-acre property, for $1,242.18. (Figure 13.2)

"You know, Alice, I've always wanted more land," Otho continued. "Henry and Samuel are doing so well buying property, that I feel *we* need to take this chance to buy more," Otho said, trying to persuade his wife to agree with his way of thinking.

Alice's fist covered her mouth. Her brow furrowed, and her eyes squinted. She wanted to say the right thing. After a brief pause, she said, "Well, Otho, you know I don't like being in debt for the first five acres. I am afraid that if we add more, we certainly won't be able to pay it back. We could lose everything. It is already too much stress on your shoulders with all of these babies. Are you sure you want to buy more and get into more debt?" Alice questioned.

After Otho's assertive nod of his head, she acquiesced, saying, "Well, okay husband, if you think it's best."

"We need to take this chance, Alice." Confident on the outside, Otho wasn't so sure on the inside. He had started having occasional chest pains and brief bouts of dizziness. He thought it was from lifting the hand plow the wrong way. Or maybe he was just too tired. Or maybe he was worrying that he couldn't pay off the medical bill for little William Franklin Wheeler Williams, named after Dr. Wheeler who helped William survive a complicated birth.

Otho felt sure God would intervene and make everything work out.

This was the chance Otho had been waiting for. Otho now had a built-in workforce, as did many farmers. Sons Edgar, then 10; Samuel, 7; and Otho Sherman, 5, helped their father plow the fields, sow the seeds, and pluck the weeds. They primarily grew wheat on their five acres and used some of their extra pasture-land for cattle. Surplus wheat was loaded onto carts pulled by mules and taken to Roxbury Mill down the road from his house, or Newcomer's Mill, or Edward Ingram's Mill for processing.[144] During harvest time, Otho got help from his brothers, Hez and Henry, or from other people he could hire during that busy harvest time of the year. When the boys were old enough, they helped him take the harvest to Mr. Newcomer's mill a few miles down Beaver Creek.

The 1880s were hard years. It got harder and harder to keep up with the mortgage, the taxes, and the Williams ever-growing family. By 1883, they had seven living children under the age of 14.

"Alice," Otho said one day, "the slope is getting slippery with each new child, and the prices for wheat are falling faster than we can catch up. I don't need to remind you that we were late with last year's taxes. Sam Funk told me this morning they purchased the 1879 debt that we took on with Joseph Eavey. Now we owe the Funks a total of $1,240, for the first five acres we bought, and the additional nineteen acres they included in the new deed for $600. They think we can make it now that the children are getting a little older and can help out more. We might even be able to hire a gang of workers in town." Alice looked doubtful.

The tide of Otho and Alice's fortunes must have turned for the worse, for a deed was executed and delivered in 1888. It indicated the mortgage issued to Otho Williams in 1880 by the Funks was not paid on time. Otho and Alice's land reverted to Samuel Funk after May 8, 1888.[145]

This non-payment of mortgage may have occurred because Otho had died and his family could not keep up the payments to Sam Funk. [Note: this is only my supposition; no death records have been found for Otho Williams.]

In 1889, as a result of the public sale of Otho's estate, Edward Baker bought the five-acre property that Otho defaulted on, for only $440. This land was adjacent to Baker's existing holdings in what is called the "Baker Hill" area on the road to the old Roxbury Mills. In fact, according to local expert, Jane Neff, just about everybody who lives in that area today is a descendant of Edward Baker.[146]

One final land transaction from 1892, involved Henry A. Williams and his "wife" Alice A. Williams, and Jacob Keller. That land was located along the east margin of the Franklin Railroad from the public road leading from Maugansville to Hagerstown. I believe this was Otho's brother, Henry, and Otho's wife, Alice, who co-signed/marked their signatures on this deed.

By 1900 Alice had moved her family to Greencastle a few miles north of Maugansville, in Franklin County, Pennsylvania. Their new home was about twenty miles north of the property she and Otho had owned for two decades before it had to be sold in 1889.

* Success After Slavery? *

"You darn right we were successful!" a familiar voice popped back into my head after nearly a year of silence. Otho continued, talking faster and faster, needing me to understand that his life did matter. "Let me clearly explain precisely why we should hold our heads up high:

1. We survived slavery with our family intact at the Ingram Farm.
2. My brothers and me learned farming and blacksmithing skills we could use when we were free, and my sisters learned how to run a household.
3. We survived four Civil War battles in our backyard without being shot, starved, or diseased.
4. We purchased our father's property in Funkstown after mama died in the summer of 1868.

5. Five of our nine children lived to have families of their own, who had families of their own, resulting in this book's author.
6. We purchased five acres of land a few years after the end of slavery.
7. In 1870, our estate was worth more than all the other blacks and many of the whites out of sixty-seven of our Funkstown neighbors. Our real estate holdings of $1,000 were greater than eleven of those neighbors.
8. In 1880, we bought another nineteen acres of fine land next to our original five acres. Part of that we rented out as pasture, and the other part we farmed and sold the surplus wheat.
9. Alice and I made a respectable life for our family. We usually had enough food to eat, clothes on our back, and there was always work to do.
10. Most people called me Mr. Williams, not "boy," as heard during slavery.
11. We made friends with and had the support of many people, both black and white.
12. We were involved in seven mortgage/land deeds during my lifetime.
13. Even though I couldn't read or write, I think I did just fine, but I made sure my kids learned to read, write, and do their numbers.
14. I was on the Washington County Jury List for the Boonsboro District in 1877, like any man.
15. Yes, we struggled to make a profit, and the family eventually lost the land after I died, but I had progressed from slave to laborer to farmer in my lifetime. I think that's VERY successful!
16. Last, but not least, my second great-granddaughter, Kathy Marshall, is honoring me by writing a book about my life, about my descendants, and about my ancestors. Our family legacy of hard work and beating obstacles will live on forever."

* The Williams Family Properties *

Prince and Margaret's sons were landowners and contributing members of society. Figure 13.3 documents their land transactions. The bottom line is that my formerly enslaved black ancestors carved out a piece of the American pie once laws allowed them to live by the tenets of the U.S. Constitution. "Yes, our Williams ancestors were successful!" shout their enormously proud descendants.

First	To/from	Names	Kind	Book	Page	Year	Summary of Transaction
Henry	from	Jesse and Catherine Margaret Morrison	Deed	IN16	432	1862	Sold Henry part of "Well Done" for $225.
Henry	from	Daniel Fahrney	DofM	IN18	186	1864	Freed from Fahrney who inherited Henry from John Ingram.
Henry and Mary	from	Jessee and Catherine Margaret Morrison	Deed	IN18	687-688	1864	Sold Jesse part of "Well Done" for $25.
Henry A. and Mary	to	Sarah A Moxley	Deed	IN19	234	1865	Land in Hagerstown sold for $475
Henry A.	from	Wm Heyser & Magda.	Deed	LBN1	297	1866	William sold lot 51 in Hagerstown to Henry for $500
Henry A. and Mary	to	Henson T. Summers	Deed	LBN1	28	1866	Henry sold to Henson "Well Done" for $375
Henry	from	George Brown and Elia Jane Wagoner	Deed	76	263	1878	George sold property on Church Street in Hagerstown to Henry for $150.
Henry and Mary	to	Wm Ridenour	Deed	85	156	1884	Lot #172 in Hagerstown
Otho and Hez	from	Edward Ingram	Deed	McKK1	92	1868	Paid Edward for Lots #143 and 1/2 #144 in Funkstown. No price mentioned. Ex & deld to Newcomer May 7, 1871.
Otho	from	Ann C Beeler	Deed	McKK1	402-403	1869	Otho paid Ann $1100 for 5 acres in Roxbury Mills.
Otho and Alice, Minta and Hezekiah	to	Jeremiah Balls	Deed	McKK6	290	1874	Otho and Hez sold lots 143 and 1/2 144 in Funkstown to Jeremiah Balls.
Otho and Alice	to	Joseph Eavey	Mortg	78	95-96	1879	Otho indebted to Eavey for $600. If they do not repay Eavey within 3 years, with interest, they will forfeit their 5 acres in Roxbury Mills. Mortgage released on Feb 1, 1900.
Otho	from	Samuel Funk	Deed	78	549	1880	$1,242.18 for former Jacob Keedy 19-acre property in Roxbury Mills land along the Beaver Creek.
Otho and Alice	to	Samuel & Andrew Funk	Mortg	78	550	1880	Otho indebted for $640 to Samuel and Andrew Funk. Ex & deld Roxbury Mills property to Sam Funk May 8, 1888.
Prince	from	John Cox	BofS	PP	118	1834	Household goods
Prince	from	John Sharer & wf	Deed	ZZ	44	1842	Lot 143 and 1/2 144 in Funkstown
Samuel and Sarah	to	John W Funk	Deed	IN10	67-68	1854	Received $375 from John Funk for land in Mount Aetna.
Sarah	from	Samuel Bower & wf	Deed	IN9	320-321	1855	Funkstown lots 102-103
Samuel and Sarah	from	Catherine Erich	Deed	IN15	683-684	1861	"Kellys Delight" part of "Choice" southeast of Funkstown, $400
Samuel	from	Robert EH Boteler & Rebecca	Deed	IN19	400	1865	Robert sold Funkstown lots 101+102 for $175 to Samuel
Samuel	from	Rebecca Smith	Mortg	LBN1	665-666	1866	Mrtg in Clear Spring for $400 - is this my Samuel?
Samuel and Sarah	to	Henry Eakle	Mortg	McKK2	505	1869	$125 for lots 100 and 101 in Funkstown
Samuel	to	Sarah	Deed	McKK3	22	1870	Samuel sold lots 100-102 in Funkstown to Sarah for $175
Samuel	to	Thomas Barnum	Mortg	McKK3	301	1870	Samuel granted Thomas undivided interest in 8 acres of Kelly's Delight, southeast of Funkstown. Mortgage rel. 1883.
Samuel and ___	to	Thomas Barnum	Mortg	84	184	1883	
Samuel and Eliza	to	David Stockslager	Deed	83	608	1883	

Figure 13.3. Maryland Land Records for Prince Williams and His Children.

Kanika Marshall
welded sculpture

Chapter 14 - Generations of Ironworkers

Figure 14.1. Hand-drawn rendering of the Antietam Iron Works complex as it looked in 1820, Sharpsburg, MD. Courtesy of Wayne McCrossin, owner of the Antietam Iron Works, 2017.

Did our present-day Williams descendants genetically inherit our mechanical and metal working abilities from our enslaved ancestors? This story has been passed down in our oral family history. Proving or disproving this supposition was the fifth goal of this project.

In early April 2017, the leaves were still absent from the sycamore and oak trees which border the meandering Harper's Ferry Road in South Washington County. It was late afternoon on that sunny spring day at the Antietam Iron Works in Sharpsburg, Maryland (Figure 14.1).

I felt like I was trespassing, not only on the property, but also intruding into history. There was an eerie pall, like the ghosts of the workers and my ancestors were watching me.

It was electric, almost like their charcoal fingers were reaching toward me bidding me to come closer. I could imagine an Alice in Wonderland experience of being sucked into the massive cave-like furnace and transported back into history.

We couldn't help but survey the remains of the massive fifty-foot stone walls of a still-intact iron blast furnace, which was built in 1763.[147] The imposing wall was perched against a hill on the south side of Harpers Ferry Road, running parallel to the Antietam Creek (Figure 14.2).

Figure 14.2. Antietam Iron Works furnace, Sharpsburg, MD. Photograph: Kathy Marshall, 2017.

Those carefully stacked walls were made from limestone, rugged granite, sandstone, slate, and marble.[148] Jane, my amazing guide, parked her gold truck in a small parking lot nearby. With camera and smartphone in hand and my heart racing, we strolled toward the furnace, each step taking us back through decades of my Williams' family history.

On the opposite side of Harper's Ferry Road, the Antietam Creek gushed from the still-pristine, four-arch Antietam River bridge, built in 1832 by John Weaver (Figure 14.3).[149] This is one of twenty-one historic stone-arch bridges in Washington County. The dark water roared over large rocks in the river, causing white caps downstream. Remnants of stone structures dotted the uneven land between Harper's Ferry Road and the creek.

Water-soaked, green grasses covered the ground, and brambles stretched up the hill on which the furnace was inset. More flora cascaded down the sides of the furnace stack to the edge of the two-lane roadway. The scene reminded me of the wild, frizzy hair that surrounds my face every morning. Three evenly spaced, ten-foot tall, red brick arches in the base of the tall structure begged closer inspection.

Figure 14.3. Antietam Bridge and part of the village in the background, Sharpsburg, MD. Photograph: Kathy Marshall, 2017.

I imagined the intense furnace fires that were once in the base of those arches. Once the requisite high temperature turned freshly dug iron ore into pig iron, a crude form of iron, it could be wrought into tools, nails, and ammunition. A glossary of ironworker terms is in Appendix J.

Standing there in one of the mammoth furnaces of the Antietam Iron Works, indescribable feelings of gratitude circulated through me. Being there in that sacred place of my formerly enslaved ancestor, made time stand still. I felt transported back to the early 1800s, where the smell of wood-smoke from the charcoal fires permeated every possible surface for miles around.

Is that why I love the smell of a campfire so much and have floor-to-ceiling pictures of forests in my bedroom? Is that why I love to create outdoor sculptures from recycled metal? Is welding really in my blood from my third great-grandfather, Prince Williams?

I fell into the reverie that invited my imagination to slip into the past and imagine Prince William telling me his story.

"Yes, over two hundred years ago, I used to stand in the middle of those arches with my arms stretched wide---when the furnace don't be lit, of course," his familiar deep voice boomed inside my head.

I did not have to guess who it was since I was just thinking about him. To be sure, I turned around and glanced at his left hand. Yes, part of his thumb was cut off, just how the Freedom Certificate described Negro Prince, my third great-grandfather.

I said, "Now here you are in my nineteenth month of trying to piece together your life. This may seem like a crazy question, but I just must ask. Triple G, how did you lose the tip of your thumb?"

Laughing heartily at such an unexpected query, Prince replied. "Well, you see when I was sold to Massa John McPherson in 1800, or thereabouts, he sent me to hep' the collier, a charcoal man named Robert, over at the Catoctin Furnace in South Mountain. There were three big furnaces there with lots of forests waitin' to be cut down. If I was a bird, I'd say there were trees as far as the eye could see.

"My first job was as a woodcutter, choppin' down trees with Negro Charlie. Holdin' the long axe handle like this (he pretended to hold it like a baseball bat), Charlie and me would each swing our axe toward one side of the tree, then the other, slowly chippin' away at the trunk. Takin' turns choppin' trunks sometimes as big around as my arms, but usually only one hand across. Chop, chop, chop as the tree's waist got smaller and smaller until we heard a crackin' sound. When the tippy top of the tall tree began to sway we yelled, 'Timber!' warnin' anyone in the area that a tree was about to drop. 'Course it was usually just Charlie and me, but you never knew if a hunter was nearby lookin' for bears.

"On my second-day choppin' wood, the heavy axe handle slipped out of my right hand on the down-swing. My thumb was in the way. Before it happened, I could already see the blade reachin' toward the nail on my thumb, then slicin' right through the middle, leaving a piece of me on the ground a foot away. I couldn't stop the axe, so my vision came to pass. Part of me flew right off my hand!"

I grimaced, visualizing his bleeding digit lying on the ground.

Prince continued, "Blood squirted from the end of my thumb, and I screamed like a little girl. I began runnin' in circles, not knowin' what to do, bleedin' all over myself. That type of accident happened a lot to woodcutters—fingers, hands, arms, toes, or gashes in the leg.

"Thankfully, Charlie knew what to do. He wrapped his bandana around my thumb and cinched it real tight. He tol' me to sit down, keep my arm over my head, and press as hard as I could on the cut thumb part, usin' my second finger. He said that would stop the bleedin' quicker. I had to sit like that for 'bout an hour, just breathing deep. Charlie gave me some whiskey to help with the pain and tol' me to relax. Truthfully, I was lucky it didn't cut my thumb bone off. It healed up in a couple of weeks. After that, my thumb never felt nothin'—not touch, pain, heat, or cold.

"Every day for weeks, we felled trees, then chopped them in two to four-foot lengths, depending on how big around they were. We carefully stacked the pieces on a sled, five or six logs high, and five or six logs wide. Mules pulled the sled downhill to one of several coaling pits dug in the ground. We helped Robert place the logs in a specific manner around the center of the pit.

I asked him to describe how he placed the logs.

"First," he started, "we laid two of the thinner, shorter logs on the ground, then crisscrossed them by two more thin logs, into a square shape. More thin logs would be crisscrossed in that same manner until the stack was 'bout six-feet tall. That square design acted like a chimney, allowing air to move around, which would create a hotter fire.

"Thirty to fifty cords of the longer logs were stacked around the chimney in ever-widening circles. The finished stack looked like a rounded mound which was covered with leaves and dirt to help control the amount of air that reached the fire. The same stack-wood process was done for the other five or so pits. We had cut down almost every tree in one part of the forest, leaving only a few to regrow the woods. There were a lot of cords to char.

"To begin the charring-wood-to-charcoal process, the collier dropped hot embers in the center chimney on a cool night. Tendin' the fires was a round-the-clock job, so the collier lived nearby in a simple hut built from sticks, hardly big enough to lie down in. Most colliers, like Robert, were old guys who used to be loggers who could no longer do the physical work of cuttin' and haulin' trees. Robert watched six or more hearths that smoked and smoldered for two weeks until the charrin' was done. About 80 bushels of charcoal was burned for every ton of iron. It took a cord of wood to make six bushels of charcoal."[150]

I listened with rapt attention as Prince continued, "The charrin' process took about two weeks, finally coolin' down enough for us to take it from the pits and shovel it into wagons pulled by horses to the Antietam Ironworks. Teams of men, mostly us slaves, shoveled the charcoal from the wagons into smaller carts to be pushed up the slope to the top of the fifty-foot furnace stack.

"A gang of men would dig iron ore from the forests around Antietam Creek and as far away as Frederick. Then they shoveled the ore into smaller carts to be dumped into the top of the furnace stack. All day long, shovelin' ore, then charcoal, then ore, then charcoal—whatever the ironmaster wanted. There was times I thought my back would break under the strain. The heat and smoke comin' up the stack would choke off our breath, so we all wore bandanas around our mouths. We also wore hats with brims to keep some of the smoke out of our eyes. You don't know what dirty is until you have been an ironworker!"

"I can only imagine," I replied. "Grandpa Prince, did you ever learn blacksmithing skills or learn to shape the iron metal that came out of the forge?"

Prince nodded then answered, "A couple of years before I was freed in 1812, the ironmaster taught me a little bit about the smithy—that's another name for the small furnace. He had me heat metal in a forge, hammerin' it into shape with different kinds of hammers, and reheating it until the form was perfect. I later learned to use these skills to make horseshoes and other tools needed on every farm.[151] After I got my freedom, I worked in the Antietam nail factory next to the company store and post office (Figure 14.4). We made square-cut nails and many other useful tools and objects."

Seeing that I was so interested in what he was saying, Prince continued, "At the Iron Works, I sometimes had to help run the water wheel that was fed by the Antietam Creek (Figure 14.2); it was right across the road from the fifty-foot stack. The water wheel powered large bellows which blew a steady stream of air to keep the furnace fire hot twenty-four hours a day, seven days a week. The ironmaster knew how to place streams of air from bellows, and a continuous dumpin' of charcoal and iron ore in the stack. This would make sure the temperature was right to melt the iron ore to produce pig iron. The iron would be hammered to remove slag, then worked—called 'wrought'—by skilled workers, into bars and other shapes.

"When I was first sold away from my family in Kent County by Massa Hatcheson, I thought my life was over. Thankfully, I made a lot of friends at the ironworks, and I learned skills that helped earn extra money to buy the property in Funkstown for my family. My life changed for the better. I left the ironworks before they built the rollin' mill in 1831 and . . ."[152]

With that incomplete parting comment, Prince vanished, before I could ask him any questions about his childhood.

In the 1760s and 1770s, the then-called Frederick Forge (now Antietam Iron Works) was a critical part of the economy of the colony of Maryland. It was situated near the resources needed to make iron: water, wood, lime, and iron ore. The forge is reputed to have produced cannons for the Patriot cause in the American Revolution.

Figure 14.4. Post office and metal products manufactured at Antietam Iron Works. Photograph: Kathy Marshall, 2017.

For decades, this was the largest business in the area, with as many as 250 employees, including up to sixty slaves. Because of this employment boom, the "Village of Antietam" sprang up along the banks of the creek, primarily to house the forge workers.[153] The white house in the background of Figure 14.2 was part of Antietam Village.

A mile from the forge is the mouth of the Antietam Creek, crossed by the Chesapeake and Ohio Canal. Less than three miles to the north is the Antietam Battlefield. Indeed, my family lived and worked in an area of great historical significance, in the Revolutionary War, War of 1812, and the Civil War.

Walking north from the furnace stack, back towards the truck, Jane and I encountered a 25' by 20', red brick building. It had distressed, graying, wood plank doors. The windows were boarded with the same kind of wood plank coverings, topped by a greenish moss-tinged, corrugated metal roof. That may have been the old nail factory. There were several more out-buildings, sheds, and open-sided covered barns—filled with workbenches, tables, and tools.

Looming beyond that was an imposing multi-story, elongated building with white-framed windows (Figure 14.5). Red brick on the two upper floors and a sturdy rock façade covering the bottom floor completed the unusual architecture. This was the heart of the Antietam Iron Works containing a general store, post office, commercial kitchen, and some sleeping quarters.

The Antietam Iron Works has been cleverly restored and is used as a venue to host private parties and special events. The current owner, Wayne McCrossin, with whom I visited in April 2017, has taken great care to maintain the integrity of the original property. He has created an environment in a picturesque setting that entices the visitor with its historic lure. More information and photographs of this engrossing trip are included in Chapter 16: The Journey Home.

Standing there in front of the Antietam Iron Works building, I realized my third great-grandfather, Prince, grew into a man right there on that spot. He had a rocky start. At age 16 he assaulted Slave Isaac in 1799 in Kent County, Maryland. The trial was held in a different (unnamed) county and Prince's slave master, Sheriff Benjamin Hatcheson, sold him. Prince's 1812 Certificate of Freedom indicated that "he was sold by his former master for a term of years to McPherson and Brien at Antietam Iron Works with whom he finished his servitude."

When I first learned about Prince Williams in the fourth month on this project, I began a frantic search for anything and everything concerning his life. One of my first Google searches brought up results that forced me to rub my eyes in disbelief: "*Technological and Cultural Transfer of African Ironmaking into the Americas and the Relationship to Slave Resistance.*" This citation references a 1991 thesis by Public Historian, Jean Libby, which proposed that Africans from West Africa were specifically brought to western Maryland because of their expertise with ironworking. *Was my*

Prince the scion of African ironworkers who were brought to Maryland directly from Africa?

Believe it or not, several other historical sources that reference ironworking in the Maryland and Pennsylvania areas specifically mention a slave ironworker named Prince. Were they all the same person or related people, and were they related to my Prince?

Figure 14.5. Antietam Iron Works main building which housed the general store, post-office, industrial kitchen, and sleeping quarters for the manager. Sharpsburg, MD. Photograph: Kathy Marshall, 2017.

- In 1728, the Principio Company credited Prince, a forge man, more than five shillings for being careful. By March 1729, Principio owed Hughes over seven pounds, five pounds of which he earned by agreeing to apprentice Prince.
- From the 1730s to the 1750s the Principio Company paid slave forge men such as Prince and Dick one shilling to one shilling, sixpence for every ton of anchonies they made.
- White forge men earned at least fifteen to twenty times more than slaves for making the same amount of wrought iron.[154]

- By the 1750s one of his successors as a master finer, John Holloway, worked with Negro assistant Prince and Dick.[155]

- In 1757, Prince paid to have a "fine" shirt made to wear in place of the coarse slave shirt when appearing in public. Dick and London each ordered a coat and breeches from Joe Elliott."[156]

- The 1781 inventory of Principio Forge[157] includes one Prince, a 65-year-old founder. The job descriptions indicate Prince was doing forge work at 39 years of age in 1755. He had been with the Company for no less than twenty-six years.

Was the slave named Prince, mentioned as working at Principio and at Mount Joy Forge, the same person or a father and his son? Were they related to the Cecil County Prince Williams born in 1769? Most critically, were they related to "my" Prince who was born in 1783 in Kent County? Even though I was unable to prove whether these ironworker possibilities were my Prince's parents and/or grandparents, as discussed by the parentage theories mentioned in Chapter 8, this topic will be exciting fodder for future research in the Second Edition of this book.

My Prince's racial description "of a black color" on his Freedom Certificate made me even more interested in finding out whether Prince was directly descended from pure Africans. I was motivated to find out as much as possible about his involvement at the Antietam Iron Works. What types of skilled labor did Prince perform? Did his ironmaking skills earn him enough money to purchase land and his daughter-in-law and granddaughter, and support his enslaved family?

Figure 14.6. Kanika Marshall's welded metal kinetic sculptures, Elk Grove, California, 2017.

One of my four primary goals for this book was to determine whether generations of my family members received our mechanical/machinist skills from our enslaved ancestors. Having a proven ironworker in the family—Prince Williams—brought a small measure of credence to our family story.

This part of the Williams story particularly piqued my interest because I am a metal artist myself (Figure 14.6). I use a MIG welder[159] on discarded pieces of recycled steel, to create my Kanika African Sculptures "up-cycled" artworks. Many of my reborn kinetic art objects[160] dance and spin in the wind, reflect the light of the sun, and/or are lit from within. Some of my sculptures are enhanced with the soothing sound of cascading water, clay, glass, stone or other metals. But my welded outdoor artworks are certainly not as structurally tough as the cannons, pike poles, nails, and other metal items that Prince may have fabricated.

I read all the publications I could locate to learn about the fascinating world of charcoal making, bloomery, iron forges, pig iron, ironworking tools, and blast furnaces in Maryland, from the period of 1715 into the mid-1800s.

The first iron works in northeast Maryland was built by Robert Dutton in 1715, but it was a small bloomery producing only one hundred pounds of iron a day. To increase production to make the industry profitable, the Principio Company sent Ironmaster John England from Great Britain to supervise construction of the first blast furnace and refinery forge at Principio Forge in Cecil County (adjacent to Kent Country where my third great-grandfather was born. By 1725, that furnace was producing pig iron, and by 1728, forge workers were hammering out wrought iron. Iron was produced for export to England. At the same time, food was grown on the property to provide a measure of self-sufficiency, and there was a company store selling merchandise to workers.[161]

As with most industries in Colonial America, slaves and indentured servants were the major sources of unskilled labor; however, some slaves held skilled positions at Principio, such as foundry and forge work and clerical tasks.[162] In 1727, two white forge men, John Hughes and James Jarrett, were paid nine shillings each if they agreed to apprentice a slave named *Prince* at the furnace. I wasn't positive whether that *Prince* was related to my family or not, but I was ecstatic that it was a possibility.

Principio slowly expanded its ranks of skilled slave artisans and by the Revolutionary War, they nearly monopolized the hearths and hammers of Principio Forge.[163] In addition to forge work, slaves grew enough grain and fodder to provision themselves, in addition to sometimes building their own cabins in the woods at various forges. Most forges had to be self-sufficient, often hiring women to help with cooking, farming, and sometimes various ironworking duties.

The ironmaster implemented incentives to motivate slaves. Rewards for exceptional service were one way to make slaves more industrious.

Slave ironworkers eventually created a system called "overwork" where slaves earned cash or credit to purchase goods for any work they did which exceeded the quota for the job, usually at the same rate as free workers. Extra tasks could include cutting wood during the winter, cultivating large gardens, selling produce, hiring themselves out, or exceeding their normal work quota.

Slave ironworkers could decide for themselves which goods and services to purchase, to improve life for themselves and their families. In 1757, Prince (my fourth or fifth great-grandfather?) paid "for making his fine shirt."[164] It was important they were not immediately identified as slaves when out in social settings, so spending extra money on their appearance increased their self-esteem. Is this how my Prince was able to buy $30 of household goods in 1834 from John Cox, the Funkstown property in 1842, the astounding $1,200 in his estate that was claimed by his executors, and $145 distribution to each of his five living children?

Another interesting fact is that archeologists unearthed the remains of thirty-one enslaved ironworkers at the Catoctin Furnace in Frederick County and determined they were first or second-generation West Africans. In 1830, it appeared that Brien and McPherson had as many as twenty male slaves of mature age who could have been employed at the Catoctin ironworks. This figure dropped off considerably in 1835 and again in 1841. Those few who remained may have been either highly skilled artisans or house slaves.[165]

Ms. Libby speculated that the Catoctin Furnace ironworkers, like other African ironworkers of the period, had been imported specifically to forge iron. There is some evidence to support her hypothesis that slave traders valued Africans with skills from iron-producing regions. There also exists limited evidence that some slaves practiced their native "spirit-infused" ironworking skills in America. I reached out to Jean Libby in my tenth month on this project and she not only gifted me with an autographed copy of her "From Slavery to Salvation: The Autobiography of Rev. Thomas W. Henry of the AME" but also a copy of her "Technological and Cultural Transfer of African Ironmaking into the Americas and the Relationship to Slave Resistance."

The significance of spiritual attributes given to iron and ironworking was essential to understand African ironmaking techniques in countries like Nigeria, where iron was fundamental to the rise of several important African kingdoms like Benin, Yoruba, Ife, and Oyo. In these African countries and tribes, Ogun, the God of Iron was credited with introducing iron, as well as being the first hunter and warrior, the clearer of fields, and the founder of dynasties. Ironworkers like blacksmiths were revered and feared because of their proximity to the supernatural power that seems to turn rock into iron, which could then be fashioned into implements like swords and spears.

The Mande people believed blacksmithing skill was endemic (genetic); therefore, you were born into a blacksmithing family and apprenticed as such. In the African communities, male ironworkers were often married to female potters, who also used fire to "magically" turn clay earth into strong pottery.[166] Ironworkers and potters were the most powerful people in a tribe, aside from the chief.

Why was Ms. Libby's hypothesis so stimulating to me when I found these texts in my fourth month on this project? *If* (and this is a big *if*) I could prove my Prince's father and/or grandfather were the ironworkers at Principio and Valley Forge, and *if* I could prove the Principio or Valley Forge Princes were brought to America directly from Africa, I *might* be able to determine whether my Prince came from a long line of ironworkers from Africa. This difficult theory will be left to prove or disprove in a Second Edition of this book.

I believe Prince taught his metalworking skills to his sons Samuel, Hezekiah, Henry, and Otho. Margaret Elizabeth was listed as a servant in the 1860 U.S. Federal Census and was, therefore, unlikely to be a metalworker herself. The probate records of John and Benjamin Ingram suggest that Hezekiah and Otho were generally hired out as laborers. There was also a blacksmith's toolkit in the list of Ingram property.

Is ironworking in my family's blood and passed down from generation to generation, as the Mande people of Guinea and Mali believe about their blacksmiths?[167] While I was not able to conclusively prove that for this First Edition book, there are indicators that it is true.

Figure 14.7 shows my family members, by generation, who have utilized machinist, metalworking, or mechanical engineering skills during their lifetime.

According to the 2017 Bureau of Labor Statistics, there were 378,000 machinists in the United States, including machinery manufacturing, metalworking, fabricating metal products, and motor vehicle parts manufacturing.[168] There were 291,000 mechanical engineers, and 404,000 welders, cutters, solderers and braziers. There were 126.22 million households in the U.S.[169]

Therefore, on average, there was one machinist, mechanical engineer, welder, cutter, solderer, or brazier for every 117 households in the U.S. in 2017. There is a much higher incidence of those types of jobs which deal with metal in the direct-line descendants of Prince Williams than the average household in the United States. It seems the family lore of metalworking being in my family's blood may not be farfetched.

GENERATIONS OF WILLIAMS WITH METALWORKING OR MECHANICAL SKILLS

Gener-ation	NAME Jobs Birth-Death, States Lived			
1	**NEGRO PRINCE** Principio & Mount Joy Forge 1720?-1780? Kent/Cecil, MD?	*Note: this Williams family linkage is unconfirmed. If he is related, there would likely be another generation beteween him and Prince Williams, perhaps the Prince Williams mentioned in Vincent Hatcheson's 1755 Will, who may or may not have had any ironworking exposure.		
2	**PRINCE WILLIAMS** Antietam Iron Works 1783-1843, MD			
3	**SAMUEL WILLIAMS** 1819-?, MD	**HENRY WILLIAMS** 1824-19__?, MD, PA	**HEZEKIAH WILLIAMS** 1831-1871, MD	**OTHO WILLIAMS** 1834-1888?, MD
4	**OTHO SHERMAN WILLIAMS** Millrite/____ 1874-1948, OH			
5	**ARTHUR CARTER** Machinist, Auto Mechanic 1908-1995, OH	**CHARLES WILLIAMS** Shop Teacher 1924-Present, OH, NY, IN		
6	**ARTHUR CARTER** Molder, Auto Mechanic 1933-2006, OH	**GEORGE CARTER** Foundry, Electrical 1936-2003, OH	**DALE CARTER** Router, Machine Operator 1938-Present, OH	
7	**KATHY MARSHALL** MIG Welder 1957-Present, CA	**EVERETT SANDERS** Mechanical Engineer 1962-Present, OH	**GREG MARSHALL** Electrical, Plumbing, Building 1963-Present, CA	**ROY SANDERS** Mechanical Engineer 1966-present, OH
8	**ISAAC ANDERSON** Computer Network & Security 1985-Present, CA, NC, Japan	**DON CULPEPPER** Auto Mechanic 1988-Present	**EVERETT SANDERS IV** Mechanical Engineer 1982-Present, OH, __	**MATTHEW ANDERSON** Computer Programming & Repair 1990-Present, CA

Figure 14.7. Generations of Prince Williams' family members with metal-working and/or mechanical skills.

Chapter 15 - Williams' Family Migration

How and when did the Williams family move from Maryland northeast to Philadelphia, Pennsylvania, where my grandmother Pearl Williams Carter was born?

I was able to track the Williams family migration from Washington and Kent Counties, Maryland to Greencastle and Philadelphia, Pennsylvania. Then they migrated to East Liverpool and Barnesville, Ohio; and finally, to Mt. Vernon, Ohio. The family generally stayed close to the east-to-west "National Road" built in 1811, which makes a path through the states of Pennsylvania, Maryland, West Virginia, Ohio, Indiana, then to Illinois.

* The Rock Crumbles *

What follows is my imagined narrative told from the point of view of my great-great-grandmother, Alice Logan Williams, as her family's life is turned upside down one morning in 1888.

An undulating wail began deep in my soul and raced through my heart, my throat, over my tongue, escaping through my mouth. Breathless, pale, and still, my Otho did not wake up that morning, plain and simple. His muscular arms were crossed over each other on his still chest, his sunken cheeks flanking a placid smile on his once-handsome face.

He didn't open his deep-set dark brown eyes when I called his name. He did not move his arms or smile at me like he always did when he woke up. He did not stir in the least. "C'mon now, Otho, don't play with me, it's time to get up," I chided. No response. I began to panic as the full realization slowly spread in disbelief from my eyes to my ears, then my fingers. His body was firm and cool to the touch. "Otho," I cried again, "wake up, love, pleeeease." That's when the wail began. I couldn't believe my precious husband was dead.

Edgar, then Samuel, bounded into our room, shouting, "Mama, what's wrong?" Catching me rocking my unmoving husband in my arms, no words were needed to tell them their father was dead. No more pain or worry for my husband. No more me rubbing grease on his aching back when he came in from an exhausting day tilling our fields. No more making my homemade jam sandwiches for his lunch, or washing his grimy clothes, or listening to him worry about his work, or watching him play with our daughters and sons. My Otho was dead.

My heart pounding in my ears, I could not speak. The panic welled up inside my chest and raced to my brain. It was all on my shoulders. My husband's essence was no longer here. He left me and our children to fend for ourselves. My mind tried to keep me strong in front of the boys.

In a flash, through the haze, I started thinking that, well, Edgar is 18, and Samuel is 16, and Otho is almost 14. Could they take over and run our farm without their father? If they can't finish the plowing, we won't be able to sow the seed, or care for the plants, or harvest the crop, or sell it at the market to pay our many bills. What would we do to get out of this mess with the bank? They already gave us one extension from last year's drought, but they won't give us any more time.

My wailing started up again uncontrollably. *Would we really lose our land and home that Otho and me built over the last twenty years?*

"Boys, go get Dr. Fahrney as fast as you can," I directed the eldest boys with as much control as I could muster. "Tell him your father isn't breathing and he feels cold." I added, "Samuel, tell Alice and Mary Irene to get you something to eat from the pantry before you go."

Gazing at my husband of over twenty years, lying so peacefully on our double bed, under the beautiful white scalloped quilt his sister Mary gave us on our wedding day, my mind takes me back. I remember so clearly when Otho and I got married. It was only about twenty-two years ago, on November 2, in 1867[170].

As newlyweds, Otho and I lived with Mama Margaret on East Cemetery Street in Funkstown. It was a nice big lot and a half with a couple of log cabin houses on it and plenty of land in between to grow crops. Otho and me felt pretty safe in that neighborhood, even though there were few colored people living there.

Thank the Lord, Massa John Ingram freed Mama Margaret right after Prince died in 1843, so she could begin living in that Funkstown property. I have been told that Mama Margaret was still a good-looking woman at 45, with her long, dark, wavy hair and smooth skin the color of milk chocolate. And she was an excellent cook and seamstress. Do you think a pretty woman like that, with a house and land, is going to stay single for long? No sir. Those local colored men started sniffing around not long after poor Prince died. Well, that William handsome Hanson was the lucky winner.

William and Margaret soon married and began living together in that cute log cabin house on the East Cemetery Street side of their property, along with her and Prince's daughter Margaret Elizabeth. They grew corn and some rye and had some hogs and chickens. While William worked as a farm laborer during the day, Margaret tended her little vegetable garden and made the house a fine home. They worked that half acre of land and had tolerably good harvests nearly every year, enough to feed their family through the winter.

There was a setback, though, when those soldiers came marching through Funkstown in July 1863, during that horrible Civil War that lasted for years. Those Union forces attacked the Confederate soldiers when they left Pennsylvania, following the Battle of Gettysburg. You better believe that everyone's harvests were taken by the soldiers, as well as the hogs and chickens and anything else that could be eaten. They also trampled everything in sight.

My family had nothing left after the war, but Mama Margaret was clever and knew how to create something from just about nothing. She sometimes made baby clothes and other knick-knacks which she sold at the market on Sundays. William sometimes worked at other farms as well as his own, or worked at the brick factory. He was also good at making furniture, like tables, chairs, and fancy dresser drawers.

My goodness! Mama Margaret and her new husband sure bought a lot of things after Prince died. They did up that house real nice. She made pretty flowered curtains for the windows and laid green carpet on the floors. She was always kind to me. We enjoyed our first year living with her until she got so sick that summer of 1868, and her spirit joined her husband, Prince, in Heaven.

That sticky hot August morning after Mama Margaret died, the auctioneer had a couple of hundred household items and farming equipment to auction off. Except for the house and land, they sold everything she had collected during her life as a free woman for only $106. My husband and I bought the wardrobe, twenty yards of olive-green carpet, a couple of dishes, and some blankets and pillowcases.

I am so glad my Otho and Hezekiah were able to keep the property in the family by buying it at auction for $690. Otho and me went in as "tenants in common" with his older brother Hezekiah and his pretty wife, Minta, to buy this Funkstown property.

Yes, when Margaret died, we were just newlyweds, learning how to live together and be a good Christian husband and wife. Like every colored man, my husband Otho had to work hard all the time, usually from sun-up to sun-down. All his life, Otho had lived with his family on the big Ingram Farm that they called Meadows Green, next to the Beaver Creek where trout fishing was real good in the fast-flowing water.

Otho was often sent to work as a day laborer for Massa Benjamin South, and the Funks and Newcomers, doing whatever needed to be done on their farms. Sometimes he took his blacksmithing kit with him to shoe the horses and fix whatever equipment needed mending.

Alas, this morning my beloved husband didn't wake up. I don't know if his heart gave out from the strain and stress of constantly coming up short, but his eyes never opened. I sent my oldest boy, Edgar, to fetch the doctor. When Edgar came back with him, nothing could be done. My husband was gone. The undertaker will come tomorrow to pick up his body for burial.

Now, what are we going to do to pay the taxes? Mr. Sam Funk says Mr. Eavey will have to repossess our property if we cannot pay the bills, and I just don't know what we're going to do. I tried to get help from Otho's older brothers, Samuel and Henry, but they have their own families to care for. And my children are too young to take over the farm on their own.

* Where the Grass is Greener *

Several months pass trying to figure out what to do, but Mr. Joseph Eavey, who had been kind to us for twenty years, took back our property and sold it to Mr. Edward Baker for $440 in 1889. Now we must move somewhere else, but where?

My oldest son Edgar, now 19, thinks he knows exactly what we should do now that his daddy is gone. Our friends and family have been so helpful, bringing food and giving us advice on what to do next. Edgar is certainly stepping up to be the man of the house, and I know that would make his daddy proud. Edgar says we should just give up all this hardship and these debts and get a fresh start in Greencastle, Pennsylvania. He heard from his friends that there is some work in Greencastle for colored folk so maybe we can get on our feet again there. He says we can probably get his friends to help us pack up and leave town before the Sheriff gets here and starts throwing our hard-earned property into the street. Oh I can see Otho turning over in his grave right now.

I don't know what to do. My younger children, Alice Virginia and Mary Irene are crying all the time for their daddy. Samuel is 17 years old, and he agrees with Edgar that we should move up north. Otho Sherman isn't so sure that is the best thing to do, but in the end, we decide to pack our belongings and move. It sure is going to be strange being away from all my family here, but we have lost our land and the home that my husband treasured, and we've got to move somewhere. So in the fall of 1889, after our land passed to Edward Baker, we left our home behind. All of us moved to a little place on Jefferson Street in Greencastle, Pennsylvania. It's only twenty miles north from our Maryland home.

That first ten years after Otho died were tough on all of us. There was work in Greencastle for colored folks doing cleaning for others, being a tailor or seamstress, working as a porter, doing laundry, performing general day laborer tasks like sweeping floors and washing dishes.[171]

My son, Otho Sherman, is a stubborn boy, just like his daddy. He's not even 15 years old and telling me "I ain't going to stay here. I'm going to go to Pittsburgh or Philadelphia with my music buddies. You see, Otho Sherman taught himself to play the fiddle, mandolin, and clarinet pretty well; he sometimes earned pocket change playing in a small band for picnics and parties.

At Otho Sherman's belligerence, Edgar and Sam puff out their chests and get in Otho Sherman's face and order him to stay with the rest of the family. Their fight gets louder and louder until I can't take them fighting anymore. "Stop it! Can't you see I am still grieving my husband's death? I just want peace and a decent home," I blurted out. Thank you, Jesus, they stopped arguing.

Let me talk a little about our children, the ones who have kept me going all these years. My oldest, Edgar E. Williams, was born on a bright Saturday morning on April 23rd in 1870. We had just bought our Roxbury property the year before from Mrs. Beeler. Edgar was always a headstrong but loving boy, and he had the cutest dimples. He seemed to know what he wanted to do in life from a young age. He followed his daddy around the farm and wanted to do whatever his daddy did. By 1880, Edgar could not read or write because he was so busy working on our farm and sometimes working for the neighbors. He was mostly plowing, sowing seed, and harvesting the corn and wheat. He felt right at home working with plants. I told you earlier that Edgar stepped up to the plate when Otho died, taking the reins and suggesting that we move to up the road a ways to Greencastle, Pennsylvania.

Well, after Greencastle we moved to Pittsburgh for a while because there were a lot of jobs in the steel industry. Finally, me and most of my kids we ended up on the east side of Pennsylvania, in Philadelphia, near Germantown. Edgar was working as a janitor for most of his life. He never found the right woman; I think because he was a bitter man who thought his life should have been better. I must admit that Edgar was often difficult to live with. He died on October 15, 1933, at the age of 63, at his last residence at 1623 10th Street in Philadelphia. As far as I knew, he never had any children to carry on his name. My poor unhappy boy drank himself to death, with that cirrhosis of the liver condition. A Mrs.

Virginia Christian informed the authorities of his death, but I don't know if she was a special person to him or just a landlord. They say there was an inquest into the reason for his death, but I know it was the fault of that flask he always had close by. My Edgar was buried in the Fairview Cemetery in Philadelphia.

Our second son, Samuel M. Williams, was born on June 12, 1872. We named him after Otho's Uncle Samuel who was always so nice to us. This baby was noticeably different from our first-born. Caramel-colored Samuel was quiet and watched everyone carefully and calmly. He learned by watching. He wanted to please everyone. He was an agreeable child who gladly did whatever you asked him to do. Edgar took to being the big brother, showing Samuel how to do everything, even though he took advantage of Samuel's good nature. The younger brother did not seem to mind. Luckily, Samuel did not have to do much farming when he was younger, and he was able to go to school when it wasn't harvest time. He got a fifth-grade education and even taught me to read a little. My Samuel was a patient person who helped me in the vegetable garden. He had a knack for making plants grow.

By the turn of the century, Samuel was a single 27-year-old butler in Greencastle, Pennsylvania. I was so happy when he married that sweet girl, Fannie P. Taylor, and blessed me with my first granddaughter, Jessie Edna, in 1912. By 1920, they had three boarders living in their rented Philadelphia home on Coulter Street. They listed Samuel as a black machinist in the Jobbing industry. His daddy had taught him a thing or two about metalworking. My Samuel always kept his nose to the grindstone and made a nice home for himself and his family. By 1930, he was a chauffeur for a private family and he, Fannie and Jessie were doing well and living in a $7,500 house they owned on Winona Avenue in Philadelphia's 22nd Ward. I cannot tell you how proud I was of his and his family's efforts.

Jessie went to Roosevelt Junior High School in Germantown, Philadelphia, Pennsylvania. (Figure 15.1)

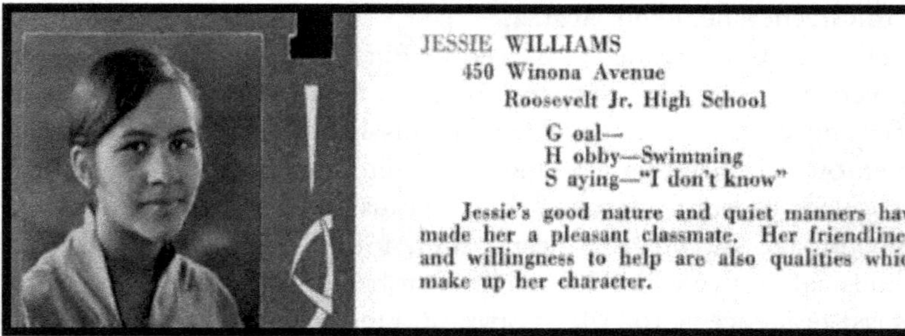

JESSIE WILLIAMS
450 Winona Avenue
Roosevelt Jr. High School

G oal—
H obby—Swimming
S aying—"I don't know"

Jessie's good nature and quiet manners have made her a pleasant classmate. Her friendliness and willingness to help are also qualities which make up her character.

Figure 15.1. Jessie Williams, granddaughter of Otho and Alice Williams, Philadelphia, Pennsylvania, 1930.

Ten years later, in 1940, Sam was a caretaker. Unfortunately, their house was only valued at $3,000 by then, presumably because the neighborhood had gone downhill. I don't know exactly if it's true, but some folks told me he and his wife and child were passing as white folks. I don't entirely blame those who "pass" because life has certainly been difficult for black folks in this country. All of my life I bragged that I would never "pass", but I guess you never know what you'll do until you're living in another person's shoes.

Samuel's last occupation was as a gardener. He died from portal fibrosis of the liver at Penn Hospital on July 13, 1962, at the age of 90, three years after his wife died. He lived his last few years quietly with his daughter at their 85 Lincoln Avenue home in Philadelphia, Pennsylvania. Jessie had married William David Coverdale, who was working at the Board of Education in Chester in 1937. Jessie had completed three years of college by the time she had a son in 1939; they named him William. Their son died in 2001 in Suffolk, New York, three years after Jessie passed away in 1998.

My third son, Otho Sherman, was born in 1874. What an interesting child he was! When my Otho died, and we moved the family to Greencastle, Otho Sherman did not want to stay with us. He wanted to explore the world with his friends. Otho Sherman was very social, and he loved music and playing cards.

Otho Sherman struck out on his own when he was about 15. He and his friends went to Pittsburgh for a short time, getting whatever work he could find, sometimes working in the steel mill as a strikebreaker; colored people were only allowed to work there when the white workers were striking.

By 1900, Otho had moved on and was working as a coachman for the rich Lee family in East Liverpool, Ohio. He had a black uniform and a flowing cloak and top hat and drove Mr. Lee to his pottery building every day. He drove the rest of the family to shops, to church, or to visit friends.

Otho Sherman met his sweetheart, Myrtle Booker, in East Liverpool. She and her sister were doing day's work for a family---laundry, ironing, some house cleaning, and light cooking. Right before Christmas in 1905, in Philadelphia—well, Germantown, to be precise—with some of our family present, Otho Sherman asked Myrtle to marry him. I was living there then, so they lived with me for a while until I got sick. Their babies started coming in 1907 with Reba Mae, then 1908 with Pearl Lavata.

I hate to admit it, but Otho Sherman was not being a responsible husband or father, according to his wife, so she up and left him. Yes, Myrtle took my darling little granddaughters, Reba and Pearl, and moved them to Mt. Vernon, Ohio, to be with her parents, Joseph Booker and Sarah Myers. Myrtle threatened to put Otho Sherman in jail for not taking care of his kids—they did that back then, you know.

My son learned really quick that he had to grow up and be a good husband and father, so he joined his wife and kids in Mt. Vernon, Ohio. Myrtle's father, Joseph Booker—a former slave from Virginia--got Otho a cleaning job at the Cooper-Bessemer engine manufacturing plant. He rented a row house from the company on the property grounds. Eventually, as more babies and grandbabies came, Otho and Myrtle had sixteen people living in their house in the 1930s and 1940s. I am proud of the man he became, even though it took him longer than some to grow into a responsible man of the house.

Our fourth child, William Franklin Wheeler, was born in 1877. He was always a sickly little boy, and it was tragic when he died at just five years, eleven months and four days of age, as reported by the *Hagerstown Herald and Torch Light* newspaper on August 4, 1882. He was partially named after the good Dr. Wheeler in Boonsboro who delivered him.

Our fifth baby, Charles Elmer, born in 1879 was Otho Sherman's favorite playmate. Charles doted on Otho Sherman, always following him around and wanting to be held by him. None of us was prepared when Charles died suddenly a few years later. Otho Sherman never forgot his baby brother and named one of his own sons Charles Elmer Williams in 1924.

After so many years of having male children, I finally had a baby girl! My precious Mary Irene Williams was born in September 1880. You better believe that I sewed her pretty little dresses and treated her like a very special little person. Her brothers also treated her gently and made sure others at school did the same.

My seventh child was Alice Virginia Williams named after me. She was born in 1883 and was a very confident girl. As an adult, "Virgie" actually moved to New York and opened her own beauty salon. Imagine that—a businesswoman in the family! In fact, she was quite successful and opened three hair salons. Dressed in her finery which clearly showed her success, she always fixed my hair when she came to visit me on the holidays.

I had birthed a ninth child right after Otho died. It was a stillborn girl. I was devastated to lose two family members within such a short time, but life went on.

All in all, I had a miraculous life. I survived slavery, married the man of my dreams who took care of me the best he could, had several children who lived their lives the best they could. It was very stressful for me after Otho died and, quite frankly, I never really recovered emotionally, but I always tried to protect my family and live a good, clean life.

* Alice in Wonderland *

Lo and behold, during the eighteenth month of continuous investigation, I finally found Alice's Death Certificate from Philadelphia, Pennsylvania.[172] She died a widow in the Philadelphia Women's South Homeopathic Hospital[173] on March 9, 1908, at the age of 58. The cause of death was viremia, a viral infection in the bloodstream, with exhaustion being a contributing factor to her death.

Alice's former residence was 1615 Alder Street in Philadelphia, where her disease was contracted. The informant, M. Battersby, the Funeral Director (Figure 15.2), said Alice's parents were from Virginia, which conflicts with the 1870, 1880 and 1900 Censuses which indicated her parents were born in Maryland. Mr. Battersby submitted the above information to the Board of Health. He indicated that she had been a housekeeper and that Dr. Ridgway treated her.

Alice had evidently never remarried because Otho was listed as her deceased husband. She was buried on Friday, March 13, 1908, between 1:00 and 2:00 PM, in Merion Cemetery, Philadelphia, Pennsylvania. She was buried in a grave that would contain three bodies. Since son Samuel Williams paid the $66 funeral bill, I presumed he and his wife, Fannie, would eventually inhabit the other two positions in Alice's grave.

Figure 15.2. Hearse for Alice Williams, Philadelphia, PA, 1908. Photo courtesy of Jim Moshinske, PhD, CPT, Funeral Director at Oak Crest Funeral Home, Texas.

To summarize the known life of my second great-grandmother, Alice Virginia Logan Williams, she bought many properties with her husband of over twenty years, bore and cared for nine children, with five of them living past the age of five, moved her family to Greencastle, Pennsylvania, for a short time then moved to Philadelphia, Pennsylvania, where she was a housekeeper until her death in 1908.

NOTE: Many stories of the descendants of Otho and Alice are contained in *The Ancestors Are Smiling!* available on Amazon.com. That book satisfies my goal #4 following the lives of their son, Otho Sherman Williams, and his wife and children, down through the generations to me, my children, and my grandchildren.

Chapter 16 - The Journey Home

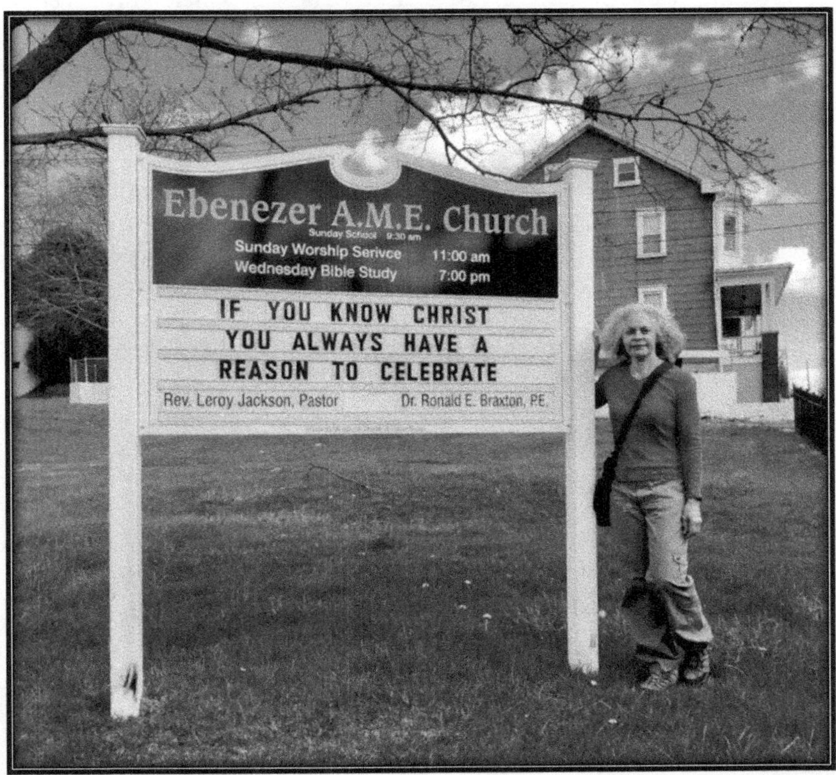

Figure 16.1. Kathy Marshall standing at the Ebenezer A.M.E. Church whose former cemetery is where Prince, Malinda, and Margaret Williams were buried.

Even with the wealth of genealogical information available online these days there is still no substitute for good, old-fashioned "field work" when it comes to finding your ancestors. There is nothing like walking in the footsteps of those who came before you, seeing the towns where they lived, looking at things from their perspective, and maybe even finding the house where they lived (or where it used to be). These are the details that bring your ancestors to life and tell you so much more about who they were as human beings, more than any name or date on a family tree ever could. All of this and more was true about my genealogy trip to Maryland in April 2017, one of the most memorable trips I have ever taken.

It seemed a bit disingenuous to have started writing this book in Sacramento, some three thousand miles away from my ancestral Maryland homeland. So, I arranged to spend the first part of my seventh month researching this project in Maryland. This is where my second great-grandparents, Otho Williams and Alice Virginia Logan, were born slaves but died free persons of color. I felt the need to explore where they lived in the 1700s and 1800s. Taking a genealogy trip like that was a critical step in understanding more about the environment of where our ancestors lived, loved, worked, and died.

My highest priorities were to see the Ingram Farm where my family members were slaves, as well as the properties that my ancestors owned after slavery. I must also see the Antietam Iron Works, where my third great-grandfather, Prince, was sold, worked for a number of years, and was freed in 1812.

I took quite a few African American history classes in college, decades ago. I planned to explore abolitionist John Brown's hideaway at Kennedy Farm where he assembled a group of family members and followers, as well as a small arsenal of weapons. He intended to incite a slave rebellion and overtake the important water transportation hub at Harper's Ferry near the Maryland/West Virginia border. Even though Brown failed in achieving his objective, and Brown himself was hanged for the action, the raid had the effect of galvanizing pro and anti-slavery positions in the United States prior to the outbreak of the American Civil War.

I needed to become part of that by experiencing the Kennedy Farm and visiting Harper's Ferry. Oddly, I yearned to expose myself to the emotional place where slaves were sold in Sharpsburg. I also wanted to experience a sunrise and sunset, which signified a normal workday for my family.

No trip would be complete without spending time at the Washington County Historical Society, the John Clinton Frye Western Maryland Room, and the Enoch Pratt Free Library in Baltimore. I also intended to drive to Germantown, Pennsylvania—an enclave of Philadelphia—where my maternal grandmother, Pearl Williams Carter, the granddaughter of Otho and Alice Williams, was born in 1908. On the way to Germantown,

I would tour the Principio Iron Works in Cecil County, Maryland, looking for clues about another black man named Prince Williams, who lived there from 1820 through 1850. I hoped to determine whether he was related to my family.

To prepare for this solo trip, I conducted an exhaustive online search for everything having to do with slaves in Washington County. This search led me to Dr. Emilie Amt, Chair and Professor of History at Hood College in adjacent Frederick County, Maryland. She has helped me immeasurably with theories about my family's history.

Next was contacting the Chesapeake and Ohio (C&O) Canal Trust to get maps of Washington County bridges that I wanted to visit; that was how I met the indomitable Jane Neff. She and I became fast friends over several months of email correspondence. She sleuthed and prodded until she found the exact locations where Prince and Otho's properties were located. She also made inroads on my behalf with the current owners of those properties. Her stalwart preparations would allow me to spend time in those places during this trip. Jane had taken a week off from work to drive me anywhere I wished. As you can imagine, Ms. Jane Neff was at the top of my "must see" list!

The time had come to visit western Maryland, the place our Williams family left over 125 years ago for Pennsylvania, and then on to Ohio. My bags were packed. My trusty Apple laptop was stowed in my oversized hiking bag. My clothes, vitamins, and daily protein bars were fitted into a bright red, forty-liter, carry-on backpack. And my hopes were flying high. This chapter was ready to capture my long-awaited "journey home" to Maryland.

* The First Day: Home Sweet Home *

I was nervous. Since October 2016, it had always been part of my initial book-writing plan to do some "boots on the ground" family research in Maryland. As the months rolled by, the excitement kept building as I found more and more clues about my enslaved ancestors.

The day of departure was April Fool's Day, 2017, the day that would have been my mother's 84th birthday. As the Boeing 737-800, Southwest Airlines plane sped down the runway at 6:05 AM, I looked up to see the most gorgeous orangey-pink sunrise streaming through the window. This positive sign from my dearly departed mother foretold a wondrous journey home.

The youthful blonde sitting next to me was a native Marylander who grew up in Washington County. What luck! Telling her about my slave research, I gladly showed her the thick manuscript I brought with me.

That hefty draft would prove to my Maryland contacts that I was serious about writing a book.

I took the opportunity to ask my new flying buddy all sorts of questions, including: "are there still colorful fall leaves on the trees in early November?" She happened to have photos from the previous November on her smartphone. I imagined what the weather might have been like when my second great-grandparents married on November 2, 1867. I was planning to write an authentic description of the wedding day from Alice's point of view.

The airplane descended through the silvery clouds over eastern Maryland airspace at 2:00 PM. From my window seat, I began taking photographs of the landscape, woods, and lakes. *Is that the Chesapeake Bay down below where slave ships first made their way to St. Mary's City, Maryland, in 1664?*[174]

I tried to imagine what my enslaved ancestor's state looked like over two hundred years ago when they worked at the Antietam Iron Works and harvested wheat and corn on the Ingram Farm near Boonsboro. *Was I really going to step into the footsteps of my ancestors in just a few minutes?* I felt a bit of emotion believing this trip would shed much light on the experiences of *my* family. That adventure of discovery would certainly enhance the authenticity of my long-awaited book.

After landing at the Baltimore Washington International Thurgood Marshall Airport, I boarded a shuttle bus to the Hertz Rental Car building five or so minutes away. Twenty minutes later, I settled into the black, faux-leather seats of my gun-metal colored Ford Fiesta and plugged the address of the D'Addios' into my smartphone travel app. My boyfriend and I met John and Heidi D'Addio on a Rick Steve's tour to Europe in August 2016. They insisted I stay as long as I liked at their home in Ijamsville, Frederick County, next door to my ancestral home in Washington County. There are good people everywhere.

After checking the mirrors and locating the lights and windshield wiper controls, I started the engine and cautiously left the parking garage, escaping into the marine gray afternoon that hinted a coming rain. The travel app took me through lightly-traveled rural roads bordered by leafless sycamore trees. Soon, I veered onto Interstate 95 toward Baltimore, then onto Interstate 70, west, toward Frederick County.

Having worked at the California Highway Patrol for thirty-six years, and sometimes with our compatriots at the California Department of Transportation, I find highway infrastructure to be quite interesting. Wherever I travel, whether in the United States or beyond, I observe whether the roads are well-maintained, or are full of potholes and uneven pavement, like many highways in often-underfunded California. In general, Maryland freeways appeared to be amazingly smooth, with only rural roads sometimes being a tad bumpy.

The rolling hills alongside the highway were beginning to wake from their winter sleep, leaving them a somewhat anemic, mousy brown. In contrast, the flatter grassy meadows were an unbelievably lush, emerald-green, looking so uniform in height that they must be regularly mowed. After thirty minutes or so, I exited the freeway and meandered through miles and miles of one-lane backwood country roads. I am a forest girl all the way, so I was in my element traveling through the heavily timbered State of Maryland. Sprawling farms, low split-rail fences, and lush green pastures were dotted with grazing horses or Holstein cows.

Centuries-old stone and brick homes were contrasted by newer housing developments in this rural area of western Maryland. At about 4:30 PM, I made it to the D'Addios hill-top mini-mansion in an exclusive area of Ijamsville. After making fast friends with their handsome Westie Terrier, Wyatt Burp (Figure 16.2), I was shown to a spacious upstairs room, in *one* wing of their 4,000 square-foot house. My daily commute to Washington County from Ijamsville would be about thirty-five minutes. It was comforting knowing I had a safe (and luxurious) place to lay my head for the next nine nights.

Figure 16.2. The D'Addios and the dashing Wyatt Burp, Courtesy of the D'Addios, 2017.

* The Second Day Home: D.C. Bound *

On my second day in Maryland, the D'Addios and the sparkling Melissa Powell—another Marylander who we met on our European tour—and I boarded the metro train and headed toward Washington, District of Columbia (DC) for a personal tour of the Smithsonian Museum.

On that cold and clear Sunday, I wanted to see as much of the Nation's Capital as possible. We started our adventure at the venerable Smithsonian Castle. It contains sample artifacts from each of its nineteen museums, as well as a compact gift shop. We spent a scant three-quarters of an hour or so in five museums.

- African Art Museum: For an artist with a business called "Kanika African Sculptures," I was on Cloud Nine. I digested with relish the exceptional African art exhibits and purchased an affordable wearable-art headband and several beaded bracelets from their colorful gift store.

- The National Air and Space Museum was impressive with its overhead planes and spacecraft hovering above our heads. The huge gift shop seemed to take up the entire basement. Of course, I had to purchase freeze-dried, astronaut ice cream and NASA tee-shirts for my space-enthusiast boyfriend back home.

- The sweeping, curvilinear facade of the National Museum of the Native American looked like it was carved out of a soap-stone mountain. The museum contained intricate totems, Native American tools and artifacts, kiosks bemoaning the numerous broken treaties from the U.S. government, and a superb restaurant.

- The most popular—based on the longest entrance line—was the Natural History Museum. I wished we could have spent hours there because it was a Noah's Ark of nearly every kind of animal, fossil and ocean-going creature imaginable. It was ludicrous to attempt to chronicle the many varied and interesting exhibits in that well-appointed museum in only forty-five minutes. I added to my Bucket List to return in the future and spend a whole day in that museum.

Figure 16.3. Visited Smithsonian Museums, Washington, D.C. Photograph: Kathy Marshall, 2017.

- ❖ We found the Modern Art Museum to be unexpectedly mundane, at least during that visit. Perhaps it was just that we were dead tired from a full day of museum hopping.

After a long day of walking and filling our heads with amazing sights and sounds, we exited the last museum hot, tired, and hungry, wondering where was an ice cream truck when you needed one?

* The Third Day Home: My Heart's Desire *

My long-anticipated genealogy adventure began Monday morning, April 3, 2017. I drove from my home base in Ijamsville, Frederick County, Maryland, onto Interstate 70-West toward Hagerstown, the Washington County seat. I looked forward to meeting Jane Neff at the Chesapeake and Ohio (C&O) Canal Trust office at 9:30 AM. She drove up in a gold-colored, half-ton truck and invited me to hop in. I had no premonition in those first few seconds of the momentous discoveries she was about to bestow upon me that remarkable day. I was thrilled beyond belief to learn that our first destination was the most coveted on my list of priorities.

Only a few months earlier, I learned the Ingram family owned my second great-grandfather, Otho Williams, his siblings, and his mother. I had dreamed about visiting the place where my Williams family had been enslaved until the end of slavery in 1864 in Maryland. No, I was not happy they were slaves, but I was driven to find out where they had lived and how they had survived that horrific time in American history.

Weeks earlier, Jane had been warned by neighbors that the current owner of the Ingram Farm would, without a qualm, shoot first and ask questions later to protect his property from strangers. I was devastated learning that I would not be able to see the slave owner's property after all.

That day Jane Neff proved she didn't give up easily. Without telling me what she had up her sleeve, she drove us to the top of a hill in the upscale Meadows Green development, where one-acre parcels with mini-mansions dotted the land. From our vantage point, we could see a long, flat pasture in the distance. She told me that was where the old Ingram Farm was located. The buildings were still there, albeit in poor shape.

I gulped audibly as I realized that Jane had arranged for me to have a reasonably close look at my most coveted destination—the place where my family were enslaved—after all.

Jane explained that we could not go onto the former Ingram property, but we could do something that would get us a tad closer. We left the safety of her vehicle. She explained that between many properties there was a scant, two-foot-wide pathway, that might be considered as public space. She had already cleared our approach with the current neighbor whose property overlooked my heart's desire.

It seemed so illicit and a little bit dangerous, but I loved that we might get to see the slave owner's farm. We walked gingerly along the footpath overgrown with weeds and occasional tree roots until we conspiratorially stood inside a mass of brambles, about two football fields away from the grassy knoll.

From 1785 until 1867, the Ingram family had owned the entire 246-acre area, called Meadows Green, located on the east bank of the Beaver Creek. This information was found in a forty-page National Register of Historic Places' document, prepared in 1979. It contained detailed plot specifications, historical information about the property, and clear photos of the inside and outside of the Georgian-period, two-story, four-bay, red brick, main house.

There were two small log cabins down the graveled road from the house, where the Ingram's dozen or so slaves probably slept. Also, there was a large barn, frame sheds, and other out-buildings. A two-bay frame addition at the west end of the house linked it with the brick summer kitchen (Figure 16.4). *Was my third great-grandmother, Margaret A. Williams, the cook for the Ingram family and the farm hands, along with her own family?*

With the aid of my zoom camera, we spied one side of the red brick main house. We also noticed the tall chimney of what was likely the log cabin where my 3x great-grandparents, Prince and Margaret Williams, may have lived with their children. I made several videos of the Ingram property, chronicling my conflicting feelings of sheer happiness, disgust, and sadness with the beauty of the bucolic setting before me.

Based on my research, it seemed the Ingrams might have been somewhat more lenient than other slave owners because four of their slaves were eventually freed: Jacob Jeffries, Samuel Williams, Mary F. Williams, and Margaret Elizabeth Williams. The two oldest slaves, Charles Solomon, and Pegg (Margaret A. Williams), were allowed to "go around as they pleased."

However, for some reason, they kept my second great-grandfather, Otho Williams, and his brothers Henry and Hezekiah as slaves. The brothers were sometimes farmed out to work for other whites until the end of slavery, according to Ingram probate records.

Here I am, fully, yet unbelievably, realizing that 150 years ago my ancestors lived down the hill from where I am standing right now!

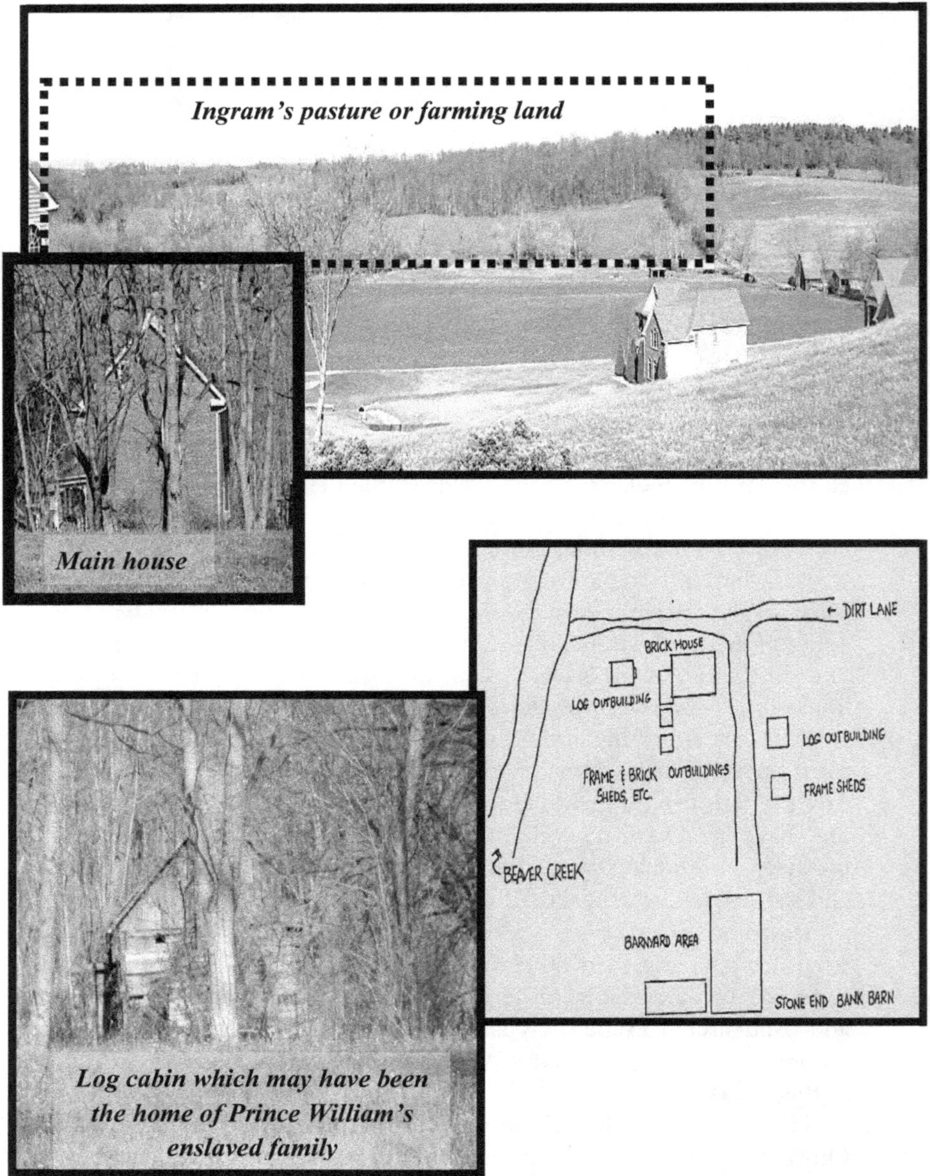

Figure 16.4. Looking onto the Ingram farm from an overlook in the Meadows Green development, Boonsboro, MD. Photograph: Kathy Marshall, 2017.

Our secret perch was from the relative safety of the near-hidden Ingram family crypt, a six-foot high, wide and deep stone structure bordering the next-door neighbor's property atop a hill overlooking the Ingram farm.

We could barely make out the names of the eight Ingram family members interred in the crypt because heavy greenish-gray lichen was eating away at the surface name carvings: Joseph, John, Benjamin, Rachel (mother), Rachel (daughter), .

We were standing in what was called the Fahrney Cemetery in the 1800s. The property was formerly owned by Dr. Daniel Fahrney, who bought my second Great Uncle, Henry Williams, in 1863 for a buck (yes, $1), after owner Benjamin Ingram died in 1862.

I mused that Henry may have been disabled in some way because his assessed "value" was only $50, according to Benjamin Ingram's probate records, compared to his slightly younger brothers' (Hezekiah and Otho) $250 value, and Henry was actually sold for $1.00. Isn't it disgusting to be speaking about a human being in this way? Interestingly, Dr. Fahrney sold some of this land to Henry when slavery was finally declared illegal in 1864 in Maryland.

Being there, next to the Ingram family crypt, standing in the middle of a mass of stickery bushes, at the edge of the next door neighbor's mini-mansion property, which looked down onto my family's owner's land and house was the first of several, surreal, priceless experiences I had on that third day of my journey home.

Over the next hour or so, we drove by or stopped at several grist mills and charming stone bridges and canal locks throughout Washington County, from Hagerstown in the north down to Harper's Ferry at the southern border with West Virginia. Jane explained the importance of those structures, as well as the 184-mile C&O canal system, which operated for nearly one hundred years as a lifeline for communities along the Potomac River.

The C&O facilitated the movement of coal, lumber and agricultural products which floated down the waterways to markets, from 1831 to 1921, at which time the railroads took over commerce transport. It was fascinating to imagine how water from the Beaver and Antietam Creeks was harnessed to power large water wheels and grinding stones for the early iron, sawmill, and grain mill industries in the area. *Were my relatives involved with these waterways in any way?*

Jane arranged for us to have a fascinating private tour of abolitionist John Brown's hideout at the Kennedy Farm (Figure 16.5), where Brown planned the slave insurrection in 1859 at Harper's Ferry. Brown's small "army" of twenty-one insurrectionists, whose mission was to foment rebellion among the slaves, stayed in this home for many months during the planning stages.

Figure 16.5. Kennedy farm where John Brown planned an abolitionist insurrection in 1859. Photograph: Kathy Marshall, 2017.

I was surprised to learn that the original owner, Dr. Robert F. Kennedy, purchased 194 acres of land from the Antietam Iron Works in 1852. That cottage was built in the late 1700s to help the slave ironworkers become self-sufficient. In 1859, Dr. Kennedy then sold the property to Isaac Smith (John Brown, incognito). I later found that the Ingrams family was peripherally involved in the original sale of the Antietam Iron Works property to Kennedy. *Did my ancestor Prince live here in this very house in the first decade of the 1800s?*

I enjoyed speaking with Jane and the current Kennedy Farm owner, Sprigg Lynn, and listening to their family connections in the Washington County area. To be exploring places and people I had only read about in history books for the last forty years, made me realize just how momentous it was to have ancestors from this area of movers and shakers—people who had a real impact on American history. Harriet Tubman, Frederick Douglass, Sojourner Truth, John Brown, and other famous abolitionists lived and worked in Maryland, partly because it was a gateway to freedom in the state of Pennsylvania, at Maryland's northern border.

The previous adventures so far that day had been pretty amazing in and of themselves, but dream-maker Jane was not finished with me. On that beautifully sunny day, she drove us about ten minutes along Harper Ferry Road, to the exterior of the Antietam Iron Works forge (Figure 16.6 where "Negro Prince" worked for a number of years until he was freed in 1812. The actual fifty-foot furnace stack was built into the side of a tall rocky hill).

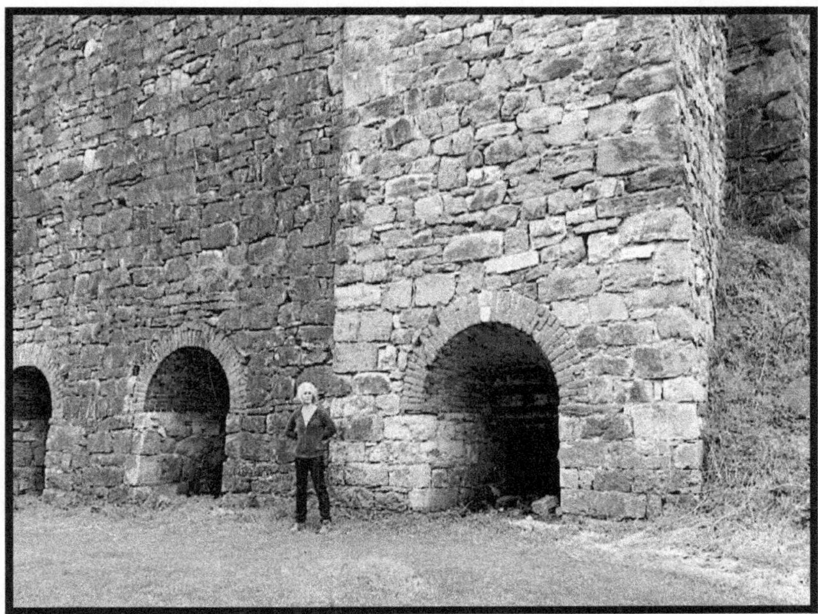

Figure 16.6. Kathy Marshall in front of the Antietam Iron Works stacks.

We had an appointment with the present owner in a couple of days. It was good we were taking pictures during that brief visit because a storm was predicted for later in the week and we might not be able to take outdoor photographs then.

Next, we got to examine a small cemetery in Funkstown where Jane's father, and many notables who I had seen in digital records, were buried.

OK, now this was just too much. My dear guide had driven me to meet her mother, who just happened to live---wait for it---one block away from the Funkstown properties owned by my second and third great-grandfathers in the 1800s! Now understand that my head had begun to explode after visiting the Ingram Farm during the beginning of the day. Half of my brain was left at the Kennedy Farm, but threads remained at the Antietam Iron Works. Driving by the Funkstown property, I was running on pure adrenalin. I was way past exhilarated—on overload from the excitement of having nearly all of my genealogy dreams come true in only a few short hours. I felt wonderful, thankful, and exhausted all at the same time.

In the warmth of the afternoon, it was a relief to take a little break and enjoy a dish of homemade Pocono Paws ice cream at Nutter's Ice Cream Shop in Sharpsburg. It was located in a building originally built in 1887 as a Masonic lodge, then as Kretzer's Market becoming Nutter's Ice Cream twenty years earlier. Sharpsburg (Figure 16.8) was the site of the brutal Battle of Antietam where 23,000 Union and Confederate soldiers died or were wounded on September 17, 1862.

I worried that I was not emotionally prepared for the next adventure. We walked the couple of blocks from the ice cream shop, past a sign that pointed the way to Boonsboro, Hagerstown, and the storied Antietam Battlefield in Sharpsburg commemorates the American Civil War Battle of Antietam that occurred on September 17, 1862.

I tried to keep my eyes on the red brick buildings proudly sporting large American flags hanging next to the front door. As Jane told me about the history of this area, I looked downward at the red brick sidewalk boarded by emerald green lawns. We turned the next corner, getting closer to our ignominious destination.

Jane and I turned the corner and continued walking slowly toward a painful, but historic monument which had been unceremoniously discarded at a now-defunct gasoline station. I brazenly mounted the "Old Slave Block" (Figure 16.7) where all slaves in Sharpsburg were sold from 1800 to 1865. The plaque affixed to the block reads:

> "From 1800 to 1865, this stone was used as a slave auction block. It has been a famous landmark at this original location for over 150 years."
>
> .

I stood on the pitted and sliced rock that perhaps hundreds of enslaved men, women and children had stood, trembling, afraid, and angry. I stood on the rock where children were sold away from their parents, and husbands were callously ripped away from their wives' embrace to be sold "Down South" to the scary southern states.

The indescribable feelings of sadness from those many enslaved

human beings was visceral, seeping up from the rock through my rubber-soled mountain boots, then surging up through my trembling, sad, angry body into my very soul.

I was processing all of that pain when suddenly a young white woman drove up to the curb, rolled down her window and flippantly asked if I was for sale. I had no comment.

However, Jane was furious at the driver and embarrassed that her community revealed its ugly racist head, clearly showing that its true feelings were still alive—at least with that woman.

Truth be told, I didn't recall seeing a single black person anywhere in that town. Perhaps it was easy to see why.

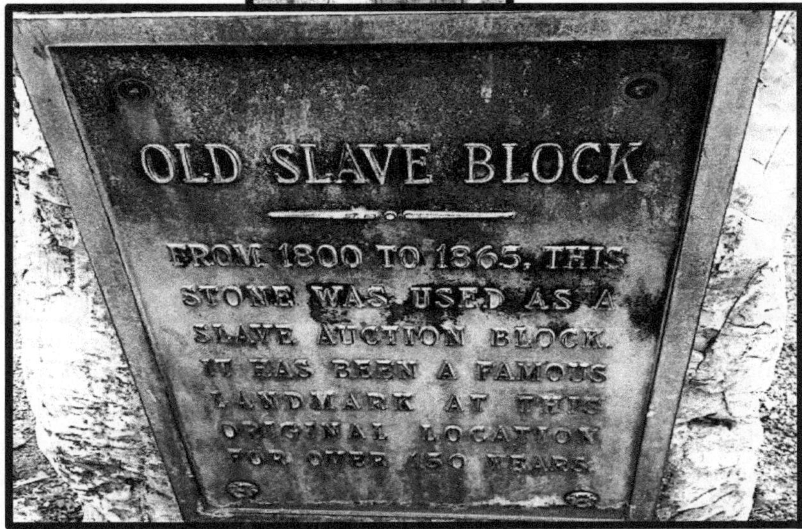

Figure 16.7. Old slave block, Sharpsburg, MD.

To cap off that phenomenal third day of my genealogy trip, Jane had gotten approval from the Rowe family to visit their five-acre property near Roxbury Mills which Otho and Alice Williams had originally purchased in 1869 (Figure 16.8), only five years after the end of slavery. I got to kiss the ground of my ancestors.

Figure 16.8. Kathy Marshall kisses the ground Otho and Alice Williams purchased in 1869 in Boonsboro, MD. Photograph courtesy Jane Neff, 2017.

They had come so far from those difficult slavery days to become landowners. Since there were (and are) so few black families in the area, I had to marvel at Otho and Alice's tenacity and spirit during that particularly inhospitable period in American history. I assume Otho and his family were personable and hard working. It was obvious they were very determined individuals. I was emotionally and physically drained by day's end, but thoroughly satiated and intensely proud all at the same time.

* The Fourth Day Home: More Surprises Await *

Almost all my genealogy dreams came true the previous day. I couldn't imagine how my capable guide, Jane, could top that experience. Meeting again at her Hagerstown office, I jumped into the passenger seat of her truck. While she drove toward our unknown-to-me destination, she gave me a history lesson about Maryland.

Jane revealed we were traveling toward Cunningham Falls State Park, located in a part of the Catoctin Mountain range that forms the north-eastern rampart of the Appalachian Mountain System. After about ten minutes following the winding road through a heavily forested area, the sun sneaked through still-denuded tree limbs, mottling the asphalt road in front of us. Jane found a safe place to park, across the street from "Isabella," the only one of three iron smelting furnaces that still stood at the Catoctin Furnace site.

Several houses originally built for ironworkers were being restored. We looked through the partially curtained windows to observe how forge men, colliers, and the ironmaster lived in the early 1800s. Before coming to Maryland, I had read that to separate iron from the raw iron ore, approximately eighty bushels of charcoal were burned for every ton of iron manufactured.

Woodcutters—generally slaves—entered a forested area and cut every standing tree, leaving one or two trees to re-seed the forest. The resulting logs were moved downhill by horse or mule-drawn sleds to a hearth where the wood was charred. Tending the fire was a round-the-clock job, so the collier lived nearby. He watched up to seven hearths that smoldered for two weeks until the charring process was complete.[175] Often, slaves or free blacks were colliers, expected to make huge batches of charcoal for the furnace. *How will I be able to prove whether my third great-grandfather, Prince, was a collier or a forge man or worked the water wheel, or made nails?*

We took cover inside the immense Isabella Furnace when the first raindrops fell. The lingering smell of what was left of thousands of acres of trees and tons of iron ore being burned there over a seventy-year period was haunting. Catoctin Furnace was originally constructed in 1774 by four Johnson brothers to produce pig iron from locally mined hematite. The furnace changed hands several times to the Bakers, Briens, and others. [176]

Noted ex-slave, Reverend Thomas Henry, ministered to the Africans, free and slave, who were working there in the 1830s. *Did my Prince become friends with Reverend Henry, who had an illustrious career as an ironworker-turned-Reverend, here at Catoctin Furnace?*

Fascinating studies regarding the Catoctin slave workers maintain that the majority were pure Negroid, likely brought there directly from western Africa.[177] John Brien owned the Catoctin furnace from 1820 to 1843, and reportedly had his slave and free ironworkers also working at Antietam Iron Works, which he owned from about 1806 to 1818. Perhaps my Prince periodically worked at Catoctin and at the Antietam Iron Works. I wanted to get a visceral impression of those places where my ancestors may have worked, hoping it would help me prove or disprove his possible descent from pure African ironworkers.

Figure 16.9. Kathy Marshall at the Appalachian Trail.

Jane noticed how excited I was to see a sign for the Appalachian Trail (Figure 16.9) and listened when I revealed that walking the trail was on my personal Bucket List. I had read books of people walking the trail and always had a yen to hike a bit of it. As an additional impromptu treat for me, Jane asked if I'd like to walk a mile or so on that famous trail that extends 2,200 miles from Mount Katahdin, Maine, down to Springer Mountain in Georgia. *Are you kidding?* "Absolutely!"

In the gravel parking lot, I asked Jane to photograph me standing next to the large billboard which indicated we were 3.2 miles from the Washington Monument to the south, and north 2.5 miles to Annapolis Rock.

We strode from the parking lot, through the encaged pedestrian walkway over the busy freeway, then down through peoples' backyards, along a somewhat rocky dirt path, through a thinly forested area. I felt like Hansel and Gretel, following the blue trail markers stuck on trees which indicated the correct direction of the uneven gravel path.

As the trail became gradually steeper, and the trees sparser, we both concluded that I had experienced enough of that dream, thank you very much. On the way back to the truck, we saw a flushed, young woman trekker hiking solo along the trail. She carried a bulging, bright green backpack on her stooped shoulders. I wanted to, but didn't have the nerve, to chat with her about her solitary journey. Even though Jane and I only walked about a mile in total, I was happy to check that adventure off my bucket list.

Next, we attempted to determine what happened to my ancestors' remains at the former home of the Ebenezer Cemetery. It seemed my Prince was one of the first to be buried there in 1843, and his widow, Margaret Williams Hanson, joined him in 1868. That nexus to the church founder, Reverend Henry, was particularly exciting, as it was a topic of conversation I'd been having with African ironworking expert, Jean Libby (see Chapter 14: *Generations of Ironworkers* for more information).

Finally, and perhaps most importantly, we visited one of the five homes currently standing on lot 143 and half-lot 144 in Funkstown (Figure 13.1). Those lots were initially purchased by Prince in 1842, and then repurchased in 1868 for $690 by his sons Otho and Hezekiah Williams, after their mother, Margaret died.

The present homeowner would only agree to let me visit if I promised to give her three, 10 to 15-year-old, home-schooled children a history lesson about my enslaved ancestors. "I'd love to," I said. It was exhilarating to explain my family story of enslavement and freedom to the white children who lived in one of the five homes on my family's former property.

Jane believed the 4' by 4' concrete pad in the middle of their backyard could be covering a hand-dug well or a cistern from the original house. We looked closely at an old hand plow and a hand pump at one of the neighboring houses from Prince's original lots. Although dated 1891 and 1900, respectively, those were probably like the implements Prince and Otho used in the 1800s.

My knowledgeable guide was sure the large rock chimney was original to the house. She also believed that the vinyl siding on the structure likely covered the original log cabin where Margaret and her second husband, William Hanson, probably lived from the late 1840s until 1868 when Margaret died. The process of cladding original log cabins in brick, vinyl or aluminum siding seemed to be the custom for upgrading colonial-era homes in Washington County.

* The Fifth Day Home: Touring with Dr. Amt *

On Wednesday, I got to meet Dr. Emilie Amt, with whom I had collaborated online for several months. She helped me fine-tune possible theories about my family's origins. I was overwhelmed by the magnitude of the family memorabilia throughout her comfortable Frederick County home. She proudly showed me the personal family objects she had collected over a lifetime.

Dr. Amt has been instrumental in writing and publishing numerous educational materials about enslaved and free persons who lived in Washington County. She also regularly gave talks to community and academic groups about Maryland's slavery past. We took her car to experience the restored Beaver Creek School House for white children because, unfortunately, we could not find the remains of the "colored" school where Otho's niece—my first cousin, three-times removed—Katie Williams, taught colored children during the 1906/1907 school year.

Dr. Amt proudly showed me where colored people sat upstairs in the St. Mark's Church in Fairplay, Maryland. We sat together, above the first-floor pews, with me silently musing about how it must have felt to be black and separated from the rest of the congregation (Figure 16.10). Except for it being uncomfortably hot in the balcony during the summer, black folk did have the best seats in the house, view-wise.

Figure 16.10. View from upstairs seats where "colored people" sat at St. Marks Church, Fairplay, MD, 2017. Photograph: Kathy Marshall.

We explored the church cemetery which housed their black parishioners, like the Warfield family. Otho's sister, Mary, gave her prized "Freedom Quilt" to their daughter as a wedding present.

I noticed a bricklayer making improvements on the building and boldly asked if I might help a bit in the restoration. "Sure," he said, so I helped him mix the mortar in the wheelbarrow for a repair he was making to the exterior of the building.

We then explored the historic Jonathan Street neighborhood in Hagerstown where three predominantly black city blocks were sandwiched between Summit Avenue and Forest Drive. It was a settling place for free blacks in the county and the site of city homes and black businesses. This is the location of the Ebenezer A.M.E. and Asbury churches, the black-owned Harmon Hotel, and the jail (Figure 16.11).

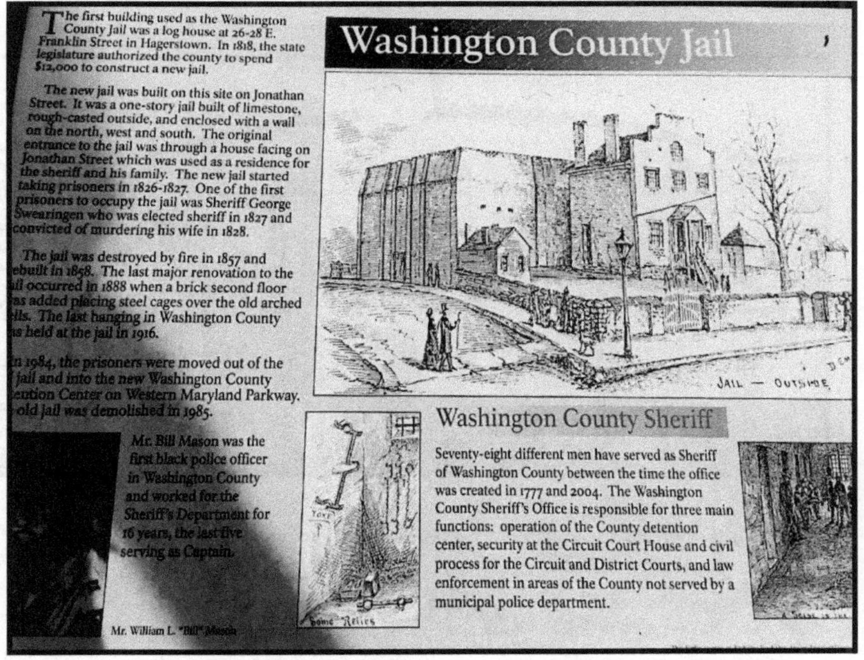

Figure 16.11. County Jail, once located in the Jonathan Street neighborhood, Hagerstown, MD

I tried to imagine a lively area where black people could feel reasonably safe, looking out for slave catchers, plotting plans to run away, selling their harvests, and worshipping together. I was gratified to learn Prince was probably one of the first people to be interred in the Ebenezer A.M.E. cemetery in 1843 since the church was founded in 1840. Until the 1960s, it was common practice to prevent members of the black community from expanding beyond Jonathan Street.

Most of our day together was spent perusing original documents at the John Clinton Frye Western Maryland Room in the Washington County Library. (Figure 16.12). That included looking through cemetery records, tax records, and even a book about the Ebenezer A.M.E. church. I enjoyed touching the actual "primary" documents that I had previously only seen in a digitized form on my home computer in California. Discussing my many theories about the parentage of my ancestors with Dr. Amt—an expert on black history in Washington County—was the highlight of my day. And I was thrilled when the Western Maryland Room and Washington County Historical Society accepted a copy of my *"The Ancestors Are Smiling!"* book.

Figure 16.12. John Clinton Frye Western Maryland Room, Washington County Free Library, where this author's *The Ancestors Are Smiling!* book now resides. Photograph: Kathy Marshall, 2017.

In the afternoon, Ms. Edie Wallace showed me the Tolson's Colored Church (Figure 12.1) in Sharpsburg which was being lovingly restored to represent a colored school arranged by the Freedmen's Bureau after the Civil War.

As always, I wondered if my family sent their children to that school. Realistically, Tolson school was about 9.5 miles from Otho and Alice's home near Roxbury Mills. Back in the day, people had to walk everywhere, unless they were rich enough to have a horse and buggy. There were seven colored schools in Washington County during the Reconstruction period following the end of slavery, but I could not determine where most of Otho and Alice's children learned to read and write in the 1880s.

* The Sixth Day Home: Rain Brings Clarity *

Thursday morning, I was on my own and spending time at the charming Washington County Historical Society in Hagerstown (Figure 16.13).

Figure 16.13. Research materials for this project spread out on the table, Washington County Historical Society, Photograph: Kathy Marshall, 2017.

Located downstairs in the Miller House, their amiable assistants were pulling boxes of slave-related materials for me. That treasure trove included original manumission documents protected with cellophane, indexes of deed records and bills of sale, original census records in hardbound books, newspaper articles about black life in western Maryland, photographs, and lists of slave owner names.

Many of the materials about blacks were compiled by historian Marguerite Doleman, who created a comprehensive Doleman Museum in her home. It contained a plethora of documents and black-oriented memorabilia she collected over a lifetime.

There were so many newspaper and other documents I wanted to review and photograph, but I had an important 1:00 PM appointment at the Antietam Iron Works. I had to tear myself away from that interesting research endeavor and leave by 12:30 PM, hoping to come back on Friday to get more clarity about black life in that locale.

For four days in a row, my requests for sunshine and tolerable warm weather were fulfilled. On the fifth day, forty-mile-per-hour-winds split open dense gray clouds that dropped their heavy wet loads on the streets of Hagerstown. As I drove toward my long-awaited appointment at the Antietam Ironworks, I could scarcely see the lines on the Sharpsburg Pike Road for the deluge pounding on my windshield. Luckily, there was a car in front of me with its red taillights as a beacon leading the way. I could only hope s/he was familiar with the road and had more effective windshield wipers than I did.

I had twenty-one minutes to get to my appointment on time, so I gripped the steering wheel, as an ocean-going ship captain must grip the wheel during a harrowing storm at sea. My rental car slowly moved through the slick, two-lane, winding roadways of rural Washington County. The nicely maintained roads were bordered by exceptionally green meadows, and still-leafless white oak, hickory, and ash trees.

A left turn onto the meandering Harper's Ferry Road brought me to my destination right on time. I parked on the graveled lot next to the gold truck of my friend and guide, Jane Neff. Buttoning up our hooded jackets and unfurling her umbrella, we dashed across the rain-soaked street and climbed the aggregate stone stairs to a glass door on the west side of the main building.

A tall, smiling man wearing a black and red baseball cap, and an open black jacket over a white cotton turtleneck shirt, stepped out to greet us. Wayne McCrossin was a retired engineer and the passionate owner and capable custodian of the Antietam Iron Works Furnace and Lime Kiln. Wayne spent the afternoon regaling Jane and me with fantastic stories about the Iron Works' history, the equipment used, and how waterpower was harnessed from the adjacent Antietam Creek in the mid-1700s to 1800s. He thoroughly described every step in the ironmaking process. (Figure 16.14).

It was clear he was serious, even dogged, about maintaining the historical value of the ironworks. He had no reservation about sharing his politically-charged views and opinions about people who misused their power and influence. He was indeed a charming man, in that special southern way.

I was there to learn all Wayne wanted to teach me about the Antietam Ironworks, and he was ready and willing to go on and on about the intricacies of the place. I loved every minute of it!

Wayne showed us numerous samples of the iron outputs produced there: nails, pike poles, hooks, chisels, wedges, and cannonballs. There was even a pair of ominous slave shackles in his collection. He took us on a memorable tour of the main building, showing us the barrel roller device in the lower level, and several outside storage buildings. Wayne and I exchanged historical documents each adding to the other's database of often obscure facts or various aspects of the Antietam Iron Works' history.

Figure 16.14. The general store in the Antietam Iron Works' main building. Owner Wayne McCrossin talks with C&O Canal Administrator, Jane Neff. Photograph: Kathy Marshall, 2017.

Jane and I were most happy to come home with a few pieces of shiny leftover slag, the stony waste matter separated from metals during the smelting or refining of ore, that had bits of colored ores and melted-silica-turned-to-glass from the iron ore rock. We even became familiar with delicious cherry moonshine, which at 180-proof, was surprisingly smooth and tasty.[178]

It was surreal, almost indescribable, knowing that my third great-grandfather, Prince Williams, became a skilled ironworker before the War of 1812 right here where I was standing.

Wayne was living in that main building where he had carefully renovated the company store, post office, and the industrial kitchen. All were likely places my Prince frequented during his tenure here. The basement held an authentic dolly-like barrel-roller with long wooden staves used to transport various goods on the nearby Potomac River to and from ships bound for various ports during the 1700s and 1800s.

Outside, Wayne had personally cleared a good swath of overgrown trees and shrubs which, over many decades, had been allowed to obscure the millrace and other important facilities at the furnace.

We stood for many minutes on the covered balcony, watching and listening to the soothing rhythm of the pouring rain splattering against the tin roof, and the powerful Antietam Creek cascading over large rocks in its course. We imagined what that place was like two hundred years ago when it was in its heyday of producing cannonballs, nails, and various other sundry metal objects.[179]

Jane and I thoroughly enjoyed the hospitality and spicy nature of our charming host.

* The Seventh Day Home: Williamsport and Fort Frederick *

On Friday, I left my home away from home at 8:00 AM on a dismally cold day to drive to Williamsport to meet up with a man I met online through DNA testing, Wayne Williams. I left earlier than necessary, so I could spend thirty minutes driving around Williamsport, the town founded by Otho Holland Williams (RevWarOtho). He was the man I had originally thought was my Otho's father or owner. I easily found the petit port and canal area where Otho Holland Williams attempted to convince George Washington in 1790 that little Williamsport should become the brand-new nation's capital.

It was way too cold that morning to walk along the tow path as I had intended, so I drove to meet Wayne at a coffee shop to talk about the intricacies of DNA research. He showed me the technical spreadsheets he had developed to track his DNA matches. I gave him all the documents I had collected on the Otho Holland Williams family since I proved they were no kin to me.

Next, I wanted to see Fort Frederick, a former military complex which had been purchased by ex-slave Nathan Williams for $7,000 on the eve of the Civil War. Inside the fort, he had added fences to pen animals and planted grape vines, produce, and a small orchard. Nathan also tilled and cultivated the fields outside the fort.[180] It was fascinating to explore the stone-walled fort and renovated rooms for officers, enlisted men, and prisoners, as well as the kitchen, dining room, hospital, laundry room and, of course, the armory.

I was furious to learn the cabin occupied by the black Nathan Williams family, who saved Fort Frederick from the ravages of time, was demolished by the National Park Service in favor of a parking lot for tourists. I felt it was a missed opportunity to have renovated their cabin as an insight and homage to the stalwart black family who had owned and cared for the fort for fifty years.

The rest of the afternoon was spent blissfully reviewing more documents at the Washington County Historical Society in Hagerstown. I was honored to be asked to provide them with some of my artwork for sale; yes, my Kanika African Sculptures artwork might be sold at my newly found Maryland ancestral home. I sent them a copy of my *The Ancestors Are Smiling!* book to become one of the research materials that others could use in their search.

* The Remainder of the Trip *

I spent the entire seventh day at my friends' Frederick County home sanctuary updating notes from my first week in Maryland.

On the eighth day, I drove toward Germantown, Pennsylvania, stopping off at Cecil County where a free black man named Prince Williams was mentioned in the 1820 through 1850 Federal Censuses (Figure 8.2). Was it possible that he fathered my third great-grandfather, Prince Williams? I did not know exactly where he had lived, but I got an idea of the terrain and towns.

I also journeyed to the remains of the Principio Furnace where a slave ironworker named Prince was mentioned in several ironworking-related books and reference documents. Whether that Principio Prince was related to my Prince is unknown, as discussed in Chapter 14, but it was an exciting possibility for future research.

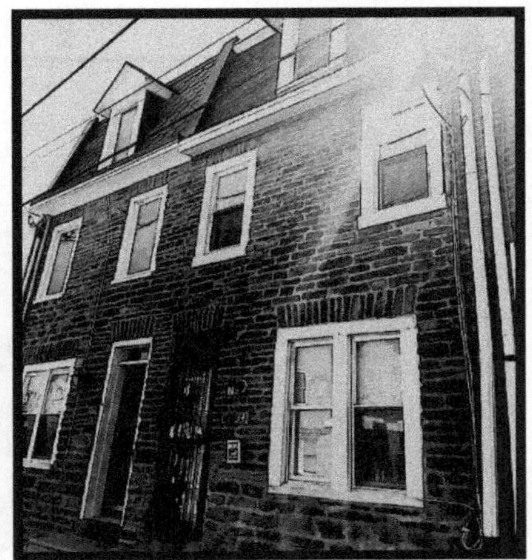

Figure 16.15. 5334 Priscilla Street, across from Otho Sherman's demolished house, Germantown, PA, 2017.

I made it to Germantown, a suburb of Philadelphia. I wanted to visit the 5335 Priscilla Street home of Otho Sherman Williams, son of the slave Otho Williams, and father of my Grandmother Pearl Williams Carter, who was born there on October 7, 1908.

I had driven back and forth several times on the narrow one-way lane that was Priscilla Street, but I couldn't find 5335 (Figure 16.15).

I asked neighbors who were playing darts outside their garage. They told me the homes on the other side of the lane were replaced with "the projects"[181] subsidized housing for low-income people, in 1953. The backside faced Potter's Field, which had been a cemetery for paupers. They said my grandmother's house would have been made from stone blocks like the one across the street.

I toured many historical sites and different segments—both the affluent and the destitute—of Philadelphia. I stayed in the comfort and safety of my rental car, soon realizing that I was not comfortable in big urban cities.

The ninth day was spent researching at the venerable Enoch Pratt Public Library and driving by various historical sites in Baltimore, Maryland.

Not looking forward to sitting another day in a research library, my vigor was renewed on the tenth day (Figure 16.16) by a trip to Bernice Bennett's home where she showed me ways I could analyze my DNA results to find our common ancestors.

Plus, it was simply delightful to meet the incredible woman who had a Blog Talk Radio show every week, called "Research from the National Archives and Beyond."[182] She interviews experts on various topics, generally, but not exclusively, on African American genealogy.

I was delighted to be her very first interview of the new year, on January 4, 2018, talking about my first book, *The Ancestors Are Smiling!* to people throughout the nation.

Figure 16.16. Genealogist Bernice Bennett helping Kathy Marshall with DNA Research, 2017.

PART IV: DNA DOESN'T LIE, DOES IT?

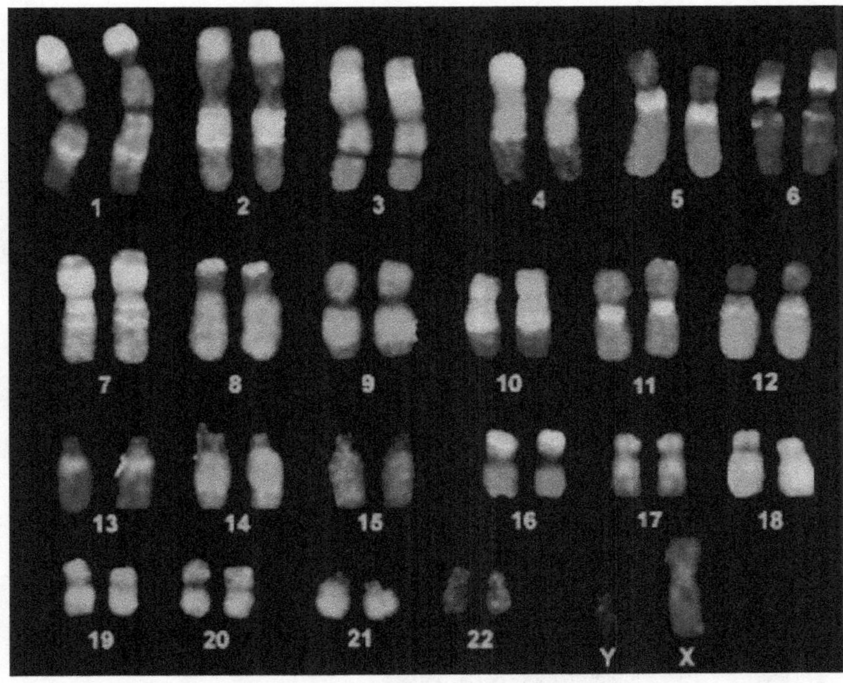

22 pairs of human chromosomes and 1 set of sex chromosomes from each parent make up our DNA.

MARY MARSHALL
That science hat looks real good on you!

Chapter 17 - A Basic DNA Primer

My father, Dr. Thomas R. Marshall, had the slim muscular build, full lips and the soft wooly hair of a traditional African, but he was over 6'2" tall and had the skimpy buttocks, full calves and skin tone of a tanned white man. Dad's powerful build and never-ending lung capacity were perfect for swimming, bicycling, long-distance running, and participating in numerous Marathons [183] and Triathlons[184] around the world.

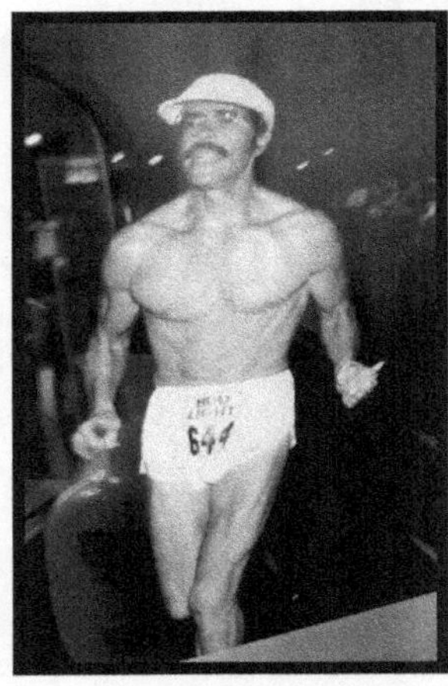

Dr. Thomas Marshall, 60 in 1991, triathlete.

My mother, Mary Carter Marshall, had an athletic but petite, pear-shaped build with full hips "made for having babies" as her obstetrician told her. She was slightly duskier in complexion than my dad, and her meaty calves and thick ankles helped her become a competitive tennis player who could safely pivot and return balls with a powerful force from any part of the tennis court.

Mary Marshall, 18 in 1952, tennis player.

Facially, some say I look so like my mother that sometimes her friends mistake me for her, which can be alarming because she died 11 years ago. Genetically, I have my dad's broad shoulders, muscular arms, narrow waist and defined abdominal muscles, as well as my mother's strong legs, which helped me become the 1987 Sacramento, California, Middle Weight Body Building Champion.

Kathy Marshall, 30, 1987, bodybuilder

Greg Marshall, 53, 2016, bicyclist in Eppie's Great Race Triathlon.

Carrie Marshall, 21 in 1980, swimmer.

My brother, Greg, is in dad's mold all the way; well, except that Greg is lucky enough to have an ample rump. Greg's masculine physique and lung capacity allow him to be a long- and short-distance bicycling competitor.

My sister, Carrie, is physically a combination of both parents: tall and slim but with an hour-glass figure. Even though Carrie had severe bouts with asthma as a child, her dad-lungs give her long-distance stamina, so she can swim fifty laps at a measured pace with little difficulty, compared to her sister (me) who can only swim two fast laps before my weaker lungs conk out.

To what may we attribute these similarities and differences between parents and children? Genetics.[185] Have you ever watched one of those afternoon tabloid TV talk shows where the "Baby Daddy" is proven to be the father of his girlfriend's illegitimate child? And how about those fascinating crime scene investigation TV shows that investigate the causes for murders? What do these two genres of TV shows have in common? That's right: DNA, genetics.

We all can identify traits we believe we received from our parents and other family members. These genetic traits can be purely physical—such as height, weight, eye color or hair type. They can be mental—such as a parent passing on a tendency for depression or schizophrenia. Genetic traits can also be physiological—such as sickle cell anemia blood disease, glaucoma eye disease, or heart disease being genetically passed onto a child.

Have you ever thought about exactly how genetic traits were passed down in your family from one generation to the next? Did you inherit your mother's full bosom, your father's paunch, or your grandmother's piercing green eyes?

Nowadays, not only doctors, scientists and forensic police have access to genetic material, but also the general public through DNA testing that is widely available through several reputable testing companies. Depending on the desired use, there are four primary types of DNA tests available to the public:

1. A Y-DNA test may be used to determine the man's paternity from son to father, back over generations of fathers to theoretical Adam.

2. An X-DNA test can point to the mother's lineage of a male or female.

3. A Mitochondrial DNA (mtDNA) test estimates the woman's direct maternal ancestral line back from mother to mother to mother, to theoretical Eve.

4. An autosomal DNA test can estimate the genetic admixture - that is, the percentage of African, European, Asian, or other ethnic percentages in your DNA from past generations of relatives. The autosomal test may be taken by men or women and is, arguably, the most important test for general genealogical analysis.

I wanted to clearly understand what DNA was so I could better determine whether it might help find our Williams family's ethnic origins and family connections. After all, finding out the reason for my pale skin color was one of the primary springboards for writing this book. Bear with me while I offer what I've learned about DNA testing. For more detailed information I recommend *The Family Tree Guide to DNA Testing and Genetic Genealogy*, by Blaine T. Bettinger.

OK. Do you have your "Bill Nye Science Guy" hat placed firmly on your head? First, let us begin with DNA - Deoxyribonucleic acid. It is a molecule that carries the genetic instructions used in the growth, development, functioning, and reproduction of all known living organisms and many viruses.[186] DNA determines whether a cell[187] is a sweat gland, a hair shaft, a fat cell, a cell in your lungs or in your eye, etc. Cells perform different functions depending on where in the body they are. A cell in the heart pushes blood all around your body. A cell in your mouth registers the taste, and so forth.

"Genes" are made up of DNA and are part of the hereditary material of a "chromosome" that can be passed from one generation to the next. A chromosome is a long chain of DNA, organized into a compact package which is often drawn to look like pairs of squiggly colored lines because that is how they look under a microscope (see the photo on the first page of Part II). Humans have 22 pairs of autosomal chromosomes. The 23rd pair, consisting of an X or Y chromosome, determines a person's sex. Women have two X sex chromosomes in that 23rd pair, but men have an X and a Y, so-called because they look roughly like the letter X and Y under a microscope. Chromosomes are inherited in pairs, one set of 23 chromosomes from each parent, for a total of 46 chromosomes.

You randomly received 50% of your genetic material from your mother and 50% from your father. Each of your parents randomly got 50% of their traits from each of their parents; that means you *randomly* got 25% of your traits from your mom's mother, 25% from your mom's father, 25% from your dad's mother, and 25% of your traits from your dad's father. Continue back three more generations and only about 3% of your genetic material is from your great-great-great-grandparents, as shown in Figure 17.1.

Generation	%DNA
Parents	50
Grandparents	25
Great grandparents	12.5
Great great grandparents	6.25
Great great great grandparents	3.125

Figure 17.1. Approximate percentage of traits received from your ancestors.

Think about *your* family and who you believe got which traits from which parent and grandparent.

As stated in the Introduction, I wanted to prove or disprove whether Otho Williams passed along his alleged mechanical and engineering abilities down through each generation in my Williams family to me. The chart shows that it is theoretically possible that 6.25% of my total DNA is from my second great-grandfather and grandmother, but which specific traits did I get from each of them? There is no gene for mechanical ability, of course, so it will likely be impossible to prove whether my penchant for welding or solving mechanical problems was passed down through the generations genetically, but let's explore the concept anyway.

Look at Figure 17.2 representing some made-up traits. Let's assume that the letter codes in each CIRCLE (which represents a woman) and SQUARE (which represents a man), are from my fictitious "Traits Passed Down from Your Parents and Grandparents to You" at the bottom of the figure. In this made-up example, your maternal grandmother in the top left circle was a calm person (purple-P) and had brown freckles (BR); she passed those traits down to your mother in the middle left circle (see the BR and P). However, neither of those traits were passed down to you, shown in the bottom square. So, you did not inherit a sense of calm, nor brown freckles from your mom's mom.

Conversely, your dad's father, in the top right square, was gregarious (G) and he was overweight (O). He passed down his weight problem (O) to your dad, in the square in the middle row, as well as his wonderfully gregarious nature (G). You received some of that gregarious trait (G) from your father, as shown in the square in the bottom row. It looks like you got a lot of a tendency for red cheeks (R) from your maternal grandfather, as well as his left-handedness (L). You got blond hair (Y) from your dad's mother, as well as her blue eyes (B).

You did not get your maternal grandmother's peaceful nature nor her freckles (no P or BR), and you did not get a tendency to be fat from your paternal grandfather (no O). However —*and this is important*—maybe your sister *did* get your maternal grandma's peaceful countenance and paternal grandpa's extra pounds.

The bottom line is that the traits you get from your parents and grandparents are *randomly* assigned. While you and your siblings may have the same parents, there is no pattern as to which child gets which trait. That means the traits you inherited will likely be different than what your siblings got unless you are identical twins. But why should this information matter to us?

It is critically important to understand this issue of randomly receiving different traits from your parents and grandparents, especially when it comes to DNA results. It is the key reason why you must DNA test multiple family members, not just yourself, to get a better picture of your DNA heritage.

A prime example is illustrated with Native American (NA) ancestry. There are few pure NA tribes left for DNA comparison testing. This is partially due to diseases from foreigners, but more to the relentless genocide from dominant Caucasian populations towards native peoples in America.

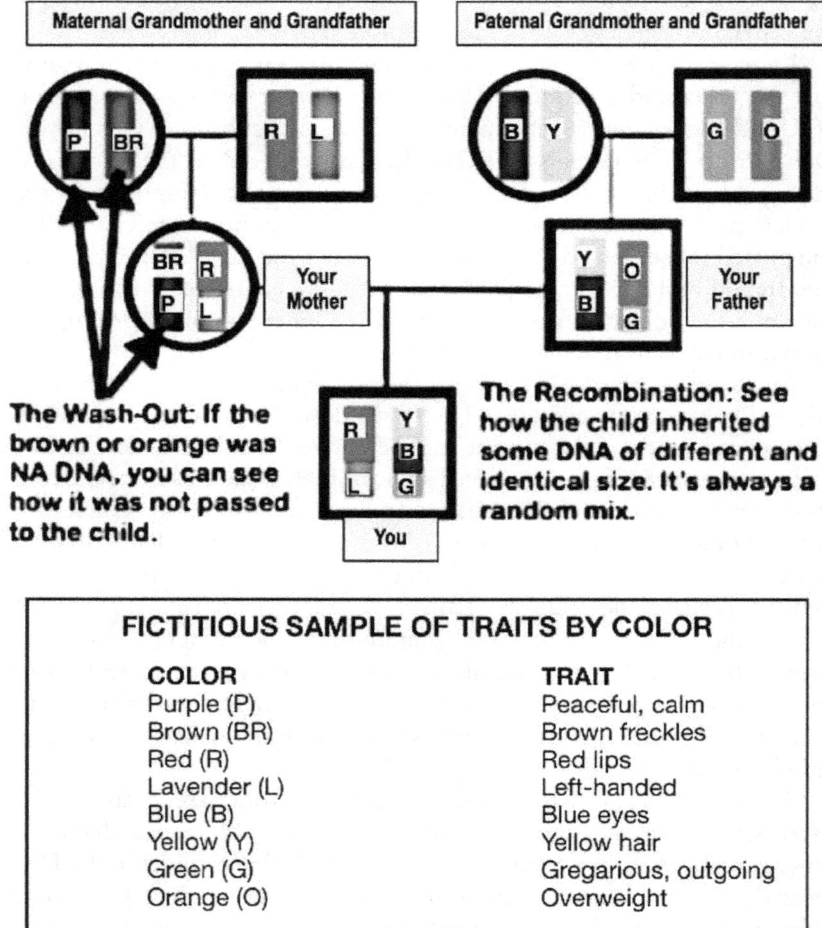

FICTITIOUS SAMPLE OF TRAITS BY COLOR

COLOR	TRAIT
Purple (P)	Peaceful, calm
Brown (BR)	Brown freckles
Red (R)	Red lips
Lavender (L)	Left-handed
Blue (B)	Blue eyes
Yellow (Y)	Yellow hair
Green (G)	Gregarious, outgoing
Orange (O)	Overweight

Figure 17.2. Traits passed down from your parents and grandparents to you.

This has resulted in the mixing of NA tribes who were forced to vacate their lands in the eastern United States for reservations in middle American states.

There is generally not a large enough reference population[188] of pure NA tribes to connect them to those of us who want to prove our NA heritage. Look at Figure 17.2 again. Let's assume this second time that the dark purple color stands for NA ancestry. As you may recall, none of the purple trait was passed down to you in our example. In our new scenario, that would mean you did not receive NA ancestry from your maternal grandmother.

The random "wash out" of some traits as they dwindle away from generation to generation, may explain why you may have NA ancestors in your family's past, but not see any evidence of that in *your* DNA test results. That is why it is so important to DNA test several members of your family, especially your elders.

In our second fictitious example, maybe your sister's DNA results do show a small amount of residual NA DNA, even though *your* results do not show any. With multiple family members testing, you may get a better picture of your family's complete ancestry.

It's a fact. DNA testing is expensive.[189] Autosomal tests that look at 22 of your 23 chromosomes from each parent cost between $59 and $199, depending on the testing company and whether they are having a sale. However, Y-DNA and mtDNA tests generally cost much more than that, in the many hundreds of dollars.[190] Truthfully, before I understood the residual DNA issue, I thought testing multiple family members was just a racket by greedy DNA companies who wanted to make more money. Well, I still think DNA testing is way over-priced, but I think it is a *requirement* that multiple family members be tested to get a more well-rounded picture of your genetic family heritage.

Family members are more likely to agree to take a DNA test if you pay for it. I shelled out about $1,000 in DNA test kits for several family members in 2016 alone. Here are two great tips for reducing the costs for DNA testing. 1) Buy DNA tests when they are on sale, usually around the holidays, to save 30% or more. 2) Ask your family members to get themselves tested instead of buying you a Christmas, birthday or anniversary present. My son took a Y-37 DNA test from Family Tree DNA (FTDNA) for my Christmas present in 2016. He upgraded to a Y-67 test in 2017 for another $100 or so. Maybe he will upgrade to a Y-111 test in 2018. More expensive tests lead to more statistically significant results, which means more surety in who your actual Y-DNA matches are.

How many family members should be DNA tested? There is no set rule, but you should *immediately* test your parents and oldest living relatives, for they have genetic material from further back in your family line. Also test at least one other sibling, first cousins, and aunts and uncles. Second cousins share the same great-grandparents, and third cousins share the same great-great-grandparents, the latter of whom were from the period of slavery.

If you are a woman, consider asking the oldest male in your family to take a Y-DNA test for you, because only men can take a Y-DNA test. I was fortunate to get three males from three of my different family lines to take Y-DNA tests, in the hope that we may find our ancestral lineage during and before slavery.

After all was said and done, within four months of starting to write this book, I had autosomal DNA results from eleven family members, one mitochondrial test, and three Y-DNA tests at the 37, 67 and 111-marker levels for our Anderson, Williams, and Marshall family lines:

- From 23andMe: (http://23andme.com) me and my Uncle Dale. This included autosomal tests and a haplogroup (a group of people who share a common ancestor in the maternal or paternal line).

- From Family Tree DNA: (http://familytreedna.com) me (autosomal and mitochondrial test), and Y-DNA and autosomal tests for my brother, Greg, my son, Matthew, and my cousin, Bob, whose Y-DNA was most directly from Otho Williams (via his father, Charles Williams, who was the son of Otho Sherman Williams, who was the son of our formerly-enslaved Otho Williams).

- From Ancestry DNA: (http://ancestry.com) autosomal test only: me, Uncle Dale (my mother's brother), "Aunt" Lavata (technically my mother's first cousin); my sister Carrie and brother Greg; first cousins Julie and Pamala, whose parents were the siblings of my mother; and third cousin Launi whose grandmother was the sister of my grandmother.

I am now ready to use this powerful DNA technology to find more clues about my family's ancestry. Come and join me on this adventure. My steps may help you to find your ancestors through DNA.

Chapter 18 - The Best DNA Testing Company?

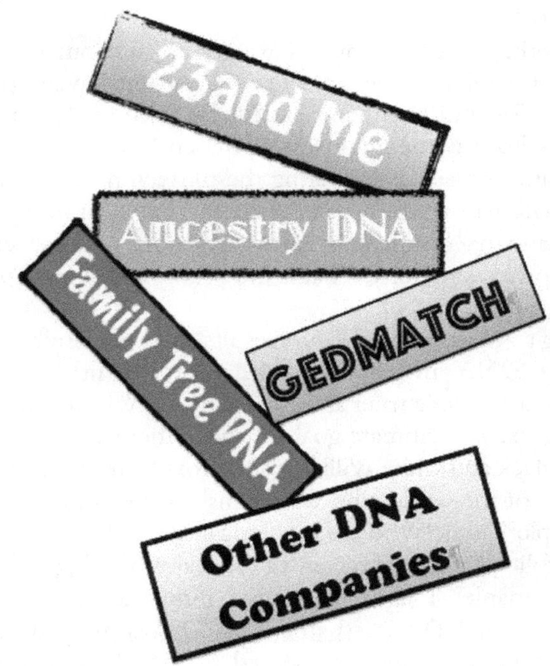

Time to put on your science hat for Chapters 18 and 19. Don't be scared. It will be fun, you'll see!]

People often ask me, "Which is the best DNA testing company?" My answer is, "It depends on what you want to discover." Different companies offer different types of tests, display the DNA information in a variety of ways, and have multiple tools to help analyze the results.

This chapter explores a few of the differences between the three major companies that I used which may help you determine which might be the best testing company for your needs. Please note that the following are the techniques and features that I used in this study. They are by no means a complete assessment of all the companies' features. Further, I am NOT a DNA expert and am still learning about this powerful tool.

By the second month on this project —November 2017—I was fortunate to get several family members to take DNA tests. I used their initials for the following charts and graphs. My sister, Carrie, is called CM, brother Greg is GM. Among my first cousins, Julie is JC, Pamala is PC and Bob is BW. Third cousin Launi is LG, and my youngest son, Matthew, is MA.

I am perhaps most happy to have gotten autosomal DNA test results from our three living Williams elders: my Aunt Lavata, (LW) 83, Uncle Dale, (DC) 78, and our then-oldest living relative, Great Uncle Charles (CW), 92 who was the grandson of my enslaved Otho Williams. Great Uncle Charles passed away during the thirteenth month on this project, after his wife had read *The Ancestors Are Smiling!* to him three times. He died knowing that his life story, as well as those of his sisters and parents, would go on in perpetuity. That is the beauty of having a published book on Amazon.com.

Having so many familial DNA results gives my family a greater chance of finding DNA matches[191] with other potential family members. Perhaps, it also gives a truer assessment of our Williams family's complete ethnic origins. The ultimate goal for this rather expensive DNA exercise is to find black and white Williams ancestors from Africa and Europe and other parts of the world who would answer the questions: "Who are my white people?" and "Who are my Africans?"

What follows is a brief review of the major offerings of the three DNA testing companies I used, and what I learned from them: 23andMe (23andme.com), FTDNA (FamilyTreeDNA.com) and Ancestry DNA (ancestry.com). I generally presented my DNA results due to privacy concerns for other family members.

Please keep in mind that DNA companies are constantly changing the look and content of their results. Therefore, the specific views and tools presented in this book, as of November 2018, may be different in the future. Figure 18.1 shows which family members took a DNA test from at least one of the companies mentioned above. Their initials will be used on charts and graphs in Chapters 18 and 19.

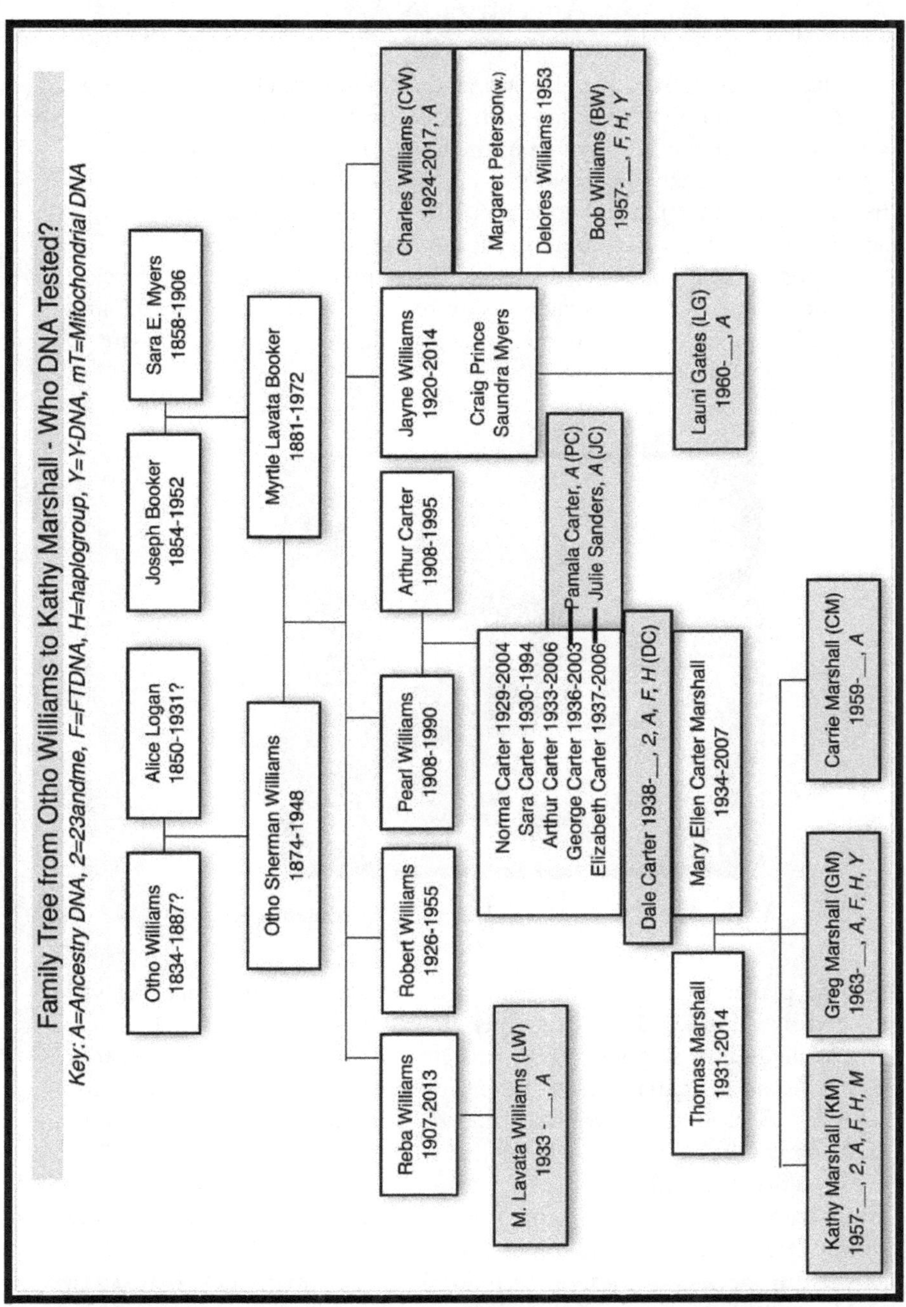
Family Tree from Otho Williams to Kathy Marshall - Who DNA Tested?
Key: A=Ancestry DNA, 2=23andme, F=FTDNA, H=haplogroup, Y=Y-DNA, mT=Mitochondrial DNA
Otho Williams 1834-1887?
Alice Logan 1850-1931?
Joseph Booker 1854-1952
Sara E. Myers 1858-1906
Otho Sherman Williams 1874-1948
Myrtle Lavata Booker 1881-1972
Reba Williams 1907-2013
Robert Williams 1926-1955
Pearl Williams 1908-1990
Arthur Carter 1908-1995
Jayne Williams 1920-2014
Craig Prince
Saundra Myers
Charles Williams (CW) 1924-2017, A
Margaret Peterson(w.)
Delores Williams 1953
Bob Williams (BW) 1957-__, F, H, Y
M. Lavata Williams (LW) 1933 - __, A
Norma Carter 1929-2004
Sara Carter 1930-1994
Arthur Carter 1933-2006
George Carter 1936-2003
Elizabeth Carter 1937-2006
Pamala Carter, A (PC)
Julie Sanders, A (JC)
Launi Gates (LG) 1960-__, A
Dale Carter 1938-__, 2, A, F, H (DC)
Mary Ellen Carter Marshall 1934-2007
Thomas Marshall 1931-2014
Kathy Marshall (KM) 1957-__, 2, A, F, H, M
Greg Marshall (GM) 1963-__, A, F, H, Y
Carrie Marshall (CM) 1959-__, A

Figure 18.1. Kathy Marshall's Family Members Who Took a DNA Test (yellow/shaded).

* Ancestry DNA *

After I retired from my day job at the California Highway Patrol in 2012, I ordered a DNA test kit from Ancestry.com. A few days later, a 4 x 6 white and green box arrived in the mail. The diminutive package had a greenish aura emanating from it—a power, a promise. As I held it in my trembling hands, I felt this innocuous item would bestow upon me the answers to my many questions about our ancestry.

I opened the DNA Kit with nervous excitement. Inside was a postcard which contained simple instructions on how to "collect my sample," and a place for me to "sign my name," thereby acknowledging my consent to have my DNA tested. (Figure 18.2).

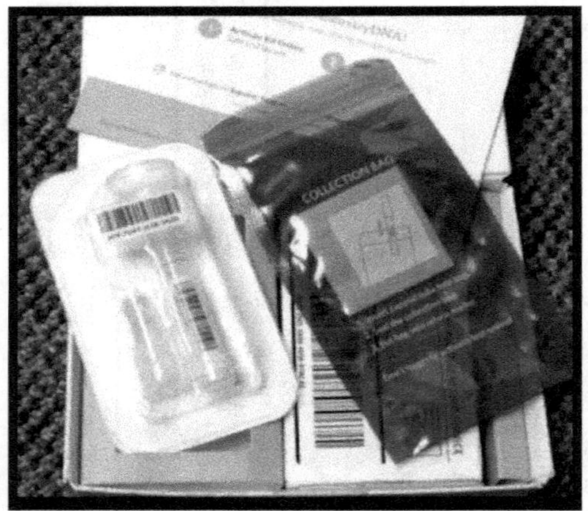

Figure 18.2. Ancestry.com DNA test kit contents.

The plastic-wrapped, white package contained a three-inch-tall vial topped by a funnel; the instructions indicated this vial would "hold my DNA-filled saliva sample." There was also a tiny capped bottle next to it with a liquid in it that was to be poured into the vial to "stabilize my sample." A clear gray envelope labeled "Collection Bag" would safely "house my DNA" on the way to the laboratory.

Would that small vial of DNA-filled saliva really tell me where my family came from decades ago, generations ago, centuries ago? Would I discover the secret of my origins? Which African or Native American tribes, European countries, or Asian locales, make up my DNA? Just as a child, I agonized waiting for Santa Claus to come down the chimney with my presents. How could I wait eight long weeks to learn my ancestral fate? But wait I did. Oh, happy day when the results came via email!

There are several different components that Ancestry DNA's autosomal test provides. 1) An Ethnicity Estimate of the countries from where your DNA originates, called your "admixture". 2) an extensive list of people whose DNA matches parts of your 22 chromosomes. 3) DNA Circles which indicate which of your DNA matches might have common ancestors with you (Figure 18.3).

The verdict? I was stunned. There was no denying the extent of the European cream in my African coffee!

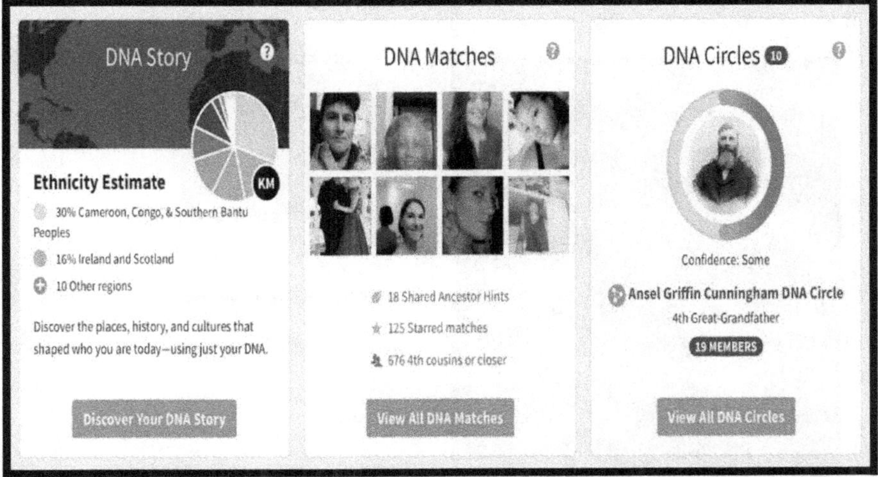

Figure 18.3. Ancestry.com DNA results for Kathy Marshall show links for the ethnicity estimate, list of DNA matches, and graph showing DNA Circles (as of October 2017).

Many American blacks have 15-25% Caucasian DNA,[192] most often due to white men having "relations" with enslaved black women before the end of slavery. My percentage of Caucasian DNA was much higher than the norm. Looking in the mirror, I should have anticipated my results. I wasn't happy seeing only 53% of my DNA came from African countries (primarily Cameroon, Congo, and Bantu regions and Benin-Togo). A whopping 45% is from Europe (primarily Ireland, Scotland, and England), with the remaining 2% from Native America (Figure 18.4).

Such a high European percentage signifies to me that *several* of my female relatives were impregnated by *several* white men long ago. After decades of denying that I—the owner of Kanika *African* Sculptures—am anything but 100% black, I must deal with the facts: I *am* mixed after all.

Being a data girl who likes knowing the facts, I was motivated to find out which Europeans and Africans contributed to my appearance. Since I couldn't answer that question from my family tree alone, I kept hoping DNA research would provide the key to unlock the

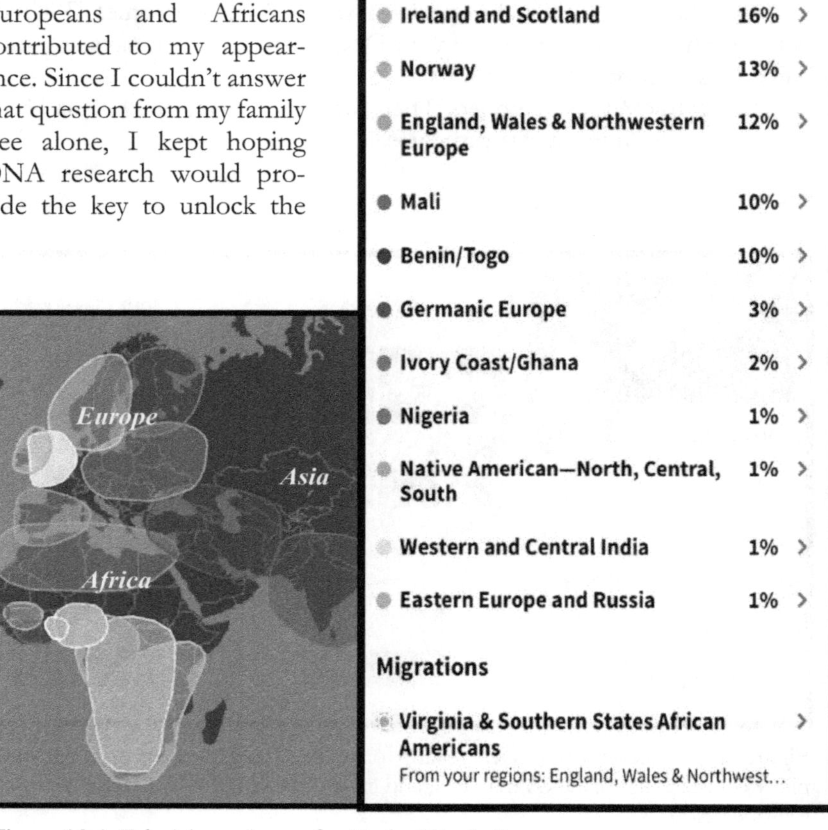

Figure 18.4. Ethnicity estimate for Kathy Marshall.

truth. A distant DNA cousin of mine, named HDG, *only* uses the scientific data from DNA testing to find the families of adoptees. I was fortunate that he was helping me find my white and African people by closely examining my family's DNA results.

Before discussing this topic further, one must understand that:

- DNA ethnicity admixture results are only estimates, not facts, sometimes based on a small reference population who tested in some countries. Estimates will change as more people are tested worldwide.

- Several family members should be tested to get more complete estimates of family ancestry, due to the randomness of DNA passed from generation to generation.

- DNA from the oldest family members provide the best results for finding ancestors because theirs contains more genetic material that matches the ancestors.

The ethnic admixture estimates for eleven of our Williams descendants are shown in Figure 18.5. On average, 57% of our collective ethnic origins are from Africa, 42% are from Europe, and the remaining 1% are from other continents. Ancestry DNA found a minute 1% amount of Native American (NA) DNA for KM (me).

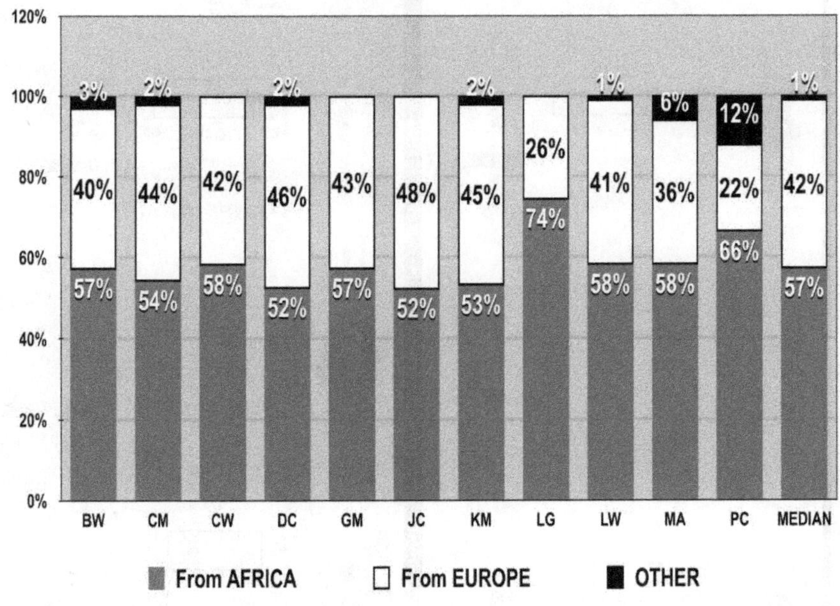

Figure 18.5. Ethnic admixture estimates for Otho Williams' descend-

Finding DNA matches allows you to sort your matches by family tree hints, the newest data results, starred matches, and migration regions, like Virginia and Southern States African Africans. You can also search by surname or location. Matches are listed by relationship: immediate family is listed first, then first cousins, then second, third, fourth, and "distant" cousins. The confidence level of the estimates is also included: "extremely high" describes how confident Ancestry is in the predicted match. Figure 18.6 shows third to fourth cousin DNA matches for Kathy Marshall and Charles Williams, the grandson of slave Otho Williams.

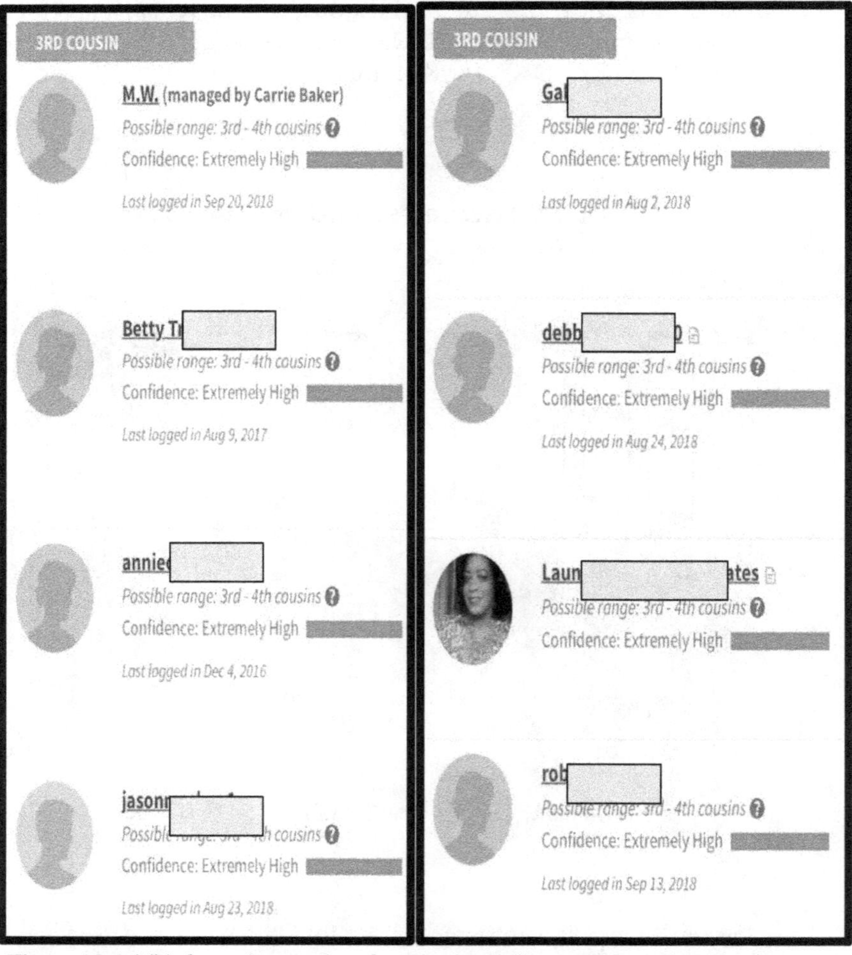

Figure 18.6. Third cousin matches for Charles Williams (left) and Kathy Marshall (right).

Finding Shared Hints Matches indicates whether your DNA matches have some of the same surnames in their family tree, leading to the name of common ancestors if both people have extensive family trees back many generations that contain common ancestors. The majority of my matches have no Ancestry DNA family tree, or their tree is private, or I have too few generations, so the Shared Hint Matches function produced only a half-dozen results. (Figure 18.7).

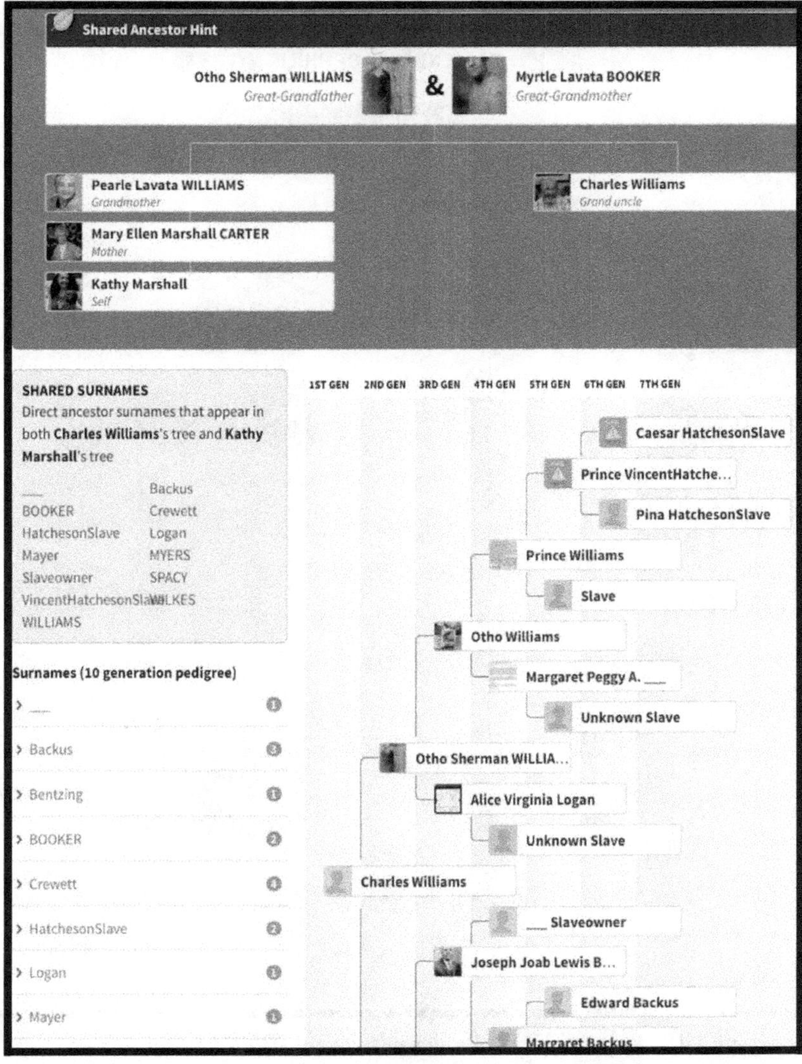

Figure 18.7. Ancestry DNA: Finding shared ancestors/relatives.

Reviewing DNA Circles (Figure 18.8) helps discover other members who are related to you through a specific ancestor. Many of the names in DNA Circles are not yet in your family tree, but they identify other potential family members who match your DNA and might match specific family members. For example, I do not yet know anyone in my Daniel Fleming Circle, but they could contain some of "my white people" whom I simply do not know about yet.

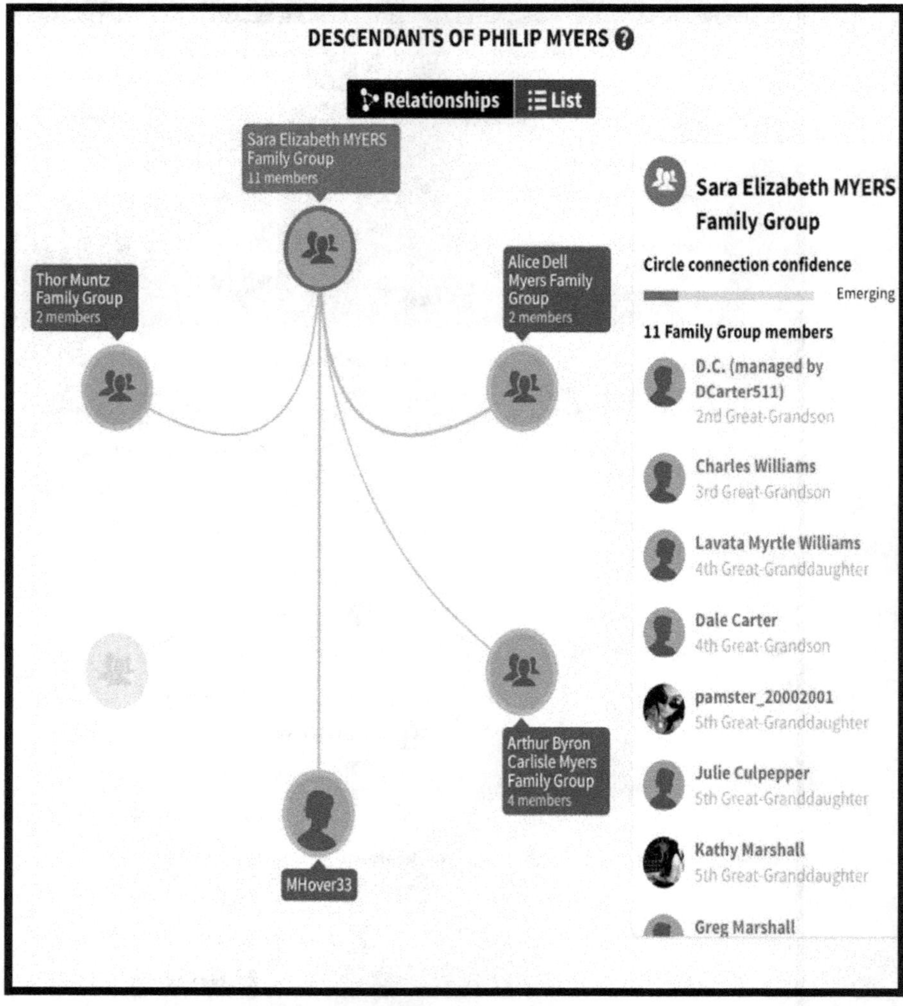

Figure 18.8. Ancestry DNA: Reviewing DNA Circles.

Examining Migration Patterns: helps determine specific places where your family may have lived before coming to America and where they settled as of 1850, as shown in Figure 18.9.

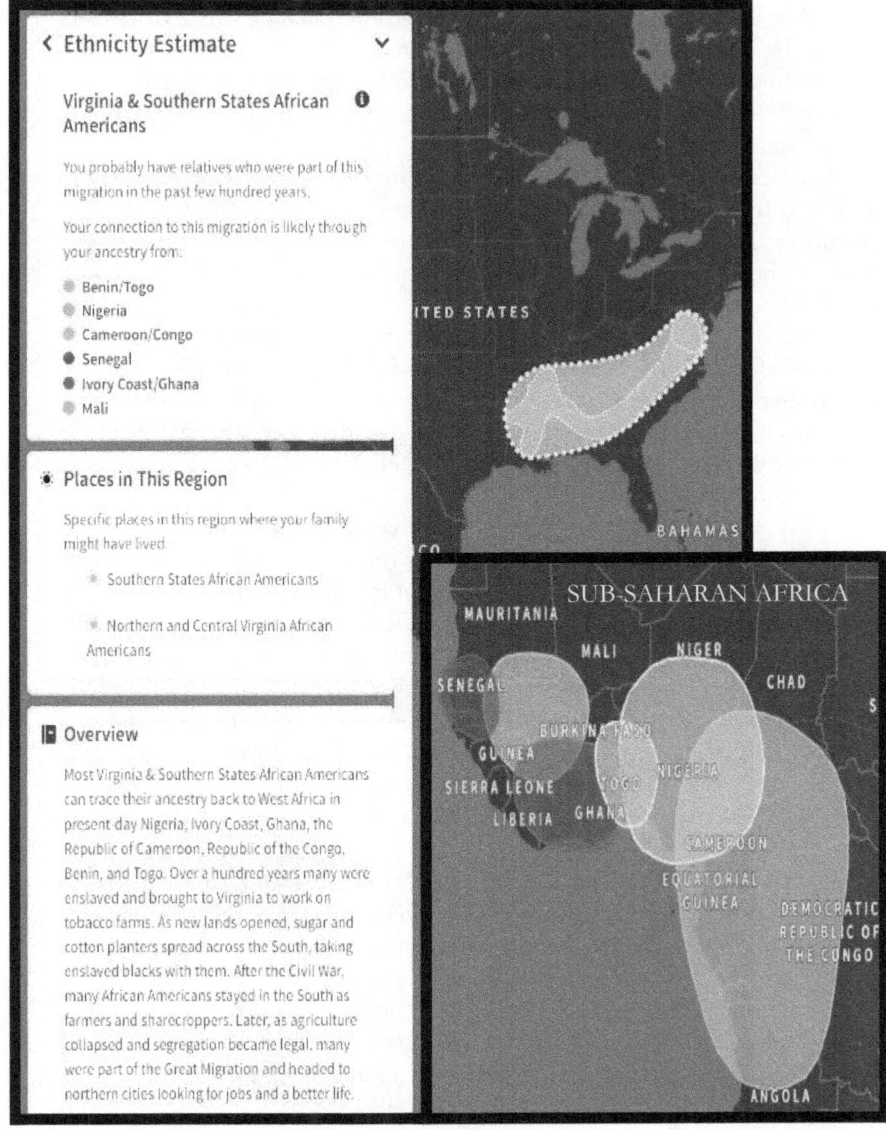

Figure 18.9. Ancestry DNA: Examining migration patterns.

* 23andMe *

I was skeptical about the veracity of my beta 2012 Ancestry DNA ethnicity estimates, so I took a second autosomal test in 2014, but with 23andMe. It provided similar European ethnic breakdowns to Ancestry DNA, but also genetic and health-related information, as well as a haplogroup (a group of people who share a common ancestor in the maternal or paternal line) indicating my mother's line of mothers back to theoretical Eve.[193]

The verdict? 23andMe says 47.7% of my DNA is from Europeans, 49.6% is from Sub-Saharan African countries, with a sprinkling of other countries. 23andMe estimates are slightly different from Ancestry DNA, but they both indicate that I am the "Oreo" and the "zebra" school kids used to laugh at. (Figure 18.10)

Ancestry DNA uncovered 1.0% Native American DNA for me; 23andMe found 1.5% Native American and .5% South Asian for me. This is admittedly a very low percentage statistically, and nothing to jump up and down about. It *may* suggest, however, that perhaps my paternal Grandmother Daisy's story about my having a Native American great-great-grandmother, was true.

Many African Americans are told they have NA blood to explain away light skin coloring or non-kinky hair, but the truth is often that a white man inseminated a female slave to *breed* lighter-skinned slaves who would become house-slaves[194]. The bottom line was that it was time for me to accept all aspects of my bloodlines, not only my African roots.

DNA doesn't lie! Who were all those white people whose DNA makes up almost half of my family's DNA? There are only a couple of white men my family knows about. One tale was a German fellow named Philip Myers who sailed to Pennsylvania as a young boy in 1766, migrated to Frederick County, Maryland, then had a mulatto son who moved to Belmont County, Ohio.

It is also family lore that my maternal second great-grandfather, Joseph Booker, was fathered by his slave owner, who may have had the surname Early. The slave master's sister taught him how to read, even though it was illegal, and that ability helped him live a successful life after slavery. I also met paternal cousins through DNA on my Grandma Daisy's line in Mississippi. Can I find white and African relatives in my Williams family line using DNA matching? Let's see what 23andMe can tell us.

Sub-Saharan African	49.6%
West African	44.9%
African Hunter-Gatherer	2.7%
Broadly Sub-Saharan African	2.0%
European	**47.7%**
British & Irish United Kingdom	16.2%
Scandinavian	2.2%
Iberian	0.4%
Ashkenazi Jewish	0.1%
Broadly Northwestern European	20.2%
Broadly Southern European	5.3%
Broadly European	3.3%
East Asian & Native American	**1.5%**
Native American	1.0%
Southeast Asian	0.3%
Broadly East Asian & Native American	0.1%
South Asian	**0.5%**
Broadly South Asian	0.5%
Unassigned	**0.6%**

Figure 18.10. 23andMe DNA: Kathy Marshall's ethnicity estimates.

Viewing the Ancestry of DNA Relatives, from the 23andMe App, gives visual clues to the larger picture of our DNA migration patterns (Figure 18.11).

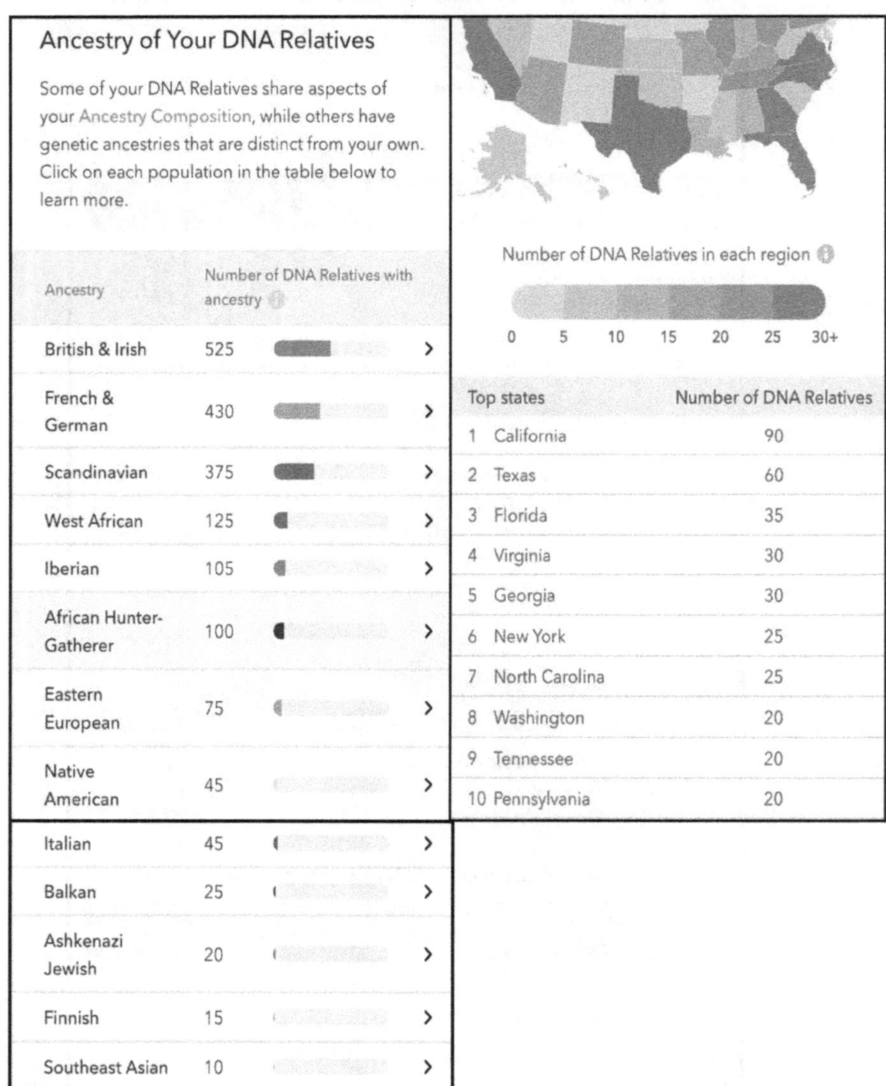

Ancestry of Your DNA Relatives

Some of your DNA Relatives share aspects of your Ancestry Composition, while others have genetic ancestries that are distinct from your own. Click on each population in the table below to learn more.

Ancestry	Number of DNA Relatives with ancestry
British & Irish	525
French & German	430
Scandinavian	375
West African	125
Iberian	105
African Hunter-Gatherer	100
Eastern European	75
Native American	45
Italian	45
Balkan	25
Ashkenazi Jewish	20
Finnish	15
Southeast Asian	10

Top states		Number of DNA Relatives
1	California	90
2	Texas	60
3	Florida	35
4	Virginia	30
5	Georgia	30
6	New York	25
7	North Carolina	25
8	Washington	20
9	Tennessee	20
10	Pennsylvania	20

Figure 18.11. 23andMe: Migration patterns of people whose DNA matches Kathy Marshall to some degree.

Participating in Health Research. With 23andMe there is a never-ending slew of research surveys one may participate in to help scientists solve medical problems. It makes me proud to know that my genetic material and survey responses may help doctors find a cure for Alzheimer's, or breast cancer, or any number of health-related concerns. Admittedly, there are privacy issues to carefully consider when allowing your DNA data to be used by others.

With 23and me, I may learn which of several medical conditions are common for people like me, healthy females in our sixties. Based on my genetics, I only have a 1% likelihood of coronary heart disease, but I might want to watch out for allergies, asthma, and cancer. I did choose to find out if the DNA sample I submitted to 23andMe indicated that I carried the BRCA breast cancer gene (thankfully I do not, but that does not mean I won't get the breast cancer that killed my mother).

There are several informative reports that 23andMe generates from our DNA, such as:

- Traits: The genetics behind our appearance and senses.
- Ancestry: The story of our ancient ancestors, our origins, and our ancestral background.
- Wellness: How our DNA may affect our response to diet, exercise, and sleep.
- Find out how your DNA may affect your body's response to diet, exercise, and sleep. [Author note: the predictions based on my DNA are all true … DNA doesn't lie].
- Caffeine Consumption: Likely to consume less than others.
- Deep Sleep Less: Likely to be a deep sleeper.
- Genetic Weight: Predisposed to weigh less than average.
- Muscle composition: Common in elite power athletes.
- Saturated fat and weight: Likely have similar weight.

These reports are interesting, but I do not peruse them much.

Painting Chromosomes visually estimates which of the DNA segments in each of my 23 chromosomes are linked to my different ethnic ancestries (Figure 18.12). I am especially interested in the yellow colors (denoted by the dotted lines circling the yellow color) noted on the chart which indicate my Native American and Southeast Asian ancestry on my X chromosome because they possibly validate my Grandmother Daisy's story that her grandmother was part Native American, as well as my exciting haplogroup findings discussed in Chapter 20.

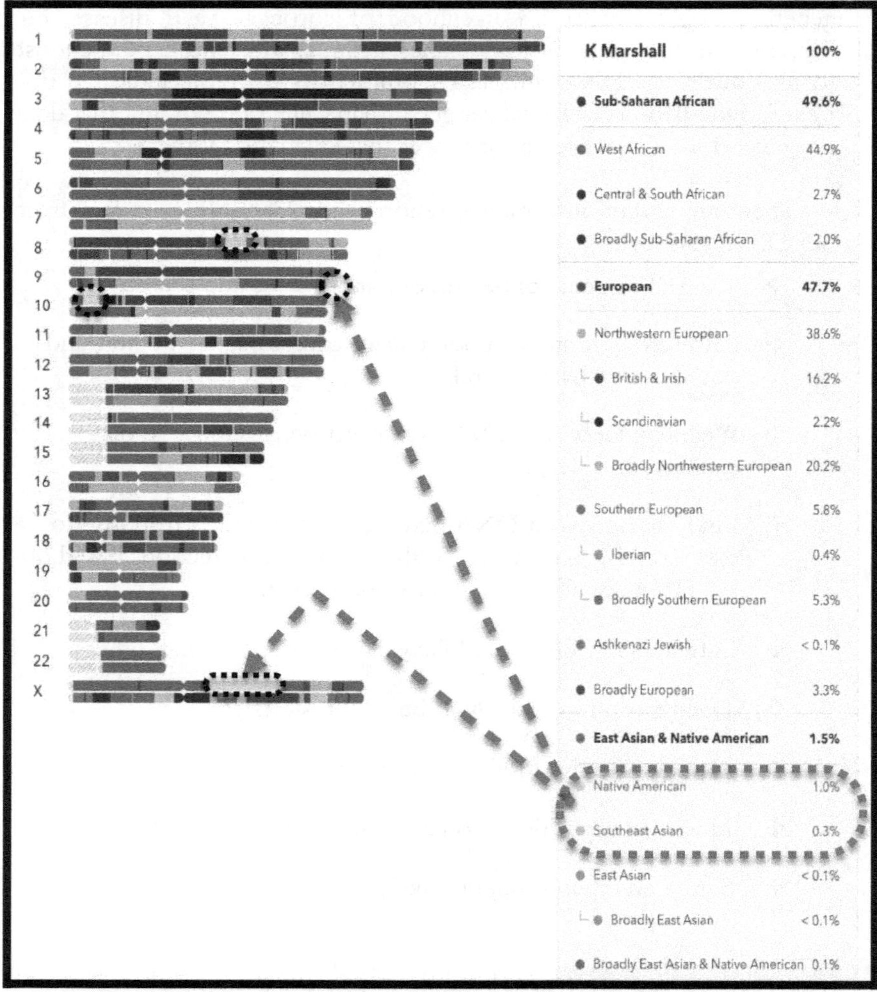

Figure 18.12. 23andMe: Kathy Marshall's chromosome DNA results.

First Step: **Identifying DNA Relatives.** This is accomplished in several useful ways with 23andMe. First is a listing of people whose DNA matches yours. 23andMe calculates the familial relationship based on the number of centimorgans (cMs) [195] shared, as expressed in the percentage shared over all 23 chromosomes, and how many total chromosomal segments are shared.

If the 23andMe member included their gender and a photograph, those are also visible. I was interested in 100% European ancestors to "find my white people." Because my closest matches are listed first, I chose to explore the first white person on my list, TMB, even though she only shares a paltry 0.51% of four of my DNA segments. She is a third to fourth cousin (Figure 18.13).

BB	Female	1.78% shared, 8 segments
LS	Linda I Female	Second to Third Cousin 1.38% shared, 6 segments
SB	Samue Male	Third Cousin 0.47% shared, 3 segments
	Tresia Bond Jeffries Female	Third to Fourth Cousin 0.51% shared, 4 segments
	Alana Carr Female	Third to Fifth Cousin 0.53% shared, 2 segments
SA	SUSAN Female	Third to Fifth Cousin 0.50% shared, 2 segments
	Windy Domi Female	Third to Fifth Cousin 0.48% shared, 2 segments

Second Step: **Determining the ethnic admixture of our ancestors.** The chart shows that TMB's ancestors almost totally came from Europe, compared to almost half of mine from Europe. This view also shows our mitochondrial (maternal) haplogroup which tracks the lineage of our mothers. My B4a1a1[196] is a Southeast Asian/Native American haplo-group, but when applied to an African American it is called the "Malagasy Motif"[197] (more on that in Chapter 20). TMB's Ia1 haplog-roup[198] is common in only a few small areas of East Africa, West Asia, and Europe, including the Lemko people of Slovakia, Poland, and Ukraine, the island of Krk in Croatia, the Department of Finistère in France and some parts of Scotland.

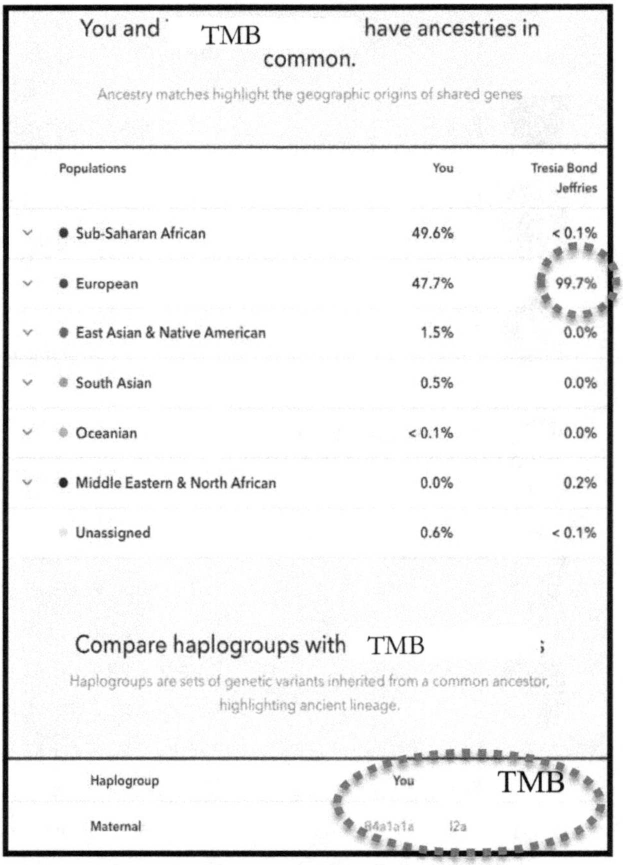

You and TMB have ancestries in common.

Ancestry matches highlight the geographic origins of shared genes

Populations	You	Tresia Bond Jeffries
Sub-Saharan African	49.6%	< 0.1%
European	47.7%	99.7%
East Asian & Native American	1.5%	0.0%
South Asian	0.5%	0.0%
Oceanian	< 0.1%	0.0%
Middle Eastern & North African	0.0%	0.2%
Unassigned	0.6%	< 0.1%

Compare haplogroups with TMB

Haplogroups are sets of genetic variants inherited from a common ancestor, highlighting ancient lineage.

Haplogroup	You	TMB
Maternal	B4a1a1a	I2a

Figure 18.14. 23andMe: Determining the ethnic admixture of our ancestors.

Third Step: **Predicting our familial relationship.** 23andMe calculates that TMB and I may be third or fourth cousins who share a second great-grandparent (Figure 18.15). Since TMB's ancestry is 99.7% European, our common second great-grandparent is *likely* European; but it is possible that our connection is through her 0.03% Sub-Saharan Africa ancestor.

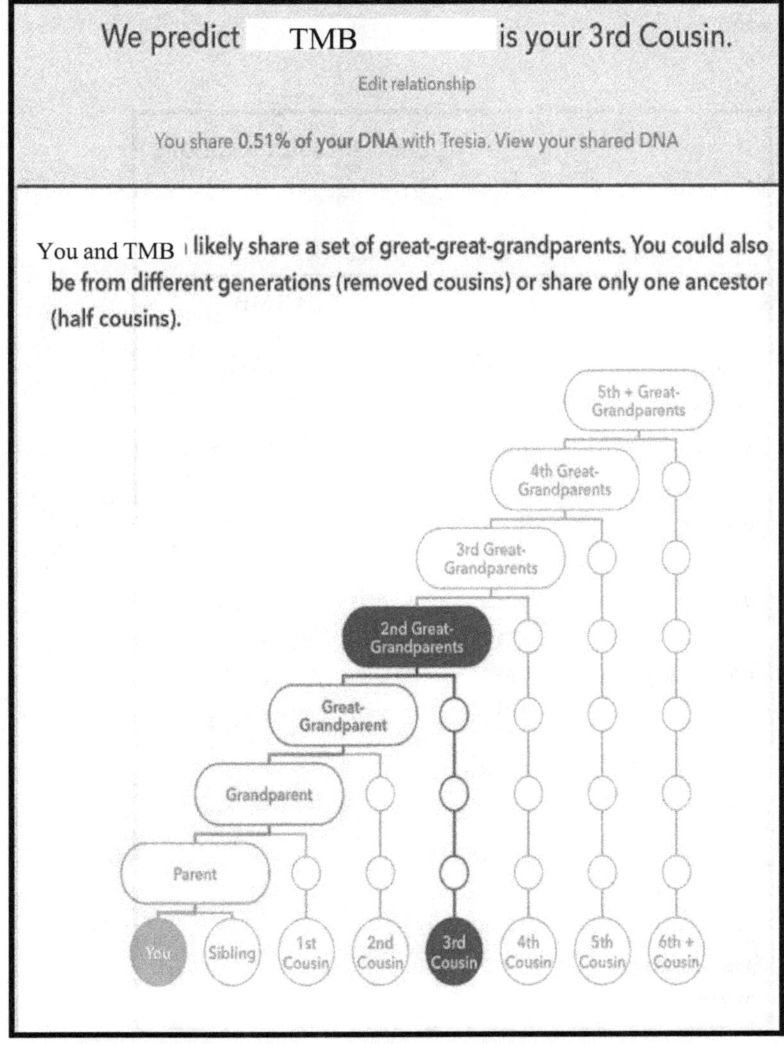

Figure 18.15. 23and Me: Predicting your familial relationship.

Fourth Step: **Identifying ancestral locations** depends on information supplied by the user. This comparison indicates that both TMB and I have parents and grandparents who were born in the United States. However, TMB indicates that she has family members from Scotland and the United Kingdom (Figure 18.16). As shown in Figure 18.10, 36.4% of my DNA is reportedly "British and Irish United Kingdom" and "Northwest European" according to 23andMe. TMB may provide exactly what I am looking for: white ancestors to help explain my light skin coloring.

TMB included **ancestor locations**

Locations can highlight the geographic origins of shared genes

	You	TMB
Mom's Mom	United States	United States
Mom's Dad	United States	United States
Dad's Mom	United States	United States
Dad's Dad	United States	United States
Other Ancestor Birthplaces	AL, GA, MD, MO, MS, OH, PA, Germany, England Washington County, Maryland, United States	Scotland, United Kingdom
Ashkenazi Jewish (self reported)	No	Yes

Figure 18.16. 23andMe: Identifying ancestral locations.

Fifth Step: **Determining relatives in common** is a critical step. Essentially, 23andMe is triangulating (see Figure 19.2), identifying which people match both my and TMB's chromosomal segments. In the past, this process was extremely laborious for most of us, necessitating the hand-searching of common matches from numerous printouts of DNA information for each person. 23andMme does it for you in seconds, indicating the predicted relationship (e.g., third cousin) and the percent of total DNA shared between TMB and me. Most importantly, the last column shows whether we share DNA with other people (Figure 18.17). If the Shared DNA column reports "No," then TMB and I do not share DNA with that third person. If the column entry is "Yes" then we do share DNA on the same parts of specific chromosomes with that third person, and we may proceed to the exciting next step to find our most recent common ancestors.

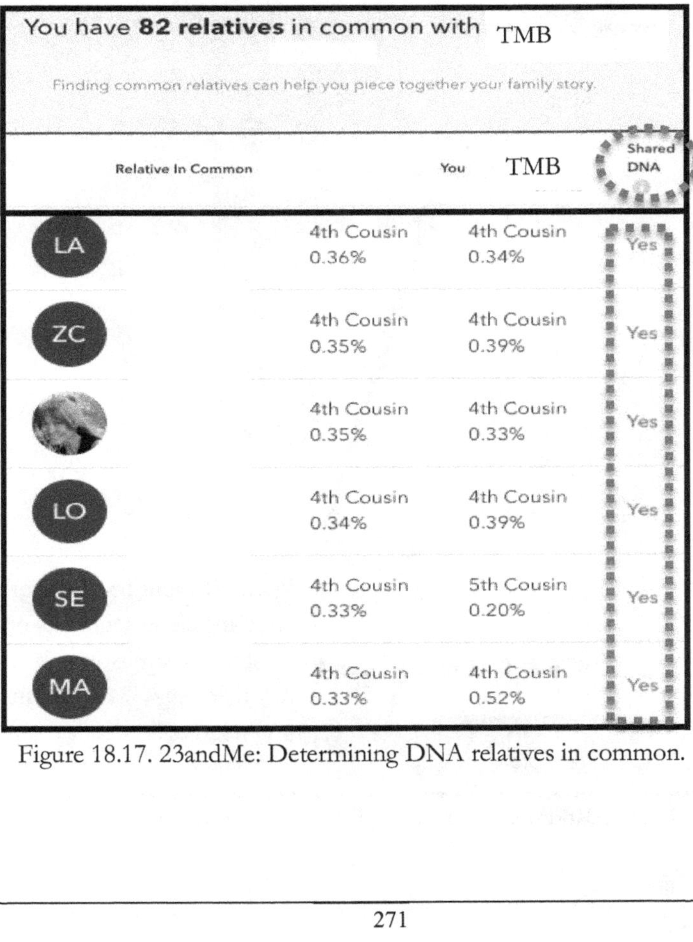

You have **82 relatives** in common with TMB

Finding common relatives can help you piece together your family story.

Relative In Common	You	TMB	Shared DNA
LA	4th Cousin 0.36%	4th Cousin 0.34%	Yes
ZC	4th Cousin 0.35%	4th Cousin 0.39%	Yes
	4th Cousin 0.35%	4th Cousin 0.33%	Yes
LO	4th Cousin 0.34%	4th Cousin 0.39%	Yes
SE	4th Cousin 0.33%	5th Cousin 0.20%	Yes
MA	4th Cousin 0.33%	4th Cousin 0.52%	Yes

Figure 18.17. 23andMe: Determining DNA relatives in common.

Sixth Step: **Comparing Triangulated Chromosomal Segments** (Figure 18.18) shows five people who match chromosomes two (2) and nine (9) with TMB and me. The chart also denotes how many chromosome segments and cMs match us (30 cM denotes about a fourth-level cousin match). These results suggest that I should contact TMB, LO, JB, DA, and HL to learn whether we can identify the most recent common ancestors (a third great-grandparent) in our family trees. Huzzah!

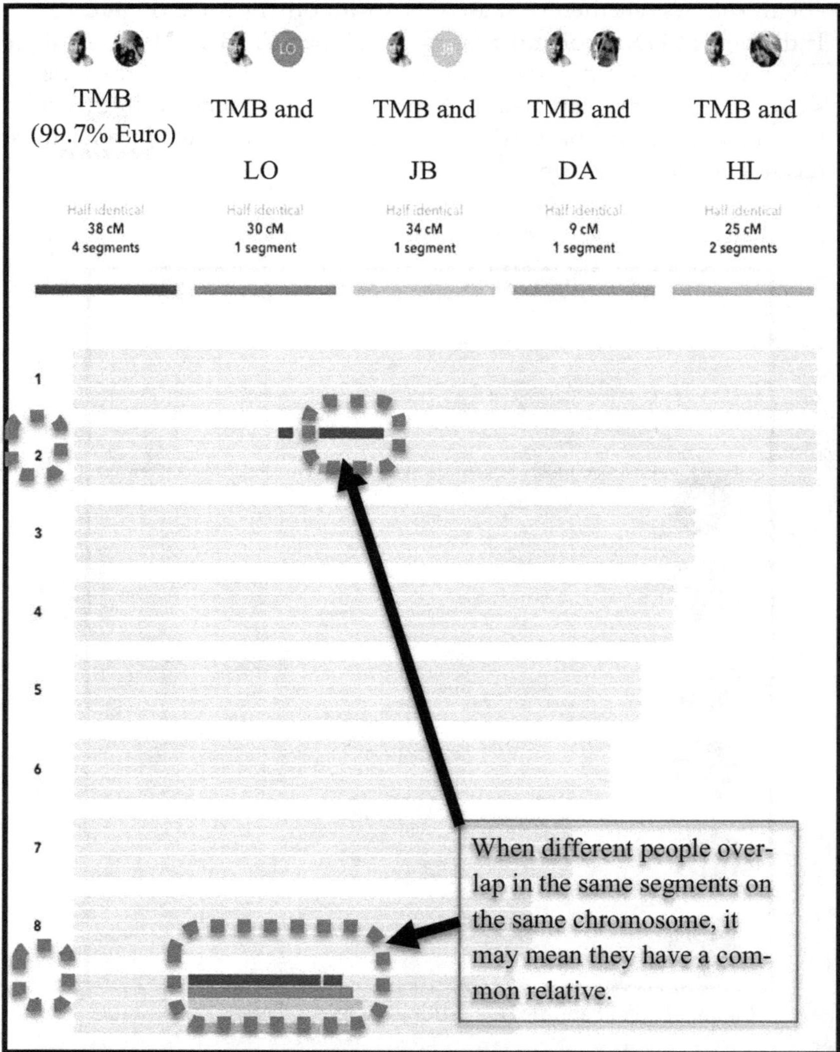

Figure 18.18. 23andMe: Determining DNA relatives in common.

* Family Tree DNA (FTDNA) *

Family Finder identifies people who are strong matches to segments of our 22 "autosomal" chromosomes (Figure 18.19). This view shows DNA matches to my Great Uncle Charles Williams. His top match, son BW, is correctly listed as having a "Parent/Child" relationship[199] with Charles. They share 3,382 cMs of about 7,000 total cMs, which means almost half of BW's genome comes from his father, with a little more than half from his mother.

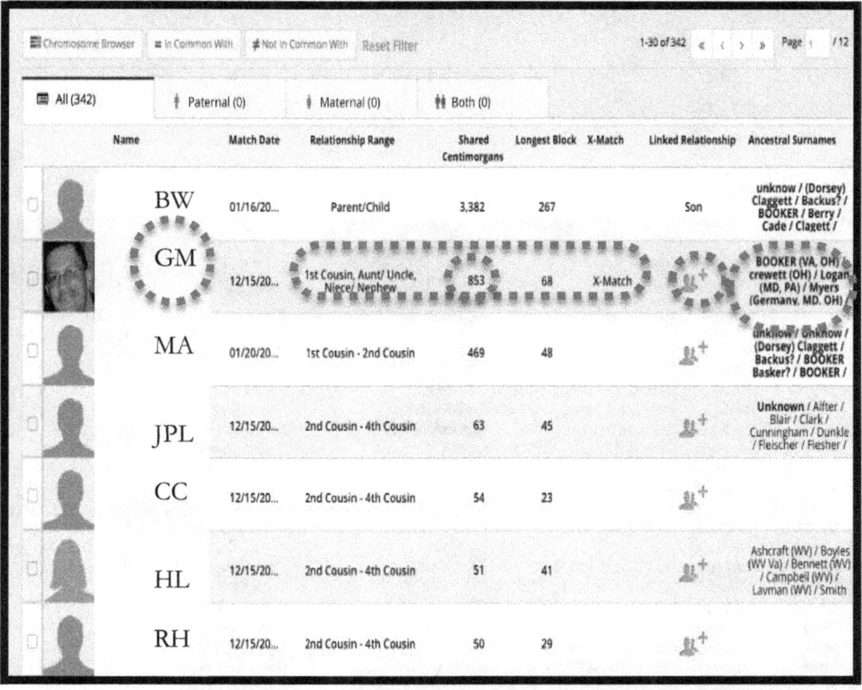

Chromosome Browser | In Common With | Not In Common With | Reset Filter | 1-30 of 342 | Page 1 / 12

All (342) | Paternal (0) | Maternal (0) | Both (0)

Name	Match Date	Relationship Range	Shared Centimorgans	Longest Block	X-Match	Linked Relationship	Ancestral Surnames
BW	01/16/20...	Parent/Child	3,382	267		Son	unknow / (Dorsey) Claggett / Backus? / BOOKER / Berry / Cade / Clagett /
GM	12/15/20...	1st Cousin, Aunt/ Uncle, Niece/ Nephew	853	68	X-Match		BOOKER (VA, OH) / crewett (OH) / Logan (MD, PA) / Myers (Germany, MD, OH) /
MA	01/20/20...	1st Cousin - 2nd Cousin	469	48			unknow / Unknow / (Dorsey) Claggett / Backus? / BOOKER Basker? / BOOKER /
JPL	12/15/20...	2nd Cousin - 4th Cousin	63	45			Unknown / Alfter / Blair / Clark / Cunningham / Dunkle / Fleischer / Flesher /
CC	12/15/20...	2nd Cousin - 4th Cousin	54	23			
HL	12/15/20...	2nd Cousin - 4th Cousin	51	41			Ashcraft (WV) / Boyles (WV Va) / Bennett (WV) / Campbell (WV) / Layman (WV) / Smith
RH	12/15/20...	2nd Cousin - 4th Cousin	50	29			

Figure 18.19. FamilyTreeDNA.com: Family finder example for Charles Williams.

On the other hand, GM (my brother), only shares 853 cMs with his uncle. Based on the amount of DNA they share, GM could be Charles' first cousin, his uncle or his nephew, as shown in the "Relationship Range" column. Appendix K shows a chart which explores differing familial relationships based on the number of shared cMs.[200] The "X-match" indicator shows that Charles is related to GM on GM's mother's side. In the far-right column are surnames in the match's Family Finder tree; as an example, Charles' male match named "JPL" has the surname Cunningham in his family tree; this becomes very important in Chapter 19.

FTDNA also offers a suite of specific tests for the 23rd chromosome—the sex chromosome. For men only, a Y-DNA test examines 37, 67, 111, or more, genetic markers to find the most recent common ancestor in a man's patrilineal ancestry, i.e., father to father, back to theoretical Adam. Women may use a mtDNA test to learn about their matrilineal heritage, i.e., mother to mother, back to theoretical Eve.

For those doing specific research in different locations, or particular surnames, FTDNA offers almost 10,000 specialized "projects" one may join. Figure 18.20 compares the SNPs—a change in your DNA code at a specific point[201]—of men in the Williams Surname DNA Project. My first cousin, BW, is third from the bottom; his data indicates that Prince Williams is his oldest paternal ancestor name. Because so few black people have taken the Y-DNA test, and because Prince Williams was not likely born a true Williams, BW's Y-DNA will not likely find a match in the Williams Project.

Kit Number		Paternal Ancestor Name	Country	Haplogroup
Hap'group A				
B50739	Williams	Philop Mathews	Unknown Origin	A-M31
Hap'group E - unmatched				
385057	Kearley	Richard Kennedy, b. 1800 and d. 1862	United States	E-M96
424912	Watkins	John Joe Watkins, b. 1856, Nebraska, US	United States	E-L117
31356	Phillips	Solomon Phillips, d. 1797, Edgecombe Co., NC	United Kingdom	E-M35
B27212	simmons	Elzie McCarley b. 1869 and d. 1927	United States	E-M96
240685	Williams		Unknown Origin	E-M96
B83873	King	Robin King 1816	Unknown Origin	E-M96
Hap'group E1b1a1 - ne[illegible]oject				
237674	Williams		Unknown Origin	E-M2
B217809	Williams			E-M2
A4396	Williams	Paul Ricard b:1835	United States	E-M2
N24059	Horton	William H. Horton (1775- 1822?)	England	E-A930
B6429	Williams	Henry St Clair Williams, b. 1830	Unknown Origin	E-Z16130
587388	Anderson	Isaac Ismael Anderson, 1888 OH -1955 CA	United States	E-M2
110439	Williams	frederick williams 1912-1991	Unknown Origin	E-M2
9968	Williams	Paul Elisha Williams, DOB 1909 Youngstown, Ohio	Unknown Origin	E-U174
B11108	Williams	Berry Hamilton Williams b. abt 1820 and d. abt1886	Unknown Origin	E-M2
86168	Williams	Charles Williams, b. 1895, Waynesboro, GA	Unknown Origin	E-M2
Hap'group E1b1b1 - Ge				
180501	Williams	John M. Williams b 1829-1831 Gallatin Co., IL marr	Unknown Origin	E-BY8404
325658	Prather	John G Prather 1763 MD-1826 OH son of Samuel [HMP]	United States	E-BY8439
Hap'group E1b1b1 - to t				
U2547	Williams	John Williams1810 -1867	Unknown Origin	E-M35
Hap'group E1b1b1 - Un[illegible]oject until others upgrade or join				
569952	Williams	Prince Williams, b. 1783, d. 1843, MD	United States	E-M2
59504	Williams	George Coan	Germany	E-L117
B5666	Coker	Simeon Coker, 1818 South Carolina -1893 Florida	Unknown Origin	E-FGC11447

Figure 18.20. FTDNA: Williams Haplogroup Project - Partial View.

My cousin BW and my son MA have the E-M2[202] haplogroup, which usually signals a Sub-Saharan African paternal lineage. More about African matches will be explored in Chapter 19. My brother, GM, on the other hand, has an I-P37/I2a1 haplogroup which is the most common paternal lineage in the former Yugoslavia, Romania, Bulgaria, and most Slavic countries. This means that my Marshall males' Y-DNA lineage likely came from what is now Eastern Europe many generations ago. Interestingly, my brother's haplogroup is the same as TMB's who we studied a few pages ago. More about European matches will be explored in Chapter 19.

To find more people who match our family's Y-DNA and mtDNA, I enrolled my male family's results in several FTDNA projects, including Maryland DNA Project, Williams, African, Black Potomac Valley, and England GB Groups. I enrolled my mtDNA in the Malagasy Project.

As shown in Figure 18.21, my son's DNA matches the most black people, with sixty-nine total people. I have thirty-one mtDNA matches of many ethnic origins, but primarily black. My first cousin Bob Williams has fifteen total black matches. My brother GM, with his expensive 111-marker test, has only eight total white matches, which is not much bang for our big buck to find white ancestors, but it is something.

	Haplogroup		Number of Individuals Matching at Various Marker Levels:						Exact Matches:
Family Member, Relation to author	Haplo-group	Countries of Origins	12*	25*	37	67	111	Total	(Genetic Distance=0)
GM, Brother	I-P37	Eastern Europe	1	3	1	2	1	8	5
BW, 1st cousin	E-M2	Sub-Saharan Africa	1	2	6	4	2	15	5
MA, son	E-M2	Sub-Saharan Africa	20	8	25	11	5	69	25
Kathy, me	B4a1a1	Madagascar						31	12
*NOTE: the 12 and 25 marker levels have less precision and confidence than the 37, 67, and 111 marker levels									

Figure 18.21. FTDNA: Y-DNA or mtDNA matches at various marker levels.

FTDNA does not provide detailed ethnic breakdowns. For example, 47% of my brother GM's DNA is from West Africa, 2% from South Africa, 27% from the British Isles, 12% from West and Central Europe, 3% from Southeast Europe, and trace amounts from other places. This is disappointing, compared to the plethora of detailed African origin estimates from Ancestry DNA. With that said, detailed ethnicity results are only general estimates anyway.

* GEDmatch *

What happens when some family members test with Ancestry DNA, but others use FTDNA, or 23andMe, or some other testing company? It is hard to compare those disparate results because they are in separate testing databases. GEDmatch.com is a third-party website that accepts raw DNA files from many testing sources, generally for free. It offers numerous charts and analytical tools. GEDmatch issues a six-digit "kit number" that identifies your raw data file. If a kit number begins with an "A," the DNA comes from Ancestry DNA. If it begins with an "M," the data is from 23andMe. If the kit starts with a "T," the raw DNA came from FTDNA. If it is an "H" it is from My Heritage, (Figure 18.22).

Some useful GEDmatch tools used for this research:

- "One-to-many" comparison lists people who match a kit.
- "One-to-one chart" compares two specific persons' kits.
- "Ethnic Admixture" breakdown indicates whether the person's DNA primarily comes from Caucasian, African or Asian countries.

Of the thousands of people who match my DNA, it is important to find my closest relatives. After performing a "One-to-Many" comparison (Figure 18.22), I study the "Autosomal Total cM" column. Those with the highest numbers have a closer relationship to me. Generally, anyone with about 3400 cM indicates a parent-child relationship, where 50% of their DNA is from the father and another 50% is from the mother (my son, MA, who got 3581 cM from me).

A sibling might exhibit a range of about 2300 to 3900 cM (see GM and CM). An aunt/uncle/niece/nephew might show about 1800 cMs Around 900 cM could be a first cousin, etc. Appendix K has a chart that shows those predicted relationships based on shared cMs. Cousin7, shown in Figure 18.22, shares 42.4 total cM with me, which indicates she could be a second cousin once removed, or a first cousin three times removed. BW, at 432.4 cM, is my first cousin once removed, even though BW and I were born in the same year (he is the great-grandson of slave Otho and I am the great-great-granddaughter).

					Haplogroup		Autosomal				X-DNA			Person
Kit Nbr	Type	List	Select	Sex	Mt	Y	Details	Total cM	largest cM	Gen	Details	Total cM	largest cM	(
▼▲					▼▲	▼▲		▼	▼	▼▲		▼	▼	
M1(^^^^	V3	L	⌜	F	B4a1a1a		A	3585.8	214.5	1.0	X	187.9	98.8	KM
T9(	F2	L	⌜	M		EM2	A	3581.3	277.4	1.0	X	196	196	2
A2(#	F2	L	⌜	M		I-P37	A	2760.3	174.1	1.2	X	82	36.1	MA
A69 s	F2	L	⌜	F			A	2595.2	191.6	1.2	X	196.1	196.1	GM CM
A1(	F2	L	⌜	F			A	980.7	63.1	1.9	X	96.1	96.1	JC
A75	F2	L	⌜	M			A	913.6	72.4	2.0	X	8.7	8.7	CW
A68 s	F2	L	⌜	F			A	533.1	47.2	2.4	X	76.5	76.5	LW
T49 a	F2	L	⌜	M		E-M2	A	432.4	47.4	2.5	X	0	0	BW
A41 n i	F2	L	⌜	F			A	176.2	51.5	3.2	X	53.9	53.9	LG
A71 t	F2	L	⌜	M			A	82.5	31.0	3.7	X	12.3	12.3	1
A51 i	F2	L	⌜	M			A	53.3	30.9	4.0	X	0	0	2
A91 z e	F2	L	⌜	F			A	51.4	29.5	4.1	X	0	0	3
A03 d	F2	L	⌜	F			A	51.4	29.5	4.1	X	0	0	4
M82	V4	L	⌜	M	L2a1c3	R1b1b2a1a2d3a	A	47.7	16.5	4.1	X	0	0	5
M1	V3	L	⌜	F	L2a1c3	R1b1b2	A	44.3	13.3	4.2	X	0	0	6 7
A2(ᴊᴊᴊ	F2	L	⌜	F			A	42.4	42.4	4.2	X	0	0	

Figure 18.22. GEDmatch: One to Many Comparison - Sample of matches with Kathy Marshall. Right column key: Kathy is KM; her siblings are GM and CM; son is MA; elders are CW, LW, and DC; first cousins are JC and BW; and third cousin is LG.

I decided to examine more closely LG, my second cousin once removed, who has 176.2 total autosomal cM to me, as shown in Figure 18.22. I want to discern exactly where we match on our 22 autosomal chromosomes. I ran a "one-to-one" GEDmatch.com Autosomal Comparison. Figure 18.23 indicates that *LG and my DNA matches on eight different chromosomes: 2, 3, 4, 5, 8, 9, 14, and 16.

So, what does all that mean? Truthfully, I mostly care about the total cMs that we share and how strong a relationship that is, and how closely we overlap on various chromosomes, which could help point to a common ancestor when compared to other test takers who match on the same segments of those chromosomes. Some genealogy geneticists find the "largest segment shared" detail important.

Comparing Kit A709123 (*Kanika) and A415619 (*L.G.)

Minimum threshold size to be included in total = 500 SNPs
Mismatch-bunching Limit = 250 SNPs
Minimum segment cM to be included in total = 7.0 cM

Chr	Start Location	End Location	Centimorgans (cM)	SNPs
2	234,899,831	242,656,041	17.2	1,464
3	134,760,425	174,876,118	38.5	4,798
4	101,441,465	111,640,026	8.5	1,054
5	75,995,248	96,083,069	20.4	2,425
8	3,836,158	37,578,682	51.3	6,847
9	78,571,283	88,715,269	13.9	1,734
14	20,024,850	22,358,249	9.4	688
16	30,085,308	54,869,275	16.2	1,621

Largest segment = 51.3 cM
Total of segments > 7 cM = 175.5 cM
8 matching segments
Estimated number of generations to MRCA = 3.2

404031 SNPs used for this comparison.

Figure 18.23. GEDmatch: One to One Autosomal Comparison.

2-D Chromosome Browser. So what if we match on parts of specific chromosomes? What does that mean? This two-dimensional chromosome browser allows us to pictorially view where other people match specific segments of our chromosomes. Theoretically, if multiple people overlap the same segments of a particular chromosome, it is possible we may have the same common ancestor. Although difficult to easily discern from a black, white and gray rendition from the original that was color-coded, Figure 18.24 illustrates how seven of my family members overlap segments on chromosome #1. MA, CM, GM, CW, and Cousin2 overlap the first third of that longest chromosome, as illustrated inside the dotted lines.

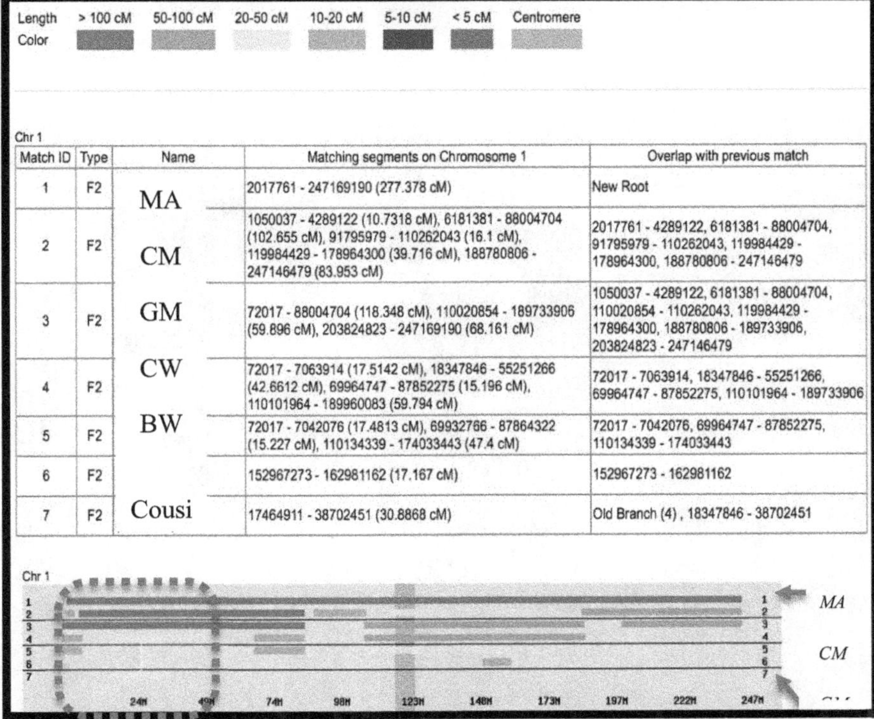

Length	> 100 cM	50-100 cM	20-50 cM	10-20 cM	5-10 cM	< 5 cM	Centromere
Color							

Chr 1

Match ID	Type	Name	Matching segments on Chromosome 1	Overlap with previous match
1	F2	MA	2017761 - 247169190 (277.378 cM)	New Root
2	F2	CM	1050037 - 4289122 (10.7318 cM), 6181381 - 88004704 (102.655 cM), 91795979 - 110262043 (16.1 cM), 119984429 - 178964300 (39.716 cM), 188780806 - 247146479 (83.953 cM)	2017761 - 4289122, 6181381 - 88004704, 91795979 - 110262043, 119984429 - 178964300, 188780806 - 247146479
3	F2	GM	72017 - 88004704 (118.348 cM), 110020854 - 189733906 (59.896 cM), 203824823 - 247169190 (68.161 cM)	1050037 - 4289122, 6181381 - 88004704, 110020854 - 110262043, 119984429 - 178964300, 188780806 - 189733906, 203824823 - 247146479
4	F2	CW	72017 - 7063914 (17.5142 cM), 18347846 - 55251266 (42.6612 cM), 69964747 - 87852275 (15.196 cM), 110101964 - 189960083 (59.794 cM)	72017 - 7063914, 18347846 - 55251266, 69964747 - 87852275, 110101964 - 189733906
5	F2	BW	72017 - 7042076 (17.4813 cM), 69932766 - 87864322 (15.227 cM), 110134339 - 174033443 (47.4 cM)	72017 - 7042076, 69964747 - 87852275, 110134339 - 174033443
6	F2		152967273 - 162981162 (17.167 cM)	152967273 - 162981162
7	F2	Cousi	17464911 - 38702451 (30.8868 cM)	Old Branch (4) , 18347846 - 38702451

Figure 18.24. GEDmatch: Chromosome segment matching two-dimensional view.

The colored bands give a visual idea of the magnitude of the overlap in the chromosomal segments. The more overlaps and total cM shared, the more likely all those people may share a common ancestry. If those overlaps have an "X" in the X-DNA column in Figure 18.21, one may surmise the common ancestor is on the mother's line.

3-D Chromosome Browser. This graph shows the total cM among my 22 autosomal chromosomes that other people matched. The colors indicate the magnitude of those matches, with salmon-colored cells (the top shaded half) being the higher-numbered matches and the white cells representing no shared chromosomal segments. The more the segments overlap different people, the greater the chance that they have a common ancestor.

Figure 18.25 is an example of the strength of matches to me and each other. We would expect my close family members to exhibit the larger numbers. The user named *Griff shows a fairly strong match with Great Uncle CEWilliams. After emailing *Griff to find out how he and Charles were related, we found that they both descend from my maternal third great-grandmother, Margaret Booker

Total Shared cM (Chr 1-22):

K	Name	A709123	M163047	A266176	A755675	T498984	A690940	A683369
A70	*Kanika	-	3585.8	2760.3	913.6	423.7	2595.5	533.1
M16	*Kanika2	3585.8	-	2751.1	912.2	429.6	2573.1	530.3
A26	*GF	2760.3	2751.1	-	1041.2	543.5	2761.4	709.4
A75	CEWilliams	913.6	912.2	1041.2	-	3565.7	788.5	1845.3
T49	*BWill	423.7	429.6	543.5	3565.7	-	326.4	968.2
A69	CLMarshall	2595.5	2573.1	2761.4	788.5	326.4	-	611.5
A68	Lavata Williams	533.1	530.3	709.4	1845.3	968.2	611.5	-
T90	*MANDERSON	3562.2	3574.2	1900.7	500.9	186.4	1736.9	267.8
A10	Julie Sanders	980.7	981.8	933.5	759.8	312.6	1076.2	363.6
M06	DONNA HARRIS	17.4	17.4	55.2	None	None	72.1	None
A06	*david dorsey	18.3	15.0	None	26.5	22.7	None	None
A13	*Griff	10.9	10.9	32.9	129.2	70.7	29.6	35.8
T27	Ada Ruth Cole	29.9	29.9	33.9	8.2	7.5	40.0	24.8

Figure 18.25. GEDmatch: Three-dimensional view of total centimorgans matching Kathy Marshall's 22 chromosomes.

Admixture Utilities offer several models to list ethnic proportions for each of the 22 autosomal chromosomes, among various populations throughout the world.[203]

The darker the shaded area, the more heavily weighted that proportion of DNA is.

The top three categories shown in Figure 18.26 represent my European ancestry, by chromosome, from North Atlantic, Baltic, as well as from the West Mediterranean regions. The middle eight categories are generally Asian or Middle-Eastern.

The last two categories are Northeast African and Sub-Saharan, which many African Americans have a higher proportion than the other regions of the world.

On my Chromosome 1, 39.9% of that DNA is from Sub-Saharan Africa; 6.8% matches that of people from Northeast Africa. Almost 50% matches people who come from Europe, and 3.5% is American Indian (on chromosomes 1, 4, 5, 6, 8, 17, and 20).

23andMe indicates that 1.5% of my DNA is Native American, whereas Ancestry DNA predicts 1%.

Population	Chr->1	2	3	4	5	6	7	8	9	10	11	12	13	14	15	16	17	18	19	20	21	22
North_Atlantic	21.2	28.6	22.7	24.6	16.5	12.8	36.9	8.9	24.6	29.5	15.4	5.1	18.2	-	43.5	21.3	31.3	22.3	32.5	7.5	13.4	-
Baltic	9.8	1.0	10.6	2.4	7.2	-	17.3	10.0	6.3	6.9	17.0	20.3	1.1	12.1	2.4	13.8	11.5	22.7	5.3	7.3	-	-
West_Med	14.8	6.6	8.9	4.1	7.1	7.7	6.9	8.9	10.9	3.0	-	7.8	24.5	-	-	-	12.6	-	22.3	-	9.1	-
West_Asian	4.0	1.5	7.4	-	-	0.4	10.9	-	-	-	19.4	-	12.8	-	0.1	-	1.5	11.5	4.7	0.5	-	-
East_Med	-	4.9	8.3	2.3	-	10.9	-	-	-	11.2	-	17.1	8.5	-	-	-	14.2	-	2.5	-	-	-
Red_Sea	-	1.5	-	-	1.2	-	7.3	6.2	-	-	-	-	-	-	1.5	-	-	0.9	3.2	-	-	1.5
South_Asian	-	4.5	-	-	2.6	-	-	13.1	-	0.2	6.5	-	-	2.8	-	13.1	-	3.3	-	-	-	-
East_Asian	-	-	0.1	-	0.9	-	-	2.9	2.4	4.3	-	-	3.6	-	-	-	-	-	-	-	0.6	2.5
Siberian	-	-	2.6	-	0.1	1.4	-	-	0.3	-	-	-	-	-	-	-	-	0.8	-	-	-	2.2
Amerindian	3.5	-	-	1.5	1.3	0.4	-	2.2	-	-	-	-	-	-	-	-	1.4	-	-	3.5	-	1.1
Oceanian	-	-	-	-	2.3	-	-	4.4	-	3.7	2.2	0.8	0.3	-	-	-	2.0	-	-	-	0.1	-
Northeast_African	6.8	-	-	6.2	6.4	3.9	-	-	-	1.2	-	3.0	-	10.7	7.8	5.6	6.0	1.7	-	1.5	15.0	-
Sub-Saharan	39.9	51.4	39.4	59.0	54.3	62.4	20.8	43.4	55.5	40.0	39.5	45.9	31.0	74.4	44.7	46.1	19.5	36.7	29.4	79.8	61.9	92.7
Number of SNPs eval:	14425	14695	12587	10596	11197	12171	9870	10389	9181	9960	9157	9015	6750	6195	5828	5867	5113	5746	3423	5040	2926	2574

Figure 18.26. GEDmatch: Kathy Marshall's admixture proportions Chart.

After this brief walk on the wild side of three DNA testing companies, here is a summary of my pros and cons of each.

Ancestry DNA is easy to use, well-established, with a huge database. As of April 2018, it had twenty billion records, eighty countries of origin, one-hundred million family trees, and ten billion family connections. Seven million people have purchased the Ancestry DNA test. It is a perfect platform for the least technically oriented people who are mainly interested in learning about their ethnicity (ancestors' countries of origin), conducting traditional genealogical research, and finding people to add to their online family tree. The negatives are that it costs about $300 per year to access one's records and only offers a few of the analytical DNA research tools that the other two companies have gratis.

Family Tree DNA requires the most technical and genetics knowledge of the three companies. If you are not flummoxed by scientific inquiry, algorithms, SNPs, cMs, and enjoy getting down and dirty in raw data, then FTDNA is your baby. For people who know just a few family members—like adoptees, orphans and those with a single-parent upbringing—the no-frills FTDNA may be for you. It is the only one of the three to offer Y-DNA and mtDNA tests (not cheap though!) and reveals your haplogroup. You may compare your results with others in special "projects" by surname and location. FTDNA has 661,000 Y-DNA records and almost 300,000 mtDNA records, and 10,000 group projects, as of 2018.

23andMe falls between Ancestry DNA and FTDNA regarding complexity and size. As of February 2018, 23andMe had sold five million test kits. It is the only one of the three that offers genetic testing that can alert you to different types of health risks. 23andMe offers a haplogroup, invaluable analytical tools such as a chromosome painter, admixture view, and triangulation. It is easy to use, has a helpful "Matching Relatives" feature, and 150 ethnic DNA regions. Unfortunately, raw data created after 2017 cannot be uploaded to GEDmatch, only their newer Genesis program. You get a lot of bang for your buck with a haplogroup being included with autosomal results.

So, which is the best test? All of them! I had myself tested with all three companies, including a mtDNA test with FTDNA and genetic testing with 23andMe.

Having my Uncle Dale represent my mother's genes, I had him take the AncestryDNA and 23andMe tests so I could have his autosomal, and paternal and maternal haplogroups, in addition to his Ancestry test.

Since I needed male Y-DNA results, I had first-cousin Bob Williams take the Y-DNA test to represent my Williams line, brother Greg Marshall for my Marshall line, and son Matthew for his father's Anderson line (the latter of which I may investigate in the future, if my sons, or their children, become more interested).

All my family members, except Bob, took the Ancestry DNA autosomal test. This testing methodology allowed me to compare and contrast DNA results and get the best features from each of the companies for my main family lines.

As discussed in Chapter 17, experts recommend having as many of your family members tested as possible—especially your eldest elders—and parents and cousins, to maximize the benefits of this indispensable, powerful DNA testing tool.

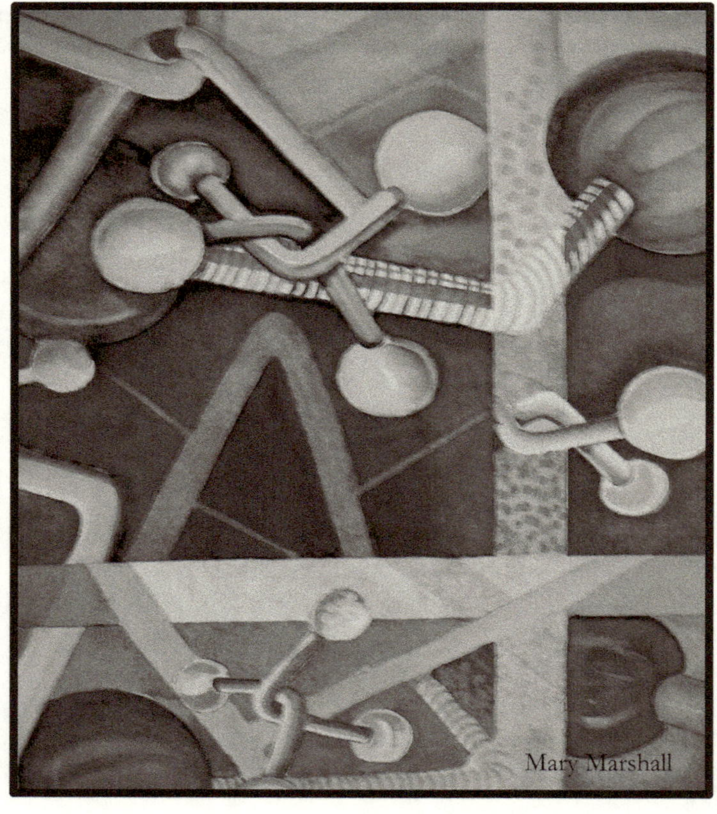
Mary Marshall

Chapter 19 - Using DNA to Find Our Europeans

What would you do *first* if you finally found your present-day African or European who shares your DNA? Would you attempt to contact that DNA match to find out more information about his/her family?

Would you try to find your DNA relative's birthplace?

Would you try finding them on Facebook, Twitter, or Google?

Would you immediately call your family members?

Would you cry tears of joy?

Would you tell your genealogy friends on Facebook?

Would you praise the ancestors for leading you to the find?

Would you meditate on your good fortune?

Would you scream an exhilarating war cry?

Would you do the Happy Dance?

Would you contact the consulate closest to your area who would know local people who are genealogists, tribal elders, librarians, or college history or anthropology professors to have them contact us directly? Starting a dialog with people in the country our DNA say we hail from is an important step to encountering our DNA relatives and/or learning about the customs and history of the country.

Would you celebrate with dark chocolate and port wine, even though it is 7:30 AM when you made your momentous find?

Well, I did all those things every time I made a breakthrough.

Now let's explore how I finally found my Europeans and my Africans. Keeping in mind that I am not a DNA expert, I did have a measure of success finding relatives. You may want to try the same techniques to see if they will help you find your ancestral family.

* Who Were My Europeans? *

Who is the cream in my Oreo cookie --- the other half of my black zebra stripes --- the *au lait* in my *café* --- the other half of my DNA? What results from the DNA testing indicate where the white side of our Williams family came from? I wanted to find which parts of the world our forebears traveled *and* find descendants of specific common ancestors who share the same DNA as my Williams ancestors. Uncovering specific people in the family trees of living people who came from Africa and Europe — the paper trail — is a long shot, but a goal I fervently wished to attain.

Nothing had been easy with this Williams project. Yes, I was thrilled to have over six hundred confirmed fourth cousins or closer in Ancestry DNA alone, with more in 23andMe, FTDNA, and GEDmatch. I was disappointed I had not confirmed any most recent common ancestors (MRCA) that match both the paper trail and DNA with my Williams family. *Who were my African and European common ancestors?*

I began to feel I was drowning in the tumultuous DNA ocean of cMs, color-coded three-dimensional chromosomal segments, single nucleotide polymorphisms (SNPs) and complex triangulations.

Are you still with me?

I reviewed websites, read books, and spoke with numerous genetic genealogists about how to approach this important goal. Before I published this book, I needed to find at least one European and one African person in the family tree of someone who matches the DNA of my Williams family. You'd think it would be simple with over one thousand people whose DNA matched mine? Well, it wasn't.

I reached out to my many experts. Ms. Bernice Bennett, genealogist and blog talk radio personality[204] spent an afternoon with me at her Maryland home during my seventh month on this project. She showed me the concept of color-coding overlapping chromosomal segments to help isolate DNA matches who might have an MRCA with me. 23andMe makes the process simpler by figuring out for us which segments of chromosomes we both share.

Further, Anthony May[205] helped me figure out an important Nicholson white slave owner connection on my father's Marshall line. Genealogist Andre Kearns proposed using GEDmatch Utilities to access the "one-to-many matches," "Triangulation Groups" and "Chromosome Segment Matching" tools.

I used all the recommended DNA tools on *my* DNA results, and those of my Uncle Dale Carter, my Great Uncle Charles Williams, and my sister and brother. The results were ambiguous and did not bring me any closer to finding my white people or my Africans. Aarrgghh!

In the fifteenth month on this project, I received an email from a distant DNA cousin named HDG whom I had contacted four years earlier regarding our very slight three cM, DNA connection. He saw one of my recent internet posts on the "Our Black Ancestry" Facebook page where I implored people to help me figure out my lineage. He remembered my name and responded to my S.O.S. for help to "find my white people."

HDG is an expert at helping adoptees find their families using DNA analysis. In a three-hour telephone call, he taught me how to more effectively use GEDmatch and 23andMe tools to determine the ethnic admixture of my third to fourth cousins. Those tools helped me understand whether a DNA match was mostly a white person, mostly African, or mixed like me (see Figure 18.26 for example).

HDG also taught me how to perform a deep analysis of those autosomal matches so I could hone in on which of them might result in a common ancestor. I was ready to dip my big toe of my size eleven foot into the water then slowly lowered myself into the swirling DNA research pool, holding onto my experts for support.

Remember the "Baby Daddy" paternity test examples we discussed at the beginning of Chapter 17? One must know the correct paternal ancestry for the Y-DNA test to give useful results. As shown in the pedigree chart in Figure 19.1, Robert "Bob" Williams and Charles Williams *should* have been ideal test subjects for my analysis, as they are in the direct descendant line from Otho and Prince Williams.

At the outset of writing this book, I just *knew* one of the many white Otho Holland Williams in Washington County, Maryland, was the father of my enslaved ancestor Otho Williams. Who else would name their child—even a slave child—Otho? To prove my assertion, I had first cousin Bob take a Y-DNA test in the second month on this project, because I was so sure Bob was a direct-line descendant of my Otho Williams. Therefore, if I found a present-day descendant from one of the three white Otho Holland Williams families in Washington County, I would surely be able to prove our genetic relationship to them. Simple. Using Ancestry DNA, I searched long and hard for males who were the descendants of the white Otho Holland Williams families in Maryland.

One morning, I woke thinking, "Oh no! My base theory was wrong.

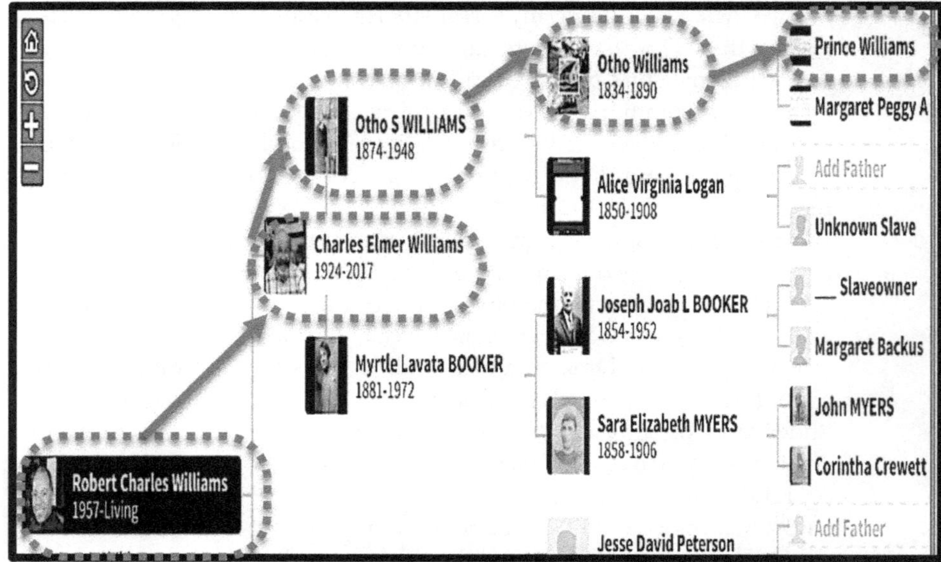

Figure 19.1. Pedigree Chart from BW to Prince Williams

It wasn't until the fourth month that I learned that *none* of the white Otho Holland Williams likely fathered my Otho. I also learned that my Otho's *probable* true father, Prince Williams, had *chosen* the Williams surname after he achieved freedom in 1812. So, who really knows what genetic line Prince actually came from? It could be anybody.

Cousin Bob's E-M2 haplogroup suggested that his Williams line of fathers came from Africa. Since Bob is a direct-line male descendant from our formerly enslaved Otho Williams, does that mean we should conclude that Otho and Prince's male genetic line absolutely descended from Africans? Probably, but that is not 100% assured because the following mulatto question had to be rectified first.

It is a fact that Otho Williams and his siblings were classified as mulatto on different historical records, indicating it is likely one of their parents was a white person, or a mulatto themselves.

It is a fact that Prince was described by County Clerk Otho Holland Williams as "of a black color" leading one to believe Prince was a darker-skinned black man whose DNA was likely much more African than European. Therefore, Otho must have achieved that "mixed-race" status from his mother, right? Maybe, or maybe not. As discussed in Chapter 6, Joseph Ingram's Will described Margaret as "my *black* woman Pegg." So, what is the truth about the mulatto question?

The elephant in the room might answer this dichotomy: Prince Williams *may not* be the biological father of my light-skinned Otho and some of his siblings. Some of my expert muses had suggested that perhaps the unmarried slave owners, John and/or Benjamin Ingram, or their father, Joseph Ingram, was Margaret's and/or my Otho's biological father. With that in mind, I rigorously attempted to find DNA matches with people from Maryland, and from adjacent states in my cousin-match family trees who had Ingram surnames. The result? Nix, nada, nothing. No proven Ingram DNA matches.

What I did know is that the expensive Y-DNA test I purchased for my first cousin Bob was likely money down the drain, because Otho probably did not have any actual DNA from a true Williams bloodline. Bob's E-M2 haplogroup suggested his paternal bloodline came from Africa. The Y-DNA results confirmed that there were no Williams surnames who matched Bob. He had no Y-DNA matches at the 67-marker level and none at the 37-marker level. The five men who matched Bob at the 12-marker level with a genetic distance of zero have surnames of "Fleets, Ortiz, Beauchamp, Holloway, and Duncan." The surnames of the eight men who match Bob at a genetic distance of one are "Burr, Wright, Harris, Maynard, Taylor, Ben-Yehuda, John, and Davison." The latter, Mr. Davison, and I communicated on numerous occasions about our possible common ancestors who were likely from Maryland or Pennsylvania.

Was it difficult to follow the previous paragraph? The bottom line was that I was not able to use the expensive Y-DNA test to find white relatives who matched the grandson (Charles Williams) or great-grandson (Bob Williams) of our former slave Otho Williams. That is not to say I won't *ever* be able to locate the true genetic and paper trail ancestors of my Williams family, but it did mean I may have to rely on other methods to "find my white and African ancestors," other than cousin Bob's Y-DNA test.

Confused? Me too!

Chapter 18 presented several descriptions of the cousin-matching tools available on 23andMe. My DNA guru, HDG, recommended identifying my DNA relatives and keeping track of the resulting relationships in a database, so that's what I did.

* One Case: Trying to Find Common European Ancestors *

As shown in Figure 18.11, I had 1,065 cousins in the 23andMe database—black, white, and mixed-race relatives who match my DNA. I downloaded all my matches from 23andMe, Family Tree DNA's Family Finder, GEDmatch and some of Ancestry DNA relatives into two spreadsheets—one for primarily Africans and one for Europeans.

This massive spreadsheet contains the chromosome numbers and segments of chromosomes that we match, their family surnames and locations, haplogroup, sex, birth year, birth country of parents, generations, etc. I added a few more columns for %European, %African, GEDmatch kit number, total cM, date email sent, and miscellaneous notes. The spreadsheet allowed me to keep track of who I contacted, the information that documented our matches and, hopefully, our common ancestor.

HDG called my attention to a fourth-cousin DNA match named TMB who was a 99.7% European match. She had an Eastern Europe haplogroup of I2a which, by the way, is the same as my brother's Y-haplogroup (Figure 18.14). Predicting our familial relationship (Figure 18.15), I learned TMB was one of my highest European matches on 23andMe and may share a second or third great-grandparent with me. Otho and Alice Williams are my second great-grandparents, so I hope TMB and I might find a connection there.

To learn more about TMB to see if I could identify our common ancestor, I used a tool called *triangulation.* According to Figure 18.16, she wanted to find out more about her Scottish ancestors. TMB has fifteen surnames she was investigating, including Bond, Bailey, Mastey, McGonald, Freud, Resse, Holward, Rawlins, Brownler, Canpenter, Bouch, Feldon, Shringer, Fretcher, and Smith. The only surname I recognized from my family tree was Smith; Israel Smith was my second great-grandfather and his daughter, Mary Smith, was my first great-grandmother on my father's side. *Were my father's Smiths related to TMB's Smiths?*

That was where the power of 23andMe tools came through. The next step was to determine which other DNA relatives do TMB and I have in common? This is called triangulation, which is the primary goal of genetic genealogy.[206] The concept is simple but executing it without the help of GEDmatch and 23andMe tools was difficult (Figure 19.2).

Figure 18.17 listed six of the eighty-two total relatives with whom TMB and I shared a small amount of DNA. The relatives who had a "YES" in the Shared DNA field overlapped the same segments of chromosomes that TMB and I share.

I emailed about two hundred of my highest matching cousins on Ancestry DNA, 23andMe, Family Tree DNA, and GEDmatch. I provided them with the names, dates, and locations of my third great-grandparents so that they could compare my family surnames to their family trees. Some returned my inquiries and tried to find our common ancestors. TMB, for one, sent me a detailed listing of her family tree. Others gave me entry to their online trees, family biographies, telephone numbers, etc.

WHAT IS TRIANGULATION? Think of a triangle:

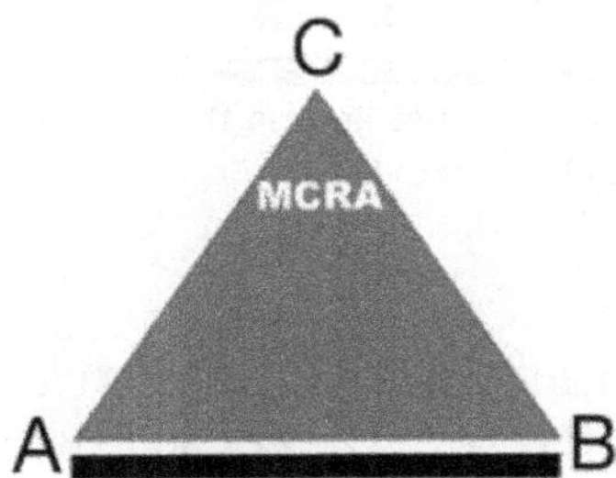

- Persons A & B match genetically (e..g, share DNA) and that forms the base of the triangle.
- Person A (e.g., me, the author) has a paper trail (e.g., genealogy family tree) that goes back in time.
- Person B (e.g., TMB) has a paper trail that goes back in time.
- The top of the triangle, C, is the most recent common ancestor (MRCA). If the DNA of Person A & Person B match, and the paper trail includes the MRCA, then it helps prove Person A and Person B are related both genealogically and genetically.

Those people became part of my very important "Common Ancestral Community" of DNA cousins. Ancestry's "DNA Circles" embody this concept of a common ancestral community. For this to work, both parties must have a well-documented family tree to identify common ancestors.

I wanted to find which of my Williams family surnames were in the family trees of other close DNA matches, hoping the synthesis of surnames and family connections would eventually lead to my finding a paper trail of the most common, recent, ancestor between us. I noted some of the common surnames from the 1,300 cousins on my spreadsheet. A subset of those surnames is shown in Figure 19.3.

Baker	Bennett	Bond	Carter	Cunning-ham	Davis	Logan	Marshall	Smith	Walker	Williams
39	14	17	13	5	23	9	3	25	12	22

Figure 19.3. Common surnames among the cousins of Kathy and Greg Marshall. Source: FTDNA Family Finder, GEDmatch, 23andMe, and Ancestry DNA.

TMB had her primary family tree on WikiTree.com. I noted that her ancestors from Maryland were Davises and Bonds from Cecil County, Maryland. Since we had the surname Smith in common, to observe whether any lived near my dad's Marshall family, I also searched her tree for Smiths from Alabama and for her ancestors who lived in Georgia. I scoured my spreadsheets for her Bonds to find commonalities there. My link to TMB's family is still a work in progress. We shall keep the communication lines open until we find our connection.

I tried another avenue using the handy Ancestry "Search Matches by Location" function to list all people who matched me and who were from the following Maryland areas: Washington County, Funkstown, Boonsboro, Beaver Creek, Hagerstown, Kent County, and Cecil County. I found many people who matched my Great Uncle Charles Williams, Uncle Dale Carter, and me, and who had ancestors born in Maryland, with surnames I had come across through my research, such as those in Figure 19.3, as well as: Beall, Claggett, Dunn, Hanson/Hensen, and Magruder. Unfortunately, I could not *prove* a relationship to anyone from Maryland—my prime directive—who might have matched my Williams family.

* Could There Be a Match to Ingram Slave Owners? *

After a year and a half of daily searching, I found the Mother Lode in a distant, six cM, DNA match named Pam who had my slaveholder Ingrams in her family tree! Yes, that was what I had dreamed about since finding the Ingrams early in this book-writing process. I twirled on my toes, maracas in hand, doing the Happy Dance, my spirits soaring through the shimmering silvery clouds over my head. I could now say with surety that one of the Ingram boys *was* related to me. Whether it was from fathering Otho or Margaret, I didn't know or care. I had finally found my white people and can prove it with DNA!

I composed a quick message to my DNA match savior, Pam, informing her of our incredible Ingram common ancestor.

Pam responded, "Looking at our trees, I see we do seem to have a distant DNA relationship. I do know that there are slave owners in my tree from across the south. My family starts in America in Pennsylvania, Maryland, and Virginia and moves South and West through the Carolinas, Kentucky, Tennessee, Alabama, Arkansas, Mississippi, and Texas. As to the Ingrams, they are in my ex's family and therefore in my son's section of the tree, but I am happy to share anything that I have found. My son has not done DNA testing and hasn't warmed to the idea, but I keep hoping!"

Her response was not the slam dunk I coveted. Her son — my needed proof — has not, and probably will not take a DNA test, even if I volunteered to pay for it. I knew that Pam only matched my sister Carrie and me, not any of my mother's direct line who took the DNA test. This meant she likely matched my father's family, not my mother's Williams family. My internal thermometer dropped from my sizzling hot Happy Dance to the deep-freeze of knowing that my connection with her might not work out after all.

After a minute of repose, I put a new battery into my Energizer Bunny's brain and theorized that perhaps one of the Newcomers, Bakers, or Funks who intermarried with the Ingrams, and who were involved with Otho and Alice's land transactions, could have a descendant related to us.

More manic hours adding family members from the Newcomers, Bakers, Logans, and Funks into my faux online family tree resulted in *no* additional DNA matches, not to me nor any of the family DNA kits that I managed. More hopes dashed, like a Jenga tower whose blocks are removed one by one until the tower falls. That's my life as a genealogist.

Now, Kathy, until you have explored every Ingram descendant and the descendants of the Newcomers and Funks and Logans with whom they married or did business, you cannot be sure this is a dead-end. You need to find out whether a white man fathered Otho and/ or his mother Margaret.

OK. Driven to finish this book, it was driving me crazy! Every morning I woke before 6 AM to analyze my latest genealogy data and compose coherent sentences. I stole precious hours throughout the day to research and type more paragraphs. Edit. Concoct an interesting turn of phrase. Contact more DNA matches about our connections. Document DNA findings in my computer spreadsheets. Compose my findings. Create graphic images to describe the findings. Clarify. Print. File documents (sometimes) correctly. Write. Do the same steps over and over.

That schedule was my never-ending and all-consuming daily life for two years. I had a hard deadline (in my mind) to get my manuscript to a copy editor to prepare it for publishing by the end of 2018. By mid-2018, though, I still had to correctly format over two hundred-plus citations and the bibliography entries, as well as structuring the book layout according to Chicago Book of Style dictates, and the front and back cover created.

Moreover, I still hadn't found white people or Africans who I had proven were related to my Williams relatives. Darn it! How could I finish this book without those very important components?

* Triumph in The Deep South *

Since I hadn't had any luck with a DNA/paper trail match to my Maryland Williams, and I was running out of time to finish this manuscript, I chose to turn my efforts toward my father's Marshall family to "look for my white people."

Many of my DNA matches appeared to be related to my father's mother, Daisy Dooley Marshall, whose family came from Noxubee County, Mississippi, and Calhoun County, Alabama. Grateful that my brother, Greg, had taken a Y-DNA test, it made it possible to prove Y-DNA matches to our paternal Marshall ancestral community.

My generous DNA expert, HDG, indicated "If your brother is showing significant shared allele matches (a visible DNA coding that occupies a given position on a chromosome) with Caucasians, and those Caucasian-matches document their Marshall ancestors to the late 1700's to 1865 in the same location as your brother's Marshall ancestors, then that white person's family tree will likely include the most recent common ancestor relevant to your brother's Marshall line."

HDG further mused that "My interpretation of the probable connection to your paternal Marshall Y-origins, is that Nicholas Marshall born circa 1500 in the United Kingdom, may well suggest that your Marshall line is that of the slave owner, Supreme Court Justice Thurgood Marshall. If so, then I would suggest that you keep an eye open for descendants of this Marshall line. There should be a Pedigree of this family and loads of contemporary descendants online." That sounded like an exciting lead to investigate in the future when writing the Marshall Family book.

I had already found and proved two shared black ancestors with a third cousin named Clevlyn Bankhead Anderson (clbankhead). She and I had tested on 23andMe and Ancestry DNA and had uploaded our raw DNA to GEDmatch a few years prior. Ancestry's "Shared Ancestor Hint" clearly showed our common third great-grandparents, Wilson L. Nicholson and Emily Nicholson of Noxubee, County, Mississippi (MS) (Figure 19.4).

I was delighted beyond belief when we proved our common ancestors! I had been working on unraveling my first-great-grandmother Julia's lineage since 2001. Because Julia's mother, Fannie Cunningham, married so many times, and there were so many misspellings of surnames on various records, I never knew whether Julia's maiden name was Nickerson from Tennessee (TN), or Clayton, Nickleson, or Nicholson from Alabama.

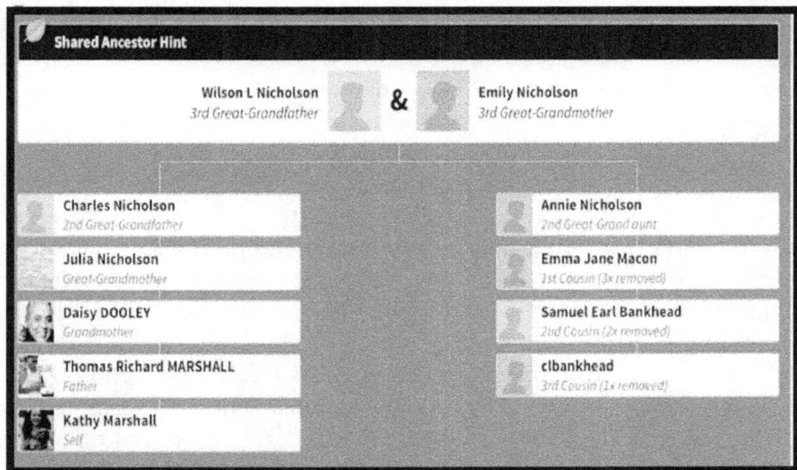

Figure 19.4. Ancestry DNA: Common ancestors for Kathy Marshall and clbankhead.

According to HDG, finding one's common ancestral community is especially important for slave research. Slaves were isolated, mated, and married within a relatively closed community. They were not permitted to drive down the road and meet guys and gals from a larger community. Thus, a Cunningham may have taken this surname from the slave owner at a given time; later to become a Nicholson; later to become a Clayton, etc.[207]

What clbankhead and I *did* know was that black Wilson Nicholson was born in 1830 in Tennessee. He married Emily Nicholson sometime before 1853 in Noxubee County, Mississippi, when their first child, Charles Nicholson, my second great-grandfather, was born. They had eleven children between 1853 and 1877. Ace genealogist Anthony May determined that Wilson's slave owner was Joel Barrett. What we didn't know was whether Wilson's father was white. We were back at square one again. What can we try next?

* DNA Circle Triangulations Are the Key! *

Ancestry had indicated I was in five DNA Circles, three of which related to my mother's Myers family. Excited by that news, I had to acknowledge I am an oddball for many things to be sure, but this time it was because I was the only lucky family member who was linked to two additional DNA Circles: Mary Jane Brown and Thomas Fleming Daniel. Truth be told, I had glanced at the twenty-three members in the Brown/Daniel DNA circles a few times over the prior two years. Most seemed to be from Kentucky. Because I was not aware of any family members who lived in Kentucky, I had glossed over those data circles, but kept them safe in the far recesses of my overworked brain.

As my self-imposed editing deadline for this second manuscript fast approached, I *needed* to find something positive about DNA testing to feel proud of my investment for this book. I snatched those two abandoned DNA Circles from their distant lofty perch and plunked them down in front of me for intensive scrutiny. Who were those white people from Kentucky in the Brown/Daniel DNA Circles? To find out I performed several steps:

I studied the comprehensive spreadsheets I developed, composed of seventy people whose DNA came almost entirely from Europe ("European matches") and sixty people with 50% or more of their DNA coming from African countries ("African matches"). I could tell at a glance how many cMs matched my DNA, indicating how close a match they were to me. I also noticed which people matched us on the same chromosomes, the largest block of chromosome segments they overlapped, etc., to estimate which of them might share a common ancestor with me. (Chapter 18 describes this process in more detail).

I summarized the surnames of my 130 closest cousin matches from those two spreadsheets (sample in Figure 19.3), so I am alerted when those surnames pop up in my research. Then I utilized various data analysis tools and interpreted the results for my 130 spreadsheet cousins, as described in Chapter 18.

I contacted cousin Clevlyn, and with the help of DNA expert Anthony May, we confirmed that my paternal first great-grandmother was mulatto Julia *Nicholson* Dooley, born in Noxubee County, Mississippi. Julia's mother was mulatto Fannie *Cunningham* Nicholson, born in Calhoun County, Alabama. Fannie's mother, my third great-grandmother, was mulatto Julia *Borders* Cunningham, from Georgia (Figure 19.4). Those surnames are now in the forefront of my brain when analyzing new data. Would I finally be able to find white ancestors from this branch of my father's family?

I checked Ancestry's "Member Connect" feature to see if anyone was searching for Julia Borders, Fannie Cunningham, or Julia Nicholson. Two interesting stories cropped up using that methodology. Ancestry member, known only by the alias, WWalk, told me Fannie Cunningham was his great-grandmother. His grandmother was Stella Clayton near whom my great-grandmother, Julia Nicholson, was raised. WWalk was told the following incredible story from his elderly cousin, who is also their family historian:

> "Born into slavery, Julia (Borders) was in the kitchen when she saw a sea of men in blue uniforms marching toward the house. It was the Union Army. Julia's daughter, Fannie (Cunningham), was present and outside. A soldier picked Fannie up and placed her on the fence post to hold the gate open for the soldiers. The soldiers entered the property and asked Julia to prepare them some food. Julia advised them that her master would be upset. The soldiers told her that she did not have a master anymore and that she was free." Ancestry member WWalk was also told by his cousin that: "John Cunningham owned Julia and fathered Fannie with her."

Can't you just picture this scene? A slave woman is cooking in the over-heated kitchen, getting a meal ready for her owner's lunch. She looks out the window at the battle-ravaged landscape all around her home. She spies strange men—Yankees—picking up her precious five-year-old daughter and placing her on top of the four-foot tall whitewashed fence post. What alarm must have rushed into her head, as she bounded out of the building to get her child, then to be told by these men, her liberators, that she is free. She is free! Imagine the excitement around the plantation, especially since the owner wasn't there at that precise moment. Imagine that the remains from the food larder were hastily made into a celebratory meal with the soldiers and newly freed men, women, and children. Glory be!

I can tell you there was a joyful noise inside *my* head hearing that plausible tale! The names are right. The historical timing is right. The location is, well, I don't know, but this was a real possibility that we got to see a glimpse of my then-young second great-grandmother, Fannie Cunningham, and her mother, Julia Borders!

Keeping that fascinating story in mind, I explored my Thomas Fleming Daniel and Mary Jane Brown DNA Circles, adding hundreds of their family connections to my not-wholly-confirmed working family tree. I began to notice that some of those Daniels and Browns were married to Borders and Cunninghams. I saw other surnames I had seen in my spreadsheets. Some of those folks lived in Calhoun County, Alabama, like my

Cunningham kin! The joy of opening a new avenue of exploration burst through me like a 4th of July fireworks finale.

I decided to do an Ancestry "Search Matches" function by location, specifying Noxubee County, Mississippi. I took special note of Ancestry member "J.C." because of his last name. Ancestry's Shared Matches indicated we both had Borders, Carter, Cunningham, Griffin, Hopton, and Knox in our family trees. His family tree had a John Borders (1779-1873), Narcissus Virginia Borders (1813-1889), and Michael Bader Borders (1751-1807) in his tree (Figure 19.5). Who were those people and were they related to me? NOTE: Some names in the following figures have been obscured for privacy.

Ancestry Member	Names in their tree	cMs	Segments
Carl	Barnes Has Michael Borders mother, Anna Maria Schneider in tree	6.6	1
Cha atlock	Borders	9.2	1
D.D.	Borders	24.8	2
E.B.	**John V** (1756-1817) Mary Polly (1796-1863)	12.3	1
Jame	**John V** (1756-1817) Mary Polly (1796-1863) Thomas F. Daniel (1841-1915)	24.7	1
J.C.	John (1779-1873) Michael (Bader) (1751-1807 Narcissus Virginia (1813-1889) Several Cunninghams	6.2	1

Figure 19.5. Ancestry DNA: Partial matrix of people whose DNA matches Kathy Marshall and "Borders" surnames in their family trees.

I checked Ancestry's "Member Connect" feature, to observe whether any members in the Mary Jane Brown DNA Circle were searching for John or Narcissus Borders, or Michael Bader/Borders. If so, they might be genetically related to me. I couldn't believe my eyes when Ancestry members "Honey" and "D" who had these Borders and Cunningham names in their family trees showed up on my DNA match list! (Figure 19.6) It is a distant match at only 6.6 cMs, but a match all the same. That was to be expected since we were comparing generations from the 1700s and 1800s. That was exactly what I had been hoping for: people who matched my DNA and had the same people in their family tree.

Next, I performed the "Search Matches" function on Calhoun County, Alabama. Names that were unknown to me the previous week were now recognizable welcome sights, like old friends, coming to my finding-common-ancestors party. One near the bottom of the list, was J.C.; the same one who was in the Noxubee County search listing (Figure 19.7). He had a Michael, Matthaus, and Anna Maria Bader from Germany in his family tree. I noted that his DNA kit was being managed by someone with a moniker of ACS.

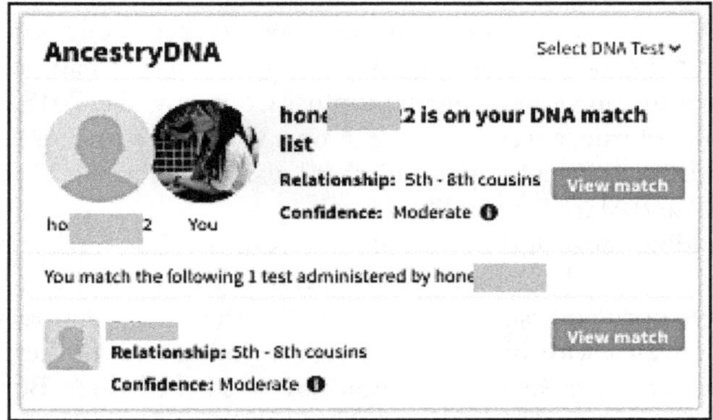

Figure 19.6. AncestryDNA: Cousins on Kathy Marshall's DNA match list.

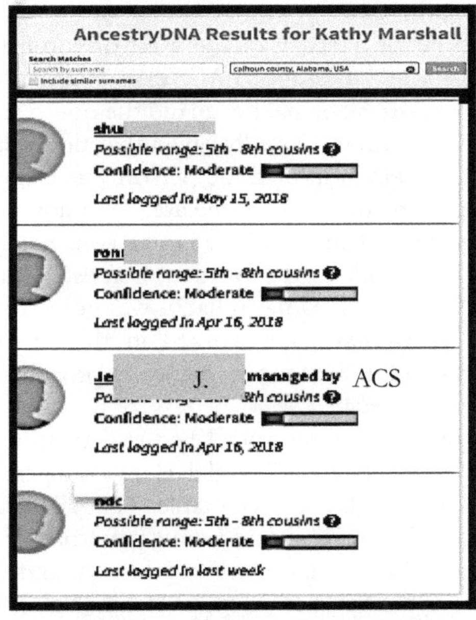

Figure 19.7. AncestryDNA: Calhoun County, Alabama, matches.

Another Ancestry member, named "Carly" also matched me on John Borders. *Hold your horses.* Was I getting closer to the truth? Had I finally found white people who not only matched my DNA but also contained the same people I was investigating in their family tree? *Stop biting your fingernails. Just slow your roll and savor this adventure . . . I need something right now to calm my eagerness.*

After eating a handful of walnuts (instead of truffles), I performed the "Search Matches" function on the surname "Borders". Twenty-eight of my DNA matches had Borders surnames in their family trees! Were they all "my" Borders? Could that be the Mother Lode I had been digging to find for the previous eighteen months? Could my May 2018 birthday wish be coming true, a week late, but a most welcome surprise? Could I prove genetically, and via a paper trail, that I was related to the Thomas Fleming Daniel and Mary Jane Brown clans?

Adding more and more generations to my faux family tree, I learned that John Borders' father was Michael (Bader) Borders (1751-1807). He was born and baptized in Baden-Württemberg, Germany, arriving in Pennsylvania with his father, Matthaus Bader, and mother, Anna Maria Schneider, when he was one-year-old. It seemed these Borders/Baders from Germany were some of my white progenitors, at last. Certainly, much more is needed to precisely determine the exact nature of our common relationship, but my hunter's bow is closer to finding my ultimate mark.

With a bit of trepidation and a lot of adrenalin fueling my thudding heartbeat, I sent a message to ACS explaining my likely connection to the Cunninghams in Alabama. I even did the no-no and mentioned that I was doing slave research. I usually saved that tidbit until I had made contact with a white person in case the person was turned off by an interaction with an African American. Some are, you know.

I was surprised and overjoyed to be congenially conversing with ACS. She sent me a link to the Borders homestead in the town of Oxford, Calhoun County, Alabama. What? I was going to see where my enslaved Borders family may have worked in the 1800s (and maybe earlier)? I couldn't stand it. Sometimes my joy approached mania. I had to focus, breathe, and relax.

The previous few months, I had chosen to move my study materials from my "research library" (which is my youngest son's former bedroom) to my seven-foot dining room table. That allowed me to lay out my laptop, backup disk drive, bound draft paperback book, genealogy binders of pertinent documents, stacks of history and genealogy books I had purchased, synonym dictionary, pens, and a glass of water.

A bigger payoff to this arrangement was being able to gaze onto my lush backyard landscape, full of bright green privets, aromatic gardenias, and my colorful welded steel art pieces interspersed throughout the garden. One dozen ancient hot-pink and scarlet-red geraniums preened, lifting their huge heads toward the sun, vying for my attention. Sometimes when I could hardly sit still from the excitement of a long-awaited find, I focused on the sound of water coursing out of the neck of my 40-inch tall ceramic goddess waterfall cascading into the tiny above-ground pond. Lilting birdsong added to the perfection that is my personal retreat.

It took me several minutes to compose myself before clicking on the link ACS sent. Before my eyes appeared several photographs taken in 1933 showing the exterior and interior of the former Border plantation house (Figure 19.8) as part of the Library of Congress' Historic Map Works, Residential Genealogy™ historical map collection.[208] The two-story home looked in reasonable shape in 1933 when the photographs were taken. ACS said it was still standing eighty-five years after those photos were taken, has been renovated, and is being lived in. The photo in Figure 19.8 is one-half of the "Big House" where the Border slave owners lived. The two-story portion of the structure, flanked by two chimneys, likely contained the bedrooms.

Figure 19.8. Blackmon-Borders House, Oxford, Calhoun County, Alabama.

The one-story "bump out" is flanked by two smaller chimneys, probably to heat the main living spaces just inside the back-door entrance. I assumed that underneath the light clapboard exterior was a log cabin home. I suspected the home was jacked up a few feet to avoid flooding during the winter and the lower two or three feet sided with brick. The wooden stairwell leading to the second floor, and the flooring shown in the upper right of the picture, looked pristine and structurally sound.

More plantation photographs, census, and other documents proving the thrilling details about the Caucasian and African American relationships I found on my paternal side via DNA testing are available in my third book, *Finding Daisy: From the Deep South to the Promised Land*, due for release in 2019.

Suffice it to say that the 1860 Slave Schedule indicated there was a slave owner named John Borders (1779-1873) who had thirty-five slaves. John Borders was a neighbor of "NV" Cunningham who had fifteen slaves, four of whom were listed as mulatto. A little sleuthing brought forth information that NV Cunningham was Narcissus Virginia Borders, the daughter of John Borders. She married Ansel Griffin Cunningham in 1830, and they had a son named John Borders Cunningham (1833-1912). Once again, I wondered whether I could determine the connection between John Borders and Narcissus Borders Cunningham to my family.

The hitch was "proving" that the slave master, John Borders was not only the owner of my third great-grandmother, Julia Borders, but also perhaps her father. According to the 1860 Slave Schedule, Calhoun County, Alabama, John Borders was the owner of a 25-year-old "black" female slave. Could she be Julia Borders who was born around 1834-35? Would the black scion of the white slave master always be described as a mulatto, whether or not she was dark-skinned?

NV Cunningham had mulatto female slaves, age 40, 30-something, and 18, along with an 18-year-old male mulatto. I did not know whether those mulattos were a male Cunningham's children, or whether they had anything to do with my Julia Borders.

The DNA Circles—a type of triangulation—identified over one dozen people who share my family's DNA and who have the same ancestors in their family trees. We share 7 to 228 centimorgans with non-direct line matches in the John Borders Cunningham, Ansel Griffin Cunningham, Narcissus Virginia Borders, John Borders, Fleming C. Daniel, and Mary Jane Brown DNA Circles. I also have "Shared Ancestor Hints" with two dozen DNA matches who have Cunninghams and Borders in their trees.

Ancestry member WWalk was told by his family historian that my Julia Borders had "married" her former slave master, John Cunningham. There are quite a few John Cunninghams in Alabama and Georgia. Could John Borders Cunningham, son of Narcissus, be the most likely subject? He was roughly the same age as my Julia and they likely grew up next door to each other.

Was John Borders Cunningham (of Irish ancestry) my third great-grandfather, and father to my second great-grandmother Fannie Cunningham (Figure 19.9)? Had DNA helped me find my white people? I staked my claim that the Borders/Bader German and Cunningham Irish heritage were part of my heritage too, as suggested by the many DNA matches I had with people of their lineage. It would take a bit more work to firmly close this case, but there was a lot of fuel to keep my fire stoked for some time to come.

For the moment, port wine and dark chocolate truffles would suffice on my shockingly red sofa in the front room that I consider the energy center of my house. The ancestors are smiling, and so am I!

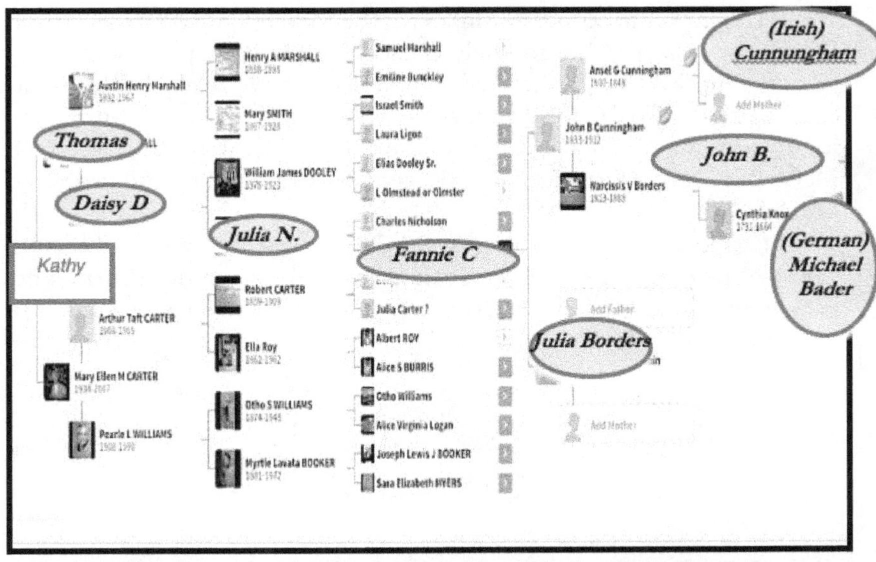

Figure 19.9. Pedigree tree showing relationship of Kathy Marshall to John Borders: Thomas Marshall, Daisy Dooley, Julia Nicholson, Fannie Cunningham, Julia Borders, to John Borders, who was the son of the German, Michael "Bader" Borders.

* Another DNA Success Story *

Let me tell you the astounding DNA success story of my brother-in-law, Bruce Anderson. He knew at the age of 10 that he had a different father from my husband's. He met his birth father in 1979 when he was thirty-three but didn't find out his grandfather was white until March 2018 when he received the results of his Ancestry DNA test. That was my seventeenth month on this project without any luck with DNA testing for my Williams family. (No, I was not jealous of his good fortune . . .)

Bruce was so lucky! Upon uploading his raw data results to GEDmatch.com, Bruce learned that someone named C.C. shared 1,946 cMs with him, indicating C.C. and Bruce are half-brothers, about 1.4 generations apart.

Bruce and C.C. are both very tall, attractive men, with a man-of-the-world complexion. Meaning, they look like they could be African American, South American, Portuguese, Puerto Rican, or even Asiatic. Their more-than-tanned skin coloring suggests African rhythms mixed with some European features, and their eyes a hint of the Asian Silk Road.

Bruce, age 72 and my 27-year-old son, MA match at 1,005 cMs, 1.9 generations apart. There were three other people who matched Bruce at the 241 to 750 cM second cousin level. The thrilling outcome of Bruce's DNA test was that he not only made contact with these new close relatives but also learned they had identified extensive family trees. In just two short months, Bruce met a first cousin that is 100% European, which led to learning about his extensive McCoy family. Yes, he is the real McCoy! Is DNA worth the cost? Bruce gives a resounding and unequivocal "ABSOLUTELY!"

My experience finding common white ancestors is very difficult, because my potential white progenitors were five or more generations back in time, and we have slavery as a major confounding issue.

Chapter 20 - Who Were Our Africans?

I wanted my Kunta Kinte experience! After reading the masterwork, *Roots: The Saga of an American Family*, by Alex Haley, in 1976, about African teenager, Kunta Kinte, who was stolen from his African home and forced into slavery in America, I had wanted to learn which African tribes produced my family.

I adopted the name Kanika—which means black cloth in the Swahili language—and established my Kanika African Sculptures business in 1993. I believe my African ancestors work through my fingers to create each of my ceramic masks, clay statues, clay figurines draped with African fabric, carved platters, wearable-art jewelry, and kinetic welded-steel garden-art sculptures.

A Caucasian friend recently visited my house, which is a veritable shrine to my African roots, with African art and artifacts gracing every wall in my home. She asked why I don't also celebrate my European roots. I explained that my light skin color represents the rape of my black female ancestors; thus, my white blood is not to be celebrated, but mourned. To better explain my feelings, I shared with her an excerpt from my *The Ancestors Are Smiling!*

> "As I got older, my sensitivity to racial inequalities really began to bubble to the surface. I noticed there were only two pages in our high school history books about black folk in America, and they were only about slavery. The Civil Rights movement was in full force as I entered the integrated and troubled Hiram Johnson High School in 1972. There were daily uprisings and fights between the black, white, Asian and Hispanic students at our school.
>
> "'Say it loud, I'm Black, and I'm Proud!' was our black students' motto. We proudly wore our thick black Afro hairstyles with a cake cutter sticking out of the top of our hair. We wore vividly patterned jersey shirts, the-shorter-the-better hot pants, big hoop earrings, and thick-soled Famolare shoes. We watched the 'Soooouuullll Train' music TV show on Saturdays. After being denigrated as a race for so many centuries in this country and around the world, we just enjoyed

being black! The Black Panther Party for Self-Defense was the leader in this newly proclaimed black self-love fest. They practiced militant self-defense of minority communities against the U.S. government and fought to establish revolutionary socialism through mass organizing and community-based programs. However, the newspapers rarely covered their positive food and education programs for poor and black people, only covering stories about 'uppity Negroes' with guns."

Figure 20.1. Kathy Marshall's 1975 ink and felt pen drawing and photos of 2015 metalwork.

During that exciting and difficult period of civil unrest, though, my blossoming artwork became 100% Afrocentric. (Figure 20.1)

The more I found out about slavery and Jim Crow segregation that existed in many parts of the country (then and now), the stronger my militant feelings became. More than anything I wanted to be *black enough*.

My college career started at Sacramento City College in January 1975, after graduating (escaping, really) mid-term from high school. I felt like a bird soaring, free at last! It was wonderful to be taking classes that interested me, like African-American History and Women's Studies. We students openly talked about topics that would have gotten our black ancestors lynched, and we *loved* the freedom of expression! Can you dig it?

This is why I have been absorbed with "Finding my Africans" for the last forty years. So far, I haven't succeeded in satisfying my heart's desire of identifying and visiting my African tribe(s).

While I was more than unhappy to find that little more than half of my DNA came from Africans, I was excited to find that my original people came primarily came from Benin/Togo, the home of accomplished metalworkers, especially bronze castings like that in Figure 20.2.

Figure 20.2. Unknown jeweler/metalworker Nigerian brooch of a Portuguese face, hip ornament, Edo, Court of Benin.

The same basic process described in the "Finding My Europeans" section was used to find my African connections. Instead of looking for people who primarily came from European countries, I looked for those who had at least 50% African admixture. Believe me, that was much more difficult than finding people of primarily European heritage. There has been so much miscegeny between blacks, whites, and Native Americans that there aren't many pure Africans who match our Williams DNA.

My DNA expert, HDG, also pointed out that the major DNA companies have not generally sent a representative number of DNA kits to African countries, so it is difficult to match Africans still living in Africa.

To help us "lost children" in America find our African roots, the "Imperial African History and Genetic Genealogical Society Reconciling the African Global Family, One Genome at a Time" organization has a goal to facilitate reconciliation between the Autosomal DNA Tested African Diaspora (for example, we African Americans) with Autosomal DNA Tested Africans born on the continent of Africa. This organization attempts to coordinate this reunification through language classes, naming ceremonies, and other enriching events after our African DNA results have been matched to an African person living on the vast African continent.[209]

There is a relatively simple way to learn whether one's DNA is related to the Royal Africans. First, the raw DNA from Ancestry DNA or the other major American testing companies must be uploaded to GEDmatch's "Genesis" tool [note: complete instructions are on the Genesis.GEDmatch.com website].

One must then run the "One to Many" option, perform a "Find" on the search term "Royal" to identify matches from the Royal African project. In my case, and the case of the rest of my Williams family, there was only one Royal African who matched my Uncle Dale at the time of this writing. Privacy concerns prohibit my mentioning the African's name. I was not able to make contact with that match prior to publishing this book.

The following website, http://DNATestedAfricans.org has more information about this interesting service to match descendants of the African diaspora with their African relatives.

Hearing drumbeats in my head as my fingers tap-tap-tapped on the computer keyboard, I utilized additional techniques to find my African relatives. Several ideas which you may want to try are briefly described on the following pages.

* My Kunta Kinte Moment *

I decided to revisit Ancestry DNA's "Search Matches" function that I had tried many times before with no satisfactory results. First, I refreshed myself on the current names and locations of African countries (Figure 20.3) so I could better visualize where my relatives lived. I desperately wanted to find out where my African roots came from so I could eventually visit the "Motherland" and experience the African culture that Alex Haley imagined with us in *Roots: An American Family*.

Figure 20.3. Map of African countries, 2018. Source: Google maps.

* Madagascar *

I intended to search each African country, one at a time, to see if there were people born there who matched my DNA or the DNA of my other family members. Holding my breath, I started with the biggest island off the east coast of Africa.

I typed "Madagascar" into the "Birth by Location" field (Figure 20.4). Would anything be different this time? I held my breath without realizing it until I took in a deep breath when the search delivered its bonanza. Huzzah! My ship had turned. The horizon was bright. My fortunes were made. In front of my eyes was one 5th to 8th distant cousin born in Madagascar, in the family tree of someone named JQ!

Clicking on "View Match" I found that JQ's DNA came from Nigeria, Ivory Coast/Ghana, Benin/Togo, Cameroon/Congo, with trace regions in Senegal, Mali, Great Britain, Ireland, Europe West, Asia South, Caucasus, Finland, and Asia Central. Even though it was obvious JQ was not a

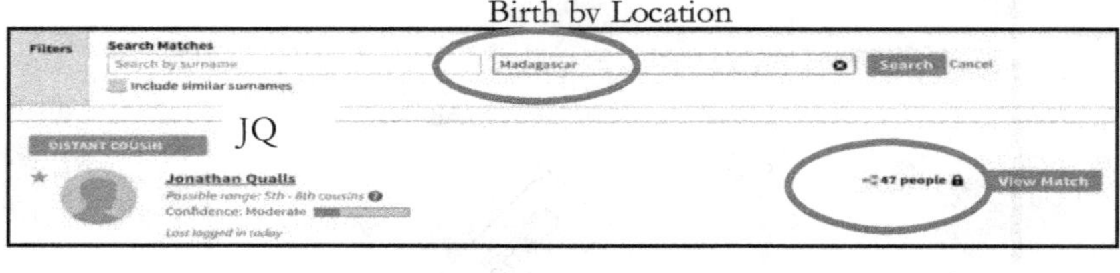

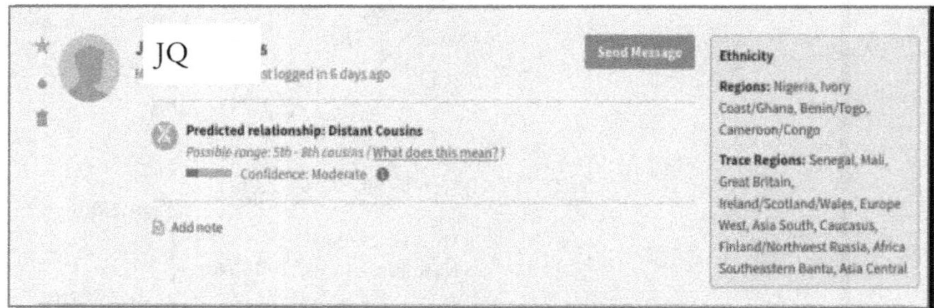

Figure 20.4. DNA match to Kathy Marshall from Madagascar.

100% pure African, I jumped and stomped and shook my tail feathers! That was the first time I had seen any mostly-African person, born in Africa, matching my DNA. Had goal #3 for this book finally been met? Had I finally found my long-sought-after African ancestor? Unfortunately, JQ's family tree was private so I could not see the extent of his tree or where exactly his people lived and died.

Again, I pondered. What would you do *first* if you found your forty-year-old heart's desire? Would you attempt to contact your DNA match right away? Would you search birthplace information for your match? Would you try to find your DNA match on Facebook, Twitter, or Google? Would you cry tears of joy? Would you tell your family and genealogy friends that you finally found your African ancestor? Would you praise the ancestors for leading you to this long-awaited find? Would you meditate on your good fortune? Would you do the happy dance? Would you celebrate with dark chocolate and port wine, even though it was 7:30 AM when the find was made? Well, I did all these things in no particular order!

* Nigeria *

Reminding myself to keep breathing I rolled the dice again. Using the same methodology, I checked every African country against my DNA, starting with Nigeria.

"Al" was a Nigerian match. To find out how Al was related, I sent an email.

"I just noticed that you have a relative from Nigeria: JD Reynolds. That is so exciting! I am trying to find Africans who match my family's DNA. You may be that link. Do you know much about JD besides she was born in Nigeria in 1812, was married to HReynolds and died in Pennsylvania in 1924 or 1925? Do you know whether she had been brought to America as a slave or whether she was a free woman?" I was unable to make concrete linkages for this book.

I also checked for Nigerians who matched my Great Uncle Charles Williams' DNA. Oh my goodness! There were four people born in Nigeria who matched him! (Figure 20.5).

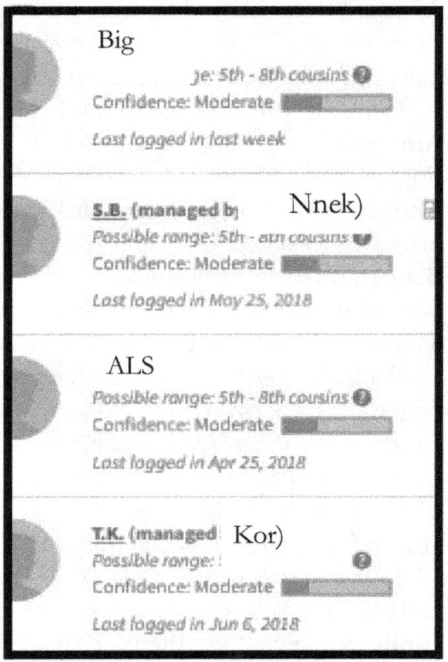

Figure 20.5. People born in Nigeria who match Charles Williams' DNA.

The first person in Charles' match list was "Big" whose ethnicity regions were Nigeria, Benin/Togo, and the Ivory Coast/Ghana, with trace regions from Cameroon/Congo, Mali, and Africa Southeastern Bantu. That was more exciting than I could possibly describe. He was a pure African! The only way to make that better would be actually to speak with, and visit, our newly found African cousins. Perhaps I could in the future.

I could not help but peek at the handful of people in his public family tree. The only name listed was J. Igwe (1890-1964). The other four were not listed so I assumed they were alive and their names were not listed due to privacy concerns. I attempted to "View Full Tree" hoping there was more to the exciting mystery than just one person. Hmm . . . J. Igwe was married to a woman named Anna (1900-1978).

Using Ancestry and Google, I attempted to find more information about J. Igwe from Nigeria, but there were too many possibilities. Next, I composed a message to "Big" telling him briefly about my genealogy search and asking if he knew any more about his family. I crossed my fingers that he'd respond, then proceeded to research the other three matches on Charles' list.

The second person on Charles' DNA match list was "S.B." whose DNA test was managed by a member named "Nnek". According to Anestry.com's assessment, S.B.'s DNA came from Nigeria, Benin/Togo, with trace regions in Mali, Ireland, African Southeastern Bantu, Senegal, African South-Central hunter-gatherers, Ivory Coast/Ghana, and Cameroon/Congo. There were five people in her public family tree, with one named: Ambrose O. It appeared S.B. was the granddaughter of Ambrose.

Clicking on the "Map and Locations" option, I observed that Ambrose was born in 1943 in Port Harcourt, Rivers, Nigeria (Figure 20.6). Further clicking on "View Details" indicated Ambrose was living in Silver Spring, **Maryland**, as of 2001. An audible intake of breath broke the silence as I realized my expert genealogist friend, Bernice Bennett, lived in the same suburb of Annapolis, Maryland. What were the odds that Bernice knew Ambrose, S.B. and Nnek and that their ancestors were somehow related to my Prince Williams?

With the fervor of a mad woman, I typed "Port Harcourt, Rivers, Nigeria," into my laptop's Google browser to find out more about Ambrose's birthplace. I learned that before the area became Port Harcourt in 1912, it was part of the farmlands of the Diobu village group of the Ikwerre, an Igbo sub-group. Are the Igbo one of my long sought-after African tribes? Is this finally my Kunta Kinte moment?

I wondered how, why, and when, Ambrose's family decided to emigrate to America, whether they still lived in Maryland, and how my family connected to them. I did a Google and Facebook search for "Nnek" to see if I could discover anything about the administrator of S.B.'s DNA results. I also sent a message through Ancestry to see if we could chat about our family connection. My crossed fingers and toes were rewarded a few months later when she responded.

She told me a fascinating story about how her father, Ambrose, came to America on an Arts scholarship to make a better life for his family (whom he sent for in 1977 after he had established himself in this country). Nnek admitted she believed my Great Uncle Charles' DNA matched on her ten-year old daughter, S.B's *father*, not Nnek's DNA. S.B.'s father is African American, and he has no interest in finding his ancestors. My hopes were dashed again. No connection to an actual African after all?

Good news. Nnek had begun investigating her husband's genealogy and found his family lineage also came from the Igbo tribe in Nigeria. His people were taken by slavers from a town not too far from hers. What a small world!

She proceeded to describe her hometown of Orlu and her husband's ancestral town of Mbaise, which has a museum that tells the story of slave traders who came and stole Igbo tribe members from a village named Vim. The museum has art sculptures depicting the slaves being taken and how they passed through the village.

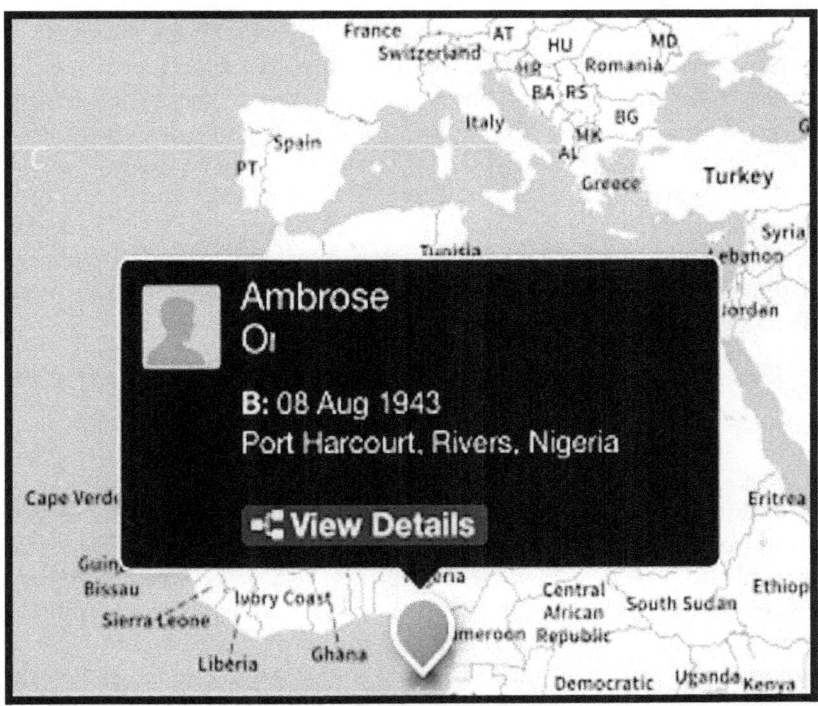

Figure 20.6. Ambrose O, grandfather of S.B. whose DNA Matches that of Kathy Marshall's Great Uncle Charles Williams.

Nnek and I have become pen pals and vow to explore our familial relationship further. My goal is to visit the country of our common ancestry within the next few years. My Kunta Kinte moment is within reach!

Third on Charles' DNA list of discovery was named ALS. Her primary DNA regions were in western Europe and Nigeria, with trace regions in Benin/Togo, Senegal, Ivory Coast/Ghana, Mali, and a few others. Reviewing her two small online families, the most interesting ancestor, named Sarah, was born in Nigeria in an unnamed year. The only surname listed was Kelly, a man born in 1750. Was it likely that an Irishman traveled to Nigeria and perhaps brought a Nigerian woman named Sarah back with him to Great Britain, where they had a mixed-race son named G. Kelly? That would explain the mixed-race lineage of ALS. I sent her the same message I sent other DNA matches, hoping to get clarification of our distant connection.

* Senegal *

Next was a search for cousins born in Senegal. Charles' fourth-to-sixth cousin, PWill, was a 22.9 cM. She and Charles were members of the Lydia Louisa Wilkes and Philip Myers DNA Circles. PWill was descended from Senegalese slave, Banna-ka, who married Molly Walsh, an Englishwoman, in 1796 in Maryland. Their daughter, Mary Banneker married a slave named Robert. They had a son named Benjamin Banneker[210] (1731-1806), who was famously noted as a black mathematician, astronomer, compiler of almanacs and writer from Maryland. PWill was distantly related to our Myers family line. Is my family is related to Benjamin Banneker?

* Liberia *

Searching for people born in "Liberia" produced a match to AM whose ancestor, Estella, was born and died there. AM's DNA was primarily from Nigeria, Mali, Benin/Togo, Ivory Coast/Ghana, with trace regions in Senegal, and Europe West. The resulting state of Liberia, sandwiched between Sierra Leone and the Ivory Coast, would become the second (after Haiti) black republic in the world. In the 1830s, the "Back to Africa" movement was very strong in Maryland, in particular, after the Nat Turner rebellion in 1831. Many whites, concerned the free black population would encourage their slave brethren to run away to freedom, became proponents of the "send blacks back to Africa" movement. Many began freeing their slaves in droves to send them to Liberia. Between 1822 and 1867, 13,000 blacks migrated to Liberia. Unfortunately, AM did not respond to my inquiry.

* Ghana *

A search for persons born in "Ghana" produced a DNA match to JMK, whose DNA was from Mali, Benin/Togo, Cameroon/Congo, Nigeria, and Ivory Coast/Ghana. His 370-person tree had a female ancestor named Sethe who was born in Ghana in 1735 and died in Patapsco Hundred, Baltimore, **Maryland** in 1812. JMK had four Carters in his tree, with William L Carter born in 1848 in Virginia and died in 1920 in Denton, Texas. The DNA from AR comes from Benin/Togo, Cameroon/Congo, Mali, Ivory Coast/Ghana, Senegal, and Africa Southeastern Bantu. His mother said her grandfather, J. Bodoe, was a Ghanaian Chief. Figure 20.7 shows a photograph of an unknown Chief dressed in the typical colorful regalia of Kente cloth with lots of beautiful gold ornamentation. Just dazzling! When I think of African Kings and Chiefs, this is exactly the bountiful, golden scene that comes to mind. Ghana was part of the "Gold Coast" after all.

Figure 20.7. Typical Ghanaian Chief.

* Family Tree DNA African Project *

What happened to those expensive Y-DNA and Matrilineal-DNA tests that I purchased in late 2016 at the beginning of this adventure?

As described in Chapter 18, both my first cousin, Bob, and my son, Matthew, exhibited an E-M2 haplogroup, which meant our Williams and my sons' Anderson family lines were probably from sub-Saharan Africa.

There were only two Y-DNA testers who matched nine of eleven SNPs with Bob Williams; one had ancestors from Sierra Leone and the other, from the United States. My son, Matthew, had three Y-DNA matches at the Y-37 level; one had ancestors from Nigeria, Haiti, and Jamaica. My brother, Greg, had one P-I37 European haplogroup and understandably had no close matches in the African Project. I could not determine from any of those DNA matches specific family members in common.

The bottom line was that the expensive Y-DNA tests did not help much in finding common ancestors, at least not at the time of this writing.

* Is My Matrilineal Line from Madagascar, Africa? *

I first took a mitochondrial mtDNA, women-only, test in 2014 using 23andMe, then another in 2017 using Family Tree DNA. I was hoping the results would uncover information about my mother's Crewett matrilineal family line, perhaps verifying whether I had Native American DNA.

Wait, do I have that right? Let's look at a pedigree chart of my family, starting with me, then my mother Mary Ellen Carter (born 1934), her mother Pearl Williams (born 1908), her mother Myrtle Booker (born 1881), her mother Sara Myers (born 1858), her mother Corintha Crewett (born 1842), and her mother Adella "Free Dell" Chandler Crewett (born 1829), who was my fourth great-grandmother (Figure 20.8).

My mtDNA results suggested that I had a rare B4a1a1b haplogroup, which traced back to a woman who lived approximately 5,500 years ago. That haplogroup was virtually universal in Polynesia (really?), but hard to find anywhere else. I thought the results were a mistake for I have almost no DNA from Asia and only a scant 1% Native American according to Ancestry DNA, with 1.5% Native American from 23and me. *Grandma Daisy, what happened to the Blackfoot Indian you said we had in our lineage?*

On his "Finding Your Roots" genealogy television show, Dr. Henry Louis Gates described an interesting occurrence when the B4a1a1b haplogroup was attributed to African Americans. That special case was called the "Malagasy Motif" which suggested that very small numbers of people from remote, Southeast Asian Islands 3,000 and 1,000 years ago made their way to Madagascar in boats and merged with Africans.

In *Exchanging Our Country Mark*, Michael Gomez describes how Madagascar's inhabitants, the Malagasy people, possessed light skin and facial features very akin to people in Southeast Asia and Indonesia. Geneticists determined all the Malagasy people descend from Africa and Asia, specifically Borneo. As time passed in America, Africans from Madagascar were believed to be "Indians" or "Black Indians."

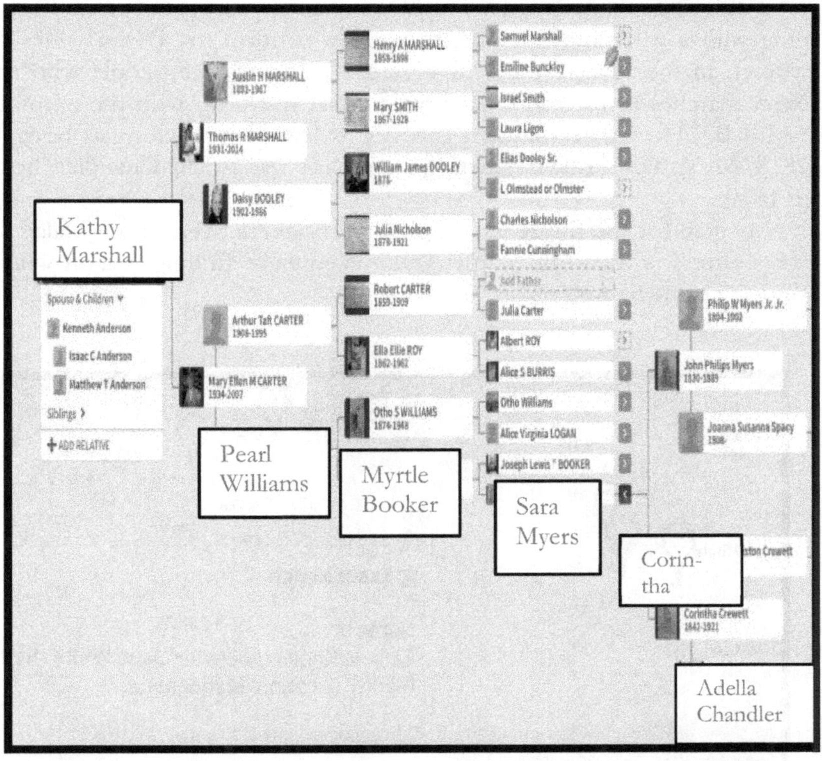

Figure 20.8. Example of mtDNA mother-to-mother test from Kathy Marshall, to Mary Carter, to Pearl Williams, to Sara Myers, to Corintha Crewett, to Adella Crewett .

In my mind, the most exciting thing about the B4a1a1b haplogroup was there were very few ship disembarkations of enslaved Africans from Madagascar between 1678 and 1721 that came through to Virginia and New York.[211] To me, that meant I could *conceivably* track my matrilineal line to one of those Malagasy women who may have landed in Virginia or New York and whose descendant was my fifth great-grandmother, Adella Chandler. It is possible that I may eventually learn the name of that original Malagasy woman in my lineage! I looked forward to exploring that possibility in the Second Edition of this book.

Teresa Vega's *"Radiant Roots, Boricua Branches: Musings on My Black and Puerto Rican Ancestry" website* (http://radiantrootsboricuabranches.com/) is a must-read for those wanting to learn more about their Malagasy roots. I also recommend *Memories of Madagascar and Slavery in the Black Atlantic* by Wendy Wilson Fall, Ph.D.

Twelve people matched my mtDNA results with a generation of zero, nine with a generation of one, helping to confirm my B4a1a1 links to women in the Malagasy Motif. Figure 20.9 shows the people who are exact matches to my mtDNA from a DNA test-taker with the moniker "ALR-B." Her earliest known ancestor is Jean White who was born in 1818. My earliest known matrilineal ancestor was Adella Chandler, born in 1829.

My goal for the future will be finding more relatives whose Malagasy progenitress is the same as mine and, eventually, finding out on which ship she came to America.

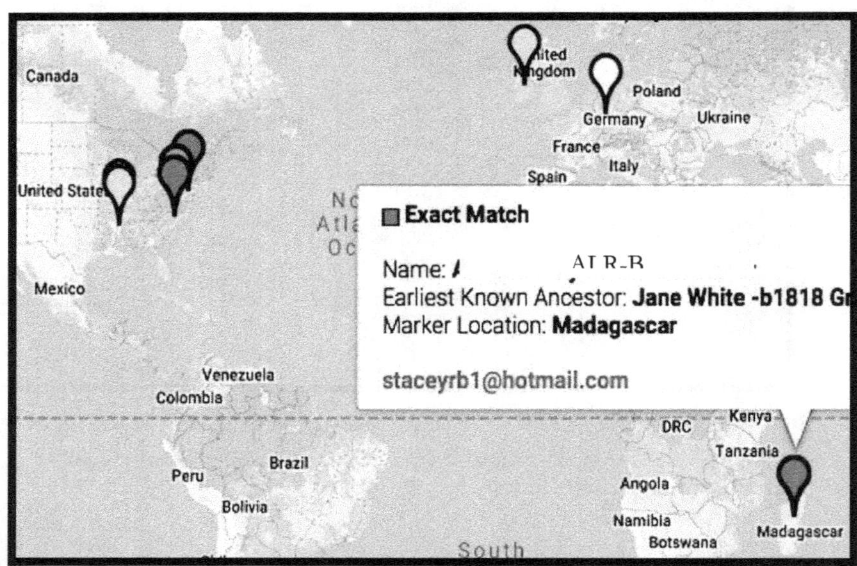

Figure 20.9. Kathy Marshall's B4a1a1b haplogroup is an exact match to ALR in Madagascar. Source: Family Tree DNA.

* Are We Melungeons? *

"Are you mixed?" still comes up as a topic of conversation among black people (almost never among whites). Through this lengthy, but rewarding process, I must admit that my heritage is mixed. I still did not know all the pure Europeans and pure Africans who provided the mixtures, but DNA doesn't lie.

My DNA expert, HDG, strongly believed that, for generations, my family of mixed-race people married other mixed-race people, moving to sanctuary cities that treated mixed-race people fairly. He explained the general term for mixed-race people composed of white, black and Native American blood is "Melungeons."

Most modern-day descendants of Appalachian families traditionally regarded as Melungeon are generally European American in appearance, often (though not always) with dark hair and eyes, and a swarthy or olive complexion. Descriptions of Melungeons have varied widely over time. In the nineteenth and early twentieth century, they were sometimes identified as "Portuguese," "Native American," or "light-skinned African American." Stories and claims abound as to how this group of people descended from Portuguese, or Turks and/or Moors who navigated to the American shores with the Portuguese, and who intermarried with Native Americans before English settlement.[212]

Some of the most prominent surnames claimed as potentially associated with a Melungeon identity include Bowling (Bolin), Bunch, Chavis (Chavez), Collins, Epps, Evans, Fields, Francisco, Gibson, Gill, Goins, Goodman, Minor, Mise, Moore, Mullins, Osborn(e), Phipps, Reeves (Rives, Rieves, Reeves, Reaves), Ridley (Riddle), Rodrigues, Stowers, Vanover, Williams, and Wise. This limited partial list should not be taken as suggesting that every family using this surname is necessarily considered to be Melungeon.

Some experts suggested that large slave-owner families *bred* slaves. Lighter-skinned female house slaves were bred with the master to produce lighter-skinned offspring. Consequently, many of today's mulatto, Melungeon, and passing-for-white folks descended from them. Clusters of people who were designated "not black," but historically "not white," were scattered across the U.S. All these groups, dubbed by anthropologists and sociologists as "tri-racial isolates," or "maroons," are an interesting part of our troubled racialized history and current notions of "race," "ethnicity," ancestry, and genetics. Some of the descendants from these slave-owner families have a Kentucky, Tennessee, Cincinnati, Zanesville, Ohio, Melungeon ancestral history.

In the sixteenth month of research, HDG, my most treasured DNA expert, concluded the data supported that my family is clearly mixed-race

Melungeons. I had heard the term, especially related to the populations in Zanesville, Ohio, where mixed-race people abound. My parents met there on a blind date at the roller-skating rink in 1952. HDG confirmed that Greencastle, Pennsylvania; East Liverpool, Ohio; and Barnesville, Ohio, are also well-known Melungeon communities. Those are the cities my Williams family migrated to from Washington County.

Further, most African Americans are mixed-race—whether people want to acknowledge it or not. According to esteemed African American genealogy guru, Henry Louis Gates, Jr., in his 2013 article, *"Exactly How 'Black' Is Black America?"* the average black person was 74% sub-Saharan African, 24% European, and 2% Native American. These averages came from Ancestry DNA, 23andMe, Family Tree DNA, AfricanDNA[213], and National Geographic. That meant it would be difficult to find a present-day African who matched me unless I take the $299 African Ancestry DNA test.

The "Ethnicity Regions" in Ancestry DNA estimate which countries the DNA came from between 500 and 2,000 years ago. For example, my top third-cousin match, HSW, shares 135 cMs across seven segments with me and has some African ethnicity regions (Figure 19.14). Unfortunately, I could not easily tell her total percentage of African DNA versus that of Finland, Ireland, and Great Britain. That person, like many, had no family tree or had a private tree, so I could not see if we had a paper trail match. I left several Ancestry DNA messages asking to see her tree. I also looked up her Ancestry name on Facebook, GEDmatch, and 23andMe. I also Googled her name and found her in Cleveland, Ohio, my birthplace. I could find no other records or connection in the Public Member Trees with others searching for her. I hoped she would respond so we may learn about our connection.

HDG and others suggested that the reason I couldn't easily "find my white people" or my Africans was that they came into my gene pool in the 1700s. My family tree, and that of most black folk who have slave issues, generally do not go back that far.

Another third cousin match, BD, paid a surprise visit at one of my 2017 book signings in Sacramento, California. His ethnicity regions are Great Britain, Mali, Ivory Coast/Ghana, Nigeria, and Ireland/Scotland/Wales. He has my same coloring, but we cannot compare family trees because his mother gave him away at birth. We have several GEDmatch's in common, clearly on my father's side of the family, who overlap chromosomes 1, 4, 6, 7, 8, 12, 18, 20, and 23. That might indicate that we shared a common ancestor. I would attempt to find our commonality for his sake, as well as my own.

To summarize, it seems that generations of my family were Melungeons who tended to move to other mixed-race communities where they felt safe and comfortable, could open businesses, marry, and become educated. They intermarried with others in the community, people who also tended to be mixed-race. Some decided to pass for white. I chuckle at the knowledge that many so-called white people are surprised when their DNA results come back indicating they have North African or Sub-Saharan African DNA. So far, the 98% or more white people who have some African DNA and matched my DNA seemed kind of jazzed that they had something other than pure white blood.

Well, folks, I guess I am mixed after all! It has been very difficult for me—owner of Kanika African Sculptures—to come to grips with, accept, and even permit myself to feel OK about being mixed-race after a lifetime of wanting to find belonging in my darker-hued community. My "us" versus "them" thinking must be eradicated. Like a true Gemini child, I must not favor the darker twin over the lighter one. We are equally valid. We are equally children of the Earth.

* Is DNA Testing Worth the Cost? *

In general, Y-DNA testing was not worth the cost for this *Finding Otho* project, as I found no Williams ancestors who could be verified through Y-DNA testing. However, mitochondrial DNA testing led to my unexpected B4a1a1b haplogroup which may, in the future, allow me to isolate the exact slave ship that brought my female ancestor from Madagascar to New York or Virginia.

Autosomal testing was definitely worth the cost! DNA testing not only revealed which parts of the African, European and Asian continents our ancestors were from but also put me in touch with over one thousand people whose DNA results from the three major companies matched mine to at least the fourth cousin level. Since my first DNA test in 2012, I have communicated with hundreds of DNA cousins to try to find our common ancestors. While I did not find a common ancestor on my Williams family line, I did find several on my other family lines.

Even though it was frustrating that half of my DNA matches have either no family tree online, or they keep it private, my research has been greatly enhanced by all these interactions. I suspect that many of the new-found relatives who match my DNA will become lifelong friends.

An unexpected benefit of autosomal testing was that our Family Historian, my Aunt Lavata, found a second cousin on her father's family line. Lavata never knew who her father was so it was wonderfully gratifying for her when she visited my home in June 2016 and telephoned that long-lost cousin. Along those lines, my brother-in-law, Bruce Anderson, successfully found generations of his little-known father's family within a scant two months after receiving his DNA results.

DNA TESTING IS DEFINITELY WORTH THE COST!

EPILOGUE

* It's a Wrap *

On October 1, 2016, I had five main goals in mind for this book:

1) Find my great-great-grandfather, Otho Williams', parents.
2) Uncover information about Otho's slave owner.
3) Explore how DNA analysis could link my family to the descendants of specific European and African people to our family tree.
4) Commemorate the life stories of Otho's descendants.
5) Determine whether we genetically received our tendency to be mechanically inclined, from our enslaved ancestors.

The first few days on this absorbing project were spent developing a framework and outline for this book, determining what page layout to use, and developing a list of questions to answer.

The first two months were spent writing the stories which my family already knew about Otho's descendants. During this period, I encouraged eleven other Williams relatives to take DNA tests to provide a scientific angle for this research.

Nights and days during the third and fourth months were deluged with researching the history of western Maryland in general, and Washington County in particular, with a narrow focus on the life of free and slave African Americans. I purchased and read numerous books and biographies written from, and about, black people in Maryland. I happily met my primary stated first goal—to find Otho's parents, and the second—to find his owner.

The fifth and sixth months of work were spent filling out the book outline and refining and asking others to help edit the initial manuscript.

Touring various sites in Maryland and Pennsylvania during the seventh month gave me a much better understanding of the environment in which my ancestors lived in the 1700s and 1800s. I interviewed librarians, funeral home staff, neighbors, a history professor, a Chesapeake and Ohio Canal professional, and historians. I shot hundreds of photos and hours of video to record all aspects of the journey for later recall and inclusion in this book.

The fourth goal—to write family stories about the descendants of the formerly enslaved Otho and Alice Williams—was met in the tenth month. *The Ancestors Are Smiling!* was published in July 2017 on Amazon.com, in libraries, on my website, and in a local bookstore.

I got greedy and set about to find the progenitors and slave owners of my third great-grandparents, finding one slave owner in the tenth month, and developing plausible theories about my fourth and fifth great-grandparents in the eighteenth month.

Finding common ancestors proven by DNA evidence—was the most difficult task and was minimally accomplished for my Williams line. However, there were resounding successes on my father's family lines, with being able to prove DNA and family tree relationships to specific African and European relatives.

In Chapter 14, a compelling case identifies my fifth goal: that my family is genetically more mechanically-inclined, or at least more oriented toward metalworking, than the average American family.

My ardent desire was to pep up the facts and figures with interesting qualitative descriptions about the lives of my enslaved and free ancestors from Maryland. To that end, I joined three writing and critique groups to help me learn to write imaginative dialog from my ancestors. I also ensured this "Finding Otho" book was professionally copyedited and proofread to achieve my intention.

* Let the Truth Be Told, But Don't Cheat 'n Peek *

The last step in the Genealogical Proof Standard was to summarize my exhaustive research, completed citations, data analysis, and resolution of conflicting evidence into a coherently written conclusion.

For those of you who like to read the last page of a brand-new book, it's OK. We all do it every now and then. Let the truth be told here and now.

I started this research knowing almost nothing about my great-great-grandfather (second great-grandfather), Otho Williams. He was born in 1834 and died around 1889 in Washington County. I had no idea who his parents, siblings, or slaveowner(s) were; exactly where he lived; what he did as a slave; and what his life was like after slavery.

The 1870 and 1880 Census provided a glimpse into the community in which he lived, indicating Otho and Alice were the only non-whites to own land in my sample of 67 families.

For years, I had entertained several theories about whether any of the white Otho Holland Williams who lived in Washington County were my Otho's owner or father. Based on Maryland land records and other documents, I begrudgingly concluded that none of the white Otho Holland Williams was Otho's father or owner.

It was apparent that after slavery, our Otho had participated in several land transactions during his lifetime. The first involved purchasing lot 143 and one-half lot 144 in Funkstown in 1868 with someone named Hezekiah Williams. I theorized that Hezekiah was Otho's brother. That deed also associated the property with a fellow named Prince Williams, but I did not immediately grasp what that connection was.

The Maryland land records indicated that Prince Williams had purchased household items and a cradle in 1834, the year my Otho Williams was born. In 1842, Prince Williams bought that same Funkstown property that Otho and Hezekiah bought 26 years later.

To find out more about Prince Williams, I researched probate records, finding two entries for him. The first indicated Prince died in May 1843, leaving an eye-opening Will. It confirmed that Prince liberated and set free his unnamed son's wife, Sarah Williams, and her infant daughter, Jane. This shocking revelation indicated that Prince had been a slave-owner. Prince's 1843 Will named "Margaret A." as his wife. The Will requested executor John Ingram to convey Prince's estate to Margaret as though she were a free woman. Last, the Will specified the remainder of Prince's estate be given equally to *all* of his children (but no names were listed).

Who were the Ingrams? Three slave-related Maryland land records involved Ingrams, freeing Mary Williams in 1848, Samuel Williams in 1854, and Margaret Elizabeth Williams in 1860. Sadly, no records were found for Otho Williams.

In 1834, Joseph Ingram's Will named seven slaves as part of his "young family of Negroes" and bequeathed them to seven of his adult children still living at home. The slaves included: Sam, Henry, Hezekiah, Mary, Patsy, Matilda (or Malinda), and Margaret E., as shown in Figure 6.7. John Ingram was Joseph's eldest child still living at home and he was the executor of Joseph and Prince Williams' estates.

There were additional Negroes listed in Joseph Ingram's 1834 Will, namely: Pegg, who was to remain a slave, but be rewarded by whomever she wished to work for; Charles who could act for himself; and Jacob Jeffrey who was to be freed. Again, nobody named Otho was mentioned (perhaps because he wasn't born until 1834).

After Prince's death in 1843, Margaret married William Hanson; they were living at the Funkstown property by the 1850 Census. Margaret signed her name as "Pegg Hanson" on some documents helping to prove that Prince's wife, Margaret A., was nicknamed Pegg--the black woman named Pegg mentioned in Joseph Ingram's Will fifteen years earlier.

Prince's second probate entry was dated 1868, when his widow, Margaret "Pegg" Williams Hanson, died. Those documents named five still-living children to inherit the remainder of Prince's estate, namely: Samuel, Henry, Hezekiah, Margaret Elizabeth, and **Otho**; each received $145. This was the first time my Otho was associated with Prince *and* Margaret Williams in a legal document, proving that Otho and Hezekiah were brothers. Prince Williams was deemed by his executor, attorney John Ingram, to be the legal father of Samuel, Henry, Hezekiah, Margaret Elizabeth, and Otho, but was he the biological father of all of Margaret's children?

The story of Prince Williams and his parents and slaveowner was fascinating as it unfolded over another year of diligent research. In 1783, my third great-grandfather, then called Negro Prince, was born in Kent County, Maryland, on the eastern shore of Chesapeake Bay. In 1799, during the teenage prime of a 16-year-old, then-slave Prince assaulted another slave named Isaac. The assault case had to be tried in another county, presumably because Prince's owner, Benjamin Hatcheson, the Sheriff of Kent County, could not be involved in the trial of his own slave. Prince was sold to new owners, John McPherson and John Brien, at some point after 1799 to serve an indenture at the Antietam Iron Works, located in Washington County.

Negro Prince received his Certificate of Freedom by January 1812 at the age of 28, while working at the Antietam Iron Works for an unspecified number of years. He was described as being 5'6", of a *black* complexion, and missing the first joint of his left thumb.

My strongest theory of Prince's parentage is that his father was also named Prince. Benjamin's grandfather, Vincent Hatcheson's 1755 Will from Kent County, indicated he owned a slave name Prince. I believe my Vincent Hatcheson's Prince was my fourth great-grandfather?

Additionally, white men surnamed Comegys, Hanson, Hopewell, and Frisby bequeathed slaves named Prince to their families between 1735 and 1803. Some also had a male slave named Caesar and female slave named Diner/Pina. I hypothesized that Caesar and Diner/Pina *could* be my tentative fifth great-grandparents who had a son named Prince and a grandson named Prince (Figure 8.9). I intend to revisit those plausible suppositions in a future Second Edition of this book.

There were some exciting mentions of ironworkers named Prince at Principio Forge in Cecil County and at Valley Forge in the early-to-mid 1700s. I still wonder whether those ironworkers were related to my family.

Otho and his older brothers, Hezekiah and Henry Williams, were never freed from bondage and therefore, never fought in the Civil War. Some military records suggested older brothers, Samuel and Prince, may have been registered for the Civil War in 1863.

Various stories were presented from the point of view and voices of my industrious and sometimes saucy Williams ancestors. For example, I explained the contents of the 1870 and 1880 Census to Otho. Alice described her and Otho's 1867 wedding. Otho reminisced about buying his daddy's property, then buying his own land. We glimpsed Margaret and her children conducting their daily chores. We saw the Civil War through the eyes of slave Otho, and Alice described the family's migration from Maryland to Pennsylvania and to Ohio.

The dearth of evidential information was particularly onerous regarding my female ancestors. Nothing concrete could be found about the parentage, owner, siblings, or early life of Otho's wife, Alice Virginia Logan, except her maiden name. Nor could the ethnic derivation of her family be proven in this edition.

It was also difficult to determine Margaret's parents and siblings, and when, how and where she met Prince. Was Margaret's family already owned by Joseph Ingrams' parents? Was one of her parents white?

In 1869, Otho and Alice obtained a mortgage to buy five acres of land along the public road to Roxbury Mills, within eight miles of where he grew up. Otho's growing family consisted of Alice and sons Edgar, Samuel, and Otho "Sherman" by 1874. They had six more children by 1883: William, Charles, Mary Irene, Alice Virginia, and two additional—likely stillborn—children.

Otho and Alice bought more property in 1879-1880. They likely hired white and black workers to help with the annual grain harvests until about 1888, when they apparently could not pay the mortgage. The property reverted to Sam Funk, the mortgager, then was sold to Edward Baker whose family had lived in the area for decades. Otho disappeared from the records after 1889, presumably dying at the age of 54.

After they lost the land, Alice, Edgar, Samuel, Otho Sherman, Mary Irene, and Alice Virginia, moved to Greencastle, Pennsylvania. Before 1900, 15-year-old Sherman reportedly had a tiff with his older brother and stubbornly left Greencastle to fend for himself in Pittsburgh, Pennsylvania, then traveling west to East Liverpool, Ohio. There, he worked as a coachman for the Lee family, who owned and operated a clay pottery. Because I use clay and welded steel in my Kanika African Sculptures, I was more than thrilled to learn my ancestors were associated with clay and iron.

Otho Sherman and Myrtle Lavata Booker met in East Liverpool and married in 1905, in Philadelphia, Pennsylvania's suburb of Germantown. My Grandmother Pearl Lavata Williams and her sister, Reba, were born there, then the family moved to Mt. Vernon, Ohio. Otho Sherman found work at the Cooper-Bessemer machine manufacturing plant, utilizing his mechanical abilities to keep the compressors and other equipment running smoothly. Sons, Charles and Robert, and another daughter, Jayne, were born in Mt. Vernon after 1919.

Pearl married Arthur Carter in 1929 in Dayton, Ohio. She bore seven living children with her erstwhile husband, but due to his many absences, the family had to live with Otho Sherman and Myrtle. My mother, Mary Ellen Carter, was the middle of the seven children. Mary married Thomas Richard Marshall in 1955 and they had three children over the next six years: me, Carrie and Greg. The descendants of Otho and Alice narrated their family stories in my predecessor book, *The Ancestors Are Smiling!*

The most vexing unsolved question is whether my second great-grandfather, Otho, or some of his brothers and sisters were fathered by the Ingrams, or other white men, instead of by Prince Williams. Questions arise when some of his children are described as "mulatto" with lighter skin coloring, instead of "black" like Prince and Margaret are pictured.

Utilizing DNA technology, on average, eleven of my family members who were DNA tested, indicate that 57% of our DNA comes from African countries, 42% from Europe, and 1% from other places. Who were our African and European progenitors who contributed to our DNA results?

I employed a tremendous amount of data analysis, spreadsheet comparisons, triangulations, and communications with hundreds of people who matched our DNA. I had less than stellar luck finding Africans and Europeans who we could prove by DNA *and* a family tree paper trail were connected to my Williams family. However, I had great luck using DNA to verify relatives matching my Marshall, Dooley, and Myers family lines.

Another glimmer of excitement was finding astounding information about the origins of my mitochondrial DNA. My B4a1a1b haplogroup suggested that hundreds of years ago a female ancestor from Madagascar, Africa, was one of only seven thousand slaves brought to Virginia or New York before. In a future edition, if the winds blow true, I may be able to pinpoint which of the seventeen known slave ships brought my female ancestor to America from Madagascar!

THE BOTTOM LINE: I am thrilled beyond belief with the information uncovered and presented in this book, meeting all five of the original research goals! I thoroughly enjoyed every aspect of this amazing journey and this writing experience, although at times becoming depressed or angry about the unequal treatment of black folk.

I found Otho, his parents, and his slave owner, used DNA technology to find relatives and you can too. By providing questions, theories, detailed examples and numerous figures in this book, it is my mission to help others find their ancestors too (see "Solving Your Mystery"). Whether you come from slave stock, immigrants, or adoption agencies, many of the ideas presented in this book may be readily adapted to find historical documentation on your ancestors.

I have experienced emotional highs and lows, brilliant discoveries, dashed hopes, sore eyes, long nights, and more excitement and joy than I have had in my entire life. It was all worth it! Otho, his parents, and his descendants now live on through the pages of this book.

Our Williams ancestors are indeed smiling!

ACKNOWLEDGEMENTS

The ancestors want their stories told. They have persistently encouraged me to adopt different approaches to my previous forty years of largely ineffective research efforts. I finally began following the recommendations of expert genealogists and have reaped the benefit of remarkable discoveries about my enslaved ancestors, which now reside in two published books.

Chip Canty, a cousin, met through a common family tree match in late 2012, challenged me to interview my then-105-year-old, Great Aunt Reba Williams. Six weeks after Chip's encouragement, I flew into Columbus, Ohio, where I made the biggest breakthroughs of my family history career to date.

My beloved mother, Mary Ellen Carter Marshall, passed away in 2007, but her "Reflections from a Mother's Heart" first-hand accounts of growing up in the home of the son of Otho Williams, are an important resource. Additionally, some of Mom's watercolor paintings are proudly displayed in this book.

This achievement would not have been possible without the family research accomplishments from our family historian, M. Lavata Williams. Great Uncle Charles Williams, Uncle Dale Carter, sister Carrie Malenab, and brother Greg Marshall, also provided helpful memories. Many thanks to twelve of my family members who agreed to take various types of DNA tests, as described in Part IV.

Many thanks go to Anita Henderson, the creator of the Genealogist's Writing Room online writing group, who revealed two critically important secrets which gave me the impetus to begin writing this book in 2016.

Genealogist Carol Wait, a possible cousin met through DNA testing, provided me with insightful transcriptions of the slave owner's probate and cemetery records.

The most fascinating breadcrumb trail I followed was of pure-African ironworkers who may have been brought to Colonial Maryland for their ironworking skills. I was fortunate to establish a relationship with Jean Libby, Public Historian, one of the lauded primary research experts on this topic, which became a fascinating ingredient in this ancestral recipe.

I would not have been able to accomplish the incredible discoveries in this book without the assistance of several kind people in Maryland who politely listened to my incessant questions and theories, or volunteered to take me on tours of places where my ancestors lived and worked. Innumerable thanks go to the following individuals:

- Jane Neff, Office Administrator, C&O Canal Trust, constantly fueled me with helpful information about specific locations where my family lived, as well as other people and places relevant to my research. I am forever indebted to Jane for knocking on doors to secure permission for me to visit certain sites and for driving me wherever I wanted to go during my April 2017 "Journey Home" visit to Maryland.

- Dr. Emilie Amt, Department of History, Hood College, provided an erudite sounding-board for my many parentage and slave owner theories, encouraging me to consider alternatives and prove my assertions. She drove me to the Western Maryland Room and other significant places, and helped focus my research. Her Foreword adds credibility to this effort.

- Director John Frye and Assistant Director Elizabeth Howe, at the John Clinton Frye, Western Maryland Room, Washington County Free Library, Hagerstown, Maryland. They patiently entertained my many questions about Otho and his potential family ties. Joseph Berger, Project Manager Historic Newspaper Index, graciously responded promptly to my numerous online requests for obituary and marriage documents.

- Bernice Alexander Bennett, professional genealogist, invited me to visit her Silver Springs, Maryland, home where we discussed DNA analysis at length. She asked me to be her first guest of 2018 on her weekly "Research at the National Archives and Beyond!" Blog Talk Radio program, talking about my first book: *The Ancestors Are Smiling!*

- Al Feldman, librarian, who developed the Allegany County African American History website and contacted Dr. Amt.

- Erin C. (Wolfe) Anderson, Communications Manager, City of Hagerstown Technology & Support Services, taught me how to research the indispensable online Maryland Land Records.

- Edie Wallace gave me a private tour of Tolson's Chapel, which also served as a "Colored School" in Sharpsburg, MD.

- Carol Miller-Schultz and Krista Markham helped review original documents at the Washington County Historical Society.

❖ Wayne McCrossin, the current owner and custodian of the Antietam Iron Works, provided me with a memorable private tour of the place where my ancestor worked over 200 years ago.

❖ Sprigg Lynn, whose family has long lived in Washington County, gave me a private tour of abolitionist John Brown's 1859 slave staging home at Kennedy Farm.

❖ Marguerite Doleman (deceased), whose tireless efforts to pioneer the compilation of Black history resources and data in Washington County, helped me find answers to some of my questions.

Particular thanks go to author Denise Griggs, Glass Tree Books, who volunteered to read the entire manuscript in the seventh month on this project. Her comments guided my decision to break the research into two separate books: 1) *The Ancestors Are Smiling!* and 2) *Finding Otho: The Search for Our Enslaved Williams Ancestors.*

Several genealogy and writing critique groups provided research tips and/or content editing of the manuscript, including The African American Genealogical Society of Northern California, Elk Grove Senior Center writing group, and the Greater Sacramento African American Genealogy Society.

My copyeditor, Jennifer Grainger, kindly came to the rescue to tackle my manuscript and get it in to shape for publishing. Several invaluable proofreaders double-checked the grammar and punctuation of the Finding Otho manuscript, including: family historian Barbara Slater Nelson, author of *Old Settlers of Mecosta, Isabella and Montcalm Counties in Michigan*; and avid readers Virginia Harbridge Marshall and Robin A. Harris, M.Ed. Westley Turner provided helpful tips about book layout and design.

Immeasurable thanks go to my significant other, Michael K. Fitzwater, for helping proofread early versions of my drafts, wading through online self-publishing website guidelines with me, providing the photograph on the back jacket of this book, and listening to my daily high and low musings about "The Book".

And last, but certainly not least, I pay homage to my ancestors who were gently pushing me every step of the way on this adventure to find answers about our Williams' heritage and to self-publish two books on the topic. Their life stories now live on in the world via Amazon.com; in research libraries in Maryland, Ohio, and California; and in the personal libraries of people who loved their life stories.

SOLVING *YOUR* MYSTERY

I have been researching the lives of my African American family for four decades, creating the requisite genealogy binders full of vital records, census and other documents for six of my family lines, including the Williams, Bookers, Marshalls, Dooley, Carters, and Myers.

An alarming thought entered my head in May 2016 when I began my sixtieth year of life. There are only three people older than me in my mother's family and three older in my father's. Soon I may be the matriarch of the family. If I don't write a book about my ancestors, who will? Now is the time to commemorate the lives of those enslaved and free people who have gone before me, and of those of us still living who are their proud descendants. I have a burning desire to ensure that my family is remembered in a tangible, written way.

After a gentle push from my spirited ancestors, I began writing *The Ancestors Are Smiling!* on October 1, 2016 and published it in July 2017. The next fifteen months were spent solving the mystery of my enslaved relatives in *Finding Otho: The Search for Our Williams Ancestors.*

There are a number of reasons why I was finally able to accomplish this momentous goal successfully. I had heard most of the following how-to tips numerous times over the years, but this time I ACTUALLY DID WHAT WAS SUGGESTED.

Please note that the following ideas are only one way to write a book about your family, but they are steps that worked well for me. Will any or all of them work for you? Give them a try. See if they will help you to get started (and finished) with your book.

* Planning to Write Your Book *

1. Adopt an **ATTITUDE THAT YOU MUST PUBLISH THE BOOK,** before all else. Your mantra must be: "I live and breathe to publish a book about my family." Otherwise, any mundane activity will divert you from your goal to leave a written legacy for your family.
2. **FOCUS ON ONE** specific family line, or one person, or one specific aspect of the family, for example, a specific enslaved ancestor from one of your family lines.
3. Determine the **SCOPE** (extent) of the book. I wanted to find my third great-grandparents, write about their lives, then publish this book. What, specifically, do you want your book to be about?
4. Develop a **LIST OF QUESTIONS** you want to answer (e.g., who were my third great-grandparents, what jobs did they do, where did they live, who were their slave masters?).
5. Understand that you may not be able to answer all your questions but accept that it is OK. Write about the **steps you DID take and** present what you *did* and *did not* find. Indicate that you may resume your inquiry in the Second Edition when more information becomes available.
6. Decide on the **AUDIENCE** for your book (e.g., children, family, genealogists, the public).

* Developing the Book Framework: Type Book as You Research * *(This will make you feel so successful!)*

7. Decide on a computer **WORD PROCESSING PROGRAM** for your book, such as Microsoft Word or Apple Pages.
8. Open a **NEW DOCUMENT and NAME IT** (e.g., My Family Book) and **SAVE** it to a folder on your computer.
9. Be sure to **SAVE** your word processing manuscript every hour or so and **BACK UP** your book file every day (e.g., keep a copy on the Internet cloud or on a portable backup drive).
10. Develop a **BOOK OUTLINE** in your new word document, like the following:
11. **Title of your book** on the first page.
12. **Copyright** on the second page (copyright.gov).
13. **Dedication** on the third page.

14. **Filler** on the 4th page: add a picture, or a quote, or a poem, or a **Foreword** from a professional.

15. **Table of Contents (TOC): Microsoft** Word and Apple Pages automatically generate the TOC with the "Styles" Function.

16. **Acknowledgments** page thanking people who helped you write your book.

17. **Introduction** that explains what the book is about; write it early in the process, then refine it.

18. **Timeline** of historical events, if desired.

19. **Chapters** about certain characters or topics (NOTE: Start chapters in the printed book on an odd-numbered, right-side page for chapter headings in the header).

20. **Epilogue**/Conclusion/Coda/Wrap up to summarize your efforts.

21. **Appendices**, lists of tables and maps (if appropriate).

22. **Bibliography** listing which sources you used to develop your ideas in the book.

23. **Endnotes** (optional) with complete the citations, using this basic format: Author, *Title*, (Publisher State, Publisher, Year), page number.

24. Refine the **book layout** after some of the manuscript has been written (e.g., add photographs or quotes to the first page of each chapter, if desired).

* Writing Your Book *

25. **START WRITING TODAY** with what you already know (e.g., your life story, parents, grandparents). Don't worry about perfect sentences; just type your thoughts and revise them later.

26. **COPY AND PASTE** into the correct chapter any documentation that has already been written. For example, a memory about your fifth birthday party would go into your chapter; your grandparents' wedding picture would go into their chapter, etc.

27. **TYPE THE BOOK** as you are conducting your research and getting stories. Include your emotions at that time when they are fresh.

28. Include **FOOTNOTES/CITATIONS** citing your information sources as you write.

29. **RECHECK YOUR FOCUS** and scope often, to remain on track with what your book is about.

30. Consider writing the passages as though you are telling the story directly to your audience or writing the stories from the **POINT OF VIEW** of your family members.

31. **READ OUT LOUD** what you have written to uncover awkward sentence structure or to notice missing words and to hear whether the text is too conversational or too technical, keeping in mind your audience.

* Gathering Information *

32. **INTERVIEW YOUR ELDERS** and other family members and type their stories in the book.

33. Do **DNA TESTING NOW** for yourself, your elders, and other family members. The major DNA companies are: ancestry.com, 23andMe.com, FamilyTreeDNA.com, My Heritage, and Living DNA. For more information, check https://isogg.org/wiki/List_of_DNA_testing_companies.

34. Gather **FAMILY PHOTOGRAPHS**, using your camera or smartphone to take high-resolution photos. Copy the photos to a folder on your computer. Save them as 300 dots-per-inch (dpi) resolution for printing. Label the photos with the date, place, and names of the subjects.

35. Read **PROBATE, CENSUS, and LAND RECORDS** documents pertinent to your family.

36. Visit family **HOME SITES** and **CEMETERIES** (search Findagrave.com**)**, take photographs and type your findings, and **YOUR FEELINGS,** about visiting these places in your book.

37. **PRINT DOCUMENTS** within each family line and organize them into separately named **GENEALOGY BINDERS**.

38. Start an **ONLINE FAMILY TREE** (e.g., ancestry.com, familysearch.org) with names, dates, locations, etc., and **KEEP IT PUBLIC** so others may connect with you and share information about your family.

39. Also keep **FAMILY TREE DATA ON YOUR COMPUTER** (e.g., Family Tree Maker).

40. Use **ONLINE GENEALOGY SITES** (e.g., ancestry.com, familysearch.org, USGenWeb.com, WikiTree.com, newspapers.com, fold3.com, and Genetic Genealogy Tips and Techniques.

41. Become a member of **GENEALOGY FACEBOOK PAGES** and other web pages (e.g., Our Black Ancestry, Our Black Legacy, Research at the National Archives and Beyond, Black ProGen Live).

42. Watch free **GENEALOGY HOW-TO VIDEOS** from ancestry.com or youtube.com.

43. Do a simple **online Google search on your ancestors' names and states** to see if any books or other resources contain their name. Recheck these resources often.

44. Take **GENEALOGY COURSES** and join genealogy guilds to learn the best genealogy practices. Conduct an exhaustive search. Document accurate citations. Analyze information. Resolve conflicting evidence. Develop a reasoned written conclusion.

45. **DEVELOP THEORIES** and prove or disprove them, but do not be too rigid. Review and revise theories and update the book accordingly. Avoid obsessing on preconceived ideas from family lore.

46. Discuss your book ideas and theories with other authors, editors, and family, and **ASK THEM TO GIVE FEEDBACK** on your work in progress.

* Self-Publishing Your Book *

47. Have the book professionally **COPY EDITED** and PROOFREAD to ensure the manuscript is perfect before publishing.

48. Export your book manuscript to a **.pdf FILE** on your computer.

49. If you want to sell books, obtain an International Standard Book Number (**ISBN**) through bowker.com ($295 for 10 or $125 for one); include one ISBN on the back cover of your book file.

50. **COPYRIGHT** your book (e.g., copyright.gov).

51. Choose a **SELF-PUBLISHING WEBSITE** (e.g., lulu.com or Kindle Direct Publishing) and read their online instructions on uploading a .pdf copy of your book. Create an online account for your book. Choose a book size and number of pages. Upload an initial .pdf of your manuscript.

52. Use the self-publishing website to create a **BOOK COVER** (front, back, and spine). Alternatively, make your own cover on your computer, or pay someone to make one. Be sure to use the precise measurements supplied by the self-publishing service. Export your book cover to a .pdf file.

53. After your book manuscript is perfected, export it to a .pdf file, then **UPLOAD THE MANUSCRIPT AND COVER .pdf** to the self-publishing website. Make sure you review any corrections the book website suggests (like ensuring the photos are 300 dpi), make the changes, then upload the .pdf files again.

54. Prepare a summary of the book, and other information, for the online **DESCRIPTION** of your book (you may use the text on the back jacket of your book). Look at several amazon.com memoir book examples to see what kinds of things are written in the book description. Make it pop!

55. Decide on a retail PRICE for your book. The book service will tell you how much revenue you will earn depending on your retail price, the book size, and number of pages.

56. Once the manuscript is submitted for printing, order an **ADVANCED READER COPY** to be mailed to you. Carefully **REVIEW** the printed book, make corrections, create a new .pdf, re-upload the file, recheck the uploaded file, order another Advanced Reader Copy. When you are absolutely certain there are no errors in your manuscript submit it for **FINAL PRINTING**. It takes 24-hours for book approval and about a week to print the book(s). Shipping can take another week or more.

57. If using Amazon.com's Kindle Direct Publishing, choose **MARKETING CHANNELS** for your book (e.g., Amazon in America and/or Europe, resellers, research channels).

58. **MARKET** your published book (e.g., amazon.com, Facebook page, webpage, newsletter, blog, local bookstores, donate to research libraries, and/or offer to be a volunteer speaker at local networking groups and service clubs).

* An Alternative, Simplified Book Style *

59. Instead of a narrative, self-published book as described in the previous steps, you could create hard-cover, photo album style books. Simply upload your high-resolution (300 dpi) .jpg family photos, charts, graphs, or maps to shutterfly.com or photo.walgreens.com or costco.com or other online photo book services. Get on their mailing lists to get periodic discounts. This is an easy way to commemorate your ancestors' lives, and/or to write story books of any kind.

* Always Remember *

Be so passionate about commemorating your ancestor's stories that you have an overwhelming need to publish your book. Be focused on writing about a specific person or family line. Create a book template and begin typing what you already know into it and type all your new findings into it. Include source citations as you enter information. These most important actions will result in the quick development of a manuscript that looks like a ready-for-printing real book. I hope these lessons I learned help you write and self-publish your own family stories. Remember, when the ancestors call, we must listen. **The Ancestors Are Smiling!**

LIST OF FIGURES

12.1 Tolson's "Colored Church" reenacted to a school, Sharpsburg, MD. Photographs by Kathy Marshall, 2017.
13.1 Kathy Marshall at Otho and Alice's five-acre property, Barnes Road, from the old Roxbury Mill to Boonsboro, MD.
13.2 Funkstown lots 143 & half-lot 144 purchased by Prince Williams in 1842, repurchased in 1868.
by Otho and Hezekiah Williams. Photograph by Kathy Marshall, 2017.
13.3 Maryland Land Records for Prince Williams and his children.
14.1 Hand-drawn rendering of the Antietam Iron Works complex as it looked in 1820, Sharpsburg, MD. Courtesy of Wayne McCrossin, owner of the Antietam Iron Works, 2017.
14.2 Antietam Iron Works furnace, Sharpsburg, MD. Photograph: Kathy Marshall, 2017.
14.3 Antietam Bridge and part of the village in the background, Sharpsburg, MD. Photograph: Kathy Marshall, 2017.
14.4 Post office and metal products manufactured at Antietam Iron Works. Photograph: Kathy Marshall, 2017.
14.5 Antietam Iron Works main building which housed the general store, post office, industrial kitchen, and sleeping quarters for the manager, Sharpsburg, MD. Photograph: Kathy Marshall, 2017.
14.6 Kanika Marshall's welded metal kinetic sculptures, Elk Grove, California, 2017.
14.7 Generations of Prince Williams' family members with metalworking and/or mechanical skills.
15.1 Jessie Williams, granddaughter of Otho and Alice Williams, Philadelphia, Pennsylvania, 1930.
15.2 Hearse for Alice Williams, Philadelphia, PA, 1908. Photo courtesy of Jim Moshinske, Ph.D., CPT, Funeral Director at Oak Crest Funeral Home, Texas.
16.1 Kathy Marshall standing at the former Ebenezer A.M.E. Church whose cemetery is where Prince, Malinda, and Margaret Williams were buried.
16.2 The D'Addios and Wyatt Burp, courtesy of the D'Addios, 2017.
16.3 Visited Smithsonian Museums, Washington, D.C. Photograph: Kathy Marshall, 2017.
16.4 Looking onto the Ingram farm from an overlook in the Meadows Green development, Boonsboro, MD. Photograph: Kathy Marshall, 2017.
16.5 Kennedy farm where John Brown planned an abolitionist insurrection in 1859. Photograph: Kathy Marshall, 2017.
16.6 Kathy Marshall in front of the Antietam Iron Works stacks.
16.7 Old slave block, Sharpsburg, MD.
16.8 Kathy Marshall kisses the ground Otho and Alice Williams purchased in 1869 in Boonsboro, MD. Photograph courtesy: Jane Neff, 2017.
16.9 Kathy Marshall at the Appalachian Trail.
16.10 View from upstairs seats where "colored people" sat at St. Marks Church, Fairplay, Maryland, 2017.
16.11 County Jail, once located in the Jonathon Street neighborhood, Hagerstown, MD.
16.12 John Clinton Frye Western Maryland Room, Washington County Free Library, where Kathy Marshall's *The Ancestors Are Smiling!* book now resides. Photograph: Kathy Marshall, 2017.
16.13 Research materials for this project spread out on the table, Washington County Historical Society. Photograph: Kathy Marshall, 2017.
16.14 The general store in the Antietam Iron Works' Main Building. Owner Wayne McCrossin talks with C&O Canal Administrator, Jane Neff. Photograph: Kathy Marshall, 2017.

APPENDICES

A: Project Framework

B: Partial List of Research Questions

C: African American Heritage Guide

D: Maryland Population Statistics

E: Two-Minute Ancestry DNA TV Commercial Proposal

F: Who Was the Cream in My Coffee?

G: Accessing Maryland Land Records

H: Kent House of Representatives Delegates

I: Partial Ironworker Vocabulary

J: Williams Family DNA Ethnicity Comparisons

K: Williams Family DNA Ethnicity Comparisons

L: Distribution of Shared DNA for Given Relationships

Appendix A - Project Framework

GOAL

- To write a book that documents my Williams' ancestral history.

OBJECTIVE

- To trace the lineage of my black Williams family to their European and African roots, using oral histories, DNA, and legal and other documentation.

SCOPE

- To stay focused on researching my Williams line, back to England and Africa.

METHODOLOGY

- Create a book outline.
- Attend genealogy conferences to learn genealogy-related tools.
- Watch ancestry.com videos about genealogy research techniques.
- Seek help on how to write the book, e.g., from Genealogist's Writing Room authors.
- Develop a list of questions to answer.
- Determine which application to use, structure, bibliography, citations, etc.
- Reread genealogy books written by other blacks (e.g., Henderson and Collier).
- Type up existing notes about Williams ancestors.
- Learn how to better use Family Tree Maker (FTM).
- Ensure documents already found are cited properly in FTM.
- Learn how to interpret DNA results better by reading DNA tutorials on GEDMatch.com
- Determine what information is needed to prove black—>white Williams linkage.
- Contact genealogy organizations in MD, PA, and OH to answer questions.
- Visit Williams family sites in MD, PA, and OH (cemeteries, archives, etc.).
- Keep writing about what I already know: update genealogy data binders.

DATA FINDINGS

- Determine which charts, graphs, and photos, should be displayed in the book. Keep complete citations and bibliography notes.

WRITE THE BOOK

- Write a comprehensive draft, including detail on my mom's, Grandma Carter, Great Grandpa Williams' lives. Keep a copy for future books on different family lines.
- Seek the editing assistance of genealogists, Aunt Lavata, and other writer friends.

PUBLISH THE BOOK

- Seek the advice of genealogists and others on how the book should be published.
- Obtain an ISBN and post the book online (e.g., Lulu, amazon.com).
- Print copies for myself, my children, Aunt Lavata, Mormon Library and Allen County, MD. Public Library and Historical Society, Genealogy Center, Library of Congress.

Appendix B - Partial List of Research Questions

There were a number of questions I wanted to research when starting to write this book on October 1, 2016. They are in no particular order, just as I initially thought them up. As I answered each initial query, two more popped into my head. Here is a small sample of the initial questions I set out to answer:

- Where was Otho born?
- When was Otho born?
- Where did Otho live as a child?
- Where did Otho live as an adult?
- Was Otho a slave and, if not who was his master(s)?
- Was Otho owned by a white man named Otho H. Williams?
- Was Otho owned by a non-surnamed Williams white person?
- Was Otho owned by a black person?
- Did Otho join the military during the Civil War?
- Was Otho freed before slavery was over?
- What did Otho and his family do at the 1862 Battle of Antietam?
- Who were Otho's parents?
- Did Otho have any siblings?
- What was Otho's ethnic background?
- Did Otho become a successful person after slavery?
- What did Otho do for a living as an adult?
- When did Otho die?
- What caused Otho's death?
- Who were Alice's parents?
- Who were Alice's siblings?
- Where was Alice born?
- How did Otho and Alice meet?
- Was Alice a slave and, if so, who were her owners?
- Why did Alice and Otho's family move to Pennsylvania?
- When and where did Alice die?
- Did we receive our metalworking abilities from Otho?
- What tools are available to interpret our DNA results?
- What are my family's ethnic percentages?
- Who are our African ancestors?
- Who are our European ancestors?
- Do we have native American ancestry?

Appendix C - Partial African American Heritage Guide

TOLSON'S CHAPEL, SHARPSBURG

Founded in 1866, Tolson's Chapel was a Methodist church built on land donated by the Craig family. John Tolson was the church's first minister. A Freedman's Bureau school operated in the church from 1868 to 1870. The cemetery has burials dating back to the 19th century. **111 E. High St., Sharpsburg, MD. Open by appointment only. 240-452-7389 • www.tolsonschapel.org**

WASHINGTON COUNTY HISTORICAL SOCIETY

In recent years the WCHS has procured and catalogued nearly 250 documents related to slavery in Washington County, dating from April, 1783. Documents include bills of sale, manumission documents and census records. This growing collection is available to researchers at the Society's library. Open Tues.-Fri. 9am-4pm. **135 W. Washington St., Hagerstown, MD. 301-797-8782 • www.washcomdhistoricalsociety.org**

JACOB F. WHEATON

A unique figure in Hagerstown history. An African-American born free near Middletown, MD in 1835, Jacob Wheaton moved to Hagerstown in the 1850s where he lived the rest of his life. During the Civil War Wheaton served as a nurse, helping to combat a smallpox epidemic in early 1863. Wheaton is most widely remembered as the first African-American to vote in the state of Maryland in the spring of 1868. His grave, recently rededicated, is located in historic Rose Hill Cemetery. **600 South Potomac St., Hagerstown, MD. 301-739-3630 • www.rosehillcemeteryofmd.org**

WHEATON PARK, HAGERSTOWN

This park, named in honor of Jacob Wheaton, was opened in 1935 by the City of Hagerstown to serve the African American Community. The gazebo was the original band shell from the Hagerstown City Park. **449 Sumans Avenue, Hagerstown, MD.**

WILLIAM O. WILSON

Served in the 9th Cavalry US Army. He received the Medal of Honor for his service at the Battle of Wounded Knee on December 29, 1890. View the historical marker dedicated to his honor on historic Jonathan Street. He lived at **108 West North Street, Hagerstown, MD.**

Pictured above are black workers, in 1885, at the C&O Canal's Cushwa Wharf in Williamsport.

Frisby Tilghman placed this notice in area newspapers in 1827 after Pennington's escape.

Elizabeth Hager Center
6 North Potomac Street • Hagerstown, MD 21740
301-791-3246 • 888-257-2600

Special thanks to the Washington County Free Library, Washington County Historical Society, African-American Historical Association, Ron Lytle, and the Washington County Convention and Visitors Bureau for their help in collecting information and pictures. Designed by Ovation.

Visit Hagerstown & Washington County
AFRICAN AMERICAN HERITAGE GUIDE
A GUIDE TO HISTORICAL SITES & INFLUENTIAL PEOPLE
www.VisitHagerstown.com

Appendix C - African American Heritage Guide, continued

AFRICAN-AMERICAN HERITAGE GUIDE OF WASHINGTON COUNTY, MARYLAND

From the earliest days of the 18th century, the lives, the sacrifices and the contributions of African-Americans have left an indelible impression on Washington County, Maryland. In 1820, 14% of the population was enslaved; Maryland's average however was 26%. By 1860, there were more free African-Americans than slaves in Washington County. Slavery was abolished in Maryland in the fall of 1864.

There are many historic African-American sites in Washington County. Those described here represent some highlights that we hope will engage and encourage you to further exploration of this rich history.

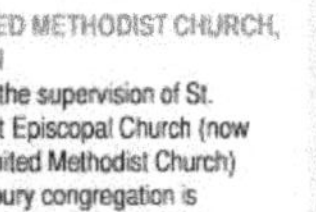

ANTIETAM FURNACE, SHARPSBURG

Manufacturer of bar iron products. The furnace was built in 1768 and produced goods for the Revolutionary War. The furnace was a large slave owner during its tenure and also employed many free blacks. The furnace closed in 1858. It reopened after the Civil War but finally closed in 1886. Three miles south of Sharpsburg on Harpers Ferry Road. **301-739-4200**

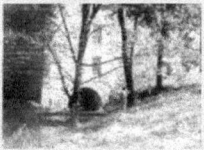

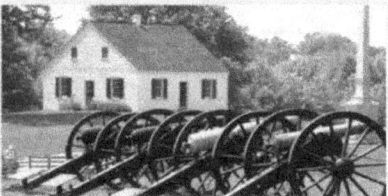

ANTIETAM NATIONAL BATTLEFIELD, SHARPSBURG

The site of America's bloodiest single day, with more than 23,000 casualties. The turning point needed for President Abraham Lincoln to rethink the opportunities for peace and issue the Emancipation Proclamation, freeing the slaves from the entire United States. No African American Union troops fought in the battle, but the effects on the lives of African Americans are significant. **Approximately 12 miles south of Hagerstown on Rt. 65. The Visitor Center Address is 5831 Dunker Church Rd., Sharpsburg, MD 21782. 301-432-5124 · www.nps.gov.anti**

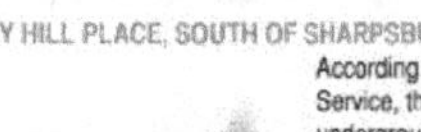

ASBURY UNITED METHODIST CHURCH, HAGERSTOWN

Founded under the supervision of St. Paul's Methodist Episcopal Church (now John Wesley United Methodist Church) in 1818, the Asbury congregation is the oldest African-American church in Hagerstown. The existing building was constructed in 1879 as a replacement for the fire damaged 1864 building. The second oldest African-American congregation in Hagerstown is Ebenezer African Methodist Episcopal Church, which was founded in 1840. The Ebenezer AME congregation was housed in a number of church buildings on W. Bethel Street, with their most recent church demolished in the late 1990s due to concerns over structural conditions. Two other community churches from the 1800s still stand, including Second Christian and Zion Baptist. **155 N. Jonathan St., Hagerstown, MD. 301-791-0498**

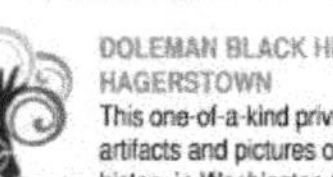

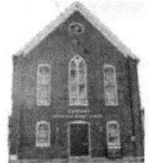

CHANEY HOUSE, FUNKSTOWN

Built in 1816, it was the home of Dr. Elias Chaney. In 1859, six men and eight women were included as property in Chaney's will. The house is currently The Hudson House Antiques Shop. **1 South High Street, Funkstown, MD. 301-733-1632 · www.hudsonhousegalleries.com**

DOLEMAN BLACK HERITAGE MUSEUM, HAGERSTOWN

This one-of-a-kind private collection contains books, artifacts and pictures of the rich African-American history in Washington County. The museum is open by appointment only. **540 N. Locust St., Hagerstown, MD. 301-739-8185 · www.dolemanblackheritagemuseum.org**

FERRY HILL PLACE, SOUTH OF SHARPSBURG

According to the National Park Service, this was sometimes an underground railroad stop built about 1812 by John Blackford. This property included a ferry that crosses the Potomac into what was then Virginia. The ferry was operated by two enslaved men, who Blackford named "foremen of the ferry". These two men, Jupe and Ned, ran the ferry with little oversight. They kept the records, purchased supplies and even hired free blacks for seasonal labor. The ferry remained in operation until 1851. **South of Sharpsburg on Rt. 34. 301-582-0813. Hours: Memorial Day to Labor Day, Friday-Sunday 10:00-3:00. C&O Canal, 301-739-4200 · www.nps.gov/choh/planyourvisit/ferry-hill-place.htm**

FORT FREDERICK, BIG POOL

The land that is now Fort Frederick State Park was once owned by a free African-American named Nathan Williams. Williams was considered the second wealthiest African-American in Washington County. He bought the property and used it as farmland. During the Civil War, Williams used the farmland to produce food which he supplied to both the Union and the Confederate Armies. He helped escaping slaves get through Maryland. Fort Frederick was built in 1756 during the French and Indian War. The fort was also used during the Revolutionary War and during the Civil War. **One mile off I-70, Exit 12 (Big Pool), 11100 Fort Frederick Road, Big Pool, MD. 301-842-2155 www.dnr.state.md.us/publiclands/western/fortfrederick.asp**

HARMON HOTEL, HAGERSTOWN

The most well known Afican-American entrepreneur in the early 1900s in Hagerstown was Walter Harmon. Prior to his death in his early 40s in 1915, he built the Harmon Hotel, a bowling alley and dance hall for Hagerstown's African-American community, and 37 houses in the Jonathan Street area of Hagerstown. The Harmon family operated the Harmon Hotel for many years into the 20th century. The hotel was important, as it was the only place for visiting African-Americans to stay in Hagerstown during the segregation era. Willie Mays stayed at the hotel during his professional debut. **Marker on Jonathan Street, Hagerstown, MD.**

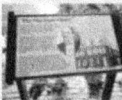

KENNEDY FARM, SOUTH OF SHARPSBURG

The planning ground for John Brown's Raid of 1859. The raid consisted of John Brown and 21 other men, in an attempt to provoke a slave uprising. The raid took over the U.S. Arsenal at Harper's Ferry and seized a sizable amount of ammunition. Some historians believe that the raid marked the beginning of the end of chattel slavery, and helped spark the Civil War. Tours by appointment only. **2406 Chestnut Grove Rd., Sharpsburg, MD. Owner-South Lynn. 301-652-2857 or 301-977-3599 · www.johnbrown.org**

LYON POST #31 OF THE GRAND ARMY OF THE REPUBLIC

Grand Army of the Republic posts, similar to today's American Legion, cropped up all over the nation as a place for Civil War Union veterans to fraternize and be of service to each other. As the posts were segregated, members of Hagerstown's white Reno Post #4 helped establish Lyon Post #31 for the "colored troops" from the area. A monument to the members of Lyon Post #31 was recently dedicated at the historic Rose Hill Cemetery. **600 South Potomac St., Hagerstown, MD. 301-739-3630 · www.rosehillcemeteryofmd.org**

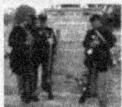

Appendix D - Maryland Population Statistics

Population of Hagerstown, Washington County, and Maryland,

total, slave and free African Americans

(Slavery abolished in Maryland 1 November 1864)

	Total population			Slaves		Free African Americans	
	Maryland	Washington County	Hagerstown	Maryland	Washington County	Maryland	Washington County
1790	319,728	15,822	N/A	103, 036	1,286	8,043	64
1800	341,543	18,650	N/A	105,635	2,200	19,587	342
1810	380,546	18,730	2,342	111,502	2,656	133,927	483
1820	407,350	23,075	2,690	107,398	3,201	39,730	627
1830	447,040	25,268	3,257	102,994	2,909	52,938	1,082
1840	470,019	28,850	3,754	89,737	2,546	62,078	1,580
1850	583,034	30,848	N/A	90,368	2,090	74,723	1,828
1860	687,049	31,417	4,132	87,189	1,435	83,942	1,677
1870	780,894	34,712	N/A	0	0	175,391	2,838

Source: Geospatial and Statistical Data Center University of Virginia Library, http://fisher.lib.virginia.edu/collections/stats/histcensus/php/county.php

Slavery was abolished in the United States with the ratification of the 13th Amendment to the Constitution on December 18, 1865

Appendix E - Two-Minute Ancestry DNA TV Commercial Pitch

Video Submitted by Kathy Marshall in August 2015 for final consideration in April 2016

ARE WE FROM ROYALTY?

Hi there. This is Kathy Marshall, and this is my Ancestry DNA story. I've been in the process of researching my African American family history for many decades and have been using Ancestry DNA for about fifteen years or so. About four years ago, I went ahead and had the Ancestry DNA test, and it showed me that only 52% of my DNA came from Africa. We've always identified ourselves as African American but where does this light skin come from? So, the DNA test showed that about 34% of my DNA came from Great Britain and another 11% from other European countries. I really wanted to find out what that nexus was.

I happened to be visiting my family in Ohio about four years ago and went into the Ohio State Archives to see if I could find some more information about our genealogy. I had my great-grandfather's name - Otho Williams - and I thought that was kind of an unusual name. I found a book from Washington County, Maryland, where my family came from in the 1800s, according to Ancestry DNA. There was an Otho Williams in that book! I typed that name into Ancestry DNA and started getting hints. Hints, hints, hints on Otho Williams. He was a Brigadier General back in the Revolutionary War, and his family came over from England, from the Otho Holland family. And lo and behold I started getting these hints and stayed up all night long until three in the morning because I was so excited. I went all the way back to 1500, then 1400, then 1300 to the Plantagenets. Yes, I am Royalty!

For those of you who don't know, for African Americans, it is very hard to find our family history before slavery. The 1870 Census is a brick wall for most of us. So, for me to finally find out where some of this skin color comes from was exciting. And I was able to do that through the Ancestry DNA and Ancestry DNA. So, thank you very much. That's my Ancestry story.

Appendix F - Who Was the Cream in My Coffee?

White Otho	1820		1830		1840		1850	
	Head Age, Where Lived	Slaves & Whites Age (#)	Head Age, Where Lived	Slaves & Whites Age (#)	Head Age, Where Lived	Slaves & Whites Age (#)	Head Age, Where Lived	Slaves & Whites Age (#)
B.(Gen.?) Otho H. Wms m.ElizaBHall:1781-1816, c. CatherineL:1808-1891, MariaA:1812-1870, LauraS:1814-1861 m.ElizabethE.VanLear: 1790-1863 c. CoraH:1828-1860	44, Hagerstown with __ **Slaves: 5** F black: <14 (1) F black: 26-44 (1) M black: <14 (2) M black: 26-44 (1) F white: <10 (2) F white: 10-15 (4) F white: 26-44 (1) M white: 26-44 (1) Otho		54, Hagerstown with Catherine, Maria, Laura **Slaves: 8** F black: <10 (1) F black: 24-35 (2) F black: 36-54 (1) M black: <10 (4) F white: <20 (4) F white: 20-49 (3) M white: 50-59 (1) Otho		64, in Hag. with Catherine, Maria, Laura **Slaves: 6** F black: 24-35 (1) mom? F black: 36-54 (1) mom? M black: <10 (2) Otho & Hezekiah? M black: 10-23 (1) M black: 24-35 (1) F white: 1014 (2) F white: 40-49 (1) F white: 60-69 (1) Otho		74, in Hagerstown with Elizabeth E. and Cora. **Slaves: 4** F black: 40+42, (2) moms? M black: 18 Hezekiah? (1) M black: 15 (Otho?) (1) F white: () F white: () M white: ()	
Otho Holland Williams m.CatherineMcDowell 1793-1821, m.AgnesAnn McDowell c.MaryEmma1826-1871, HelenM1829-1831, VirginiaW1833, AnnaM1867	35, cannot differentiate census records from him and Otho1776		45, Dist 2, Wash. Co. **Slaves: 23?** F slave: <10 (4) F slave: 10-35 (4) F slave 36-54 (3) M slave <10 (4) M slave: 10-23 (2) M slave 36-54 (3) M slave 55-99 (3) F whites: < 5 (2) F whites: 10-29 (2) M whites: 40-49 (1)		55-60, cannot differentiate census records from him and Otho1776		63, farmer, lived in SubDiv3, Wash.Co. Land value $28,000	
Otho Holland Williams 609 Park Avenue, Baltimore bequeathed to Susan 1903 m.Ann Eliza Howell: 1828-1861? c.Susan:1852-?, OthoH:1857-?							23? Lived in Baltimore City, 11th Ward with widow mom Susan, sister MaryG, brother WilliamG. 3 blk servants: Elen Warren (58), Elizabeth Planter (28), Boisey Bowser (25) Slaves: 0	
Otho Holland Williams								
Brigadier Gen. OHW, m. Mary Polly Smith:1764-95 c. WmElie:1787-1833, EdwardG:1789-1829, HenryL:1791-1826, Mary: 1793-?, Elizabeth:1794-?, *Otho:1794-1818* Laura & HarryLee & Richard workers?								

Appendix G - Accessing Maryland Land Records

1. Type www.MDLandRec.net into your Internet browser. Create an account with your email and password (you only have to do this once).
2. Get back into the www.MDLandRec.net website, type your email and password then click Submit.
3. Click on the Select County box, then scroll down the list of counties to Washington County, then click on Washington County.

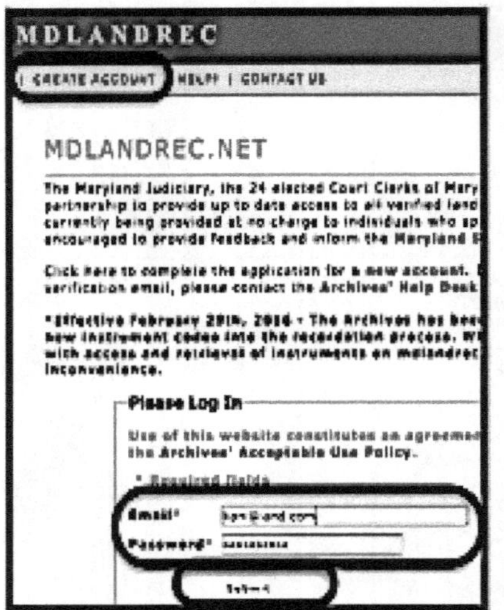

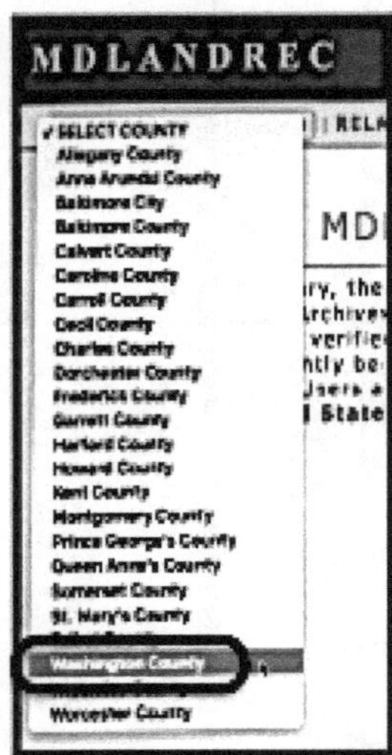

4. Click on the Active Indices option. A new screen should open.

5. Click on the up/down arrows immediately left of the "Search" option to get a drop-down box of the different Series available. Click on the desired Series, e.g., which, in my case was the "Land Records, Index, Original, 1776-1977, MSA CE 247." Click Search

6. Click on the desired Accession No., e.g., Wi-Wz, for all Williams surnames. You may have to wait as long as two minutes for each new screen page to appear.

7. The screen contains the first page of land record indices for the surname selected. The most important columns are on the right side of the screen showing the kind of instrument it is (deed, bill of sale, agreements, lease, manumission). Transactions are sorted by year, with the earliest land records listed first.

8. To see more index pages for this surname, type the page number in the "jump to new page" box shown in step number 7 and click Go! You may type in whatever page number you wish, not just the next sequential page. There can be quite a bit of hit-or-miss in trying to isolate the page you want. Note: every new page you type may result in a two-minute wait until the screen appears. You may type in a ten-page group of pages at one time, e.g., 1 to 10, but the wait time will increase proportionately; the nice thing about a group of pages though, is that you can scroll through all ten pages and you can print out all ten index pages at once.

9. There are likely multiple pages of land deeds for each surname. I advise printing them out, so it is easier to do the next step in the process. To print the page, click on the file menu, then print. Note that you will have to rescale the output from 100% down to about 55% to get the entire page to print on one sheet of paper.

10. To review individual land records, type the book and page number in the appropriate white box, then click Go!

Appendix G continued

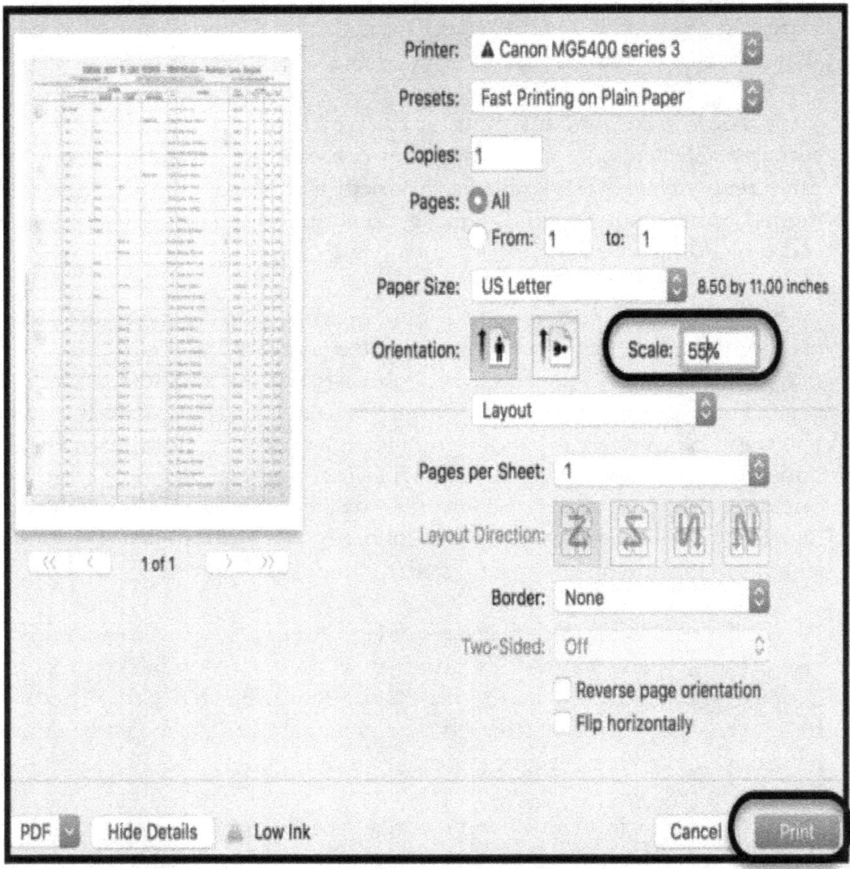

Appendix H - Kent House of Representatives Delegates

KENT COUNTY, MARYLAND, HOUSE OF REPRESENTATIVES DELEGATES

Source: Maryland State Archives, http://msa.maryland.gov/msa/speccol/sc2600/sc2685/house/html/kehouse.html

1790 Peregrine Lethrbury John Moore Thomas Ringgold William Tilghman	**1791** Cornelius Comegys Richard Miller, *dns, d* James Ringgold Thomas Ringgold John Scott, *e*	**1792, April Spec. Session** Cornelius Comegys James Ringgold Thomas Ringgold John Scott	**1792** James Ringgold Thomas Ringgold Matthew Tilghman Simon Wilmer.
1797 Thomas Angier Cornelius Comegys Henry Page James Parker	**1798** William Barroll, *spkr p.t.* William Briscoe Robert Dunn Matthew Tilghman	**1799** William Barroll Robert Dunn Matthew Tilghman James Wroth	**1800** Unit Angier Benjamin Chambers Benjamin Hanson James Parker
1801 Unit Angier, *e* Benjamin Hanson James Houston, *r* Alexander Stuart John Thomas	**1802** Unit Angier Richard Frisby Richard Hatcheson Alexander Stuart	**1803** Unit Angier Richard Hatcheson John Ireland John Thomas	**1804** Richard Hatcheson John Moore James Scott John Thomas
1805 William Gale Benjamin Hanson Cornelius Hurtt James Scott	**1806** Cornelius Comegys Richard Frisby Benjamin Hanson Gideon Pearce	**1807** Richard Brice John Gale, *d* William Moffitt James Welch	**1808** Unit Angier Richard Brice William Moffitt James Welch
1809, June Spec.Sess. Unit Angier Richard Brice William Moffitt James Welch	**1809** Unit Angier Cuthbert Hall James Harris William Moffitt	**1810** Cornelius Comegys, Jr. Cuthbert Hall James Harris James Welch	

These men were related by politics, work, and intermarried families. Several of them owned a slave named Prince. Were they all the same Prince, or generations of my enslaved family members named Prince?

Appendix I - Ingram Personal Property (Including Slaves)

It was fascinating, and at the same time horrifying, to read through the personal inventories of Benjamin and John Ingram who died in 1861 and 1862, respectively. They had a reputation of being wealthy gentlemen. Their chattel inventory listings were vast, partially described in the public sale advertisement of Benjamin's estate in Figure 10-4.

In 1862, Otho (28) and Hezekiah (31) were each valued at $275 (Figure 10-5), but Henry (38) was only valued at $50, perhaps because of an injury. There were entries for the clothing required for Otho and Hezekiah, as shown in Figure 10-6. Most importantly, are the monies paid in 1862 for slaves' work. Henry Funk paid the Ingram estate $40.50 for work performed by Hezekiah, and Benjamin South paid $85 for work performed by Otho in 1862. *Did my relatives receive any part of the fruits of their own labors?*

Many familiar names that appear in the land deeds and census records are listed on the same probate page for John Ingram's 1834 estate records. These people were paid for making clothes, or providing other goods and services on behalf of Otho and Hezekiah:

Prince's son, Henry Williams, was only mentioned once in the probate records for Benjamin or Edward Ingram: an entry for "Henry Williams for boots for Otho Slave for $4.50." This may imply that Henry was a bootmaker at that time. This notation is immediately followed by an entry that states: "Administrators of Benjamin Ingram, decd [deceased], in full of Acct. for Slave Henry Williams at the appraised value of $50.00."

<u>Page 390:</u>

One roan horse and collar:	$100
One Roan cow:	$22
One spotted cow:	$20
Half of 18 acres corn in the ground:	$126
One colored man Hezekiah Williams:	$275
One colored man Otho Williams:	$275
1000 Chestnut rails:	$25
Total	$1473

Small Sample of John Ingram's Estate Sold in 1862

Debts to be paid by Executors in 1862 for:

Goods for Slaves Otho and Hez	$5.63
Shoes for Slave Hezekiah	$2.50
Goods for Slaves Otho and Hez	$7.37
Harriet Williams Col	$1.75
Sizzie Solomon Col.	$8.62
Peggy Hanson Col.	$4.00
Clothing for Slave Otho	$11.50
Clothing for Slave Hez	$6.37
Henry Williams for boots for Otho	$4.50
Acct. for Slave Henry Williams at the appraised value	$50.00

Monies received in 1862 for slaves' work:

From Henry Funk for Hezekiah's work	$40.50
From Benjamin South for Otho's work	$85.00

Appraised value of Otho and Hezekiah ...$550.00

PUBLIC SALE!

—o—

BY virtue of an order from the Orphans' Court, the subscriberr as administrators of the personal estate of Benjamin Ingram, late of Washington county, dec'd., will sell at the residence of John Ingram, on Beaver Creek, one mile south of Doub's Mill, on the road to the marble quarry,

On Thursday, 20th day of MARCH, 1862,

the following personal property belonging to the late firm of John and Benjamin Ingram, viz:

SIX HEAD OF WORK HORSES,

among which are 2 good BROOD MARES, 2 yearling COLTS,

16 HEAD OF CATTLE!

among which are 7 good MILCH COWS, 4 f..e Steers, 1 Bull, the balance young cattle;

39 Head of HOGS,

among them are 1 Boar and several Brood Sows, 1 two-horse Sleigh, 1 Buggy and Harness, 2 Farm Wagons, 1 one-horse Wagon, 1 Wagon Bed, 1 pair Wood Ladders, 3 pair Grain Ladders, 1 Grain Drill, 1 Windmill, (Watkin's patent,) 1 Cutting Box, 5 Barshear Plows, 6 double and single shovel Plows, 2 Harrows, Double and Single Trees, 4 pair Spreaders, Fifth, Breast and Butt Chains, 1 Jackscrew, 5 sets Wagon and 5 sets Plow Gears, Bridles, Halters, Collars, &c., 3 sets Carriage Harness, 2 Riding and 1 Wagon Saddle, 1 Whip,

1 Set of Blacksmith's Tools,

1 Digging Iron, Crowbar, Sledges, Maul and Wedges, Axes, Grindstone, Cross cut Saw, Grain Cradles, Mowing Scythes, Forks, Rakes, Shovels, Hoes, lot of old Iron, lot of Plank. About

43 Acres of Wheat and 3 Acres of Rye in the Ground,

Hay by the Ton, about 850 bushels Corn to be sold by the barrel, for cash; Bacon and Lard by the pound.

Household and Kitchen Furniture,

Such as Bedsteads and Bedding, 2 Parlor Side Tables, 1 Dining Table, 1 Corner Cupboard, 1 Secretary, 1 Wardrobe, 3 Bureaus, 2 Clocks, Washstands, lot of Chairs and Carpeting, 1 Parlor and 3 Ten-plate Stoves, 1 Cook Stove and apparatus, 1 Coffee and 2 Iron Kettles, lot of Vinegar, empty Barrels, Tubs, Buckets, Sausage Cutter, and many

Appendix J - Partial Ironworker Vocabulary

Sources: Merriam-Webster Dictionary, dictionary.com, or Wiktionary, or Mastering Iron: The Struggle to Modernize an American Industry, 1800-1868.

Anchonies: Through successive reheating and poundings, refiners removed enough of the impurities in the pig iron to work it into an "anchony" – a small, square knob on the end of a billet or bloom made in a finery. Turning out high-quality anchonies was the most important single job in the forge.

Anvil: a heavy specially-shaped piece of steel that is used as a small workbench to the blacksmith.

Apprentice: An apprenticeship is a system of training a new generation of practitioners of a trade.

Bar iron: wrought iron in the form of bars.

Bellows: a device for producing a strong current of air consisting of a chamber that can be expanded to draw in air through a valve and contracted to expel it through a tube.

Blacksmith: a person who makes and repairs things in iron by hand.

Blast furnace: a furnace in which combustion is forced by a current of air under pressure; especially one for the reduction of iron ore.

Bloomery: a type of furnace with a chimney, heat-resistant walls, and pipes which allow air to enter through side walls. It was once widely-used around the world for smelting iron from its oxides.

Bloom: a porous, spongy mass of iron and slag produced from a bloomery, resulting in a finished bar of iron.

Cast iron: an alloy of iron, carbon, and other elements, cast as a soft-and-strong, or as a hard-and-brittle, iron, depending on the methods of molding.

Charcoal: produced by heating wood to produce the pure carbon fuel needed for the smelting process.

Chisel: made from high carbon steel, hot chisels are used to cut hot metals and cold chisels for cutting cold metals.

Collier: A person in the business or occupation of producing (digging or mining coal or making charcoal) or in its transporting or commerce.

Degassing: A process that may be required to reduce the amount of hydrogen present in a batch of molten metal.

Forge: to form something by heating and shaping metal.

Forge man: A person who works at a forge. A blacksmith on a large scale.

Foundry: a workshop or factory for casting metal.

Fuller: for forming tools of different shapes used in making grooves or hollows.

Furnace: refractory-lined vessels that contain the material to be melted and provide the energy to melt it.

Hammering: using various hand and sledgehammers to pound wrought iron.

Hand hammer types: Ball-peen, straight-peen, and rounding hammer.

Indentured servant: a servant who is required by a contract to work for a certain period of time.

Industrial slavery: In the antebellum southern United States, industrial slaves were often the property of a company instead of an individual. These companies spanned various industries including sawmills, cotton gins and mills, fishing, steamboats, sugar refineries, coal and gold mining, and railroads.

Iron ore: a native compound of iron (as hematite, limonite, magnetite, siderite, goethite, and the bog and clay iron ores) from which the metal may be profitably extracted.

Iron: a silver-white malleable, ductile magnetic heavy metallic element that readily rusts in moist air, occurs native in meteorites and combined in most igneous rocks, is the most used of metals, and is vital to biological processes.

Ironmaster: a manufacturer of iron.

Ironworker: An ironworker is a tradesman (man or woman) who works in the ironworking industry. A structural/ornamental Ironworker erects (or even dismantles) the structural steel framework of pre-engineered metal buildings, single and multi-story buildings, stadiums, arenas, hospitals, towers, wind turbines, and bridges.[1]

Iron Works plural in form but singular or plural in construction: a mill or building where iron or steel is smelted, or heavy iron or steel products are made.

Mill: a factory for certain kinds of manufacture, like paper, steel, or textiles.

Overwork: ironworkers (usually slaves) were cajoled into high levels of productivity with payment for "overwork" beyond specific daily tasks. With that money, slaves bought coffee, tea, fancy cloth, silk hats. Some accepted cash credits instead of their annual clothing allowance to be able to select and buy their own garments.

Pence: The correct term for monetary amounts greater than pennies is pence.

Pig iron: crude iron is the direct product of the blast furnace, refined to produce steel, wrought iron, or ingot iron.

Refinery forge: A water-powered mill where decarbonized pig iron is refined into wrought iron.

Shilling: A coin worth one-twentieth of a pound sterling, or twelve pence.

Slack tub: a large container of water used by a blacksmith to quench hot metal.

Slag: the fused material formed during the smelting or refining of metals by combining the flux with gangue, impurities in the metal, etc. It usually consists of a mixture of silicates with calcium, phosphorus, sulfur, etc.

Sledgehammer: a large, heavy hammer with a long handle used by the striker.

Smelting: a form of extractive metallurgy; its main use is to produce a base metal from its ore. Smelting makes use of heat and a chemical reducing agent to decompose the ore, driving off other elements as gases or slag and leaving just the metal base behind. The reducing agent is commonly a source of carbon such as coke, or in earlier times charcoal.

Smithy: a blacksmith's workshop; a forge.

Steel: commercial iron that contains carbon in any amount up to about 1.7 percent as an essential alloying constituent, and is distinguished from cast iron by its malleability and lower carbon content.

Striker: ironworker who uses a sledgehammer to wrought iron.

Tongs: used by the blacksmith for holding hot metals securely.

Trompe: a device used for inducing a blast of air upon the hearth of a forge by means of a current of falling water.

Wrought iron: commercial iron that is tough, malleable less than 0.3 percent carbon, and 1-2 percent of slag.

Appendix K - Williams DNA Ethnicity Comparisons

Initials	CM	CW	DC	GM	JC	KM-A	LG	LW	PC	
AFRICA TOTAL	**50%**	**58%**	**55%**	**56%**	**52%**	**52%**	**72%**	**56%**	**66%**	**56%**
Af-Benin/Togo	11%	14%	3%	9%	4%	22%		12%		
Af-Nigeria	14%	18%	4%	20%	7%	12%	10%	8%	43%	
Af-Cameroon/Congo	5%	7%	15%	8%	12%	5%	29%	14%	6%	
Af-Senegal	2%	3%	2%	7%	3%	4%		5%	6%	
Af-Ivory Coast/Ghana	12%	1%	25%	11%	15%	4%	27%	6%	11%	
Af-Hunter-Gatherers		1%	3%		2%	2%		1%		
Af-Southest Bantu	6%	4%	3%			1%	2%	6%		
Af-Mali		10%		1%	7%	1%	4%	4%		
Af-Miscellaneous					2%	1%				
Af-West										
EUROPE TOTAL	**45%**	**40%**	**42%**	**42%**	**45%**	**44%**	**26%**	**43%**	**22%**	**42%**
Eu-Great Britain	11%	6%	18%	6%	29%	34%	19%			
Eu-Iberian Peninsula	9%		3%	8%	3%	4%	5%	9%		
Eu-European Jewish		2%	3%	3%		2%				
Eu-Finland/N. Russia	2%		6%	2%		2%		2%		
Eu-Scandinavia	7%	2%	2%	13%	3%	2%		3%	12%	
Eu-Ireland/Scotland/ Wales	14%	20%	10%	9%	5%			10%	10%	
Eu- South or East		4%		1%	5%		2%	1%		
Eu-West	2%	6%						18%		
OTHER TOTAL	**5%**	**2%**	**3%**	**2%**	**3%**	**4%**	**2%**	**1%**	**12%**	**2%**
TOTAL	100%	100%	100%	100%	100%	100%	100%	100%	100%	100%

*The above were tested using ancestry.com, however, two family members were tested by Family Tree DNA which has much less detailed ethnic representation, as follows:
BG: Europe = 36% & Africa = 59% & other = 5%, MA: Europe = 36% & Africa = 58% & other = 6%

Appendix L - Distribution of Shared DNA for Given Relationships

Average autosomal DNA shared by pairs of relatives, in percentages and centiMorgans			
% shared	**Total cM shared half-identical (or better)**	**Relationship**	**Notes**
100% (Method I)/50% (Method II)	3400.00	Identical twins (monozygotic twins)	Fully identical everywhere.[2]
50%	3400.00	Parent/child	Half-identical everywhere
50% (Method I)/37.5% (Method II)	2550.00	Full siblings	Half-identical on 50%/1700 cM and fully identical on a further 25%/850 cM.
25%	1700.00	Grandparent/grandchild, aunt-or-uncle/niece-or-nephew, half-siblings	
25% (Method I)/23.4375% (Method II)	1593.75	Double first cousins	Half-identical on 21.875%/1487.5 cM and fully identical on a further 1.5625%/106.25 cM
12.5%	850.00	First cousins, great-grandparent/great-grandchild, great-uncle or aunt/great-nephew or niece, half-uncle or aunt/half-nephew or niece	
6.25%	425.00	First cousins once removed, half first cousins, great-great-grandparent/great-great-grandchild, great-great-aunt/uncle, half great-aunt/uncle	
6.25%	425.00	Double second cousins	
3.125%	212.50	Second cousins, first cousins twice removed, half first cousin once removed, half great-great-aunt/uncle, great-great-great-grandparent/great-great-great-grandchild	
1.563%	106.25	Second cousins once removed, half second cousins, first cousin three times removed, half first cousin twice removed	
0.781%	53.13	Third cousins, second cousins twice removed	Up to 10% of third cousins will not share enough DNA to show up as match. See cousin statistics
0.391%	26.56	Third cousins once removed	
0.195%	13.28	Fourth cousins, third cousins twice removed	Up to 50% of fourth cousins will not share enough DNA to show up as match. See cousin statistics
0.0977%	6.64	Fourth cousins once removed. third cousins three times removed	
0.0488%	3.32	Fifth cousins	Between 15% and 32% of fifth cousins will not share enough DNA to show up as a match. See cousin statistics

Source: International Society of Genetic Genealogy Wiki (isogg.org)

BIBLIOGRAPHY

1859 William Taggart Washington County Plat Map. Beneath the Underground: The Flight to Freedom and Communities in Antebellum Maryland. Web: *African American History Timeline.* Web: http://www.blackpast.org/african-american-history-timeline-home-page

Amt, Emilie. *History: African Americans at St. Mark's before the Civil War.* Boonsboro, MD: St. Mark's Episcopal Church, 2014.

An Illustrated Atlas for Washington County, Maryland. https://jscholarship.library.jhu.edu/handle/1774.2/32766

Appenzellar, Carol, and Feldstein, Albert, *Slaves and Free African Americans, Reports and opinions from the Newspapers of Hagerstown, Washington County, and Cumberland, Allegany County, Maryland, 1790 to 1864.* Hagerstown, MD: Western Maryland's Regional Library, 2014.

Armstead, Myra B. Young. *Freedom's Gardener, James F. Brown, Horticulture and the Hudson Valley in Antebellum America.* New York, NY: NYU Press, 2011.

Ball, Charles. *Fifty Years in Chains Or, The Life of An American Slave.* San Bernardino, CA: First Rate Publishers, December 2016.

Barnett, Ida W., Mary Prince, William W. Brown, Lydia M. Child, Charles Sumner, and William Still. *Slave Narrative Six Pack 4.* U.S.: Enhanced Media, Kindle Edition 2015.

Beneath the Underground: The Flight to Freedom and the Communities of Antebellum Maryland, slavery.msa.maryland.gov/html/grants/npsreport2003/html/index.html

Bettinger, Blaine T. *The Family Tree Guide to DNA Testing and Genetic Genealogy.* Family Tree Books: Cincinnati, Ohio. 2016.

Bezis-Selfa, John. *Forging America: Ironworkers, Adventurers, and the Industrious Revolution,* Ithica, NY: Cornell University Press. 2003.

Bragg, George F. *Men of Maryland.* Baltimore, MD: Church Advocate Press, 1914.

Burke, Diane Mutti. *On Slavery's Border, Missouri's Small-Slaveholding Households, 1815–1865.* GA: University of Georgia Press, 2010.

Collier, Melvin J. *150 Years Later: Broken Ties Mended.* Charleston, SC: Write Here Publishing, 2015.

Collier, Melvin J. *Mississippi to Africa: A Journey of Discovery, Second Edition.* Charleston, SC: Write Here Publishing, Second Edition, August 2015.

Diggins, Milt. *Principio.* Cecil County, MD: Cecil County Public Schools, 2009), http://www.cchistory.org/Principio.htm, 5/18/09.

Doleman, Marguerite. *Black Heritage Museum Document Archives* (http://archives.dolemanblackheritagemuseum.org/documents/)

Doleman, Marguerite. *Black Obituaries of Washington Country, Maryland.* Hagerstown, MD: Historical Society.

Doleman, Marguerite. *Maryland Slave Holders From 1860 Census Data.*

DuBois, W.E.B. *The Souls of Black Folk*. New York, NY: Dover Publications, Inc. 1994. First published in 1903 by A.C. McClurg and Co. in Chicago, IL.

Equiano, Olaudah. *The Life of Olaudah Equiano, or Gustavus Vassa, the African*. Mineola, NY: Dover Publications. 1999. Originally published in 1814 by James Nichols, Leeds, England.

Estell, Kenneth. *African America: Celebrating 400 Years of Achievement.* Detroit, Michigan: Visible Ink Press, 1994.

Estes, Roberta, "Durham DNA---10 Things I Learned Despite No Y DNA Matches, 52 Ancestors #167," DNAeXplained—Genetic Genealogy. As of 2017, https://wwwdna-explained.com.

Ethnography Program: Gender, Age & Work Roles, National park Service, U.S. Department of the Interior, African Nation Founders, Africans in the Chesapeake, Cultural Patterns.

Fall, Wendy Wilson. *Memories of Madagascar and Slavery in the Black Atlantic.* Athens, Ohio: Ohio University Press, 2015.

Fields, Barbara Jeanne. *Slavery and Freedom on the Middle Ground, Maryland During the Nineteenth Century.* New Haven and London: Yale University Press. 1984.

findagrave.com 315 cemeteries for Washington County, especially concentrating on cemeteries near Funkstown, Boonsboro, Sharpsburg, Hagerstown, and Williamsport, Maryland. 2016.

Floyd, Claudia. *Maryland Women in the Civil War: Unionists, Rebels, Slaves & Spies.* Charleston, SC: The History Press, 2013.

Fuller, Marsha Lynne, CGRS. *African American Manumissions of Washington County, Maryland.* Westminster, Maryland: Willow Bend Books, 2001.

Gates, Henry Louis, Jr. and Cornell West, *The African American Century: How Blacks Have Shaped Our Country.* New York, NY: Touchstone. 2002.

Genealogical Proof Standard, Board for Certification of Genealogists.

Genealogy: African American Department Resource Guide, Maryland State Library Resource Center, Enoch Pratt Free Library, 2017.

Genealogy Trails History Group, "African American Research in America," http://genealogytrails.com/mary/afameresearch.html

Gilbert, Olive. *Narrative of Sojourner Truth.* New York, NY: Harper Collins, Epub Edition 2014.

Gozdzik, Gloria. *A Historic Resource Study for Storer College.* Harper's Ferry, WV: Horizon Research Consultants, Jan 2002.

Gray, Thomas R., *The Confessions of Nat Turner: Account of the Whole Insurrection.* Baltimore, MD: Thomas R. Gray: 1831.

Griggs, Denise I. *A Mulatto Slave: The Events in the Life of Peter Hunt 1844-1915.* Sacramento, CA: Glass Tree Books, 2010.

Grivno, Max. *Gleanings of Freedom, Landscapes of Slavery and Freedom*, October 2014. http://landscapesofslavery.org/project-blog/ Grivno, Max. *Gleanings of Freedom: Free and Slave Labor along the Mason-Dixon Line, 1790-1860.* University of Maryland, 2011.

Grivno, Max. *There Slavery Cannot Dwell: Agriculture and Labor in Northern Maryland.* Dissertation at University of Maryland, 2007.

Growing a Nation: The Story of American Agriculture. Source: https://www.agclassroom.org/gan/timeline/farm_tech.htm

Guide to African American Resources - Maryland Historical Society. Web: https://www.mdhs.org/sites/default/files/African_American_Resources.pdf

Guide to the History of Slavery in Maryland, A. http://msa.maryland.gov/msa/intromsa/pdf/slavery_pamphlet.pdf

Haley, Alex, *Roots: The Saga of an American Family,* New York: Doubleday & Company, Inc, 1976.

Halpern, Rick and Enrico Dal Lago. *Slavery and Emancipation.* Malden, MA Blackwell Publishers Ltd., 2002.

Hanson, George A., *Old Kent: The Eastern Shore of Maryland*, London: Forgotten Books, 1996.

Heinegg, Paul, "Free African Americans of Maryland and Delaware from the Colonial Period to 1810," Baltimore, MD, USA: Genealogical Publishing Co., 2000.

Henderson, Michael N. *Got Proof! My Genealogical Journey Through the Use of Documentation.* Suwanee, GA: The Write Image, 2013.

Herrin, Dean, Ph.D. *Maryland and the Border in the Civil War: Tolson's Chapel and the Freedmen's Bureau.* Crossroads of War. Web: http://www.crossroadsofwar.org/discover-the-story/reconstructing-the-region/civil-war-stories/

Horine, M. C. "*Many of Us Leave Farming … So We Invent Better Farm Machinery.* Source: SaltOfAmerica.com. From *A Popular History of American Invention, 1924.*

Jacobs, Harriet. *Incidents in the Life of a Slave Girl.* Mineola, NY: Dover Publications, 2001. Originally published in 1861 in Boston, MA.

Johnston, James H. *From Slave Ship to Harvard: Yarrow Mamout and the History of an African American Family.* NY: Fordham University Press. 2012.

Knowles, Anne Kelly, *Mastering Iron: The Struggle to Modernize an American Industry, 1800-1868.* Glossary. Chicago: University of Chicago Press.2013.

LaVoie, Debra E. *Documentation of the History and Physical Evolution of Hermitage Farm, Centreville, Maryland.* Philadelphia, PA: University of Pennsylvania, 2000.

"Legacy of Slavery in Maryland," website, including; case studies of biographies of slave owners, fugitives and those who assisted slaves on the run; interactive maps showing the locations of slave owners, resources, projects like "Flight to Freedom," and "Finding Freedom." http://www.slavery.msa.maryland.com.

Libby, Jean, "African Ironmaking Culture Among African American Ironworkers in Western Maryland, 1760-1850," San Francisco State University, 1991).

Libby, Jean. *From Slavery to Salvation, The Autobiography of Rev. Thomas W. Henry of the A.M.E. Church*, Mississippi: University Press of Mississippi, 1994.

Lindenmeyer, Otto, *Black History: Lost, Stolen, or Strayed.* New York, NY: Avon Discus Books, 1970.

Marquis, Catherine, The Rearing of Slave Children and The Parental Relationships Before and After Emancipation, "The Sloping Hills Review, 3.", Pittsburgh: Carnegie Mellon University, 1996.

Marshall, Kathy Lynne. *Mary Ellen Carter Marshall: The Life of a Hero, Educator, Mother, Artist, Citizen, Mentor and Friend.* Elk Grove, CA: Kanika African Sculptures and Books, 2015.

Marshall, Kathy Lynne. *The Ancestors Are Smiling!* Elk Grove, CA: Kanika African Sculptures and Books, 2017.

Marshall, Kathy Lynne. *Thomas Richard Marshall: A Life Well-Lived, 1931-2014.* Elk Grove, CA: Kanika African Sculptures and Books, 2014.

Marshall, Mary E., *Reflections from a Mother's Heart: Your Life Story in Your Own Words.* Dallas, Tx: Word Publishing, 1995 pp. 24, 35, 38, 39, 45, 70, 72, 95, 150.

Maryland At a Glance, Historical Chronology, 1800-1899. Maryland Manual On-line a Guide to Maryland and Its Government https://msa.maryland.gov/msa/mdmanual/01glance/chron/html/chron.html

Maryland at a Glance: Historical Chronology, 1700-1799. Aided by Robert J. Brugger, "Maryland: A Middle Temperament, 1634-1980." Baltimore, MD: Johns Hopkins University Press, 1988.

Maryland Historical Trust, *Antietam Iron Furnace Site and Antietam Village,* http://mht.maryland.gov/nr/NRDetail.aspx?NRID=313&FROM=NRMapWA.aspx

Maryland Slave Laws, Source: Proceedings and Acts of the General Assembly of Maryland, assembled in http://www.drbronsontours.com/

Miller, Mrs. Warren D. *Records of Cemeteries of Washington County Maryland*, Hagerstown, District 21, page 60. Vols. IV and VI.

Minges, Patrick. *Far More Terrible for Women: Personal Accounts of Women in Slavery.* John F. Blair Publisher, 2006.

National Museum of African American History and Culture: A Souvenir Book. Washington DC: Smithsonian Books, 2016.

Passano, L. Magruder, *History of Maryland* (Baltimore, MD: Wm. J. C. Dulany Company, 1901).

Peden, Henry C., Jr., *Inhabitants of Kent County, Maryland, 1637-1878*, Heritage Books, 2007.

Prince, Mary, *The History of Mary Prince—A West Indian Slave*, first published in 1831, Slave Narrative Six Pack 4, Enhanced Media, 2015.

Scharf, Thomas. *History of Western Maryland. Being a History of Frederick, Montgomery, Carroll, Washington, Allegany and Garrett Counties from the Earliest Period to the Present Day.* PA: Louis H. Everts, 1882.

Schmidt, Ashley K., *Endangering the Stability of Slavery" Black Freedom in the Upper South, 1820-1850*, James Madison University. Spring 2012.

Schomberg Center for Research in Black Culture. *Lest We Forget: The Triumph Over Slavery.* Petaluma, CA: Pomegranate, 2007.

Sellers, Janice, "Freedmen's Bureau 2.0: A Better Way to Do Slave Research (but still not perfect)" Ancestral Discoveries, http://www.ancestraldiscoveries.com/, 2017.

Slave Narratives: A Folk History of Slavery in the United States from Interviews with Former Slaves, Maryland Narratives. Washington DC: Work Projects Administration, 1941.

Slaves and Free African Americans, Reports and Opinions from the newspapers of Hagerstown, Washington County, 1790 to 1864, including "Allegany County African American history," "John Brown in Washington County," "Chesapeake and Ohio Canal," "Battle of Antietam - Herald of Freedom and Torch Light Newspaper September 1862," and "History of the Antietam Cemetery, 1867."

Slavery in Washington County, Maryland: Mid-19th Century (1845-1854). Index to Hagerstown Newspapers 1850-1854.

Spalding, Henry D. *The Encyclopedia of Black Folklore and Humor.* Middle Village, NY: Jonathan David Publishers, 1990.

Tademy, Lalita. *Cane River.* New York: Grand Central Publishing, 2001.

Taggart, William. *Washington County Plat Map, 1859*,

Thomas, Ronald A. and Burnston, Sharon A. *Archaeological Data Recovery at Catoctin Furnace Cemetery.* Frostburg, MD: Western MD Preservation Center, 1980.

Thompson, Michael D., *The Iron Industry in Western Maryland.* WV: West Virginia University, 1976.

Thompson, Robert Farris. Flash of the Spirit: African and Afro-American Art and Philosophy. New York: Random House, 1983.

University of California. *African Arts: The Benin Centenary, Part 2.* Los Angeles, CA: Autumn 1997, Volume XXX, Number 4.

Wallace, Edie. *The Significance of Tolson's Chapel in Sharpsburg, Maryland.* Sharpsburg, MD: Tolson's Chapel website. www.tolsonschapel.org

Western Maryland' Historical Library (WHILBR) website (www.whilbr.org) Collections:

Whitely, William G. and Henry. *The Principio Company. A Historical Sketch of the First Iron-works in Maryland. PA:* The Historical Society of Pennsylvania. Vol. 11, No.2. July 1887, pp. 190-198.

Williams, M. Lavata, *Myer's Genealogy and Booker, Walker, Williams.* Columbus, Ohio: M. Lavata Williams. June 1983, p. 7.

Woods, Paula L. and Felix H. Liddell. *I, Too, Sing America: The African American Book of Days.* New York, NY: Workman Publishing, 1992.

Yetman, Norman R. *When I Was a Slave: Memoirs from the Slave Narratives Collection.* Mineola, NY: Dover Publications, 2002.

ENDNOTES

Chapter 1

1 Genealogical Proof Standard (GPS) is a guideline for establishing the reliability ("proof") of a genealogical conclusion with some certainty. It is important to clearly communicate the quality of research performed, such as by a professional genealogist. It is useful to understand what is needed for high-quality research. It has five elements: 1) a reasonably exhaustive research; 2) complete and accurate source citations; 3)analysis and correlation of the collected information; 4) resolution of any conflicting evidence; and 5)a soundly reasoned, coherently written conclusion.

2 "Pathways to Freedom: Maryland & The Underground Railroad." Source: Maryland Historical Society and Maryland State Archives. As of September 30, 2018, http://pathways.thinkport.org/flash_home.cfm.

3 *John Brown's Raiders*. Source: American Battlefield Trust. As of September 30, 2018, https://www.battlefields.org/learn/articles/john-browns-raiders

4 Antietam Iron Furnace Site and Antietam Village is a National Historic District at Antietam, Washington County, Maryland. The village consists of the remains of a mid-18th to late-19th century iron furnace site, village, remnants of a wheel pit or building foundation, furnace stack, a four-arch stone bridge built by John Weaver in 1832. Source: Maryland Historical Trust, Maryland's National Register Properties. As of September 30, 2018, http://mht.maryland.gov/nr/NRDetail.aspx?NRID=313

5 Letter from George Booker to Kathy Marshall, in the author's *Finding Otho: The Search for Our Williams Ancestors* Research File. 1977.

6 The United States Census of 1880. Source: United States Census Bureau.

7 "GEDCOM" (an acronym for Genealogical Data Communication) is an open de facto specification for exchanging genealogical data between different genealogy software. GEDCOM was developed by The Church of Jesus Christ of Latter-day Saints as an aid to genealogical research. Source: Family Search Wiki. As of September 30, 2018, https://www.familysearch.org/wiki/en/GEDCOM

8 "FamilySearch" is a genealogy organization operated by The Church of Jesus Christ of Latter-day Saints. FamilySearch is dedicated to connecting families across generations by linking the best and most valuable research resources to help people discover who they are by exploring where they come from. As of September 30, 2018, https://www.familysearch.org/about

9 Ancestry.com's website indicates they are "bringing together science and self-discovery. Ancestry engineering and technology harnesses family history and consumer genomics, combining billions of rich historical records, millions of family trees, and samples from over 10 million people in the AncestryDNA database to provide people with insights about who they are and where they come from." Source: Ancestry.com. As of September 30, 2018, https://www.Ancestry.com/corporate/about-ancestry/our-story

10 "Pedigree Chart" is a tool for genetic or genealogical research. It is similar in structure to a family tree, but is more of a working document. A pedigree chart may be used for humans, but can also be useful for studying the lineage of show dogs and race horses. Source: SmartDraw.com. As of September 30, 2018, https://www.smartdraw.com/pedigree-chart/

11 "Melungeons" have a mixture of European, Native American, and African ancestry. Source: Melungeon Heritage Association website. As of September 30, 2018, http://melungeon.org/frequently-asked-questions-about-melungeons/

12 Harris, David A., *Driving while Black: Racial Profiling on Our Nation's Highways.* Source: University of Toledo College of Law, 1999.

13 "Dixie" is usually defined as the eleven Southern states that seceded in late 1860 and early 1861 to form the new confederation named the Confederate States of America. Source: Encyclopedia Britannica. As of September 30, 2018, https://www.britannica.com/place/Dixie-region

14 "The Genealogist's Writing Room - Write Your Life" is an online community for genealogists and family history researchers interested in writing their stories, either as blog posts, journal articles, short stories, or books. It teaches members to share stories of the past with the generations of tomorrow. Conceived by Anita Henderson. As of September 30, 2018, https://www.writeyourlife.net/work-with-me/the-genealogists-writing-room/

15 "RootsTech" is the largest genealogy conference in the world, located in Salt Lake City, Utah. Source: The Church of Jesus Christ of Latter-day Saints. As of September 30, 2018, https://www.rootstech.org

16 Stahle, Tyler S., *How to Successfully Apply the Genealogical Proof Standard.* Source: Family Search Blog, March 24, 2016. As of September 30, 2018, https://www.familysearch.org/blog/en/genealogicalproofstandardpart3/

17 *10 Best Yoda Quotes.* Source: The Starwars.com, Films, posted November 26, 2013. As of September 30, 2018, https://www.starwars.com/news/the-starwars-com-10-best-yoda-quotes

18 "The Wayback Machine" is a fictional time machine from the segment *Peabody's Improbable History*, from the 1960s cartoon series "The Rocky and Bullwinkle Show." It is a plot device used to transport the characters Mr. Peabody and Sherman back in time to visit important events in human history, and that is how this author feels about my family quest. As of September 30, 2018, https://en.wikipedia.org/wiki/WABAC_machine

Chapter 3

19 "Family Search Wiki" is a free, online genealogy and family history guide that lists websites, research strategies, and suggests records and resources to help you find ancestors from all over the world. Source: http://www.familysearch.org. As of September 30, 2018, https://www.familysearch.org/wiki/en/Main_Page

20 National Archives and Records (NARA) pension application records, military records.. https://www.archives.gov/research/military/genealogy.html

21 "Freedmen's Bureau." As of September 30, 2018, http://www.history.com/topics/black-history/freedmens-bureau *and* http://www.discoverfreedmen.org

22 "Juneteenth" is the oldest nationally celebrated commemoration of the ending of slavery in the United States. Source: Juneteenth.com. http://www.juneteenth.com

23 Henry Louis Gates, Jr., Meaghan Siekman and Kristin Britanik, *Lost Slave Ancestors Found: How to research the Origin of Your Family's Name.* Source: The Root, posted November 29, 2013, Filed to: Culture. As of September 30, 2018, https://www.theroot.com/lost-slave-ancestors-found-1790899106

24 "Researching African American Ancestry" contains a plethora of research ideas and sources. As of September 30, 2018, https://support.Ancestry.com/s/article/Tips-for-finding-African-American-ancestry-1460088565989-2219

Chapter 4

25 "Frequently Asked Questions: The Voyage to Marie's Land (Maryland)." Source: Exploring Maryland's Roots: Library. As of September 30, 2018, http://mdroots.thinkport.org/library/faqs_voyage.asp#big

26 "Matthias de Sousa." Source: Exploring Maryland's Roots: Library. As of September 30, 2018, http://mdroots.thinkport.org/library/mathiasdesousa.asp

27 "Governor Leonard Calvert." Source: Exploring Maryland's Roots: Library. As of September 30, 2018, http://mdroots.thinkport.org/library/leonardcalvert.asp

28 "Description of the Ark and Foods." Source: Exploring Maryland's Roots: Library. As of September 30, 2018, http://mdroots.thinkport.org/library/faqs_voyage.asp

29 "Immigrant Ships Transcribers Guild Sister Ships Ark and Dove." Source: ISTG Home Page. As of September 30, 2018, https://www.immigrantships.net/v2/1600v2/ark_dove16340325.html

30 "Maryland." Source: History.com Editors, A&E Television Networks, original published date November 9, 2009. As of September 30, 2018, https://www.history.com/topics/us-states/maryland

31 "Washington County, Maryland, History." As of September 30, 2018, https://familysearch.org/wiki/en/Washington_County,_Maryland_Genealogy#Census_Districts

32 "Indentured Servants in Maryland: Genealogy Decoded." As of September 30, 2018, http://genealogydecoded.com/tag/maryland-indentured-servants/

33 "Slaves and Free African Americans." Source: Reports and opinions from the Newspapers of Hagerstown, Washington County, and Cumberland, Allegany County, MD, 1790 to 1864, WHILBR, Western Maryland's Historical Library. As of September 30, 2018, http://www.whilbr.org/WesternMDSlaves/index.aspx

34 "The Town of Williamsport, MD, Honoring the Past, Shaping the Future." As of September 30, 2018, https://williamsportmd.gov

35 "Resistance to Slavery in Maryland, Strategies for Freedom." Source: National Underground Railroad Network to Freedom, National Park Service. As of September 30, 2018, https://www.nps.gov/subjects/ugrr/discover_history/upload/ResistanceMDRpt.pdf

36 "A Guide to the History of Slavery in Maryland," page 17. Source: Maryland State Archives, Annapolis, Maryland, and the University of Maryland College Park, http://msa.maryland.gov/msa/intromsa/pdf/slavery_pamphlet.pdf

37 "Mulatto" is a person of mixed white and black ancestry, especially a person with one white and one black parent. Source: Google Dictionary.

38 "Beaver Creek, Maryland." Source: Wikipedia. As of September 30, 2018, https://en.wikipedia.org/wiki/Beaver_Creek,_Maryland

39 Battle of Antietam was also called the Battle of Sharpsburg, and became the battle to free the slaves. Source: History.com. As of September 30, 2018, https://www.history.com/topics/american-civil-war/battle-of-antietam

40 Maryland Population Statistics, 1790 to 1870. Source: Table 35. Maryland - Race and Hispanic Origin: 1790 to 1990, http://www.census.gov/population/www/documentation/twps0056/tabs15-65.pdf.

41 "Slavery in Washington County, Maryland, Mid-19th Century (1845-54)," page xi. Source: Index to Hagerstown Newspapers 1850-1854, Herald of Freedom and Torch Light reprinted the story in 1853. As of September 30, 2018, https://www.washcolibrary.org/assets/documents/NewsIndex_Slavery1845-1854.pdf

42 Max Grivno, Gleanings of Freedom: Free and Slave Labor along the Mason-Dixon Line, 1790-1860, page 13, University of Illinois Press, 2011, Kindle.

43 "Slaves and Free African Americans, Reports and opinions from the Newspapers of Hagerstown, Washington County, and Cumberland, Allegany County, MD, 1790 to 1864." Source: WHILBR, Western Maryland's Historical Library. As of September 30, 2018, http://www.whilbr.org/WesternMDSlaves/index.aspx

44 Myra Adams, "How Slavery Birthed the Electoral College," October 12, 2016. Source: Washington Examiner Opinion. As of September 30, 2018, http://www.washingtonexaminer.com/how-slavery-birthed-the-electoral-college/article/2604291

45 "A Guide to the History of Slavery in Maryland," p. 12. Source: Maryland State Archives, Annapolis, Maryland, and the University of Maryland College Park. As of September 30, 2018, https://msa.maryland.gov/msa/intromsa/pdf/slavery_pamphlet.pdf

46 Max Grivno, Gleanings of Freedom: Free and Slave Labor along the Mason-Dixon Line, 1790-1860, page 52-61, University of Illinois Press, 2011, Kindle.

47 James W.C Pennington, The Fugitive Blacksmith, Or, Events in the History of James W.C. Pennington: Formerly a Slave in the State of Maryland, United States, London: Charles Gilpin, 5, Bishopsgate, 1850, Third Edition.

48 "Hagerstown Historic District," Source: The Journey Through Hallowed Ground, Gettysburg to Monticello, Hagerstown Convention Visitor's Bureau. African American Heritage Guide. Washington County, Maryland. As of September 30, 2018, http://hallowedground.org

49 Max Grivno, Gleanings of Freedom: Free and Slave Labor along the Mason-Dixon Line, 1790-1860, page 9, University of Illinois Press, 2011, Kindle.

50 Max Grivno, page 3.

51 Max Grivno, page 4.

52 "Mason-Dixon Line" was originally the boundary between Maryland and Pennsylvania. In the pre-Civil War period it, together with the Ohio River, was the dividing line between slave states south of it and free states north. Source: Encyclopedia Britannica. https://www.britannica.com/place/Mason-and-Dixon-Line

53 Max Grivno, Gleanings of Freedom: Free and Slave Labor along the Mason-Dixon Line, 1790-1860, page 4, University of Illinois Press, 2011, Kindle.

54 Elie Williams letter to Otho Holland Williams, Hagerstown, Oct. 26, 1782. Source: Williams Papers, MS, Maryland Historical Society.

55 Max Grivno, *There Slavery Cannot Dwell, Agriculture and Labor in Northern Maryland, 1790-1860*, page 5. Source: Dissertation submitted to the Faculty of the Graduate School of the University of Maryland, College Park, 2007.

56 "Historical Timeline—Farm Machinery & Technology." Source: Growing a Nation, the Story of American Agriculture website. As of September 30, 2018, https://www.agclassroom.org/gan/timeline/farm_tech.htm

57 Max Grivno, *There Slavery Cannot Dwell, Agriculture and Labor in Northern Maryland, 1790-1860*, page 16. Source: Dissertation submitted to the Faculty of the Graduate School of the University of Maryland, College Park, 2007.

Chapter 5

58 listing for "WILLIAMS, Gen. Otho Holland (p.n. 11) b. 27 Sep 1776 d. 11 July 1852. Source: Washington County, Cemetery Records, Volume 1.

59 The green "Shaky Leafs" are Ancestry Hints designed to aid you in your family history research. They provide other records in their database that could possibly match the individual in your tree. Source: Ancestry.com. As of: November 2, 2018, https://www.youtube.com/watch?v=bsQp6RWjcLg&feature=youtu.be.

60 Jenny B Wahl. "Slavery in the US, Slavery by the Numbers, Table 1." There were about 361,247 free and 1,775,515 enslaved black people in the original colonies in 1860. Source: Economic History Association, Historical Statistics of the US, 1970.

61 Otho Holland Williams, 1792-1802, died after thrown by a horse. Source: Wikitree.com. As of September 30, 2018, https://www.wikitree.com/wiki/Williams-38760

62 "Most Common Last Names for Blacks in the U.S." Source: Public Records Search. As of September 30, 2018, https://names.mongabay.com/data/black.html

63 Tony Burroughs, "A Recap of Tony Burroughs for the AAGSNC Meeting." Source: African American Genealogical Society of Northern California," March 21, 2015.

Chapter 6

64 Gil Wilson, "Maryland Law" summary of laws concerning slavery, excerpt from History of St. Augustine webpage, prepared in 1991 for the Maryland National Capital Park and Planning Commission. As of October 1, 2018, http://www.drbronsontours.com/PGslaverymarylandlaw.html

65 Erin Bradford, "Free African American Population in the U.S.: 1790-1860." Source: University of Virginia Library, Geostat Historical Census Browser. As of October 1, 2018, https://www.ncpedia.org/sites/default/files/census_stats_1790-1860.pdf

66 Eric Burin, Slavery and the Peculiar Solution: A History of the American Colonization Society. (Gainesville: University Press of Florida, 2005).

67 "1832 Census of Negroes" was authorized by the General Assembly to resettle recently freed slaves and free African Americans in Africa (Chapter 281, Laws of 1831). Marylanders saw colonization as a means of curtailing the growing free black population. Source: African American Research in Maryland, Genealogy Trails History Group website. As of October 1, 2018, http://genealogytrails.com/mary/afameresearch.html

68 "Ingram Farm" was part of Meadows Green, Patent Book 1, Folio 225, June 25, 1785, surveyed for J. Ingram, 246 1/2 acres. Source: National Register of Historic Places Inventory—Nomination Form, U.S. Department of the Interior, National Park Service. As of October 6, 2018, https://mht.maryland.gov/secure/medusa/PDF/NR_PDFs/NR-563.pdf

Chapter 7

69 Deed between Prince Williams and John Cox, Source: Maryland Land Records, Washington County, Book PP, page 118.

70 Deed between Prince Williams and John Sharrer: Source: Maryland Land Records, Washington County, Book ZZ, page 44, 1842.

71 Marsha Lynne Fuller, *The AA Manumissions of Washington County, Maryland,* on the 11th page indicated that "Nathan Williams, his parents and siblings, born slaves, were purchased by a Quaker woman from Washington County who freed them in 1826."

72 "Bringing Slaves in from Another State:" If a Maryland resident owns land in Virginia, Delaware, or Pennsylvania on which slaves are used, that person or legal representatives may bring the slaves into Maryland provided they were residents of the other state prior to April 21, 1783 or are descendants of them. In addition, within one month of the removal the individual must file a list of the slaves with the county court clerk for recording. Source: Maryland State Law, Acts of 1791, Ch. 57, an act supplemental to Acts of Apr. 1783, Ch. 23, re out of state slaves, passed 5-31-1783. Sec. 1: Any title stemming from inheritance or marriage must be stated on the list. As of October 1, 2018, http://www.drbronsontours.com/PGslaverymarylandlaw.html

73 "Tetris" video game was created by Russian designer Alexey Pajitnov in 1985 that allows players to rotate falling blocks strategically to clear levels. Source: Encyclopedia Britannica. As of October 1, 2018, https://www.britannica.com/topic/Tetris

74 Facebook is a social networking site that makes it easy for you to connect and share with your family and friends online, created in 2004 by Mark Zuckerberg while he was enrolled at Harvard University. As of October 1, 2018, https://edu.gcfglobal.org/en/facebook101/what-is-facebook/1/

75 Prince Williams' 1843 Probate Records. Source: Maryland Register of Wills Records, 1629-1999, Washington County, Wills: 1831-1848, liber D, folio 494; Bond: liber G, folio 62; Inventory: liber P, folio 77; Debts: liber A, folio 607; First Account: liber 13, folio 374; Second Account: liber 14, folio 94.

76 Prince Williams' 1868 Probate Records. Source: Maryland Register of Wills Records Index, 1629-1999, Washington County, Bond: liber G, folio 550; Inventory: liber W, folio 19; Sale: liber Y, folio 658; Sale RE: liber Y, folio 664; First Account: liber 24, folio 308.

77 Prince Williams' Inventory List. Source: Maryland Register of Wills Records Index, 1629-1999, Washington County, Inventory: liber W, folio 19.

78 Description of Funkstown. Source: Maryland website: As of October 1, 2018, http://www.funkstown.com

79 Prince Williams' 1868 Bond Administrator Account. Source: Maryland Register of Wills Records Index, 1629-1999, Washington County, Bond: liber G, folio 550.

80 Prince Williams' 1868 Sale of His Property. Source: Maryland Register of Wills Records Index, 1629-1999, Washington County, Sale: liber Y, folio 658.

81 Deed between Otho and Hezekiah Williams and Edward Ingram. Source: Maryland Land Records, Washington County, Book McKK1, page 92, 1868.

82 Indenturing the children of free blacks in Maryland Laws of 1793, Chapters 45 and 54. Source: African American Research in Maryland, Genealogy Trails History Group website. As of October 1, 2018, http://genealogytrails.com/mary/afameresearch.html

83 Andrew K Frank, Perspectives in American Social History, Early Republic: People and Perspectives, page 92. (Santa Barbara: ABC-CLIO, Inc., 2009)

Chapter 8

84 "Certificates of Freedom." In 1805 the General Assembly passed a law to identify free African Americans and to control the availability of freedom papers.

A typical certificate not only indicates how the black became free, but also lists physical characteristics that could be used to establish identity. These include height, eye color, complexion, and hair color and texture. Often, blacks would bring to the courthouse witnesses or affidavits as proof of freedom. Source: Maryland Laws (Chapter 66, Laws of 1805). As of October 3, 2018, http://www.genealogytrails.com/mary/afameresearch.html

85 Otho Holland Williams (1776-1852) was appointed the Clerk of the County Court for Washington County, in 1800 and continued to hold said office until 1845, according to his 1852 obituary in the Herald Freedom and Light Newspaper, Hagerstown. He had been considered as a possible slave owner or father for the star of this book, Otho Williams.

86 There were many former owners of the Antietam Iron Works. First, in 1727 Israel Friend acquired land on the Maryland side of the river from the Indian Chiefs of the Five Nations, becoming "Frederick Forge" and later the Antietam Iron Works. Joseph Chapline received over a thousand acres of land from the French and Indian War. John Brien and John MacPherson operated it in the early 1800s. Wayne McCrossin owned it as of October 2018, Source: http://www.waymarking.com/waymarks/WM4DP2_Antietam_Iron_Furnace_Sharpsburg_MD.

87 "African American Resources for Maryland," included online resources, research strategies, records of slaves and free people of color, biographies, cemeteries, census records, Church records, Emancipation records, funeral homes, genealogies, and land and property records, among many other records. As of on October 3, 2018, https://www.familysearch.org/wiki/en/African_American_Resources_for_Maryland

88 William Comegys' 1756 probate record bequeathed a negro man named Prince to his son William. Other slaves given to other family members were: men Thomas, Sambo, Chester, Dick, Joseph, Jacob; boys Michael; woman Sue; girls Rachel and Ester. Source: MD Register of Wills Records, Kent County Wills 1735-1746, volume 2, p. 33.

89 Frederick Hanson's 1738 probate record bequeathed a negro man named Prince to his wife. Other slaves given to other family members were: men Harry, Mance and Jack; boys Stephen, ? and Cupet. Source: Maryland Register of Wills Records, Kent County Wills 1735-1746, vol 2, page 95.

90 Richard Hopewell's 1741 probate record bequeathed negro men named Prince and Caesar to his son Joseph. Other slaves given to other family members were: "fellows" Harry, Will, and Tom; "women/wenches" Rachel, Mal, Rose, and Tonoy; girls Sarah, Moll, and Cato; and boys Duly and Macy. Source: Maryland Register of Wills Records, 1629-1999, St. Mary's Will books 1733-1776, vol TA1, page 177.

91 Samuel Pennington's 1745 probate record contained a slave named Prince. Other slaves bequeathed were woman Namod Aboo and girl Aminta. Source: Maryland Register of Wills Records, 1629-1999, Cecil County Wills1744-45, Liber EE, folio 5, page 114.

92 Jacob Glen's 1746 probate record contained a boy slave named Prince. Boys Joe and Hark were given to family members were. Source: Maryland Register of Wills Records, 1629-1999, Kent County Will, Liber 24, folio 534, page 22.

93 Mary Hanson's 1747 probate record contained a negro man named Prince bequeathed to her daughter Ann. Source: Maryland Register of Wills Records, 1629-1999, Kent County Will, Liber 28, folio 367, page 10. Folio 5, page 134.

94 Vincent Hatcheson's 1755 Will: Abstracts of Wills by Carson Gibb abstracted from Prerogative Court (Wills) MSA S538, Liber 30, folio 47, page 26.

95 Negroes Slave and Free 1802. Source: Maryland Register of Wills Records, 1729-1999, 4 Dec 1801.

96 Negroes Slave and Free 1803. Source: Maryland Register of Wills Records, 1729-1999, 21 Mar 1803.

97 Vincent Hatcheson sold two tracts of land, devised by the late William Hanson, to William and Martha Briscoe in Kent County, Maryland, for five shillings. Source: Maryland Land Records, Kent County, Book 2 (TW), Pages 467 and 468, MSA CE-118_32).

98 "Negros Slave and Free 1775-1898" Source: Maryland Register of Wills Records, 1629-1999, Kent County. As of October 4, 2018, https://www.familysearch.org

99 "Sheriffs: elected by Voters to 3-year terms." Source: Kent County, Circuit Court (Constitution of 1776, sec. 42). http://msa.maryland.gov/msa/mdmanual/36loc/ke/jud/sheriffs/former/html/00list.html. Also, "List of Sheriffs, with Their Years and Location of Service." Source: Kent County, MD," Maryland State Archives, https://www.ourfamtree.org/records/sheriffs.php?state=MD&county=Kent-Co&place=

100 "Washington County Taxes, 1803-1804." Source: Western Maryland's Historical Library. As of October 4, 2018, http://www.whilbr.org/WashCoTaxes1803/index.aspx

101 Benjamin Hatcheson court cases indicated his indebtedness: Archives of Maryland, Session Laws of Maryland, 1804, Volume 562, Page 104 1803, Volume 560, Page 84. Archives of Maryland, Laws of Maryland 1785-1791, November Session 1791, Volume 204, Page 632. Archives of Maryland, Volume 105, Page 41, Proceedings and Acts of the General Assembly, 1796. Archives of Maryland, Volume 105, Page 128, Proceedings and Acts of the General Assembly, November 1796.

102 Maryland Land Record said Sheriff Hatcheson was dead as of 1806.

103 "Early Colonial Settlers of Southern Maryland and Virginia's Northern Neck Counties" for Vincent Hutcheson (1721-1756). As of October 4, 2018, http://www.colonial-settlers-md-va.us/getperson.php?personID=I054106&tree=Tree1

104 "Abstracts of Wills" by Carson Gibb, abstracted from Prerogative Court (Wills) MSA S538, Liber 30, 1755-1760. As of October 4, 2018, https://msa.maryland.gov/msa/stagser/s500/s538/html/s538-30.html

105 "Middle Passage" refers to the part of the trade where Africans, densely packed onto ships, were transported across the Atlantic to the West Indies. The voyage took three to four months and, during this time, the enslaved people mostly lay chained in rows on the floor of the hold or on shelves that ran around the inside of the ships' hulls. The shelves were under a meter high and often the enslaved Africans could not sit up. There could be up to more than six hundred enslaved people on each ship. Captives from different nations were mixed together, so it was more difficult for them to talk and plan rebellions. Women and children were held separately. Source: The Abolition Project. As of October 4, 2018, http://abolition.e2bn.org/slavery_44.html

106 Maryland State Archives Guide to Government Records, Information on S378 (Decrees, Western Shore) COURT OF APPEALS, 1806-1851. Transcripts of equity cases appealed from county courts and estate cases appealed from county orphan's courts. Arranged alphabetically by name of appellant and then chronologically by court term and case number. Dates and case numbers provided through Docket, Western Shore series [MSA S414]. See also Decrees series [MSA S379], Transcripts series [MSA S434], and Transcripts, Western Shore series [MSA S436].

Chapter 9

107 Craig W Snyde, "How to Butcher a Homestead-Raised Hog." Source: Mother Earth News, September/October 1982. As of October 4, 2018, https://www.motherearthnews.com/homesteading-and-livestock/how-to-butcher-a-homestead-raised-hog-zmaz82sozgoe

108 To "Put Up" as far back as 1860 means to can fruits and vegetables. Just one step beyond cooking, canning involves processing food in closed glass canning jars at high temperatures. The heat interrupts natural spoilage by destroying food contaminants and, at the same time, removes air from the jars. As the jars cool, a vacuum seal forms – to prevent recontamination. Source: Ball and Kerr canning website. As of October 4, 2018, https://www.freshpreserving.com/jars/

109 "Maryland Crop Harvest Schedule." Maryland produce is available at farmers' markets, roadside stands, pick-your-own farms, and supermarkets.

Harvest times are approximate as weather conditions and overpicking may affect the ripening dates and availability of fruits and vegetables. Source: Maryland Manual On-Line, Maryland At a Glance, Agriculture. As of October 4, 2018, http://msa.maryland.gov/msa/mdmanual/01glance/html/agripro.html

110 Amt, Emilie, "History: African Americans at St. Marks Before the Civil War." Excerpt: "When St. Mark's was founded in 1849, all eight of the church's charter members owned slaves, and the original plans for the building were altered to include a gallery for slaves, which still exists today.

We also know very little about most of the individuals who sat in the slave balcony at St. Mark's, but we have at least the names of thirty-one enslaved men, women, and children who certainly, probably, or possibly were among them." Source: St. Marks Church website. As of on October 4, 2018, http://www.stmarkslappans.org/african-american-history-of-st-marks.html

111 "Ingram House." National Register of Historic Places Inventory Nomination Form, 1979. As of October 4, 2018, https://mht.maryland.gov/secure/medusa/PDF/Washington/WA-II-085.pdf

112 Henry Williams, 38 years old, was sold by John Ingram to next-door neighbor Dr. Daniel Fahrney in June 1862 for ONE dollar to be a slave for life. Source: Maryland Land Record, Liber IN16, page 258, 1862, MSA CE 18-11.

Chapter 10

113 Mike High, The C&O Canal Companion, A Journey through Potomac History, "Structures and Industry Along the Canal." Johns Hopkins University Press, Baltimore, MD, 2017. Page 390.

114 James M. McPherson, *Crossroads of Freedom: Antietam, The Battle That Changed the Course of the Civil War.* (New York: Oxford University Press, 2002). ISBN 0-19-513521-0.

115 Summer birds along the C&O Canal in Washington County, Maryland. As of October 4, 2018, https://www.potomacaudubon.org/birding/pvas_birdmap/canal/

116 "Battle of South Mountain." Herald of Freedom and Torch Light Newspaper articles from September 10-24, 1862, describe the wars which mightily affected Washington County, but especially between the towns of Boonsboro and Sharpsburg.

117 "The Journey Through Hallowed Ground" describes the military necessity of recruiting African Americans for service in the Union Army As of October 4, 2018, https://www.hallowedground.org/African-American-Heritage/Antietam-National-Battlefield

118 "United States Colored Troops in the Civil War." Source: Family Search. As of October 4, 2018, https://familysearch.org/wiki/en/United_States_Colored_Troops_in_the_Civil_War

119 "Black Soldiers in the U.S. Military During the Civil War." Source: National Archives, Educator Resources. As of October 4, 2018, https://www.archives.gov/education/lessons/blacks-civil-war

120 Was Otho's brother, Samuel Williams, in the Colored Troops? Source: NARA M1820 compiled military service records of volunteer Union soldiers who served with the US Colored Troops, 2nd through 7th Colored Infantry battalions, 1861-1865. As of October 4, 2018, https://www.fold3.com/search/#query=samuel+williams&t=46

Chapter 11

[121] "America's Women and the Wage Gap, September 2018." Nationally, the median annual pay for a woman who holds a full-time, year-round job is $41,977 compared to $52,146 for a man. Overall, women in the U.S. are paid 80 cents for every dollar paid to men, amounting to a gender wage gap of $10,169.1

This pervasive wage gap is driven in part by gender and racial discrimination, workplace harassment, job segregation and a lack of workplace policies that support family caregiving. Source: National Partnership for Women and Families. As of October 7, 2018, http://www.nationalpartnership.org/research-library/workplace-fairness/fair-pay/americas-women-and-the-wage-gap.pdf

122 Current Population Survey, Annual Social and Economic (ASEC) Supplement: Table PINC-05: Work Experience in 2017 – People 15 Years Old and Over by Total Money Earnings in 2017, Age, Race, Hispanic Origin, Sex, and Disability Status. Source: U.S. Census Bureau. (2018). As of October 7, https://www.census.gov/data/tables/time- series/demo/income-poverty/cps-pinc/pinc-05.html (Unpublished calculation based on the median annual pay for all women and men who worked full time, year-round in 2018)

123 Samuel Beckett, *Waiting for Godot* tells the tale of two men, Vladimir and Estragon, who meet near a tree and converse on various topics and reveal that they are waiting there for a man named Godot. While they wait, two other men enter. Pozzo is on his way to the market to sell his slave, Lucky. An existentialist play. https://www.enotes.com/topics/waiting-for-godot/themes

124 "Washington County, Marriages 1861-1919." Source: Online Washington Free Library. As of October 4, 2018, https://www.washcolibrary.org/?q=marriages. Note: only marriages from 1886-1970 are digitized; earlier records are only available in an index because a fire destroyed the original records.

125 "Jumping the broom" referred to straw brooms being waved over the heads of marrying couples to ward off evil spirits. The couple would often but not always jump over the broom at the end of the ceremony. Jumping over the broom symbolized the wife's commitment or willingness to clean the courtyard of the new home she had joined. Source: The African American Registry. As of October 1, 2018, https://aaregistry.org/story/jumping-the-broom-a-short-history/

126 "Vulcan Mind Meld" from the Star Trek television series. A touch technique that allows a Vulcan to merge his or her mind with the essence of another's mind purely by using specialized contact via fingertip-points -- on a humanoid, usually around the targeted partner's skull temples. Hypnosis-like relaxation and a rhythmic verbal device, such as "My mind to your mind, my thoughts to your thoughts," are often useful. As of October 4, 2018, http://www.startrek.com/database_article/mind-meld-vulcan

127 James O. Lehman and Steven M. Nolt, Mennonites, Amish, and the American Civil War. (Baltimore, MD: The Johns Hopkins Univeristy Press, 2007), p. 30.

128 The Assembly of 1826 began rewriting the manumission laws that would cause extreme difficulty for slave owners to allow slaves to be freed. Deeds of Manumission had to be evidenced by two or more good and sufficient witnesses. Execution of the deed had to take place before the slave reached 45 years, nor could it begin until the slave was over 10. Source: Maryland Laws. As of October 4, 2018, http://www.drbronsontours.com/PGslaverymarylandlaw.html

129 Barbara Jeanne Fields, *Slavery and Freedom on the Middle Ground Maryland During the Nineteenth Century*. (New Haven, Yale University Press, 1985) page 28.

130 "Africa's Maryland: Manumission and Emigration of Maryland's Freed People," circa 1836. Source: Laws of Maryland, 1831, chap. 281, sec. 4, encouraged free blacks to renounce their freedom. As of October 4, 2018, https://hornbakelibrary.wordpress.com/2017/02/16/africas-maryland-manumission-and-emigration-of-marylands-freed-people-ca-1836/

131 Reconstruction. The Union victory in the Civil War in 1865 gave some 4 million slaves their freedom, in the process of rebuilding the South during the Reconstruction period (1865-1877) During Radical Reconstruction, which began in 1867, newly enfranchised blacks gained a voice in government for the first time in American history, winning election to southern state legislatures and even to the U.S. Congress. In less than a decade, however, reactionary forces–including the Ku Klux Klan–would reverse the changes wrought by Radical Reconstruction in a violent backlash that restored white supremacy in the South. Source: History Channel. As of October 5, 2018, https://www.history.com/topics/american-civil-war/reconstruction

132 Marsha Lynne Fuller, African American Manumissions of Washington County, Maryland. Data chart lists the total black population per town, the number born in Maryland and the number who own property was compiled by Marguerite Doleman, Hagerstown. Source: 1870 US Census for Washington County. (Westminster: Willow Bend Books, 2001). Unnumbered.

Chapter 12

133 "History of Tolson's Chapel in Sharpsburg, Maryland." Source: Tolson's Chapel, Sharpsburg, Maryland website. As of October 5, 2018, http://www.tolsonschapel.org/wp-content/uploads/2012/12/Tolsons-Chapel-history.pdf

134 Katie Williams, niece of Otho Williams, was a teacher in the 1907/08 school year in Beaver's Creek, MD. Source: "Teacher's Year Book, Colored Schools. 1907/08."

135 David Troy, Celebrating Rights and Responsibilities, Baltimore & the 15th Amendment, May 19, 1870, An Interactive Historical Investigation by David Troy, 1996. As of October 5, 2018, https://msa.maryland.gov/dtroy/project/story.html

136 DeNeen L. Brown, "Black Towns, Established by Freed Slaves After the Civil War, Are Dying Out," Source: The Washington Post, March 27, 2015.

Chapter 13

137 Deed between Otho and Hezekiah Williams and Edward Ingram for Funkstown lots 143 and 144: Source: Maryland Land Records Book McKK1, page 92-93.1868.

138 Antietam Creek was a source of water for the grist mills in Funkstown. As of October 10, 2018, http://www.funkstown.com/history/

139 While this "David Newcomer as advocate" tale is not proven, it is plausible. According to local expert, Jane Neff, " I think back to the mortgage Otho got with Joseph Eavey. Joseph Eavey's sister married into the Newcomer family. Many of the Eavey's and Newcomer's are buried in the same Mennonite cemetery close to the Ingram farm. Mennonites are known for their belief that all are God's people.

Discrimination is not part of their lives. But, again this is only a guess with no firm corroboration of facts." October 8, 2018, email from Jane Neff to the author.

140 Deed between Otho Williams and John Eavey, Maryland Land Records, Book McKK1, pages 402-403.1869.

141 Deed between Otho and Alice Williams and Jeremiah Balls, Source: Maryland Land Records Book McKK6, page 290, 1874.

142 Nicol, Susan C., Maryland Has a Long History of Heavy Snow, The Frederick News-Post, February 17, 2003.

143 Deed between Otho and Alice Williams and Joseph Eavey, Maryland Land Records Book 78, page 95-96, 1879. Also, clarified as being Barnes Road by Jane Neff, local expert, in a October 8, 2018, email to the author.

144 Deed between Otho and Alice Williams and Samuel and Andrew Funk, Maryland Land Records Book 78, page 549-550, 1880.

145 Deed from Otho William's estate to Sam Funk. Maryland Land Records Book 78, page 550, 1888.

Chapter 14

[146] Email from Jane Neff, Washington County, Maryland, expert, providing historical accuracy concerning Funkstown, Baker Hill, anti-slavery Mennonite families like the Newcomers and Eaveys, etc. Dated October 8, 2018.

147 Antietam Ironworks built 1763. Antietam Iron Furnace – Sharpsburg, MD – Iron Furnace Ruins on Waymarking.com. As of October 5, 2018, http://www.waymarking.com/waymarks/WM4DP2_Antietam_Iron_Furnace_Sharpsburg_MD

148 The Bridges of Washington County, Maryland maps. Hagerstown-Washington County Convention and Visitors Bureau http://www.visithagerstown.com/files/Bridges-Wash-Co-Brochuref.pdf

149 The Bridges of Washington County, Maryland. Hagerstown-Washington County Convention and Visitors Bureau. As of October 5, 2018, http://mht.maryland.gov/nr/NRDetail.aspx?NRID=313&FROM=NRMapWA.aspx

150 Catoctin Mountain, Charcoal and Iron Industry, National Park Service. As of October 5, 2018, https://www.nps.gov/cato/learn/historyculture/charcoal.htm

151 John Bedell, Gregory Katz, Jason Shellenhamer, Lisa Kraus, and Sarah Groesbeck. Collier huts: The People of the Mountain Archaeological Overview, Assessment, Identification, and Evaluation Study of Catoctin Mountain Park Maryland, Final Report. The Louis Berger Group, June 2011. https://www.nps.gov/rap/archeology/PDFs/CATO%20ThePeopleOfTheMountain.pdf

152 Following the Revolutionary War, Hughes moved his operations to Principio Furnace in Harford County, and the Antietam Furnace. In 1831 a nail factory and rolling mill were set up. Antietam Iron Furnace Site and Antietam Village, Inventory No.: WA-II-031. Date Listed: 6/26/1975. Location: Harpers Ferry Road, Sharpsburg. Category: District, Period/Date of Construction: 1765-1880. As of October 5, 2018, http://mht.maryland.gov/nr/NRDetail.aspx?NRID=313&FROM=NRMapWA.aspx

153 Antietam Ironworks: At one point, the ironworks was said to employ more than 260 workers (including 60 slaves). C&O Canal Trust. As of October 5, 2018, https://www.canaltrust.org/pyv/antietam-ironworks/

154 John Bezis-Selfa. "Forging America: Ironworkers, Adventurers, and the Industrious Revolution." Cornell University Press, page 92.

155 Baltic Iron in the Atlantic World in the Eighteenth Century, By Chris Evans, Göran Rydén. BRILL, 2007, ISBN: 978-90-47-42147-4.

156 John Bezis-Selfa, "Forging America: Ironworkers, Adventurers, and the Industrious Revolution." page 92. Cornell University Press, page 94.

157 Ned and Constance Sublette, American Slave Coast: A History of the Slave-Breeding Industry. (Chicago: Lawrence Hill Books, 2016), Chapter 18.

158 Michael W. Robbins, "The Principio Company: Iron-making in Colonial Maryland, 1720-1781." (Taylor and Francis, 1986), page 120.

159 *MIG welding*, also known as Gas Metal Arc *Welding* (GMAW), is a process that utilizes a continuously fed solid electrode, shielding gas from an externally supplied source, and electrical power to melt the electrode and deposit this molten material in the *weld* joint. PraxairDirect.com. As of October 5, 2018, https://www.praxairdirect.com/Industrial-Gas-and-Welding-Information-Center/Welding-Tips-Tricks-and-Information/MIG-Welding.html

160 Kanika Marshall's kinetic art objects. As of October 5, 2018, http://www.KanikaMarshall.com.

161 Milt Diggins, "Principio Furnace," Source: Cecil County Historical Society, July 28, 2000, page 2. As of October 5, 2018, http://schools.ccps.org/ems/8th_sl/Welcome_files/Principio%20history.pdf

162 Michael Robbins, "The Principio Company: Iron-Making in Colonial Maryland 1720-1781." Dissertation George Washington University, 1972. (New York: Garland Publishing Company, 1986).

163 John Bezis-Selfa, "Forging America: Ironworkers, Adventurers, and the Industrious Revolution." Cornell University Press. As of October 5, 2018, http://www.cornellpress.cornell.edu/book/?GCOI=80140100085160

164 Ibid.

165 A History of Washington County, Thomas JC Williams, 1906, John M. Runk and L.R. Titsworth, Columbia University Libraries Digital Collections, Page 85. As of October 5, 2018, http://www.columbia.edu/cu/lweb/digital/collections/cul/texts/ldpd_8627288_001/

166 Emma George Ross, "The Age of Iron in West Africa," Heilbrunn Timeline of Art History, The MET. As of October 5, 2018, https://www.metmuseum.org/toah/hd/iron/hd_iron.htm

167 Ibid.

168 Occupational Employment and Wages, May 2017, 51-4041 Machinists. Bureau of Labor Statistics, Occupational Employment Statistics. As of October 5, 2018, https://www.bls.gov/oes/current/oes514041.htm

169 Number of Households in US from 1960 to 2017. Statista, The Statistics Portal. As of October 5, 2018, https://www.google.com/search?client=safari&rls=en&q=number+of+families+in+us+in+2017&ie=UTF-8&oe=UTF-8

Chapter 15

170 Nov 2, 1867 Otho and Alice marriage, Washington County, Marriages 1861-1949.

171 1900 US Federal Census, Franklin County, Pennsylvania.

172 Pennsylvania Death Certificates, 1906-1944, Pennsylvania Historic and Museum Commission, Pennsylvania, USA; Certificate Number Range: 029001-033000, Commonwealth of Pennsylvania, Bureau of Vital Statistics, #32017.

173 Women's South Homeopathic Hospital of Philadelphia was founded in 1861 by Ann Preston, M.D., the Woman's Hospital of Philadelphia provided clinical experience for the Woman's Medical College of Pennsylvania students and practical training for nurses. PACSCL Finding Aids. http://dla.library.upenn.edu/dla/pacscl/detail.html?id=PACSCL_DUCOM_DUCOMWM002

Chapter 16

174 Slave ships to Maryland by way of Chesapeake in 1864. A Guide to the History of Slavery in Maryland, http://msa.maryland.gov/msa/intromsa/pdf/slavery_pamphlet.pdf

175 Charcoal and Iron Industry, National Park Service for Catoctin Mountain. As of October 4, 2018, https://www.nps.gov/cato/learn/historyculture/charcoal.htm

176 Catoctin Furnace History. After selling his interest in the Antietam Ironworks, John Brien became one of many owners of the Catoctin Furnace. Catoctin Furnace Historical Society. http://catoctinfurnace.org/home/catoctinfurnacehistory.html

177 The Purity and Power of Enslaved Iron Workers at Catoctin Furnace, The History Bandits. As of October 5, 2018, https://thehistorybandits.com/2015/12/05/the-purity-and-power-of-enslaved-iron-workers-at-catoctin-furnace/

178 Guy Logsdon, Oklahoma Historical Society. "Moonshine". Encyclopedia of Oklahoma History & Culture. Oklahoma State University. As of October 4, 2018, https://web.archive.org/web/20141031120502/http:/digital.library.okstate.edu/encyclopedia/entries/M/MO013.html

179 Max Grivno, Gleanings of Freedom: Free and Slave Labor along the Mason-Dixon Line, 1790-1860, page 90.

180 Fort Frederick in the Civil War, including "The Williams Family and Fort Frederick." Maryland Department of Natural Resources. As of October 4, 2018, http://dnr.maryland.gov/publiclands/Pages/western/fortfrederickcivilwar.aspx

181 Public housing, also known as "the projects," in the United States is administered by federal, state and local agencies to provide subsidized assistance for low-income households. .. Subsidized apartment buildings, often referred to as housing projects, have a complicated and often notorious history in the United States. Wikipedia. As of October 4, 2018, https://en.wikipedia.org/wiki/Public_housing_in_the_United_States

182 Bernice A. Bennett is genealogist, author, producer, and host of the popular Research at the National Archives and Beyond! Blogtalkradio show. As of October 4, 2018, http://www.geniebroots.com/about/index.htm

Chapter 17

183 Christine Luff "How Far is a Marathon?" A *marathon* is 26.2 miles long. Although *marathons* differ in their terrain and degree of difficulty, the distance is always 26.2 miles. Races that are shorter or longer in distance have different names (such as 5K, 10K, half-*marathon*, or ultra-*marathon*). Source: Very Well Fit. As of October 5, 2018, https://www.verywellfit.com/how-far-is-a-marathon-2911427

184 Gale Bernhardt, "How long Is a Triathlon?" As of 2000, an Olympic-distance triathlon remains a 1.5-kilometer swim, 40-kilometer bike ride and a 10-kilometer run. Source: Active Running and Sports. As of October 5, 2018, https://www.active.com/triathlon/articles/how-long-is-a-triathlon-5595

185 Ananya Mandal, MD, "What is Genetics?" *Genetics* is the study of heredity. Heredity is a biological process where a parent passes certain genes onto their children or offspring. Every child inherits genes from both of their biological parents and these genes in turn express specific traits. Source: News-Medical.Net. As of October 5, 2018, https://www.news-medical.net/life-sciences/What-is-Genetics.aspx

186 "DNA" deoxyribonucleic acid, is a self-replicating material present in nearly all living organisms as the main constituent of chromosomes. It is the carrier of genetic information. Source: Google Dictionary. As of October 5, 2018.

187 "Cells" are the basic building blocks of all living things. The human body is composed of trillions of cells. They provide structure for the body, take in nutrients from food, convert those nutrients into energy, and carry out specialized functions.

Cells also contain the body's hereditary material and can make copies of themselves. Cells have many parts, each with a different function. Some of these parts, called organelles, are specialized structures that perform certain tasks within the cell. Source: Genetics Home Reference. As of October 5, 2018, https://ghr.nlm.nih.gov/primer/basics/cell

188 A "reference population" is the base *population* from which a sample is drawn at the time of initial sampling. DNA testing technology is constantly changing, and so are the efforts to engage Native American tribes to test on an individual and group basis. However, no DNA testing can "prove" an individual is American Indian and/or Alaska Native, or has ancestry from a specific tribe. Jessica Bardill (Cherokee) PhD developed a resource guide about DNA testing for tribal elders, entitled "Tribal Enrollment and Genetic Testing." Source: American Indian & Alaska Native Genetics Resource Center. As of October 5, 2018, http://genetics.ncai.org/tribal-enrollment-and-genetic-testing.cfm

189 Tim Janzen, "Autosomal DNA Testing Comparison Chart" compares the costs, DNA collection methods, and other attributes of the major DNA testing companies. Source: International Society of Genetic Genealogy. As of October 5, 2018, https://isogg.org/wiki/Autosomal_DNA_testing_comparison_chart

190 The "Big Y-500" is a Y-chromosome direct paternal line test to explore deep ancestral links on our common paternal tree. This test examines thousands of known branch markers as well as millions of places where there may be new branch markers. Additionally, the Big Y-500 tests 450 Y-STR (short tandem repeat) markers and provides you with at least 389 STR allele value results on your Y-DNA Y-STR. Source: Family Tree DNA Learning Center. As of October 5, 2018, https://www.familytreedna.com/learn/y-dna-testing/big-y/big-y/

191 "What is DNA matching?" According to Ancestry.com, AncestryDNA member matching identifies other AncestryDNA members who might be related to you. We compare your DNA to the DNA of every other person in the AncestryDNA database, and based on how your DNA matches up, we estimate how closely you're related—

whether you are siblings, first cousins, distant cousins, or not related at all. Source: Ancestry.com. As of October 5, 2018, https://www.ancestry.com/cs/dna-help/matches/dna-matching

192 Lizzie Wade, "Genetic Study Reveals Surprising Ancestry of Many Americans." According to the study, the average African-American genome, for example, is 73.2% African, 24% European, and 0.8% Native American, the team reports online today in "*The American Journal of Human Genetics*." Latinos, meanwhile, carry an average of 18% Native American ancestry, 65.1% European ancestry (mostly from the Iberian Peninsula), and 6.2% African ancestry. Source: Science. December 18, 2014. As of October 5, 2018, http://www.sciencemag.org/news/2014/12/genetic-study-reveals-surprising-ancestry-many-americans

193 A "***haplogroup***" is a genetic population group of people who share a common ancestor on the patrilineal or the matriline. *Haplogroups* are assigned letters of the alphabet, and refinements consist of additional number and letter combinations. Source: isogg.com. As of October 5, 2018, https://isogg.org/wiki/Haplogroup. Additionally, each haplogroup describes individual branches – or closely related groups of branches – on the genetic family tree of all humans. All members of a haplogroup trace their ancestry back to a single individual, [author: for example, back to theoretical Adam and Eve]. Source: 23andMe Blog, https://blog.23andme.com/ancestry/haplogroups-explained/

194 Jason Kotte, "The American Slave Coast: A History of the Slave Breeding Industry in the United States." As of October 2018: https://kottke.org/16/02/a-history-of-the-slave-breeding-industry-in-the-united-states

195 In genetic genealogy, a "centimorgan" (cM) or map unit (m.u.) is a unit of measure, like miles are for distance. This measure is a recombinant frequency which is used to measure genetic distance. It is often used to imply distance along a chromosome, and considers how often recombination occurs in a region. Source: International Society of Genetic Genealogy. As of October 5, 2018, https://isogg.org/wiki/CentiMorgan

196 Maternal "B4a1a1 Haplogroup." The common female ancestor of haplogroup B likely lived in Central or East Asia nearly 50,000 years ago. Her descendants remain common across Asia today, from Iran to Japan. The haplogroup is extremely common in parts of China, southeastern Asia and far beyond; the presence of B4'5 at levels of up to 50% among the Maori of New Zealand and native Hawaiians indicates their shared Southeast Asian heritage. Source: 23andMe. As of October 5, 2018, https://you.23andme.com/published/reports/88962ca090e3469d/?share_id=e4119903fc0b430c

197 "Malagasy Motif B4a1a1 Haplogroup" Only seventeen known slave ships came from Madagascar to North America during the Transatlantic Slave Trade. As a result, we find Malagasy DNA in the African American descendants of enslaved people, often of Southeast Asian origin. One of the goals of this project is to discover the Malagasy roots of African Americans and connect them with their cousins from Madagascar. Source: Family Tree DNA Malagasy Roots Project. https://you.23andme.com/published/reports/88962ca090e3469d/?share_id=e4119903fc0b430c

198 "Haplogroup I2" is the most common paternal lineage in former Yugoslavia, Romania, Bulgaria and Sardinia, and a major lineage in most Slavic countries. Its maximum frequencies are observed in Bosnia (55%, including 71% in Bosnian Croats), Sardinia (39.5%), Croatia (38%), Serbia (33%), Montenegro (31%), Romania (28%), Moldova (24%), Macedonia (24%), Slovenia (22%), Bulgaria (22%), Belarus (18.5%), Hungary (18%), Slovakia (17.5%), Ukraine (13.5%), and Albania (13.5%). It is found at a frequency of 5 to 10% in Germanic countries. Source: Eupedia: Genetics: Haplogroup I2. As of October 5, 2018, https://www.eupedia.com/europe/Haplogroup_I2_Y-DNA.shtml

199 "Autosomal Statistics Chart" was created by Christa Stalcup. The chart helps determine the relationship of two people based on the number of centimorgans they share. It contains eight groups of centimorgans, an estimate of the percentage of shared DNA and, most importantly, an assessment of the relationship. For example, if two people share 60 cM, they share about .78% of their DNA, and could be third cousins or second cousins once-removed (one generation apart). Source: DNA Detectives. As of October 5, 2018, http://hackgenealogy.com/wp-content/uploads/2017/03/Autosomal-DNA-Statistics-Chart.pdf

200 "Average Autosomal DNA Shared by Pairs of Relatives" chart, showing the percent centimorgans shared, total centimorgans, relationship, and notes. Source: International Society of Genetic Genealogy.
https://isogg.org/wiki/Autosomal_DNA_statistics

201 A "SNP" is a Single Nucleotide Polymorphism, which is a change in your DNA code at a specific point. Source: Family Tree DNA.

202 "E-M2 or E1b1 Haplogroup" is the most represented human Y chromosome haplogroup in Africa. Source: US National Library of Medicine, National Institutes of Health. As of October 5, 2018, https://www.ncbi.nlm.nih.gov/pmc/articles/PMC3017091/

203 "Ethnic Admixture Guide" provides guidelines on how to best utilize Gedmatch.com. GEDmatch.com is a third-party website where you can upload your raw DNA data for further analysis and matching, with people from other companies who have also upload their data. Source: Genealogical Musings, http://genealogical-musings.blogspot.com/2017/04/finally-gedmatch-admixture-guide.html

Chapter 19

204 Bernice Bennett is a Genealogy Researcher and BlogTalkRadio Host who helped the author understand DNA triangulations, as well as interviewed the author about her first book, *The Ancestors Are Smiling!* on her weekly blog talk show. As of October 5, 2018, http://www.Geniebroots.com

205 Anthony May is a former molecular biology scientist by day (in 2018 a medical student at Howard University), but transforms into genealogy addict at night, helping numerous people find their African roots.

206 "Triangulation" is a term derived from surveying to describe a method of determining the Y-STR or mitochondrial DNA ancestral haplotype using two or more known data points. The term "Genetic Triangulation" was coined by genetic genealogist Bill Hurst in 2004. Source: International Society of Genetic Genealogy. As of October 5, 2018, https://isogg.org/wiki/Triangulation

207 "Ancestral Community" explained in a May 9, 2018, email from DNA expert HDG, as not only being one's direct-line ancestors, but also people who interact with extended family lines, neighbors, etc.

208 "Historical map collection." Source: Historic Map Works. As of October 5, 2018, http://www.historicmapworks.com

Chapter 20

209 "DNA Tested African Descendants," is a newsletter and online medium that facilitates reconciliation between the Autosomal DNA Tested African Diaspora with Autosomal DNA Tested Africans born on the continent of Africa. Source: Imperial African History and Genetic Genealogical Society. As of October 5, 2018, https://www.dnatestedafricans.org

210 "Benjamin Banneker Biography, Astronomer, Scientist," Source: Biography. As of October 18, 2018, https://www.biography.com/people/benjamin-banneker-9198038

211 Henry Louis Gates and Zachary Garceau, "How Did My Enslaved Kin Get to Virginia from Madagascar?" Source: The Root. As of October 5, 2018, https://www.theroot.com/how-did-my-enslaved-kin-get-to -va-from-madagascar-1790861807

212 "Melungeon" is a term that first appeared in print in the 19th century, used in Virginia, Tennessee, and North Carolina to describe people of mixed ancestry. Melungeons were considered by outsiders to have a mixture of European, Native American, and African ancestry. Researchers have referred to Melungeons and similar groups as "tri-racial isolates," and Melungeons have faced discrimination, both legal and social, because they did not fit into America's accepted racial categories. Source: Melungeon Heritage website. As of October 5, 2018, http://melungeon.org/frequently-asked-questions-about-melungeons/ Also see Dave Tabler, "The Guineas of West Virginia," May 19, 2017. Source: Appalachian History Blog. As of October 5, 2018, http://www.appalachianhistory.net/2017/05/guineas-of-west-virginia.html

213 "**African Ancestry"** was launched in 2003 by Dr. Rick Kittles and Gina Paige and has since helped over 500,000 people discover their heritage and explore the very roots of their family trees. The company capitalizes on the fact that there aren't any other ancestry DNA testing companies that focus specifically on African descent. Source: Top 10 DNA Tests. As of October 5, 2018, https://www.top10dnatests.com/reviews/african-ancestry-review/

www.ingramcontent.com/pod-product-compliance
Lightning Source LLC
Chambersburg PA
CBHW031457270326
41930CB00006B/131